THE AMERICAN DANCE FESTIVAL

R. WADLEIGH

THE
AMERICAN
DANCE FESTIVAL

JACK ANDERSON

Duke University Press Durham 1987

To
Martha Hill,
Jeanette Schlottmann Roosevelt,
and Theodora Wiesner,
who guided the festival in the past,
and to everyone—past and present—
who has helped make the American Dance Festival
a major center for dance

CONTENTS

INTRODUCTION AND ACKNOWLEDGMENTS

A center for performances, a school, a provider of community and professional services—the American Dance Festival has been so many things to so many people that any account of it will almost inevitably seem arbitrary in both what it includes and what it omits. Quite different—and equally valuable—books about it could be written from the standpoints of dancers, choreographers, students, teachers, and therapists.

This account is by someone who is a critic, a dance lover, and an inveterate dancegoer, and it is based on the supposition that most dancegoers have found the festival exciting because it is, first of all, a sponsor of performances by some of the greatest choreographers and dance companies of our time. Therefore the emphasis here will be upon the festival's performances, while its activities as a dance school and as a site for conferences, seminars, and symposiums will receive secondary attention.

But deciding to stress performances does not in itself solve all problems of organization. In addition to public performances for paying audiences, there have been innumerable student and faculty concerts, workshop showings, experimental efforts, and al fresco "happenings," and the number of these events has increased markedly since the late 1960s. Here, again, the emphasis will be upon the programs most dancegoers who were not also students came to the festival to see: the public performances. However, "fringe" activities have included many productions of genuine merit, as well as some notable for the oddity of their content or the controversy they aroused. A few of these will be at least briefly mentioned in passing.

Finally, any author telling the story of the American Dance Festival must decide when and where to begin. In recent years, the festival has quite rightly called attention to the fact that it is an outgrowth of the Bennington festivals of the 1930s. However, in 1948, when the festival opened at Connecticut College, its leaders, for reasons that will be made clear in this book, regarded their undertaking as a new departure, as well as a successor to an older project. Since a fine chronicle of the Bennington festival already exists (Sali Ann Kriegsman's *Modern Dance in America: The Bennington Years*), this book will merely summarize the Bennington achievements and then proceed to examine the festival in detail after its new beginning in Connecticut.

Many people have assisted me in the writing of this book. Charles L. Reinhart, Stephanie Reinhart, and Martha Myers, the festival's current leaders, have been unfailingly helpful and cooperative, as have the festival's former directors, Martha Hill, Jeanette Schlottmann Roosevelt, and Theodora Wiesner. Terry Sanford, president of Duke University at the time of the festival's move to North Carolina, graciously granted me an interview. Nancy Trovillion and her staff in the festival's Durham office have done much to make it pleasant as well as informative to rummage through festival files. Similar thanks also go to Genevieve Oswald and her staff at the Dance Collection of the New York Public Library at Lincoln Center.

Other welcome advice, information, and assistance have come from Linda Belans, Bonnie Bird, Susan Broili, Trisha Brown, Nathan Clark, Selma Jeanne Cohen, Laura Dean, Senta Driver, Jane Dudley, Doris Hering, Deborah Jowitt, Pauline Koner, Sali Ann Kriegsman, Richard Kuch, Elizabeth Lee, Sophie Maslow, Edgar Mayhew, Vicki Patton, Ted Rotante, Helen Priest Rogers, Doris Rudko, Laura Shapiro, Marcia B. Siegel, Dorothy Berea Silver, Paul Taylor, Lucy Venable, and David Voss. Joanne Ferguson has been my infinitely patient editor; Elizabeth Gratch, editorial assistant at Duke University Press, has been amazing in her ability to track down missing programs and reviews. As I wrote this book, George Dorris heard about my research problems and the festival's productions again and again; his good cheer and encouragement have proven invaluable.

1

THE FOUNDING OF
THE FESTIVAL

Since 1948 the American Dance Festival has played a major role in the encouragement of modern dance in this country. At its original home at Connecticut College in New London, Connecticut, and in its home since 1978 on the campus of Duke University in Durham, North Carolina, the festival has trained innumerable dancers and teachers and has offered more than two hundred new works.

Yet it could not have come into being if it had not been for the precedent of the earlier institution of which it is an outgrowth, an institution known throughout the dance world by a single word: Bennington. As Martha Hill, Bennington's codirector, once put it, "We all enjoyed Bennington so much we thought, let's do it again!"[1]

As used by dancers, "Bennington" refers both to a school and a festival. The school was the Bennington School of the Dance, founded in the summer of 1934 at Bennington College in Bennington, Vermont. That year Bennington was only a school, offering courses in modern dance technique. But in 1935 the Bennington Festival was established and Bennington began to produce new works. In 1939, as a sign of the national importance its summer activities had assumed, Bennington temporarily moved its dance program to Mills College in Oakland, California, returning to Vermont the following year.

One of the things that made Bennington remarkable was its diversity. Modern dance is an art that proclaims the importance of individual creativity. But, because of this very emphasis, it can be shaken by factionalism. What Bennington managed to do was to bring factions together. The principal teachers and choreographers for its summer sessions included Martha Graham, Doris Humphrey, Charles Weidman, and Hanya Holm. By the 1930s Graham, Humphrey, and Weidman had established themselves as major choreographers; in fact, the period's only other major American modern dance choreographer was Helen Tamiris who, for reasons that still remain shadowy, was never invited to Bennington. Holm represented the influential German modern dance and was a pupil of that style's most distinguished exponent, Mary Wigman. Yet, as a teacher in America, Holm did not simply pass on what she had learned in Germany; she also adapted German theories of dance training to the specific demands of the New World.

Among the significant works that received their premieres at Bennington were Graham's *El Penitente*, *Letter to the World*, and *Punch and the Judy*; Humphrey's *New Dance*, *With My Red Fires*, and *Passacaglia in C Minor*; Weidman's *Opus 51*, and Holm's *Trend*. The festival also gave choreographic opportunities to such younger artists as José Limón, Eleanor King, Erick Hawkins, Jean Erdman, Jane Dudley, Sophie Maslow, William Bales, and Anna Sokolow; and although Bennington was considered a bastion of modern dance, it nevertheless presented the debut concerts of Ballet Caravan, a company featuring new American ballet choreography that was founded in 1936 by Lincoln Kirstein, who later became the director of the New York City Ballet. Thus, through both classroom activities and public performances, the Bennington School of the Dance lived up to the statement of intention that had been published in the *Bennington College Bulletin* of February 1934:

> The modern dance, in common with the other arts of this period, is a diversified rather than a single style. At the same time it possesses certain identifying characteristics which are common to all of its significant forms. The most advantageous plan of study is, therefore, one which reflects this diversification and, by affording comparisons, aims to reveal the essentials of modernism in the dance.[2]

Bennington came about through the idealistic vision and practical planning of three people: Robert Devore Leigh, the president of Bennington College, who, unlike some other academics of the time, believed that dance could be a serious art; and Mary Josephine Shelly and Martha Hill, the summer school's directors. Shelly (known as "Mary Jo" to her associates) had been an administrator and physical education teacher at

New College, an experimental college within Columbia University Teachers College from 1932 to 1933 and from 1935 to 1938 taught at the University of Chicago. She joined the staff of Bennington College in 1938 as an assistant to Leigh, served in the WAVES during World War II, and came back to Bennington in 1946 as director of admissions. In 1951 she left to direct women's programs in the Air Force, then returned to Bennington in 1953. The following year, she became a director of the Girl Scouts of America. She retired in 1966 and died in 1976.

Whereas Shelly made her greatest contributions to dance at Bennington in the 1930s, Martha Hill has continued to be one of America's most important dance teachers and administrators. Born in East Palestine, Ohio, Hill was graduated from the Kellogg School of Physical Education in Battle Creek, Michigan, in 1920, and taught ballet and Swedish gymnastics there until 1923, when she was appointed director of dance at Kansas State Teachers College in Hays, a post she held until 1926. That year she visited New York, where she attended the choreographic debut of Martha Graham and was so impressed that she immediately signed up for classes with Graham. Inexhaustibly energetic, Hill divided her time so expertly during the next few years that she was able to dance professionally, teach dance, and study both dance and academic subjects. She received a B.S. from Columbia University in 1929 and an M.A. from New York University in 1941. She danced with Martha Graham's company (1930–31) and taught at the University of Oregon (1927–29) and Columbia University Teachers College (1929–30). In 1930 she began teaching dance in the Department of Physical Education of the School of Education of New York University. However, the following year, at the recommendation of Graham, she also joined the dance faculty at Bennington, spending two days a week in Vermont and the rest of her time in New York. She held these dual teaching posts until 1951 when she gave up both to head the new dance department of the Juilliard School in New York. Erect in bearing, hearty in manner, and unquenchable in vitality, Hill has been a crusader for contemporary dance all her life.

However, even the determination of Shelly and Hill could not prevent gasoline rationing and the austerities of World War II from making the Bennington summer school impracticable, and its last official session was held in 1942. Nevertheless, there were scattered dance events at Bennington throughout the war: the Graham company was in residence there during the summers of 1943, 1944, and 1945, and on 11 July 1946,

Louis Horst, composer,
teacher, critic, and mentor
to several generations of
dancers, was associated
with the festival,
1948–63. Photo, courtesy
Nina Fonaroff.

Martha Hill, director,
1948–58. Photo,
Thomas Bouchard.

Jeanette Schlottmann, director, 1959–62 above left. (Photo, Matthew Wysocki.) Theodora Wiesner, director, 1963–68 above right. Charles Reinhart, director, 1969–; Stephanie Reinhart, associate director, 1983–,right. (Photo, Jay Anderson.)

a new company directed by José Limón made its debut at Bennington. This company, with Doris Humphrey as its artistic adviser, would eventually be of crucial importance to the American Dance Festival.

When World War II ended, Martha Hill began to investigate the possibilities of a new festival. She was prompted by more than enthusiasm. For one thing, she believed in giving dancers as many opportunities to dance as possible. "A performing art that doesn't allow performers to perform is a sick art,"[3] she says. Moreover, she wished to promote high standards of dance training. Thus, like Bennington, the new project was to give equal emphasis to dance as an art and to dance as an educational discipline: it would stress the relationship between theory and practice, studio and stage.

Bennington College itself could no longer serve as the festival's home. Its theatrical facilities were limited, and a rearrangement of the college's academic calendar meant that more people would now be on campus in summer — and competing for the use of space and equipment — than had been the case before the war. Therefore the festival would have to be somewhere else, and, though it could be said to be inspired by or modeled on Bennington, it was not literally a continuation of Bennington and the name it eventually adopted — the American Dance Festival — had never been used at Bennington. Nevertheless, throughout its early years the festival was dominated by people who had been dancers or teachers at Bennington.

Hill was encouraged by Jay B. Nash, head of New York University's physical education department, and by two of the university's deans, Ernest O. Melby and Ralph E. Pickett. They even wondered if a summer dance festival could be held in New York in Washington Square near the university's School of Education building. But in those days, Hill says, theater and dance fans liked to escape the summer heat by going to performances out of town, and she feared no one would attend a festival in Manhattan. She began to inspect colleges in the New York area in search of a possible festival site. Then John Martin, the dance critic of the *New York Times* and a champion of modern dance, told her he thought he had found one. Martin owned a summer house in Connecticut, and, on his journeys through the state, he had been favorably impressed by Connecticut College for Women in New London.

A former whaling town that remained one of the finest deepwater ports on the Atlantic coast, New London had been the home of the U.S. Coast Guard Academy since 1932. Yet by the mid-twentieth century it had become an industrial center as well as a city devoted to seafaring, and though there were many parks, beaches, and other tourist attractions in its vicinity, it was not a particularly picturesque community. What made it a possible site for a dance festival was the fact that the Connecticut College campus boasted a well-equipped 1,330-seat theater, the Frank Loomis Palmer Auditorium, which had opened in 1939.[4] Almost equally important for Hill was the fact that the school's modern dance teacher was Ruth Bloomer, who had been a student at the first Bennington session and had received both her B.S. and M.A. degrees from New York University.

Bloomer, who told Hill that she was a descendant of Amelia Jenks Bloomer, inventor of the woman's garment of that name, had taught at the University of Oregon, the University of Michigan, and Denison University before she came to Connecticut College in 1945. With her background, it was only logical that Bloomer would be sympathetic to the notion of a new dance festival.

Although her red hair gave her the nickname of "Rusty," Bloomer was by no means fiery in temperament. *Dance News* once even characterized her as "an unobtrusive little figure quietly and efficiently taking care of her organizational responsibilities." Yet that same article also noted that she had "an indomitable will."

Many of her former colleagues would agree. Thus Jeanette Schlottmann, who succeeded her as director of the American Dance Festival, says, "Rusty was a real New Englander, a straight-from-the-shoulder, matter-of-fact person with no phoniness or pretensions." Everyone appears to have been impressed by her administrative abilities. Therefore the combination of Hill's missionary zeal and Bloomer's attention to detail helped get their new project off to a sound start.[5]

It was also a cautious start. To make sure that Connecticut College had proper studio space and could attract dance students, Bloomer invited the teacher and choreographer William Bales, with Betty Horner Walberg as his musical adviser and accompanist, to conduct a special summer course in 1947 for dance teachers, members of college dance groups, and other young dancers.[6] His reports must have been favorable, for a full-scale festival was planned for 1948.

Located on a hilltop commanding a fine view of the Thames (locally pronounced *Thaymes*) River and Long Island Sound, Connecticut College for Women was founded in 1915, although agitation for its establishment went back at least as far as 1909 when Wesleyan University declared it would no longer admit women as students and the state of Connecticut was thereby left without an institution of higher learning for women.[7] A "Preliminary Announcement" for the college dating from 1914 proclaims that it is through education that "women can enter high up" in the world and "function powerfully therein." For many years Connecticut College devoted itself to the education of what was known as "the New Woman," the woman capable of being a leader in society. As women were increasingly able to enter the professions and schools dropped their prejudices against women students, the college somewhat changed in its tone. However, the dance critic Marcia B. Siegel, an alumna of the college, says that as late as the 1950s, when she was a student there, the presence on campus of older teachers and members of the administrative staff, many of whom had been active in the suffragette movement, made an earlier era of feminism still seem very much alive. In 1959 a graduate school, Connecticut College for Men, was established, and in 1969 the entire college became coeducational under the name of Connecticut College.

Before World War II the college was usually quiet in summer. But from 1941 to 1943 summer programs were instituted in response to wartime needs. In 1944 such programs were officially recognized as an integral part of the college's operations and John F. Moore of the English department was placed in charge of them. During the war years, summer offerings included special institutes on politics and public affairs, employment training programs, and courses for servicemen and veterans. Then, in 1945 and 1946, Moore helped organize a Summer School of the Arts, offering courses in music, graphic arts, poetry, and drama. Although the Summer School of the Arts did not continue, its existence served as a precedent for the School of the Dance and Moore, who enthusiastically supported the dance school until his sudden death in 1948, was appointed co-chairman, with Martha Hill, of an administrative board drawn from both New York University and Connecticut College that would enable a dance festival to be held under the auspices of the two institutions.

This joint sponsorship existed for the festival's first three seasons. According to Hill, Connecticut College and New York University handled all financial matters, including the salaries of teachers and performers, and summer students could receive academic credit from either of the project's sponsors. Using her experiences at Bennington as a precedent, Hill—perhaps overconfidently—told officials that she expected the Connecticut program to break even.

Just as the Bennington School of the Dance might not have been able to flourish without the encouragement of Bennington's president, so the Connecticut College School of the Dance was helped by the support given it by the college's president, Rosemary Park. She came from a family of clergymen and educators: her father, the Rev. Dr. J. Edgar Park, was president of Wheaton College in Massachusetts; her brother, the Rev. Dr. William E. Park, became president of Simmons College in Boston, and at her own inauguration as president of Connecticut College her father was heard to remark, "This family has spent all of its life walking in academic processions."

Park received her B.A. and M.A. from Radcliffe College, did further work at the universities of Tübingen and Bonn and was awarded a doctorate from the University of Cologne. She came to Connecticut College in 1935 as a teacher of German, was appointed dean of freshmen in 1941 and president in 1947, leaving Connecticut in 1962 to become president of Barnard College. In 1965 she married Milton Anastos, professor of Byzantine Greek at the University of California at Los Angeles, and in 1967 was appointed vice chancellor for educational plans and programs at UCLA, a post she held until her retirement in 1974.[8]

Although a lover of the arts as well as a lover of scholarship, Park had never before been involved with dance. Yet, like Robert Devore Leigh at Bennington, she became convinced of the importance of dance as an art and even wrote occasional editorials in American Dance Festival programs about the relationship between dance and higher education. Thus in 1956 she commented:

> It is a long way from the construing of Latin roots, once the core of education, to the modern dance, but the society which prized the former has ceased to exist. If the devotion and discipline once formed in Latin grammar can be cultivated through Dance, virtue has not entirely passed from us. Surely it is the duty of our educational institutions to preserve the merits of tradition even though they may appear in untraditional guises.

In 1957, on the occasion of the American Dance Festival's tenth anniversary, she wrote about how important it had become for colleges to be supporters of the arts in a democratic society:

> As a college administrator, I prefer to believe that colleges are assuming today the protection and assistance of the creative artist which was in earlier days the prerogative of kings. We are neither as gener-

ous nor as demanding as the monarchs, but in pleasing us the artist pleases audiences of hundreds, not just the favored few.[9]

On 15 February 1948 both the *New York Times* and the *New York Herald Tribune* announced that a dance festival and a coeducational dance school, directed by Martha Hill and Ruth Bloomer, would be established at Connecticut College that summer. The school would enable students from around the country to study modern dance with master teachers, while the festival would permit the general public, as well as students, to see distinguished examples of modern dance on stage. In order to emphasize these dual objectives, the entire summer program was called the Connecticut College School of the Dance, and the series of public performances that served as its climax was referred to as the American Dance Festival. However, American Dance Festival became the term by which both the school and the performances were popularly—and, later, officially—known.

John Martin was delighted by the prospect of the festival and school. Writing in *Dance Advance*, a student publication at Connecticut College, he stressed the value to modern dance as a whole of

a school in which the widely divergent points of view of a number of artists and teachers are all validly and convincingly presented. This is in large measure to preserve the very existence of the art itself, for the modern dance is not a method, a technique, a system, but a principle. It depends entirely upon the production of creative movement out of individual experience.[10]

Martin was also excited by the notion that annual festivals could educate the public:

There is no question that the general level of dance taste over the country is extremely low. . . . The reason, of course, is not that the capacity for appreciation outside New York is in any way inferior, but only that opportunity for growth has never been provided. A dozen strategically placed festivals such as the forthcoming one in New London could completely alter the national picture in the course of a very few years.[11]

No efforts were made to establish any other "strategically placed" festivals—at least, not by the Connecticut festival's staff. Nevertheless, the American Dance Festival did much to influence modern dance across the nation.

II

SEASON BY SEASON

1948–1958

---------- **1948** ----------

The official name for the dance project that got underway in New London on 13 July 1948 was New York University–Connecticut College School of the Dance. The public performances that concluded the summer's activities, 13–22 August, were called in the programs, with what now seems almost undue modesty, An American Dance Festival.[1] Three companies participated in the festival, and dancers from those companies were in residence at Connecticut College throughout the summer as members of the faculty.

The notion of having dancers in residence for an entire summer so that students could become acquainted with them as teachers and artistic mentors was an idea borrowed from Bennington, and the companies themselves were guided by choreographers who had participated in the Bennington festivals. Yet more than nostalgia was responsible for inviting them to Connecticut, for these three companies—the Martha Graham company, the José Limón company, and one jointly directed by Jane Dudley, Sophie Maslow, and William Bales—could be said to represent some of the liveliest trends in modern dance during the 1940s.[2]

By 1948 Graham was unquestionably the most celebrated single figure—and, to many of her friends and enemies alike, the veritable high priestess—of American modern dance. Less known to the general public, but considered Graham's choreographic peer by some dancegoers, was Doris Humphrey, who now served as artistic adviser to the Limón company. Forced to give up her dancing career because of a hip ailment in 1944, Humphrey continued to choreograph and in the Limón company found dancers sympathetic to her ideas. Limón himself was considered a promising choreographer, and his craggy figure made him an imposing presence on stage. The Limón company also included Pauline Koner, an experienced dancer and choreographer who was what she has termed a "permanent guest artist" with the company, dancing with it for much of the time, but also producing independent programs of her own. In addition to Limón, the younger generation was represented by Dudley, Maslow, and Bales, who had been working together since 1942, sometimes as a trio, at other times as heads of a larger company of dancers drawn from the New Dance Group, the New York school at which the three directors taught. Because their political sympathies inclined toward the Left, their dances often showed an awareness of social realities and utilized themes from American folklore; on many occasions, Woody Guthrie appeared as guest artist with them in Maslow's *Folksay*. But no matter what the theme of their works may have been, Dudley, Maslow, and Bales knew how to make an evening of modern dance a lively occasion.

New works at the 1948 festival were offered by Graham, Humphrey, and Erick Hawkins (at that time a member of the Graham company). The major event proved to be the premiere of Graham's *Diversion of Angels*, a joyful lyric dance that remains in her company's repertoire. However, in 1948 it was called *Wilderness Stair*, a title that was soon discarded. In 1948 it also possessed a decor by Isamu Noguchi consisting of a pearl-gray background curtain that, according to Doris Hering of *Dance Magazine*, "was stretched taut and then cratered and carbuncled as though some huge hidden finger had poked at it playfully." But the decor was abandoned along with the original title.

A celebration of the pleasures and pains of young love, *Diversion of Angels* had, as program note, a text by Ben Belitt, a poet (and professor of English at Bennington) who had long been one of Graham's admirers:

> It is the place of the Rock and the Ladder, the raven, the blessing, the tempter, the rose. It is the wish of the single-hearted, the undivided: play after spirit's labor: games, flights, fancies, configurations of the lover's intention: the believed Possibility, at once strenuous and tender: humors of innocence, garlands, evangels, Joy on the Wilderness Stair, diversion of angels.

The dance was unusual in several ways. First of all, it was a vehicle for the younger dancers of the company and Graham did not appear in it. And, although it came at a time when Graham was choreographing convoluted works inspired by Greek mythology, it was a radiant, exuberant piece with only a hint of a theme. Therefore Nik Krevitsky, a critic for Louis Horst's influential *Dance Observer*, wondered whether it might be a choreographic "turning point. There is in it a new element—or a return to an old—in the use of pure dance without dramatic intent, program notes notwithstanding."

According to Cecil Smith of *Musical America*:

> In formal construction Wilderness Stair is one of those rare composi-tions which seem entirely spontaneous and almost improvised, and yet is actually tightly and cogently constructed, without a waste movement or an irrelevant passage. It is a complex counterpoint of individual movement patterns, each designed with a shrewd under-standing of the qualities and potentialities of each member of the company.

Hering summed it up by calling it "as young as a cartwheel, as old as loneliness."[3]

Erick Hawkins, who on 7 September 1948 married Martha Graham, offered the premiere of *The Strangler*, a complex mythological dance-drama about Oedipus (or Oidipous, as Hawkins rendered the name) and the Sphinx. Because that story turned upon the solving of a riddle, it could be argued that it was inherently unsuitable for choreographic treatment. To make sure that his intentions were clear, Hawkins included a poetic text by Robert Fitzgerald that was recited by Joseph Wiseman as the action progressed and wrote a long program note that gave his own, decidedly psychoanalytical, interpretation of the myth:

> The SPHINX, half lion and half woman, represents the father and mother in the primal scene, her wings are a symbol of the physical ecstasy of the parents, and her name, in Greek meaning the Strangler, refers to the danger of parental fixation or domination.
>
> OIDIPOUS overcomes the Sphinx by discerning in her the child's phantasy of the primal scene and by deciphering her riddle to mean the four-legged being of the primal scene, the two-legged image of the naked human being, and the three-legged image of the physically creative man. His name in Greek is a euphemism, Swollen Foot.

For many of the critics, *The Strangler* was all talk. Walter Terry, of the *New York Herald Tribune*, found it "peculiarly undramatic" because "the action rarely reflects the drama inherent in the situation upon which the legend is built." What action there was, said Robert Sabin in *Dance Observer*, "consisted of about four basic movements, repeated in no apparently logical sequence at least a score of times." Hering complained of Hawkins's basic choreographic approach:

> When Erick Hawkins mounts a dance of his own devising, he reminds one of a fly caught in a bottle. He buzzes about frantically bumping his head against all manner of intellectual and theatrical problems and solves them not as the breath-taking dancer he could so easily be, but as a silly old professor wearing flyleaves of the Encyclopedia Britannica as blinders.[4]

Doris Humphrey's controversial *Corybantic*, for the Limón company, allegorically depicted conflicting forces in a destructive battle. Yet, because Humphrey always refused to succumb to despair, these forces at last evinced a desire for harmony. There were dancegoers who found *Corybantic* confusing. Although he realized that its theme was conflict, Krevitsky nevertheless thought that "there is a strange feeling among the five performers that they are members of five different schools of thought; certainly, they bring no unity of style to their interpretation of the dance." Hering disliked the very appearance of the work, thinking that Pauline Lawrence's costumes made the performers resemble "the kind of figures they put in drug store windows to advertise abdominal supports and elastic stockings." And even after Humphrey revised *Corybantic* in 1949, Louis Horst, in the *New London Evening Day*, the community's newspaper, still pronounced it "aimless scurrying" and concluded that "the net result of all this 'sound and fury' seems to add up to just what Shakespeare said it did."

However, *Corybantic* had its defenders. Terry called it "a masterful job" and, far from being confused, he wrote that Humphrey's "allegory is clear and of dramatic moment, and the movements themselves, in addition to serving the theme, are of compelling power as sheer action." Years later, Limón recalled the failure of *Corybantic* as being "one of the cruel experiences" of his career, and he maintained, "I believe this was a great work. The public hated it. It probed deeply and unearthed a most unpalatable truth—that we carry within us depths of malice and depravity which need only a pretext to erupt into corybantic fury and madness. It was a heroic failure."[5]

Despite the failure of one or two individual works, the festival as a whole was an artistic success. It attracted a total audience of eight thousand people, whereas it was estimated that all the Bennington festivals combined attracted no more than thirteen thousand.[6] The school had an enrollment of 119 dancers, coming from forty-six states, England, China, and France; and Martha Graham told Walter Terry that the student body was younger in general than that of Bennington and had a higher technical level. Courses were offered in modern dance, folk and square dancing, composition, music, and dance notation, and Ben Belitt led a special workshop on poetry and dance, his students giving demonstrations at which they danced while reciting Wallace Stevens, e. e. cummings, and William Blake. Terry thought it remarkable that these various courses "were all so thoroughly integrated" and reported that Martha Hill hoped that the festival might develop into a year-round dance center.[7]

But the festival was also accompanied by problems. For one thing, it helped bring about the final separation of Martha Graham and Louis Horst, who had been her musical adviser (and confidant) since her debut concert in 1926. Conducting an orchestra drawn for the festival from the Juilliard School, Horst became so dissatisfied with the playing of the musicians that he kept interrupting rehearsals until Graham finally told him, "Look, Louis, this has got to stop." He thereupon put down his baton, walked out, and wrote a letter of resignation. However, a true professional, he conducted the scheduled festival performances. But after that he never again conducted for Graham.[8]

A problem affecting the festival as a whole was a deficit of $6,500 — not a large sum by today's standards, but a considerable one in 1948. It was also an unexpected one, for Martha Hill had assured her academic sponsors that Bennington had always broken even and she predicted Connecticut would do the same. Some officials, she recalls, started muttering, "Our schools don't intend to go into show business, you know." Therefore, to demonstrate that supporting her festival was not as risky as investing in a Broadway play, Hill organized a fund-raising drive that included two benefit performances on 28 November 1948 at New York's 92nd Street YM-YWHA. As a result of her efforts, a second festival was assured.[9]

—————————————————— 1949 ——————————————————

If *Diversion of Angels* helped make 1948 choreographically memorable, then 1949 was unquestionably the year of *The Moor's Pavane*. José Limón's retelling of *Othello* became the most acclaimed item in his company's repertoire. Its popularity has never diminished, and in recent years it has even been staged by such classical ballet companies as American Ballet Theatre, the Joffrey Ballet, and the Royal Danish Ballet. In fact, *The Moor's Pavane* may be the best known single work in all of modern dance.

The four dancers of its cast—who correspond to Shakespeare's Othello, Desdemona, Iago, and Emilia—never leave the stage; instead, they dance out their passions within the formal confines of what appears to be an elegant Renaissance court dance (although no specific court dance is literally imitated), and the resultant tensions between the restraints of court etiquette and the intensity of the characters' feelings give the choreography its dramatic power. Some basic knowledge of Shakespeare's plot may be necessary to make the stage business with Desdemona's handkerchief comprehensible. But, otherwise, the action is clear, and *The Moor's Pavane* is a remarkably successful choreographic distillation of a literary work.

Critics hailed it as a creative breakthrough for Limón. Summing up the majority viewpoint, John Martin noted in the *New York Times* that "Limón has until recently been a satisfactory but not especially distinguished choreographer . . . with this latest work he has definitely made a place for himself among the best of them." Martin praised the work for being "none of your mimed plays with danced interludes; it is a simon-pure dance composition, and a very beautiful one." Indeed, for Martin, it was "quite unlike anything else in the modern dance repertoire."

Although most critics would still assent to that judgment, there was in 1949 at least one dissenting voice: Doris Hering, at that time critic for both *Dance Magazine* and the New York *Daily Compass*. Writing in the *Compass*, she conceded that the work possessed "a clever idea." But, she added, "it is an idea that requires endless experimentation to achieve just the right counterpoint between the dramatic and the formal. At present the dance resembles a dressed up game of 'find the handkerchief' with Mr. Limón rather hammy in the role of the Moor."[10]

In addition to being a triumph for Limón, *The Moor's Pavane* was indirectly a triumph for his artistic mentor, Doris Humphrey. Working

Pauline Koner, Lucas Hoving, José Limón, and Betty Jones in Limón's *The Moor's Pavane,* 1949. Photo, Matthew Wysocki.

with him the way an editor for a publisher might work with a novelist, she pointed out weak spots and gave him suggestions for revision. It was also Humphrey who, upon hearing that Limón wished to choreograph *Othello,* suggested that he use music by Purcell, which was specially arranged for the dance by Simon Sadoff, the Limón company's musical director.[11]

Humphrey enjoyed a success of her own that summer when the Limón company gave the premiere of her *Invention.* A work in which Limón first danced happily with Betty Jones and then in a more melancholy fashion with Ruth Currier, *Invention* could be regarded as a purely formal study, and Walter Terry analyzed it in formal terms: "Here in 'Invention' one beholds the statement of a movement theme; its development spatially and dynamically; its variations, achieved through use of new directions, new accents, new juxtapositions of dancing bodies; its conclusion, echoing kinetically the basic statement and its successive motor commentaries." Though formally intricate, *Invention,* said Terry, was also "warm, jubilant and as alive as that human body which is the only instrument of dance." Hering agreed that *Invention* was interesting for the way Humphrey invested her formal structures with expressive power: "One can look at *Invention* as the depiction of the changes in a man's personality wrought by two women. Or the work can be viewed for its structural balance alone. Actually, it is the ability to synthesize the two opposing elements that marks Miss Humphrey as a composer in the best classical tradition."[12]

Like the Limón company, the Dudley-Maslow-Bales company was again in residence, and, this time, it presented several premieres. One, Sophie Maslow's *Festival*, though warmly received, was only a fragment of a work-in-progress inspired by the stories of Sholom Aleichem that would be seen in finished form in 1950.

Out of the Cradle Endlessly Rocking, a solo by Jane Dudley, proved unexpectedly controversial. In it, Dudley was what Hering termed "a personification of All Womankind," and the dance symbolized the cycle of life. What caused the critical uproar was the way Dudley manipulated a piece of red chiffon cloth to make it represent the various phases of life. Everyone who saw the solo seems to have agreed with Walter Terry that it bore "a close resemblance to the scarf dances and romantic lyricisms of an earlier day" of modern dance. But whereas Terry thought that because of "her inherent dignity and grandeur of presence," Dudley was able "to keep the most romantically impetuous movements from becoming senti-mental self-expression," other critics—including some of modern dance's fiercest partisans—were horrified. Louis Horst denounced the solo as "an inexplicable regression," and John Martin called it "a curious anachronism." Apparently, these critics had very decided notions of what constituted the limits of "the modern."[13]

Another solo by Dudley, *Vagary*, fared better. A study of someone "phasing out of reality into fantasy," according to the choreographer, it was described by Hering as "nothing short of pure delight. She [Dudley] dances a duet with herself—goes through the patterns of correct social behavior and at the same time seems immersed in some wonderful world of fantasy. She seems to hear voices, see forms, float in the air—never really detached, never really present. Yet there is no overstatement, no silliness."[14]

Judith, William Bales's premiere, retold the Apocryphal story to no one's satisfaction. Martin dismissed it as "downright bad. It simply relates the story of Judith and Holofernes with an almost synoptic directness, without comment, without choreography, without composition of any kind."[15]

The third resident company for 1949 was not Graham's, but that of Valerie Bettis. Unlike Limón, who soon came to regard the summer season in Connecticut as one of his company's most important engagements of the year, Graham did not wish to commit her group to New London. Bettis, Graham's successor at the 1949 festival, was a vibrant dancer who favored an eclectic and highly theatrical choreographic style.

She created two new works. *It Is Always Farewell* was a section of what was obviously a still unfinished work. Nik Krevitsky found it reminiscent of the moody ballets of Antony Tudor. Yet he had to admit that, in its present state, it was "vague in theme and characterization."[16]

Domino Furioso, the other premiere, was one of Bettis's many ambitious attempts to unite movement with the spoken word. With a text by John Malcolm Brinnin, it resembled a variation on Pirandello's *Six Characters in Search of an Author*. Here, however, it was the author who was in search of characters until he conjured Pierrot, Harlequin, and Columbine, as well as their alter egos, out of a box. Then everyone proceeded to quarrel until they annihilated one another. Terry tried to be kind: "'Domino Furioso' is tragedy and comedy, philosophical dissertation and farce, and it is my guess that one of the troubles with it is that it cannot seem to make up its mind which to be or whether to fuse all elements to a single dramatic purpose." Martin had no use for its entire conception: "Apparently all dancers have to learn sooner or later that even more to be avoided than sprains and charley-horses is the Commedia Dell'Arte and Miss Bettis has undertaken to learn the hard way." No one seemed pleased by Brinnin's deliberately arch text. Krevitsky dismissed it as "too much verbal ibbitty bibbitty sibbitty gibbery ad lib," and Martin warned, "If Miss Bettis is not careful she will talk us all to death."[17]

Thus, in 1949 as in 1948, the festival attracted some harsh reviews. Yet it held enough of interest to keep critics well disposed toward it. The festival also tried to be enterprising by taking dance to the surrounding community. Lecture-demonstrations were offered at a sanitarium and a public beach, students and members of the resident companies provided entertainment for floor shows at two hotels, and the festival hosted a community square dance party.[18] This was the first of many attempts to interest New London in dance. The results, over the years, can only be called inconclusive.

──────────────────────── **1950** ────────────────────────

Martha Hill and Ruth Bloomer might well have wondered what the previous summer's campaign to make New London dance-conscious had accomplished, for the third American Dance Festival failed to attract large audiences, even for performances by José Limón, who had already established himself as a star attraction.[19] The 1950 season was the last under the joint auspices of New York University and Connecticut College. Martha Hill says that NYU officials had concluded that the festival was essentially a Connecticut venture. But because Rosemary Park continued to support modern dance at Connecticut College, the festival's future was assured and the academic parting of the ways was amicable.

The Limón and Dudley-Maslow-Bales companies were again in residence. The festival also tried to widen its horizons by inviting five other choreographers to appear as guest artists, and the policy was instituted of having performances shared by several choreographers. All the guest artists offered works from their repertoires, and their performances included no premieres. One of the guests, Pauline Koner, was already known on campus as an artist with the Limón company. The other four —Merce Cunningham, Nina Fonaroff, Katherine Litz, and Pearl Primus —were truly guests from the outside.

At the time Cunningham, who had danced and choreographed at Bennington, was known for strange choreographic mood-pieces that puzzled some dancegoers. Nevertheless, reviews of the solos he presented in Connecticut tended to be favorable. Walter Terry was especially impressed by the unaccompanied *Before Dawn*, in which "the dancer succeeded remarkably well in making the beholder feel that he was accompanied by silence. The quality of the movement, cool and remote, and the manner in which Mr. Cunningham phrased his actions convinced one that a living, present stillness was the stimulus for his dance designs." Nik Krevitsky had high praise for *Two-Step*: "The effortlessness with which gravity-defying leaps are accomplished and the bonelessness with which middle-body contractions are achieved add to the wonder of the piece."[20]

Pearl Primus introduced black dance to the festival, although not with complete success. Primus was highly regarded as a compelling performer and choreographer. Yet her festival presentations were termed uneven by John Martin. Krevitsky, who found them disorganized, said, "Until she is ready to perform in a style befitting her reputation and with

Sophie Maslow Dance Company in Maslow's *The Village I Knew*.
Photo, Jane Rady.

the verve we remember from her earlier works, it would be better to just remember than to see Miss Primus do a half-baked performance."[21]

The festival's choreographic hit was Sophie Maslow's *The Village I Knew*, the completed version of her *Festival*, which had been shown in 1949. Set in a Jewish community of czarist Russia and inspired by the stories of Sholom Aleichem, *The Village I Knew* included a Sabbath ritual, a holiday festival, and vignettes about an orphan who is taken care of by the rest of the villagers, a girl who wants to marry a fiddler, and a long-winded chatterbox of a housewife who drives a rabbi to distraction with her prattling. However, as a reminder of the social conditions in which these charming people lived, the work ended with the dispersal of the villagers as the result of a pogrom. Krevitsky praised the dance for its universal appeal: "It might be Breughel as well as Chagall, Boccaccio or Mark Twain as well as Aleichem. One need not be an authority on Jewish life in Czarist times to appreciate its delicious good humor." Moreover, he liked the way in which "each member of the highly integrated company has an opportunity to become a unique personality of the village."[22]

The Dudley-Maslow-Bales company could not only be called integrated because of its harmonious dancing style, it was racially integrated as well. The political convictions of its three directors made racial prejudice abhorrent to them, and they therefore headed a racially mixed company years before such companies were common in the modern dance world.

Jane Dudley contributed a work-in-progress, *Passional*, a dance she had originally planned to call *Sonata*. But the fancier title was suggested to her by Ben Belitt. Like *Out of the Cradle Endlessly Rocking*, this piece for a cast of six reminded reviewers of Isadora Duncan, although this time the comparisons were not invidious. For Terry,

> Miss Dudley, in using the sort of sculptural approach which Isadora Duncan would certainly have employed in dancing to such music, has avoided the "living statues" pitfall through a use of dynamically strong, expressional actions. Her inventions, in terms of detail or in large scale designs, are generally affecting, usually smooth and exhilarating in their freshness.

Even though they acknowledged that it was still incomplete, some viewers were puzzled by the intent of *Passional*. Thus Krevitsky thought that "where the dance is pure it is highly evocative; when it becomes dramatic a kind of story begins to intrude." For Doris Hering, this thematic material comprised "a highly emotional and somewhat erotic picture of a woman searching for fulfillment." But Krevitsky found that "the confusion between these two kinds of expression complicates the work."[23]

William Bales's *Impromptu* was only a brief solo. But Terry considered it snappy, as well as short:

> Like the music of Satie to which it is set, "Impromptu" is thin (not shallow) and clean of line. The choreographic pattern is one of arcs, circles and spirals and variations thereof. Sometimes they are to be seen in the line of the body itself, later in an extended arm, again in the designs which the moving figure creates in space, or perhaps in combination of these. The floor patterns, however, generally pursue straight lines, and these, added to the swift, semi-percussiveness of the footwork and the sharp accents accorded each phrase of

movement, complement and give contrast to the arcs, circles and spirals which characterize this altogether delightful solo.[24]

There were two contrasting premieres by Limón. One could be considered a forerunner of what has become known as the "piano-ballet." As that expression is employed today, it refers to a plotless but emotionally evocative work set only to piano music; the pianist is often on stage with the dancers, and the lack of orchestral sonorities creates an intimate, chamber music effect. Most piano-ballets—including such later examples as Jerome Robbins's *Dances at a Gathering* and Eliot Feld's *Intermezzo* —are to Romantic music. However, Limón's *Concert* was to preludes and fugues by Bach. Otherwise, it was decidedly a piano-ballet, with Simon Sadoff as the onstage pianist.

The work's inventiveness pleased critics but, even though the term piano-ballet had not yet been invented, they were worried about *Concert's* relationship to old-fashioned classical ballet. Krevitsky said that *Concert* "turns out to be nothing more than a balletic series of solos, duos, trios as unrelated and undevelopable as the individual preludes and fugues which are its stunning accompaniment. Because it does and says nothing that ballet hasn't been able to do as well or better for some time, this work seems to have no raison d'etre."[25]

Limón returned to a more familiar style in *The Exiles*. Essentially, this duet concerned the expulsion of Adam and Eve from Eden. But, often, when he drew upon biblical, historical, or mythological sources, Limón tried to find contemporary parallels for the material, and he once told a Washington critic that *The Exiles* was inspired by recollections of refugees who came to America in the 1940s and would speak of Vienna or Prague with tears in their eyes. Limón also sought to give *The Exiles* universal significance by making it reflect "the dreary everyday life you and I have to endure against memories of our supremely happy moments —the knowledge that once we lived in Paradise."

Terry thought that *The Exiles* did indeed convey "the lostness of those who continue the search for a new Eden." Yet, said Terry, "for each freely flowing phrase, honest and forthright in the conveying of the dance plan, there seemed to be one which was labored, forced, even contrived." John Martin also found "forced" and "contrived" movement when he reviewed the duet at a New York performance in 1952. But because he felt that this sense of constriction helped give *The Exiles* its distinctive character, his comments may be worth quoting, even though they were not made at the festival. Declaring that the action of *The Exiles* was "keyed in terms of excited tensions," he immediately went on to say that "under this dramatic surface is a skeleton of curiously inhibited narrative pantomime, and on this contrast the values of the piece are built."[26]

1951

In many ways the 1951 festival was a happy one. Although the only performances were on 16–19 August (whereas the 1948 and 1949 festivals had lasted for most of two weeks and the 1950 festival was spread across three weekends), attendance was up. Walter Terry wrote that he was impressed by the enthusiastic audiences, and John Martin noted approvingly that the festival was scheduling dance classes for the community's children.[27]

The first brochures for the summer school contained what to knowledgeable dance lovers must have been the startling announcement that Mary Wigman, the great German Expressionist dancer and choreographer, would be a member of the faculty. For several years Martha Hill and Ruth Bloomer had been trying to bring her to America, but Wigman was always unable to obtain a visa, presumably because she had stayed on in her native Germany after the Nazis came to power. Eventually, however, she fell out of favor with the Nazis, who closed her school. Following the war she lived until 1949 in the Russian zone of occupied Germany. Given this complicated political past, the American government was reluctant to allow her to visit the United States, and her visa was once again denied in 1951.[28]

Nevertheless, the festival did possess an international flavor, thanks to an arrangement between Connecticut College and the Mexican government that permitted four students from the Mexican National Academy of Dance—Valentina Castro, Marta Castro, Rocio Sagaon, and Beatriz Flores—to study in New London during the summer and to participate in a special Mexican program prepared by the Limón company as a tribute to its director's native land. The bill included *La Malinche*, Limón's terse dance-drama about the Mexican conquest; *The Moor's Pavane*, his acknowledged masterpiece; and two works that Limón had choreographed the previous winter when he was a guest teacher in Mexico City, *Tonantzintla* and *Dialogues*.

The former, in which the Mexican students appeared, was inspired by the Baroque decorations in the Indian church of Santa Maria Tonantzintla and was dominated by its sumptuous decor by the Mexican painter Miguel Covarrubias. These stage designs, said Doris Hering, resembled "a child's dream of a candy world—all pink and cerise and red and blue and gold and sparkling." The dance brought sculptural figures in the church to life and dealt with the birthday celebration of a celestial mermaid. Hering summarized its strengths and weaknesses: "The body balance of the dancers bordered on the balletic. The hands curved inward as though they should contain castanets. And the patterning was naive and archaic. But the conscious mixture of styles didn't jell. The dances seemed heavy-handed when they should have had the fragility of spun sugar."

Dialogues, a pair of duets for Limón and Lucas Hoving, commemorated the struggles between invader and defender that have been a recurrent feature of Mexican history. The first duet concerned Montezuma and Cortés; the second pitted Juárez against Maximilian. Nik Krevitsky said:

What *Dialogues* does which is novel is to present a contrast in the treatment of the adversaries, showing first the naivete of the Indian Emperor whose throne and empire are seized by the conquistador, and second the ultimate strength of democracy over imperialism. It is accomplished in an interesting fashion by having an actual combat in the first section, and a psychological encounter in the second, where the adversaries never meet face to face. At present the dance seems overdrawn and lengthy, although there is a great deal of fine solo and duet movement. Mr. Limón's own movements as Montezuma are a new departure for him, the gestures, obviously inspired by Aztec glyphs, imparting a strange two-dimensionality and authenticity to the movement patterns.[29]

The Limón company—once again (along with Dudley-Maslow-Bales) one of the festival's resident attractions—was forced to cancel the announced premiere of Limón's *The Queen's Epicedium* because of an injured dancer,[30] yet it did stage a new work by Doris Humphrey that became a staple of its repertoire. At the festival it was simply called *Quartet No. 1*, after the musical composition by Priaulx Rainier to which it was set. Since it was about a sleeper and his dreams, Humphrey had originally planned to call it *The Dream*. But her son persuaded her that that title was too prosaic. On tour after the festival, says Pauline Koner, the dance was occasionally billed as *Illusions*, and then it acquired the title it still bears: *Night Spell*.

The dance showed a sleeper struggling with various dream figures. Whereas one represented some sort of ideal, two others seemed both menacing and vague, and that was probably why John Martin declared that, for him, too little really happened. Humphrey, who had no intention of choreographing a psychoanalytical fantasy, may have foreseen the possibility of such a reaction, for she wrote in her journal that she suspected some viewers would be "looking for fancy Freudian meanings which are not in the piece." What helped make *Night Spell* compelling was its performers, each member of the cast being a fine dancer and a vivid stage personality. As Selma Jeanne Cohen, Humphrey's biographer, recalls: "It was one of those remarkable instances in which she [Doris Humphrey] had created roles wonderfully suited to the talents of her company: José, the noble dreamer, was tormented by nightmare visions of Betty Jones and Lucas Hoving, menacing with staccato stabbings, sharp and strong; then saved by the tender, unearthly ministrations of Ruth Currier."[31]

The Dudley-Maslow-Bales trio gave two premieres: one, lyric; the other, dramatic. Sophie Maslow's *Four Sonnets*, the lyric piece, was something of a departure for this choreographer. Although she had been associated with Americana and dance-drama in the past, Maslow here created a Romantic plotless work to Schumann. By so doing, she violated the accepted choreographic practices of the day. She says, "Back then, the feeling was that you did modern dance to modern music." If a composer wished to employ older music, scores from the medieval to the baroque periods were considered acceptable. But the Romantic period was associated both with the sentimentality to which modern dance was supposed to be an antidote and with ballet, which was still viewed with suspicion by some modern dance theorists. Nevertheless, because Maslow liked Schumann, she went ahead and used his music.

Terry thought that *Four Sonnets* "compensated for its few cloying passages with sections quite lovely in their delicacies." However, Martin found the choreography unduly harsh and said that Maslow's style "was not able to cope with music of this sort. It is too brusque, too short of phrase, too little concerned with the lower registers of dynamism, too lacking in delicacy. One found oneself longing for the lightness and legato of Isadora Duncan's approach to movement," and Martin confessed that he now realized how much Duncan's approach had been "maligned for its alleged lack of technique."[32]

Like Eugene O'Neill's *Mourning Becomes Electra*, William Bales's *The Haunted Ones* transported the mythological figures of Clytemnestra, Orestes, and Electra to nineteenth-century America and, for Martin, did so very interestingly: "The movement he [Bales] has evolved is in no sense pantomimic, yet neither is it pure dance. It is an interesting kind of phrased motor dialogue, and with it Mr. Bales has created passages of great power." But Krevitsky was bothered by quirks of both casting and choreography: Jane Dudley, as The Daughter (corresponding to Electra) appeared "severe and maternal," whereas Sophie Maslow, as The Mother (Clytemnestra), danced movements that gave her "the quality of appearing to be the sister of Mr. Bales, The Son."[33]

The festival's choreographic guest artists were Pauline Koner and Charles Weidman, Doris Humphrey's partner before arthritis forced her to retire from the stage. Koner and Weidman were teamed together in the premiere of Koner's *Amorous Adventure*, a comedy with scenario and designs by the cartoonist Abner Dean, whose own description of the action suggests the dance's tone: "It is the story of a girl with amatory hiccups, an unbalanced equation and several men who have a peripheral influence on her personal mathematics. The dance resolves no world problems and at its conclusion, 'X' still represents the unknown." In a setting dominated by giant wishbones—a recurrent image in Dean's drawings—*Amorous Adventure* showed a bored wife repeatedly leaving her husband to follow various more attractive men, while the husband tried to win her back by bumblingly imitating each new type of man to whom she took a fancy. Weidman played the husband, Koner was the wife, and Lucas Hoving impersonated all the other men in her life.

Since the three dancers were known to be skilled comedians, critics hoped *Amorous Adventure* would be fun. But Krevitsky was forced to conclude that it was "a bit labored to be called hilarious, though it is a very whimsical piece." Martin thought it contained too much Dean and not enough Koner: "The action is almost entirely literary, dramatic, pantomimic, with scarcely a true choreographic phrase to be seen. This is, in effect, merely reading aloud Mr. Dean's scenario without adding the magic of creative presentation which is the function of the choreographer."[34]

A Song for You, Weidman's new solo, was dedicated to the memory of Elsie Houston, a Brazilian singer with whom he had hoped to collabo-

rate before her death in 1946. In the dance, the singer's spirit was symbolized by a shaft of light and the choreography, set to some of Houston's
recordings, emphasized delicate hand and arm gestures. The solo was
very much a danced memorial, and Krevitsky found that it had "a strange,
evocative quality."[35]

Reflecting upon the festival as a whole, Martin observed that, although
no masterpieces were numbered among its new works, "there was not
one that fell below the mark of high integrity." Therefore this was "in
many ways the most successful of all the festivals to date."[36]

----------------------------------- 1952 -----------------------------------

By 1952 the festival's basic programming pattern had become firmly
established: during the course of a long weekend (Thursday through
Sunday), in addition to concerts featuring the resident companies (Limón
and Dudley-Maslow-Bales), there would be performances by guest artists
or companies—in this case, Pearl Lang's company, the choreographic
team of Emily Frankel and Mark Ryder, and solo appearances (in his own
choreography) by Ronne Aul, a member of the Dudley-Maslow-Bales
company. Walter Terry found the guest dancers "uniformly expert, although
some of their dances were not," and he had special praise for Lang's
"personal radiance and sweetly commanding presence."[37]

Of the guests, only Aul offered a premiere. A black dancer known for
his speed and virtuosity, he made great use of these qualities in *Mostly
Like Flight*, a solo that Doris Hering called "an experiment in spatial
exploration and use of head and arms in rapid, birdlike gestures. It was
performed in Mr. Aul's usual sharp, strong fashion, but as he ran and
hopped along imaginary zig-zags, one had the feeling that the dance had
been devised without much emotional expenditure." Terry also had doubts
about the choreography, but not about Aul:

> Here is a dancer with a body-instrument trained to obey every
> command. He can move with incredible swiftness . . . sustain a move-
> ment sequence with pure legato style. He can leap, jump, fall, twist
> or turn with the utmost ease. . . . One is fascinated watching him
> even when his dances, as they sometimes do, fail to travel very far or
> suffer from blurred dramatic purpose.[38]

The Limón company's premieres were all slightly out of the ordinary,
the most unusual of them being *The Queen's Epicedium*, the work to

Purcell's elegy on the death of Queen Mary in 1694 that had been canceled the previous summer. The Latin text calls the deceased monarch the Queen of Arcadia and tells how the inhabitants of a pastoral realm mourn for her. As it showed a regal figure join some mourning muses, then remove her crown and assume a pose of statuesque grandeur, Limón's choreography echoed some of the textual imagery and, for Hering, it recalled "the rather specialized neo-classicism of a Puvis de Chavannes painting."

"In robes of black and with a crown of jet, Letitia Ide," said Terry, "was superb as the lamented one, sadly gracious for the tribute accorded her and, in the final passages, triumphant as the symbolic star shining secure in the heavens." But the work's most demanding role was that for Betty Jones who, as she moved, had to sing Purcell's cantata. A trained singer as well as a dancer, Jones, to judge from reviews, managed very well in her dual assignment, Terry praising her for moving "with easy grandeur through the patterns of dance while singing the taxing music with great beauty of tone and sensitivity for musical as well as textual nuance."[39]

In *The Visitation* Limón once again turned to the Bible, telling a story of a peasant couple visited by a mysterious stranger. As the action proceeded in what Pauline Koner remembers as "an absolutely spellbinding work," the peasants were revealed to be Mary and Joseph, and the stranger proved to be the Angel of the Annunciation. Among Limón's ingenious choreographic touches was the use of a plank to suggest Joseph's trade of carpentry and to prefigure Christ's death on the cross. The characterizations of Koner and Limón, as Mary and Joseph, were much praised, Terry saying, "At first they are not so much awed as terrified. They are unsure, they are doubting, they are angry. They are even petulant. For they are humans unprepared for such a visitation."[40]

Doris Humphrey's premiere, to Mozart, was *Fantasy and Fugue in C Major and Fugue in C Minor*, although that cumbersome, but musically accurate, title was often shortened to *Fantasy and Fugues* for the sake of convenience. A plotless piece, it nevertheless had emotional resonance. Louis Horst said that the first of its three sections created "the impression of entering some place for the first time." Hering also singled out that section for possessing some "especially striking moments, the most outstanding being Mr. Limón's entrance. As he paused between two scrims, clad in crimson tights, head upthrust, leg powerfully extending, it seemed as though the music should not only swell but that cymbals should crash and the light should become brighter. It was as though Jupiter had descended." This section gave way to a quiet duet for Pauline Koner and Ruth Currier that Horst found "suggestive of a mother-daughter relationship." Then, said Horst, the final fugue brought the composition to "a great close."[41]

The Dudley-Maslow-Bales company's new works were Sophie Maslow's *The Snow Queen*, a retelling of Hans Christian Andersen's fairy tale, and Jane Dudley's *Family Portrait*. Both were shown in a still-unfinished state, and Terry said he was unable "to arrive at any conclusive judgment about them." *Family Portrait* was at least eye-catching. A set of comic sketches of family life as seen through the eyes of a little boy, its set resembled a giant Tinkertoy construction; its characters included dancers representing such things as a toy gun and a cowboy jacket; and its incidents included a birthday party, bedtime, a tantrum, and a Sunday outing.[42]

1953

There were both signs of change at the 1953 festival and signs that the festival was relying very heavily upon certain tried-and-true choreographic friends. Martha Hill had married Thurston Davies the previous year, and because she was busy during the winter at Juilliard and wished to have some time with her husband, her visits to New London became less frequent. The notation "advisory" appears after her name as codirector in the 1953 bulletin, and subsequent bulletins would list her as being "on leave." This made Ruth Bloomer directly responsible for the administration of the summer program. However, Hill remained an active member of the board of directors for the dance school and the festival.

Another sign of change was the fact that this summer's resident company other than that of Limón was officially billed as "Sophie Maslow and Dance Company (with Jane Dudley and Donald McKayle, guest artists)." A back condition had forced William Bales to stop dancing, and Dudley began to go her own way as a dancer, choreographer, and teacher.

Welcome innovations in the summer's curriculum were courses reflecting the German style of modern dance. Mary Wigman was still unable to come to Connecticut. But the festival did manage to engage Margret Dietz, a teacher from the Wigman school in Berlin who later

Donald McKayle with technique class, Connecticut College. Photo, David L. Arnold.

settled in America. Other highlights of the school term included the demonstrations given for summer students by the Children's Dance Theater of Salt Lake City, under the direction of Virginia Tanner, an authority in the field of children's dance.[43]

The festival offered nine new works—the greatest number of premieres to be presented in one season thus far. All festival programs were shared by several companies or solo dancers, with the exception of one program given over to the Limón company. Henceforth at the festival, however many shared programs might be scheduled, at least one would be reserved entirely for Limón. Such a policy could be taken as a sign that festival officials believed that the Limón company was entitled to what in television would be referred to as "prime time." In retrospect, it also seems significant that most of the 1953 guest artists came from one or the other of the resident companies. In addition to giving their own works, Pauline Koner and Lucas Hoving and Lavina Nielsen (who were husband and wife, as well as dancing partners) were associated with the Limón company, and Ronne Aul danced with Maslow. If it was only logical that choreographers who were already on campus should be allowed to create dances there, the continuing reliance upon only a few sources of choreographic talent could—and, to some critics, eventually did—limit the festival's range.

The one guest choreographer from outside the festival was John Butler, a former dancer with Graham, whose company offered the premiere of *Malocchio*, a dance-drama set in an Italian village that told of how a woman, scorned by her neighbors, is protected by a stranger only to be deserted by him when he is informed that she possesses the "evil eye." Walter Terry thought it "a striking study in the cruelty of superstition." But Louis Horst was disappointed because it "did not attain the artistic results one hoped for."[44]

Aul showed two new solos. As its title suggested, *Sonata for Dancer and Piano* attempted to be a choreographic equivalent of a classical sonata with a dancer as the featured solo instrument. Instead, said Doris Hering, it was "an embarrassing piece of self-display" in which Aul "posed and preened in a dance-structure that said little more than 'look at me.'" Hering much preferred Aul's *30th at 3rd*, an excursion into social commentary that emerged as

a sensitive study of poverty and pride.

The dance began in an air of aimless drabness. A man, searching his pockets for money, pulled out the two empty linings. Calling upon the familiar state of humor-in-adversity, he tugged at the linings and drew them into a gay dance. Suddenly the mood changed. He shoved the linings back into his trousers and hurled himself into a dance of fury and rebellion.

One of the most interesting aspects of the dance was the use of ethnic material to reveal character.[45]

Hoving and Nielsen contributed two new duets. According to its program note, *Perilous Flight* derived from the notion that "to some primitive peoples the soul is a bird that cannot be allowed to escape," and Horst said the dance "possessed the strange and evocative quality of a primitive mystery." *Satyros*, the other duet, parodied the archaic Grecian choreographic style of such works as *Afternoon of a Faun* in a manner that Horst called "hilarious."[46]

Pauline Koner took a gloomier view of ancient Greece and, by implication, human nature in her solo *Cassandra*. Although she had made her reputation as a solo dancer, she had not been interested in solos for some years. Yet she felt drawn to the prophetess Cassandra who, for Koner "represents truth staring people in the face—and people still don't see it." Today, Koner thinks Cassandra might cry out against nuclear weapons. But in 1953 she was alarmed by the accusations of Senator Joseph McCarthy, the investigations of the House Committee on Un-American Activities, and the prospect of what she feared might be unprincipled attacks upon liberals in all the arts. Therefore she created *Cassandra* as a warning against hysteria.

The solo, said Horst, revealed Koner's "virtuosic technique, an unfailing clarity of design in movement, and an unerring musical sense of phrasing." It did something else as well: it made Koner resemble Martha Graham. Both dancers were short, dark-haired, and intense. And Graham, at the time, was choreographically preoccupied with mythology. Moreover, after *Cassandra*'s premiere Koner learned from Horst that, by setting her work to Aaron Copland's Piano Variations, she had unwittingly used the same score that Graham had employed for *Dithyrambic*, a solo of 1931. Critic after critic compared Koner with Graham. Thus, for Hering, "when the curtain first opened to reveal Miss Koner leaning in tragic gesture against a black drape, one almost thought she *was* Martha Graham." And Terry professed to see the influence of Graham in "those swift contractions of head, shoulders and neck that are used to give overt form to the hidden pangs of anguish."

Yet, Koner says, "I never took a Graham class in my life. We're really very different in style." The critics, too, became aware of this, once the initial shock of Koner's appearance wore off. Koner, Terry concluded, "remains a distinct personality with a distinct rhythmic attack." And Koner was especially touched when Doris Humphrey told her that she thought *Cassandra* was Koner's finest work.[47]

The resident companies contributed two premieres. Sophie Maslow's *Suite: Manhattan Transfer* took its title from a novel by John Dos Passos because Maslow thought it "a very New York title." But she borrowed nothing else from that novel. Instead of being dramatic, her *Manhattan Transfer* was a jazz—specifically, a boogie-woogie—suite that pleased many viewers, including Terry, who, after noting that it had "the slickness and the swiftness of a Broadway revue number," cheerfully warned that "Broadway choreographers had better watch out for a new rival." Hering, though conceding it to be "a light-hearted bit of dancing fun," still feared that Maslow

> overlooked the refinement of gestural and rhythmic detail that would really give her work finish.
>
> This particular composition must inevitably be compared with Jerome Robbins' *Interplay*, for it bears the same tri-partite jazz form; it concerns a group of young people letting off steam; and it is similar in costuming. But *Interplay*, with its smooth-flowing phrases and careful stylization, is a far more subtle work.[48]

José Limón was also in a lighthearted mood in his *Don Juan Fantasia*, which tried to retell the story of Don Juan's love affairs in a broadly humorous manner. However, Limón seldom attempted comic choreography and was rarely successful at it. Although Horst generously called the piece "fine and ribald," its own worst critic was Limón himself. Looking back upon it years later, he admitted, "I fell flat on my face with *Don Juan Fantasia*. I shudder at the recollection of the entire depressing episode. It was a parody built on a parody . . . I'm not good as a comedian."[49]

Towering over all the other premieres in conception—and, for many commentators, in artistic achievement, as well—was *Ruins and Visions*, one of Doris Humphrey's most complex creations. Inspired by Stephen Spender's "The Fates," a poem from his book, *Ruins and Visions*, and set to the first movement of Benjamin Britten's First Quartet and the entirety of his Second Quartet, the dance had an enigmatic scenario concerning reality and illusion. In the first scene, a mother and son sat on a real garden swing and, by means of her gestures, the doting mother tried to shield the boy from the outside world. The second scene found them in the theater where, though the play was a horrific melodrama about a man's murder of his mistress, their only response was apathetic applause. Walking home through the streets, they disdained the rowdy people around them and ignored an agitated newsboy selling papers that presumably reported catastrophic news. Finally, after a declaration of war, the son went off to the front and was brought back dead.

The dance, which Martin regarded as one of Humphrey's "most beautiful achievements," dealt with the ways people may vainly try to isolate themselves from the world, and Limón, in a reminiscence, said that, like themes in a two-part musical invention, the two themes of illusion and reality

> were played sometimes singly, at times juxtaposed in contrapuntal order, or played in unison. The effect was one of fluid ambiguity. Reality and illusion lost their identities, their definite contours. Good and evil, wisdom and fatuity, innocence and guilt became fugal motifs, entwined around each other in discordant counterpoint, were augmented, inverted, manipulated as variations, reiterated and, with the inevitability of all fugues brought to a resolution. A catharsis. In this case an overwhelming one.

Limón may have been referring to the finale in which, Martin wrote, "all eight of the dancers, now translated as if into monumental symbols, move forward in rigid, staccato style to the sharp, widely spaced chords of the music in one of the most stunning final statements imaginable."

The finale's optimistic implication that the characters had learned to face reality ran counter to the pessimistic spirit of Spender's poem, but was in perfect accord with Humphrey's own moral outlook. This was pointed out at the time by a young critic, Selma Jeanne Cohen, in an essay on *Ruins and Visions* published in *Dance Observer*. Cohen, who later became a prominent dance historian and aesthetician—as well as Doris Humphrey's biographer—found that *Ruins and Visions* afforded her an opportunity to explore some aesthetic theories. The differences between Spender's poem and Humphrey's dance, she claimed, were signs of choreographic strength, rather than weakness, for they indicated that the dance

Charles Czarny, Pauline Koner, Lucas Hoving, and Crandall Diehl in Humphrey's *Ruins and Visions,* 1953. Photo, Peter Basch.

possessed "a structure distinct from that of the poem." She argued that those who were troubled by the dance's obscurity did not fully understand the nature of dance as an art:

> Such persons believe that a choreographer's purpose is to convey simple facts, whereas he is artistically communicating a feeling about facts, simple or complex. The primary aim of the dance creator is not clarity but, rather, the stimulation of a particular emotional effect. To state a fact plainly is the function of the scientist. The artist's purpose is more complex: he asks not only that the audience perceive a fact but that they react emotionally to it.

Therefore there can be moments when the artist may "have to sacrifice immediate clarity for immediate effectiveness."[50]

Looking upon the season in retrospect, Martin acknowledged that the number of premieres made it rich in quantity; but quality was another matter, and he was bothered by "too many insignificant little solos and

Lucas Hoving and José Limón in Limón's *The Traitor*, 1954. Photo, Matthew Wysocki.

the like, too heterogeneous a programming plan. It is reasonable to demand of a festival that it consist in the main of substantial works worth a pilgrimage to see."[51] Using Martin's standard, it therefore could be argued that, in 1953, only *Ruins and Visions* and *Cassandra* were dances worth a pilgrimage.

1954

For the first time the festival directly commissioned a new work out of its operating budget: José Limón's *The Traitor*. The administration of a more straitlaced institution, or one less supportive of dance, than Connecticut College might have been startled by the results. *The Traitor* was a work for an all-male cast, and, even though they were not so identified in the program, the two leading characters were clearly intended to be Judas and Jesus Christ, while the ensemble of six men represented the disciples (Limón having found six disciples more economical to assemble than the

Gospel's twelve). At one point the dancers stretched out a tablecloth and grouped themselves around it in a tableau inspired by paintings of the Last Supper. And, to make matters possibly even more controversial, Limón told reporters that he created *The Traitor* as a result of his reflections upon the fate of Julius and Ethel Rosenberg, who had recently been executed on the charge of having stolen atomic bomb secrets.

Yet no one cried, "'Sacrilege!' Reviewers were fascinated by *The Traitor*. Walter Terry likened its pictorial effects to the "thematic grandeur, the rich and royal colors and the dramatic immediacy of the religious painting of the Italian renaissance." Doris Hering called attention to the dance's movement qualities:

> In form, *The Traitor* consisted of bursts of convoluted movement that twisted upon themselves like the roots of a tree. At intervals the convolutions froze (but did not actually resolve) into sculptural formations as though the conflicting action were temporarily stalemated, only to begin anew. We found this lack of sustained line in the dance phrases extremely provocative.

The twisted movement, said Terry, helped establish the characterizations of Limón as Judas and Lucas Hoving as Jesus: "Clearly, frighteningly, the consuming jealousy of Judas is portrayed in angry gestures, great exhortations, twisted insinuations and clearly and strongly the unquenchable fire of Jesus' mission glows through actions revelatory of purpose, dedication, faith and a strangely appealing kindness steeled with sternness." Finally, Louis Horst even speculated that the forcefulness of the male choreography might "open the door to a wholesome future for all male dancers who suffer under the popular misconception that all dance of an artistic nature is sissie."[52]

Doris Humphrey's new *Felipe el Loco* told of a Spanish dancer (portrayed by Limón) torn from his native land to appear with a classical ballet company in some distant northern country. The cultural differences he sensed eventually drove him mad. The scenario had a parallel in real life, for it recalled the story of Felix Fernandez, a Spanish dancer hired to teach traditional Spanish dance to members of Diaghilev's Ballets Russes, who were then rehearsing Léonide Massine's Spanish ballet, *The Three-Cornered Hat*; when he learned that he would not perform the leading role in the work, Fernandez sank into a depression and suffered a breakdown.

In choreographing *Felipe el Loco*, Humphrey was faced with the stylistic problem of how to make a group of modern dancers resemble both ballet dancers and Spanish dancers. John Martin thought the problem remained unsolved and that the Mexican-born Limón was miscast as Felipe:

> Her [Humphrey's] group moves in something closely akin to the style of the academic ballet (and in this she and they are not unacceptable), and her central figure works in what can best be described as unauthentic Spanish dance. Now Mr. Limón is not a Spanish dancer, authentic or unauthentic, and he can beat his heels against the floor with all his energy without convincing anybody that he is one.

But Hering, who was more favorably disposed toward *Felipe el Loco*, considered the fuss over authenticity irrelevant because "the essence of the work was not a lack of technical understanding between Felipe and the ballet dancers, but a lack of human and temperamental contact."[53]

In addition to the Limón company, festival programs included works by Yuriko, Pauline Koner, and Margret Dietz (all of whom were on the faculty), as well as Daniel Nagrin and Charles Weidman for his Theatre Dance Company. All but Koner and Weidman presented premieres. Nagrin's contribution was a joyous solo, *Man Dancing*, about which Hering said,

> Mr. Nagrin so loves to dance that it seems difficult for him to impose the confines of subject matter on his dancing. Energy just seems to spill out of him. While this joy-in-dancing gave his solo (a depiction of a peasant man on a holiday) great charm, it also injected a note of structural naivete more suited to the popular theatre than to the concert stage.[54]

Yuriko offered *Four Windows*, a set of four mood studies ("the first two rather pensive, the third violent and rebellious, and the fourth again pensive," said Hering), and a dramatic work, ". . . *where the roads* . . . ," about twin sisters who become psychologically separated when one falls in love with a man. Hering thought it contrived: "Yuriko made the dance seem more like a study than an event of the heart."[55]

Much more striking was the Wigman-trained Margret Dietz in *A Dream*, a solo which, said Terry, was a "revelation of the fantasies, the tortures, the strange and hypnotic images of a dream." Hering commented:

> The dance, with its emphasis on a leit-motif of the hands spread above and below the face, was a fascinating combination of tension

and relaxation, panic and great dignity. The hands, arms, and face seemed to play a more important part than the torso in the creation of a movement picture. Yet the total effect was cohesive and balanced. It certainly made us want to see more of Miss Dietz—and of other Wigman-trained dancers.[56]

1955

With 155 students from twenty-five states and five foreign countries, the 1955 session had the highest enrollment thus far in the summer school's history. A three-year grant of $33,400 from the Rockefeller Foundation supported the scholarship program, helped pay faculty salaries, and enabled new works to be commissioned.[57] The one resident company was that of Limón. Of the festival's guest choreographers, only Pearl Lang (who did not offer a premiere) came from outside the Limón company, the other choreographers being Ruth Currier, Lucas Hoving, and Pauline Koner. Therefore, though the festival prospered that summer, it could also be argued that it was becoming artistically inbred.

Currier contributed two new duets. *Idyll*, for herself and Richard Fitz-Gerald, was described by Doris Hering as "a dance of love—romantic yet real, fluid in style yet formal in outline. After a flower-like solo for the girl and a sturdy one for the boy, there was a soaring climax with the girl held high so that her chiffon costume and golden hair seemed to pour over the boy."

The Antagonists, for Currier and Betty Jones, was more disquieting. According to Hering,

Two women (with mother-daughter overtones) engaged in a savage struggle for domination. They sprang leopard-like upon each other; pressed each other's heads down in a gesture of drowning; snatched at each other blindly. The mother figure . . . was vanquished. As she lay inert, the "daughter" . . . was suddenly confronted with isolation. With the panic of a lost child she attached herself to the waist of the "mother," now rising from her stupor. She trellised up the mother's body, swung between her legs to impede her from walking. But the "mother" extricated herself and plunged offstage, leaving chaos in her wake.

The bluntness of *The Antagonists* startled its first audience, and Walter Terry was particularly struck by the way the duet employed "movements of great physical strength almost shocking to see in women."[58]

Lucas Hoving added sections to *Satyros*, his comic satyr-play of the previous season. But these new scenes, concerning marriage and infidelity, were found "less appealing, more forced in their humors" by Terry.[59]

Other choreographers were also in a lighthearted mood. Doris Humphrey's *Airs and Graces* was inspired by the quaint names given to ornaments in eighteenth-century music. Its protagonist was a music lover, played by Lucas Hoving, who was discovered reading a musical treatise; when he came upon a term that intrigued him, he pronounced it aloud, whereupon the whimsical implications of the name were acted out by the three graces. The terms to which Humphrey gave choreographic life included "Double Relish," "Quinta Falsa, the Devil's Interval," "Quaver with Four Tails," "Wave of the Sea," "Passing Shake," and "Springer." As might be expected of someone who was a composer as well as a critic, Louis Horst considered *Airs and Graces* "a deliciously bustling and high-spirited concoction of fanciful manifestations," whereas, for Terry, "Not every bit of every episode is as entertaining as one would like, but on the whole it is good fun."[60]

Once again, Limón choreographed a work for an all-male cast. But whereas *The Traitor* was somber, *Scherzo* was a romp. It had a percussion score by Hazel Johnson, and Limón attempted to "weave movement and percussion into a rhythmic whole," as P. W. Manchester wrote in *Dance News*. Richard Fitz-Gerald was given a long solo in which he accompanied his own dancing on a drum, and in the finale the drum was passed, like a ball in a ball game, from dancer to dancer. *Scherzo* pleased Manchester, who described it as being "full of big leaps, and high jumping turns."[61]

Limón was equally joyous in *Symphony for Strings*, a plotless work that reminded Hering of "a radiant celebration for men and women in a harmonious ideal world." Calling it "an opulent dance," she went on to say,

> One of the most satisfying aspects of *Symphony for Strings* was the opportunity it gave various members of the company for virtuoso dancing. Pauline Koner was like some fiery bacchante as she tore through leaps and sharp shifts in direction. One is so accustomed to thinking of her as a dramatic dancer, that it is always a revelation to see how dazzling a technician she is.

John Martin, however, pronounced much of the choreography "diffuse" and "overwrought."[62]

The new work that proved to have the longest life was Pauline Koner's *Concertino in A Major*, a gracious piece to Pergolesi for three women who, said Margaret Lloyd of the *Christian Science Monitor*, could have been "ladies from some remote court playing at being shepherdesses at a refined fête champêtre." Hering likened the first of *Concertino*'s three movements to "a lilting feminine conversation"; the second movement included a melancholy solo, then all three women danced "a peasant-like finale." Summing it up, Lloyd said, "One has nothing to do but enjoy it. It was most refreshing." Many audiences have found it so, for Koner has revived it for ballet companies, as well as for modern dance groups.[63]

1956

If the 1955 festival could have been called slightly insular, the 1956 season was enterprising, even experimental, for it included solos by two leaders of European modern dance and a program by one of America's most controversial groups, Alwin Nikolais's Henry Street Playhouse Dance Company. Nikolais, who had studied at Bennington, was now both amazing and bewildering dancegoers with his multimedia spectacles in which, by encasing dancers in strange costumes and attaching sculptural constructions to their bodies, he created a whole universe of his own populated by fantastic beings.

Nikolais offered *Kaleidoscope*, a suite of nine dances featuring such objects as discs, poles, straps, and capes. Although not a premiere, it nevertheless seemed novel to festival audiences. John Martin called Nikolais's company "about as different from the run-of-the-mill dance group as can be imagined," and Walter Terry listed *Kaleidoscope* among the "high points of the festival." But virtually every critic who saw it, including Martin and Terry, found it, as Terry put it, "without human feeling." And Martin complained, "There is not an emotion anywhere on the premises." Other critics, including Louis Horst, feared that Nikolais's mixed-media trappings threatened to overwhelm his choreography. Yet Horst conceded that Nikolais deserved credit "for his untiring experimentation in the fields of dance, theatre, and music. That the experimentation, as in the case of *Kaleidoscope*, was stressed to the detriment of choreographic invention and to the glory of theatrical ingenuity and surface excitation should not disturb us conservatives unduly." What certain later commentators have found significant about that review are two words: "us conservatives." Horst had championed the modern dance that flourished in the 1930s and 1940s. But now he saw modern dance developing in ways that were not entirely to his liking.

One writer who defended Nikolais was George Beiswanger, the critic and aesthetician who analyzed festival attractions in a series of articles for Horst's *Dance Observer*. Nikolais, said Beiswanger,

> wants things to move, to be seen, and to be heard, and he wants the resulting aliveness of things to be apparent even when the things are dancers. Hence the props dance and the dancers prop (not that they do not dance as well). Now one may take this in two ways, as dehumanizing the dancer or as animizing the thing. I am inclined, perhaps perversely, to the latter view.[64]

Almost equally puzzling to some viewers were the solos—*Winter, Music for Strings, Percussion, and Celesta, Movement,* and *Persephone Dance*—by the Swedish modern dancer, Birgit Akesson, a choreographer fond of meditative stillness and almost hypnotic slow motion. Martin dismissed her as "the virtual negation of dancing." Doris Hering was more sympathetic: "Unlike so many dancers on the Festival, Miss Akesson was not afraid of stillness—the stasis sometimes after only a tiny movement. But hers were not poses. They were pauses, as though the movement were going on innerly and would soon again quietly manifest itself on the outside." But even Hering felt that Akesson had not "conquered the problem of monotony."

Beiswanger became Akesson's defender. He began his discussion by wondering whether some of the adverse criticism of Akesson might have been tainted by chauvinism; he feared Americans might have been saying to this Swedish visitor, "Everything you do, we do better, or did long ago." And he had to admit that Akesson's solos were unquestionably slow: "They crawl and writhe like a slug or an upended caterpillar, hardly moving at all." He added that each one of the solos "opens as if nothing were going to happen. A precisely drawn, cleanly sculpted figure is spotted center stage. It stands there, fixed. . . . Some music gets going or none at all. One looks and looks—there is plenty of time."

But, he insisted, there was really plenty to see:

> A tiny bit of movement is ventured, repeated, amplified, added to. It may be a turn of the wrists, each palm flicked outward as if a petal or

a birdwing. It may be a twist of the head or arm, slight but clear as a sleighbell's tinkle. It may be a curl of the body, floored on the shoulders and an arm, the torso and legs upsprayed.

In the beat and the venturings a pattern begins to emerge and build. Slowly, inevitably, the dance gets on its way. It is the inexorability of the movement which keeps coming back to me, not sluggish really, but steady and relentless, a spreading consequence of the beat. If one is in a hurry, not willing to bow to the patient rhythm, it can become unbearable, but if one lets the movement have its way, it generates a compelling, almost hypnotic, beauty.[65]

A new solo by Margret Dietz, *Of Burden and of Mercy*, also inspired controversy. Its program note consisted of two statements, "And ye shall weep and lament. . . . But your sorrows shall be turned," and the dance depicted tears and consolation. Terry acknowledged the dancer's "high level of accomplishment," yet found the dance all "schmalz and schmerz." Beiswanger, however, was fascinated by the disparity he noted between the actual movement and the dancer's expression as she moved:

The movement is lyric, finely so, deeply felt, singing and secure. There are slow spinnings, sweeping turns, delicate touches, gestures that open a full arc. The dance makes its own brooding space, which it inhabits and absorbs. There are eloquent doings with a cloth of gold, signifying humiliation, violation, blood, agony, bereft glory, grief, and the cover of mercy—if I read the changing symbol aright.

But as for expression,

The mask, the face-and-body countenance which the dance *persona* presents, is the puzzle. To me, it cuts across the dance. In the aura of its immediate gesturing there is that which the lyric movement does not embody nor imply: something of resentment, of rage, of defiance, of mocking, yet of wooing and a shy, almost sly appeal. It is as if the imposed burden was inexcusable upon one of such imperial estate—it should have been another's. It is as if the proferred mercy were an insult to be given and a condescension to accept—it should have been the burdened one's to bestow. All this may be why the second portion of the dance fails to brighten in tempo, why the sense of mercy offered and accepted is not realized, why the unburdening does not come through, why the sorrow is not really turned.[66]

Although the festival included, in addition to the resident Limón troupe, Anna Sokolow's Theatre Dance Company and Ruth Currier and Dance Group, there was only one premiere by an American choreographer, Pauline Koner's *The Shining Dark*. Its subject matter startled many dancegoers, for it was inspired by the life of Helen Keller. Koner played a handicapped person, comparable to Keller, and Lucy Venable and Elizabeth Harris were teachers and counselors who could be interpreted as symbolic representations of Annie Sullivan and Polly Thomson, Keller's own teachers. Koner says she did not consider Helen Keller to be an inappropriate subject for a dance, for the young Helen Keller, being blind, deaf, and dumb, had to communicate entirely through movement and gesture. The dance explored the process of communication, a gauzy cocoonlike tent symbolizing isolation and the failure to communicate.

Margaret Lloyd declared that Helen Keller was such a familiar historical figure that "all was completely understood before the dance began," and Terry wrote that, choreographically, Koner "got herself into a lathery emotional bath." Yet Horst believed that Koner treated a "difficult and dangerous" subject "with intelligent and resourceful courage," and Beiswanger argued that Koner's dance achieved a truly classical dignity:

> In Helen Keller she found not the pathetic but the noble, the person of shining inner worth pitted against a "world of nothingness" which threatened to wall up her light and silence her voice. Note that it is with the head, the seat of aristocratic pride, that she rebels, twisting it in anguish this way and that beneath the smothering gauze. (In the same way Achilles sulked in his tent, his honor and *gloire* affronted.) What Miss Koner took from the Keller legend was not a bourgeois heroism which overcomes obstacles and achieves success but the noble ideal, the assertion of one's own shining being and eloquent voice against the surrounding silence and dark.

Continuing in this vein, he compared the other two women to figures in a classical tragedy, likening one of them to "the *paedagogos* of Greek drama" and the other to "the adult companion who tends the distraught and angered soul."[67]

Whatever one may have thought of the dances of Nikolais, Akesson, Dietz, and Koner, they were not commonplace. And that is no doubt why Hering called the festival "more imaginative this year than in recent seasons."[68]

──────────────────────── **1957** ────────────────────────

The festival's tenth anniversary got off to an impressive start on 8 July with a special tribute at which Rosemary Park received a sterling silver plate and Ruth Bloomer a leather-bound desk set, both gifts inscribed with the names of the summer's faculty members. Martha Hill praised the achievements of Park and Bloomer in a speech and expressed the hope that the festival could "look forward to endless years ahead."

There was much to be excited about. The summer school's enrollment of 175 included an unprecedented twenty-one men. With Simon Sadoff as conductor, an orchestra drawn from the New York Philharmonic was in the pit. A special lecture series included a symposium on the teaching of dance composition, a demonstration of Indonesian dance, and a lecture-demonstration by Martha Graham at which her company appeared in New London for the first time since 1948 for a single performance of *Diversion of Angels*.[69]

Premieres were offered by Doris Humphrey, José Limón, Alwin Nikolais, Daniel Nagrin, and Dore Hoyer. Other choreographers showing works were Ruth Currier, Pauline Koner, and Mary Anthony, whose Mary Anthony Dance Theatre was praised in *Threnody*, Anthony's adaptation of Synge's *Riders to the Sea*. In addition to the official festival performances, there was a Little Concert Series, a set of programs featuring young or comparatively unknown choreographers. The participants included Beverly Schmidt, Murray Louis, Michael Hollander, Diane and Durevol Quitzow, David Wood, Dance Quartet (a group consisting of Virginia Freeman, Miriam Rosen, Patricia Wityk, and William Hug), and Dore Hoyer. Conceived as workshop events, the Little Concert performances were, with one exception, not considered attractions for critics to review, the exception being the program of solos by Hoyer, who also offered the premiere of *The Great Song* at one of the regular festival performances.

With the retirement from the stage of such key figures in European modern dance as Mary Wigman and Gret Palucca, Hoyer (who had studied with Palucca and whose work, for some critics, showed the influence of Wigman) was generally conceded to be the most important modern dancer in Germany. She proved to be an austere artist—too much so for Louis Horst, who complained that "her choreographic style seems uniformly undramatic and remote according to our American standards." Yet Horst admired her "truly superlative technical equipment" and called *Signal*, one of her solos in the Little Concert Series, "an exciting use of semaphoric arm movements plus superb articulation of percussive and ingenious footwork." Doris Hering had no reservations about Hoyer: "Miss Hoyer was to us a revelation in pure movement-intuition. Watching her was like revisiting the essence of modern dance — movement rising from a deeply personal source to assume universality."

The Great Song, Hoyer's most ambitious undertaking, was a five-part suite, each of its parts bearing a separate title, and the first and fifth parts being choreographically identical. Between the repetitions of this solo — the "Dance of the Divine Possession" — came "Dance of the Pure Simplicity," "Dance of the Brutal Force," and "Dance of the Sublime Sorrow." But it was "Dance of the Divine Possession" that created the stir. Here, with "her face painted anonymously and her hair concealed," said Hering, Hoyer revolved on her own axis while also traveling across the stage in circles, her skirt swinging outward like a bell. Whereas this solo might be said to prefigure Laura Dean's use of spinning movements, it caused critics at the time to compare Hoyer with Wigman's earlier experiments with spinning. Reviewing for the New York Herald Tribune, P. W. Manchester said that Hoyer

> is gentler and less dynamic [than Wigman] and is in no sense a copyist, but there is the same intense inner concentration and in this particular dance it would be impossible not to recall the famous "Monotony" [of Wigman], though, instead of revolving endlessly without moving from the same spot, Hoyer revolved on her own axis, while also revolving in sweeping circles. . . .

For Hering, these sweeping circles looked as if Hoyer were "cleaning and purifying the dancing ground."[70]

The premieres by American choreographers were not as striking as Hoyer's efforts. Yet Doris Humphrey's brief Dance Overture was certainly lively. Designed as a dance to open programs and introduce the members of the Limón company to new audiences on tour, it was hearty in manner. Hering thought it too busy: "It piled impulse upon impulse like a gong struck repeatedly before the initial reverberations have vanished." But, totally satisfied with it, Horst declared, "Never has Miss Humphrey done anything brighter."[71]

With Blue Roses, José Limón attempted a choreographic adaptation of Tennessee Williams's The Glass Menagerie. But critics charged that he never transcended his literary source. Manchester said of the work, "It is evocative and moving when suggesting an atmosphere, but falls down completely when Limón departs from fantasy and tries for a straightforward telling of the tragi-comic gentleman caller scene." Limón himself portrayed the gentleman caller in what Horst said was "a convincing, finely etched characterization." But, to Manchester, he was "possibly for the first time in his life . . . utterly ineffectual."[72]

Alwin Nikolais combined student dancers with members of his own company in *Runic Canto*, a ritual dance in which critics found traces of cabalistic symbolism. Manchester thought that the two groups of dancers meshed "without any observable disparity," but added that "the work fell away badly after an impressive opening." Horst, in *Dance Observer*, called it "a splendid and exciting piece of prehistoric ritualism." But in the *New London Evening Day* he wondered whether Nikolais's theatricality might be mere gimmickry and feared that "all this sensational excitement is attained to the detriment of so-called legitimate choreography."[73]

Daniel Nagrin's *Indeterminate Figure* was a solo about an indecisive man who cannot take action, despite warnings of war and destruction, until, as Horst put it, "the omens of these destructive forces are realistically and fatally brought home to him by a whistling bomb." Horst pronounced the character sketch "cruelly biting," and it became a staple of Nagrin's repertoire.[74]

Summing up the anniversary season, two critics came to opposite conclusions. Manchester declared that "this tenth festival was the best in several years." John Martin agreed that the Connecticut College campus had a festive air. But he had reservations: "The five programs that made up the festival contained so much variety, and the works were based on such distinct and even conflicting ideas concerning the nature of the modern dance, that consistent agreement on their merits could only be evidence of a lack of principle in the observer."[75] It is not often that a critic complains about "so much variety" or fears that eclecticism may signify "lack of principle." Yet Martin's argument would be rephrased many years later when certain critics once again feared that the festival had become so eclectic as to be without focus. Before that time, however, would come other seasons when critics accused the festival of being so narrow in range as to be hidebound, or even reactionary.

1958

Eclecticism prevailed again in 1958, when the Rockefeller Foundation awarded the festival its second three-year grant (this one of $40,000).[76]

Viola Farber and Carolyn Brown in Cunningham's *Summerspace,* 1958. Photo, Richard Rutledge.

New works were given by José Limón and Merce Cunningham; German modern dance was represented by Inga Weiss; Pearl Lang, Pauline Koner, and Ruth Currier offered works from their repertoires, and a second Little Concert Series included choreography by Diane and Vol (also known as Durevol) Quitzow, William Hug, Michael Hollander, Connie Keyse, Pola Nirenska, and the members of Contemporary Dance Productions (Jack Moore, Doris Rudko, and Marion Scott).

What made the festival particularly exciting to audiences interested in current dance trends was the opportunity to compare the two premieres by Limón with the two premieres by Cunningham, who was making is first visit to the festival since 1950. Since then, he had developed some controversial theories about the use of chance and indeterminacy in dance composition and the treatment of stage space as an open field; and he consistently worked with experimental composers and painters.

There were critics ready to pit Cunningham against Limón in an aesthetic battle. One of them was Margaret Lloyd who wrote, "Conflicting styles marked the celebration. Two of the premieres were by José Limón, the festival's own shining knight; the other two by Merce Cunningham, the mysterious challenger." Yet whatever factional infighting may have occurred offstage, the Cunningham company's performances received favorable notices, Walter Terry rating them as "high on the list of this year's festival delights." Even Louis Horst, considered by many to be the philosophical spokesman of modern dance's "old guard," tried hard to judge Cunningham fairly—and he was often pleased by what he saw.

He was certainly pleased by Cunningham's new *Antic Meet*, a gently zany suite involving such visual and choreographic oddities as a man with a chair strapped to his back, a movable door on wheels, a sequence in which two women mimed throwing things at each other, and a solo in which a man tried to put on a sweater that appeared to have a multitude of arms but no hole for the head. All this, said Horst, added up to "hilarious comments upon what really can happen when the wacky members of homo sapiens meet for some reason or another."

Cunningham was in a lyrical mood in *Summerspace*, which possessed a remarkable decor by Robert Rauschenberg, who spattered backdrop and costumes with colored dots so that watching the dance would be akin to watching the whorls of color that can sometimes be seen when one closes one's eyes after being out in the sunlight. In choreographing the dance, Cunningham said that he had a concern for steps that carry one through a space, and not only into it. Like the passage of birds, stopping for moments on the ground and then going on, or automobiles more relentlessly throbbing along turnpikes and under and over cloverleaves. This led to the idea of using kinds of movement that would be continuous and could carry the dancer into the playing area, and out of it.

But Cunningham said that at the premiere "the audience was puzzled."

So was Louis Horst. Yet, though he thought *Summerspace* "did not . . . realize any of the high standards so patently evident" in other works by Cunningham, Horst was more sad than hostile. Margaret Lloyd was puzzled, too. "Why," she wondered, "do the dancers now and then make gestures like scooping out handfuls of the wallpaper dots to scatter on the floor?" Her answer: "Better to relax and enjoy, than to try to explain." Audiences have come to do just that. Both *Summerspace* and *Antic Meet* became popular works in the Cunningham repertoire, and *Summerspace* has even been produced by the New York City Ballet and the Boston Ballet.[77]

Limón's premieres did not find him at his best. With *Dances*, to Chopin piano music, he created yet another example of what would come to be known as the piano-ballet. Dedicated to the Polish cities the Limón company had visited on a European tour, the new work, said Horst, was "a charming, if not significant, suite of brisk and tender dances." Yet audiences grew restless watching it, possibly because it was set entirely to mazurkas. "Just listening to an extended parade of mazurkas," said Terry, "was heavygoing and the steps and movements devised to go with them tended toward the same air of repetition."[78]

Betty Jones, who had to sing as well as dance in *The Queen's Epicedium*, did so again in Limón's *Serenata*, the songs being Paul Bowles's musical settings of poems by Federico García Lorca. Chester Wolenski had to sing and dance as well, as he and Jones incarnated the secret thoughts and feelings of two lovers, played by Limón and Pauline Koner. For Horst, the result was "a beautiful work of enchantment and quiet restraint." But, for Terry, it was too bland: "Amorous etiquette, rather than amorous adventure." Doris Hering had mixed feelings. She found the dance's initial image "sensuously lovely. The stage was inhabited by four figures on pedestals. In the penumbral light, they glowed like moon-drenched statues." But, ultimately, she said, "the dance form was static, the intent unclear. One could not tell whether it was a courtship or a satire on one."[79]

Inga Weiss, a German dancer who had settled in Chicago, performed two solos, *Etudes* (Scriabin) and *Twelve Variations* (Mozart). Whereas for Terry she was "pleasant, if not memorable," Hering thought her delightful: "When Miss Weiss began to dance, it was as though someone had opened a window in the theatre and let the summer sunshine in. She is a true lyric dancer, with a free, quicksilver style and sensitive attunement to the music."[80]

Critics seemed agreed that the 1958 festival was a pleasant one that had also allowed partisans of different schools of modern dance to engage in friendly controversy. But before the 1959 season opened, the Connecticut College School of the Dance and the American Dance Festival would experience two major losses. For years Ruth Bloomer had suffered from diabetes and a chronic heart ailment; more recently she had developed glaucoma as well, and it became impossible for her to continue as a director. Stepping down from the position in 1958, she declared that she would remain a member of the festival's advisory board. But she died of a stroke on 17 April 1959, at the age of fifty-two.

A few months earlier—on 29 December 1958—Doris Humphrey had died at the age of sixty-three. Her arthritic condition had been steadily worsening, and, as her health declined, it was found that she also had cancer. Indomitable, she spent her last months writing her memoirs and completing her much-praised book on the teaching of choreography, *The Art of Making Dances*.

With Bloomer's passing, the festival lost an administrator. With the death of Humphrey, it had, in effect, lost an artistic conscience. The festival was now in need of leadership, and, although she could serve on the advisory board, the pressure of other duties made it impossible for Martha Hill to guide the summer sessions singlehandedly. Therefore, in 1959 the festival would appoint a new director.[81]

III

OVERVIEW 1948–1958

A FESTIVAL

IN CONNECTICUT

O ver the years the festival in New London came to mean many things to many dance lovers. But everyone able to make an informed comparison agreed it was not like Bennington.

Bennington had been very special. With its idyllic campus in the Vermont hills, it was not only a creative workshop, but also something of a summer retreat, and those who gathered there took pride in being devotees of a new and still largely unknown art form. The theatrical facilities at Bennington may have been makeshift, but idealistic fervor triumphed over all obstacles.

Connecticut College, in contrast, boasted a fully equipped modern theater, New London was on a major railroad line connecting New York City with New England, and the festival's potential audience included dancegoers from New York, Boston, New Haven, and several other urban and suburban communities along what Amtrak today calls the Northeast Corridor. The festival's proximity to New York automatically drew it closer to the everyday world of the professional theater than Bennington had ever been. It is not surprising, then, that Jane Dudley can say, "Connecticut and Bennington were quite different. For me, Connecticut never had the enormously exciting atmosphere of Bennington. It was sort of an anticlimax right from the start."[1]

Ruth Bloomer readily admitted that the new festival was not a replica of the earlier one: "The zeal of the crusader was missing, for that era had ended, but the enthusiasm for basic study with practicing artists, the experience of being with others trained in different disciplines and from different sections of the country, all signified the harvesting of good growth from the seed planted in that earlier crusading period."[2]

One important difference between Connecticut and Bennington involved their student bodies. Bennington attracted many dance teachers, or physical education teachers required to teach dance, who came to the summer school to learn about new developments in the field and to acquire materials—ideas, exercises, syllabi—that they could draw upon in planning their own classes for the next academic year. Such teachers also came—and they have continued to come—to the American Dance Festival in order to be, as Helen Priest Rogers puts it, "uplifted and intellectually refreshed" by direct contact with major dance artists. Yet, from its first season onward, the Connecticut student body looked younger than the Bennington student body had been, for Connecticut was attracting aspiring dancers, some of whom had been trained (and trained well) by teachers who had gone to Bennington. Moreover, among these young people were surprisingly many who were hoping for careers not as teachers, but as professional performers or choreographers. Thanks in part to the efforts of those who had been associated with Bennington, modern dance was becoming a field in which one could make at least some sort of living; modern dance was coming of age.

Connecticut may have disappointed Bennington veterans. But to young people who had never known an important summer dance festival before, it was a revelation. As "the newest and youngest member of the Graham company" in 1948, Dorothy Berea says she found the first festival "very exciting," in part because she was surrounded by people who had attained almost legendary status because of their association with Bennington.[3] Lucy Venable, a student in 1948, considered the festival "mind-boggling," and she was inspired to continue in her dance studies until she eventually became a dance notation teacher at the festival and a member of the Limón company. Selma Jeanne Cohen, who as a young writer moved East from Los Angeles in the early 1950s, says that the festivals of that period were, for her, "simply fabulous. Everybody who was anybody at the time was there. There was a feeling of great creativity. We were surrounded by the greats of our day and everyone was eager to work."

There was dance everywhere one turned, or so it seemed to wide-eyed students. Every available inch of space was somehow used for the training, rehearsing, feeding, or housing of dancers. And if the dancers formed a special community, they did not necessarily isolate themselves from the rest of the campus. Dancers and dance teachers, particularly those who kept returning year after year, often developed lasting friendships with Connecticut College faculty members who stayed on in New London during the summer, as well as with some of the college's doctors, nurses, dieticians, and housekeepers.

A few of Connecticut College's winter faculty members grew very curious indeed about their summer visitors. One such was the aesthetician and philosopher Susanne Langer. Dancers remember her constantly following them about and badgering them with questions in the campus coffee shop. Some dancers now speak of her fondly, yet confess that, back then, they considered her a bit of a pest. Nevertheless, she was one of the comparatively few aestheticians of her day who took dance seriously as a major art form.

Hard work prevailed at Connecticut College during the summers. Yet the dancers also managed to bring a mild bohemianism to campus. The lounges of the dormitories in which students were housed served as social centers. The members of the Dudley-Maslow-Bales company stayed in a building that served as the college infirmary during the winter. Friends from New York would often come for weekend visits and bed down for the night in sleeping bags on the floor. On occasion, Woody Guthrie would be one of these visitors, and then there would be folk songs until the small hours of the morning.

A unique feature of the festival was the way in which the choreographers and dancers of the resident companies were also members of the faculty; thus young people had the opportunity to study with some of the most important figures in modern dance. But this arrangement was the one aspect of the summer program that many of the resident dancers heartily disliked. Having to rehearse, perform, and at the same time teach daily classes and be on hand to advise students—and to do all this in buildings without air-conditioning—strained the dancers' nerves, patience, and muscles. The strain could be evident on stage, as when Doris Hering observed in 1949 that José Limón "danced more like a martyr than a man" and that "the usually cohesive New Dance Group [i.e., Dudley-Maslow-Bales] looked ragged and motley." Quite rightly diagnosing what was wrong, she concluded, "They were all tired, just plain tired."[4] Nevertheless, though Jane Dudley remembers that "the teaching was a burden, and we had to dance on our nerves, rather than with our trained bodies," the chance of studying with noted dancers must have inspired students. Looking back, Paul Taylor, who was a student at the festival in the 1950s, recalls only that "all the teachers genuinely seemed to care so much about passing on what they knew."

Beginning in 1950, the festival's directors made a special point of setting aside part of each year's operating budget for scholarships. A cooperative scholarship program got under way in 1953, under which the Connecticut College School of the Dance offered to match partial summer session tuition payment from a student's regular college. The festival as a whole was immeasurably benefited by Rockefeller Foundation grants in 1955 and 1958 that made possible further scholarship assistance, faculty salary increases, a lecture series, and several special projects.[5]

Among them was a film and notation project organized by Helen Priest Rogers, who taught dance notation during the summer at Connecticut College and in the winter at Mount Holyoke College. Rogers had developed an interest in recording choreography on film as early as the 1930s when she was a student at Bennington. At Connecticut, with the encouragement of Ruth Bloomer, herself an amateur filmmaker, she attempted to film at least one dance a summer. At the same time the choreography of this dance would be recorded in Labanotation under the supervision of Lucy Venable. Rogers's early films were silent. She made her first sound film in 1962, and, after 1965, all festival films were sound. Also from 1962 onward she began to call in other film directors to assist her, including Dwight Godwin, a former member of American Ballet Theatre who had become a professional cinematographer. By 1976, when Rogers's project was awarded a grant from the National Endowment for the Arts, she had supervised the filming of seventy-five dances, including works by José Limón, Doris Humphrey, Pauline Koner, Merce Cunningham, Paul Taylor, Alwin Nikolais, Ruth Currier, Helen Tamiris, and Charles Weidman.[6]

The festival received enthusiastic support not only from Rosemary Park, but also from several other important officials at Connecticut College, including Warrine Eastburn, secretary of the college, assistant to the president, and supervisor of campus publications until her retirement in 1976, and Allen B. Lambdin, the college's business manager. Because she had been a physical education teacher before going into administrative work, Eastburn had special rapport with dancers and was sensitive to their needs. As for Lambdin, who retired in 1971, Jeanette Schlottmann says of him, "He tried to be a martinet, but he was really a softie." His duties included overseeing all campus property and equipment, and his ingenuity proved invaluable one hot summer when, even though Palmer Auditorium was not then air-conditioned, he tried to make it seem so by placing blocks of ice before its ventilators and turning on the blower system.[7]

During the earliest seasons all festival activities were under the supervision of Martha Hill and Ruth Bloomer. Yet the festival was also, as Hill puts it, something of "a communal enterprise," thanks to the existence of what was known as "the Board." To be literal about the matter, there were usually two boards: one overseeing the summer school as a whole, the other dealing with matters specifically pertaining to the festival performances. But many people were on both, and former board members tend to lump the two together in conversation simply as "the Board" —and that capital B is implied by their emphasis. Over the years, in addition to Hill and Bloomer, board members included representatives of Connecticut College (among them, the president), and such leaders of the dance world as Doris Humphrey, Louis Horst, José Limón and Pauline Lawrence (his wife), and the musicians Ruth and Norman Lloyd.

After Hill's marriage in 1952, she was unable to spend the entire summer in New London. Yet, as festival codirector, she remained on the board, which from the mid-1950s assumed increased prominence as an arbiter of festival policies and aesthetics.

The faculty also had a voice in policy-making. Every summer term concluded with a faculty meeting for all teachers, teaching assistants, and staff members that was held at the home of Connecticut College's president. Even though they realize that college presidents are expected to use their residences for ceremonial or official occasions, faculty members from the early years at Connecticut nevertheless say they were touched that, rather than schedule a meeting in a campus dining hall or neighborhood restaurant, Rosemary Park was willing to invite dancers and dance teachers into her *home*.

Park would always thank the faculty for making the summer session a success. Then she would say that she hoped there could be another festival next summer. But before she could definitely promise that, she had to consult with the college trustees. (That never seemed to be a problem: there was always a next summer.) The bulk of the ensuing

José Limón and student in class, Connecticut College.

discussion would be devoted to serious consideration of the summer's curriculum, recommendations would be made for the next summer, and the meeting invariably included a fine dinner.[8]

The festival's aesthetic orientation was significantly influenced by the Limón company and also by Louis Horst. The success of *The Moor's Pavane* in 1949 did much to make the Limón company the festival's star attraction, and, unlike Martha Graham, Limón was willing to ally his company with the festival. Graham usually taught during the first week of the summer, and representatives of her school and company taught Graham technique throughout the term. But, perhaps fearing that she might thereby be limiting its possibilities for performances elsewhere, Graham did not commit her company to annual residencies in New London.

The Limón company was ideally suited for such residencies. Comparing Limón with Graham, one festival official has said, "Martha was expensive. And she was demanding." For instance, she always insisted upon appearing with a full orchestra. Budgetary considerations might occasionally lead Limón to countenance playing the orchestral scores in his repertoire in transcriptions for chamber ensemble or two pianos. But if a dance in Graham's repertoire was set to a score for full orchestra, a full orchestra had to be in the pit at every performance of it.

The Limón company had much to offer, both artistically and pedagogically. Limón was a charismatic performer and a gifted choreographer. But any institution that hired his company got more than Limón. The group's artistic director was Doris Humphrey, one of the most important of all modern dance choreographers. Several company members, including Pauline Koner, Lucas Hoving, and Ruth Currier, were also successful choreographers. Limón himself was not really interested in teaching. But some of his dancers—among them, Koner, Hoving, Currier, and Betty Jones—were known to be fine teachers, and, in addition to upholding the Humphrey-Weidman tradition, from which the company aesthetically emerged, Limón's dancers possessed varied backgrounds of training and professional experience. Thus the Dutch-born Lucas Hoving had studied the German modern dance technique developed by Kurt Jooss and had once danced with Jooss's company. And Pauline Koner had studied Spanish dance and classical ballet, her principal ballet teacher being Michel Fokine, the greatest reformer of twentieth-century ballet. All these factors made the Limón company precisely the sort of company

Lucas Hoving and student, Joanne Robinson, in class, Connecticut College. Photo, Philip A. Biscuti.

the festival required for residencies, and Limón remained loyal, returning to New London year after year.

The Mexican-born José Limón had originally wanted to be a painter, and he attended art school in New York. But a performance by the German modern dancers Yvonne Georgi and Harald Kreutzberg inspired him to dance. He studied with Doris Humphrey and Charles Weidman and joined their company in 1930, dancing with it at Bennington. In the 1940s he appeared with several dance groups and in various theatrical productions, including a revival, in 1942, of *Fledermaus*, choreographed by George Balanchine. Then, in 1946, he organized his own company.

Limón was a striking presence on stage. The Washington critic Jean Battey Lewis recalls, "There was a singing eloquence to his gestures, an uncompromising look to the way he held his arms, a proud defiance in the line of his back and neck." Remembering the Limón company of the fifties, Deborah Jowitt of the *Village Voice* says that Limón, "with his huge gestures, stabbing footwork, often seemed to plunge into dancing

—shoulders first—like a magnificent bull." About his company as a whole, Jowitt says, "A lot of the men were built like runners. Supporting Limón in his various versions of the tragic-hero role, they emphasized qualities most Americans think of as masculine: strength, directness, a kind of brusqueness that doesn't preclude tenderness."[9]

As a choreographer, Limón was usually serious and often solemn. Although he could enjoy bawdy jokes offstage, he was never at ease in comic dances. He disliked performing them, and his few attempts at choreographing them rank among his weakest efforts. He revealed his taste in dance as early as 1946 when he wrote in an essay, "The kind of dance which interests me is that which strives to be adult. Solemn, tragic, austere dances. I do not care for the gay, carefree touch. I dislike musical comedy dancing and it is incomprehensible to me why adults should waste their time and energy upon scatter-brained puerilities." Twenty years later, in another essay, he declared,

> I try to compose works that are involved with man's basic tragedy and the grandeur of his spirit. I want to dig beneath empty formalisms, displays of technical virtuosity, and the slick surface; to probe the human entity for the powerful, often crude beauty of the gesture that speaks of man's humanity. I reach for demons, saints, martyrs, apostates, fools, and other impassioned visions.

And in that same essay he said that through his choreography he wished to ally himself with the creative visions of such composers, painters, and writers as Bach, Michelangelo, Shakespeare, Goya, Schönberg, Picasso, Orozco, Cézanne, Debussy, Ibsen, Dreiser, and O'Neill.[10]

Limón's choreography could be as high-flown as his rhetoric. Although many of his works were based upon dramatically meaningful and often essentially realistic gestures, Limón so magnified and transformed them that his choreography attained a flamboyant grandiosity. George Beiswanger called Limón's works "compact dance operas," and, developing this comparison, he said, "Besides operatic texture and scenic sense, operatic characters and plots, there is the same passionate pulse, the same gusto, the same will to broad and melodramatic effects" in Limón's dances as can be found in much late nineteenth-century opera. Beiswanger thought these operatic tendencies made Limón's style essentially turbulent: "Instead of smooth progression from step to step, the dancing is complex, knotted up, jammed with contending energies and their rhythmic imbalance."

At its best Limón's choreography could be passionate or exalted. At

Martha Graham with technique class, Connecticut College, 1957. Photo, Dora Sanders.

its worst it was accused of being pretentious and long-winded. Even Beiswanger, who was sympathetic to Limón, had to admit that there were times when Limón's choreography had the "look of a merely mannered prose" and that "the dancing does sacrifice something in pace; it is supple but seldom lightfooted; true presto passages are rare."[11]

There were people who failed to respond to Limón. Some were startled to discover that, in addition to the gentlemanliness and nobility that were among his genuine character traits, Limón possessed a capacity for violence that he could control artistically in his dances, but which could erupt unpredictably in his offstage dealings with people. Other students and dancegoers found Limón bombastic. Typically, in 1968 he told Connecticut College dance students, "You will walk as gods and goddesses walk, run with the wind, leap free of the leaden tyranny of gravity, turn as whirlwinds and maelstroms, fall with despair and ecstasies. This is the magic of the dancer."[12] To some of his listeners, such words must have been intoxicating; to others, they could have seemed hot air.

One former student from the 1950s recalls, "José was always playing the role of the inspirer. Martha Graham used to do that, too, when she came to Connecticut. But, somehow, I just didn't fall for it." This student also says that he now realizes there was nothing insincere or merely self-congratulatory in these efforts to inspire, for when Limón and Graham were young, dance was often scorned or derided, and both of them devoted their lives to demonstrating that it could be a serious and noble art. As Paul Taylor puts it, "José and Martha came from a time when if you said you were a dancer, people assumed you were either a hoofer or a hooker."

For those students for whom he was a true inspirer, Limón demonstrated that dance as a profession was a glorious calling and that dancers could indeed be godly beings. Thus, according to Lucy Venable, who was first his student and later a member of his company, "José somehow always made you feel good because he was always enthusiastic about what you did. So he made you feel you could do more and do better."

José Limón once wrote that "it was Doris Humphrey who first taught me that man is the fittest subject for choreography."[13] She taught many other dancers that same lesson.

Born in Oak Park, Illinois, Humphrey studied ballet and gymnastics in the Chicago area, went to Los Angeles to study at the Denishawn School of Ruth St. Denis and Ted Shawn in 1917, and joined the Denishawn company the following year. In 1928 she and two other young rebels, Charles Weidman and Pauline Lawrence, left Denishawn to pursue their own careers; Humphrey formed a partnership with Weidman and danced, taught, and choreographed at Bennington. Then, in 1944 arthritis forced her to retire from the stage. However, when she agreed to serve as Limón's artistic adviser in 1946, a whole new life in dance began for her. Although she could no longer perform, she now had dancers available who could carry out her ideas. Moreover, she developed an unusually successful course in dance composition, which she taught at Connecticut College and, in winter, at the Juilliard School.

While she was still a dancer, she wrote:

> My dance is an art concerned with human values. It upholds only those which make for harmony and opposes all forces inimical to those values. . . . I wish my dance to reflect some experience of my own in relationship to the outside world; to be based on reality

illumined by imagination; to be organic rather than synthetic; to call
forth a definite reaction from my audience; and to make its contribution toward the drama of life.[14]

These words suggest that Limón's prose style might have been indebted to
that of his mentor. Both choreographers were much concerned with the
drama of life. But whereas Limón, on occasion, would allow his tormented heroes to hurtle toward ruin, Humphrey was forever in search of
social harmony, and, in purely practical choreographic terms, this meant
that, though she despised cheap sentimentality, she was reluctant to give
any of her dances a totally pessimistic ending.

In 1949 Walter Terry proclaimed Humphrey "America's most distinguished choreographer." Nevertheless, since her death, revivals of her
works have not invariably been successful. When badly performed, her
dances can look dry and stilted. Deborah Jowitt, an admirer of her
choreography, acknowledges that "Humphrey was often didactic, even
priggish, about what was good for mankind." To bring Humphrey's works
alive requires dancers who, like Humphrey herself, can combine strong
feelings with a passion for order, for, as Ernestine Stodelle says, Humphrey's
choreography "wed two forms previously considered worlds apart: logic
and poetry."

Humphrey could regard the simple act of walking as a kinetic drama
in itself, and she found moral implications in the law of gravity. "Fall and
recovery," the basic concept upon which she built her dance technique,
derived from the body's capacity to yield to or resist gravitational pulls,
and Humphrey viewed the struggle with gravity as a metaphor for the
struggles of life. Humphrey, says Stodelle, was fascinated by "the reiter-
ated beat of the walk, the plunging force of a falling body, the dynamic
range of its rebound, the strident effort of ascent, the smooth, sustained
and developing succession of uninterrupted flow." In addition, says
Stodelle, for Humphrey "Abstract form . . . pulsated with life. Lines, circles,
angles and points of intersection carried drama within their precise designs
whenever and wherever the human being was involved." And Jowitt notes
that Humphrey's basic theme always remained "the perfectability of mankind through the pursuit of noble ambitions."[15]

Humphrey is remembered by many former students and colleagues
as a sedate, even aloof, woman who was always polite and helpful to
those who sought her out, yet extremely difficult to get to know. She was
a woman who apparently enjoyed solitude, and her family arrangements

allowed her much time to be alone. She and her husband, Charles Francis Woodford, were by all accounts a happy couple. Yet because he was a ship's officer working for the United Fruit Company, he was at sea much of the time. Humphrey also loved her son, Charles. But because she was so often immersed in creative work and her husband was so often away, José and Pauline Limón—who had no children of their own—served as surrogate parents for the boy. In the 1950s Charles, too, began to be absent from home: he worked as an assistant purser on a ship in 1952, and in 1956 he was accepted for officer training by the Navy. One companion with whom Humphrey could easily relax in a playful, carefree manner appeared to be Monahan, an enormous, demanding, spoiled, and domineering gray cat that Humphrey would bring to New London every summer and to which she was absolutely devoted.

Humphrey's colleagues point out that much of her reserve may have resulted from the constant necessity of having to marshal her inner resources to battle against the arthritis that was progressively crippling her. She was in pain much of the time and could only get about on crutches. Moreover, her condition noticeably worsened in the 1950s. A hip operation in 1953 granted her a brief period of apparent improvement, after which she suffered yet another setback.

When she taught a class, choreographed a dance, or conducted a rehearsal, Humphrey settled herself into a chair and never stirred from the spot until the session was over. Smoking constantly, she rehearsed and choreographed works by means of detailed instructions and evocative imagery that miraculously managed to convey to dancers sympathetic to her choreography precisely what her intentions were. And with her red hair, penetrating blue eyes, and aquiline nose, she could be an impressive figure.

In a tribute to her in 1967, Limón said,

> This woman had more guts than anyone I have ever known or heard of. Rebuffs, neglect meant nothing. The constant pain of a crippling disability was serenely ignored. The important thing, the core, the essence of existence lay in the dance, in the dancers, the studio, the rehearsals, the passion, the form, the beauty and ugliness, the lyric utterance of the human spirit.

Pauline Koner is sure Humphrey's personal philosophy must have been, "Just don't ever give in or give up."[16]

As a teacher, Humphrey was particularly noted for her classes in dance composition. Paul Taylor, one of her students, remembers them as "all having much to do with finding ways to express emotional states." Once again, in her teaching as in her choreography, she wed logic and poetry. She was adamant in her demand that all movement must possess emotional motivation. But, as she indicates in *The Art of Making Dances*, her textbook on choreography, she was equally adamant that students be able to analyze such formal aspects of composition as design, dynamics, and rhythm.[17]

As artistic director of the Limón company, Humphrey worked tirelessly with José Limón. She choreographed works for him, works containing roles that, in their day, were praised for their "virile" or "masculine" movement. Yet Norma Stahl, in the *Saturday Review*, suggests that these were male roles that only a woman could create. She says the collaboration between Humphrey and Limón led to "a series of extraordinary dance characterizations. They are depictions of the male, especially the strong, manly man—moving grandly, passionately, arrested in his sweeping course only by a woman. It is perhaps a woman's vision that has been realized, just as Heathcliff and Rochester were, novelistically, women's romantic visions of men."[18]

Even more important, Humphrey served as Limón's choreographic adviser and editor, playing Maxwell Perkins to his Thomas Wolfe. Limón would show Humphrey each new section of a work-in-progress, and she would appraise it. She saved her detailed criticisms of the work for private consultations with him. But, during rehearsals, she might offer a few remarks or indicate her feelings through a simple, but meaningful, nod or gesture. Because Limón was prone to choreographic prolixity, dancers and critics alike agreed that he needed editorial guidance, and Humphrey was a good editor who was able to suggest ways to tighten passages and discard superfluous details (as when she convinced Limón that it would be unnecessary for him to wear a Moorish mask in *The Moor's Pavane*).

Nevertheless, some observers have speculated that Humphrey, perhaps inadvertently, allowed Limón to rely on her too much. Selma Jeanne Cohen has remarked about Humphrey, "As she refused to recognize her constantly failing health, she refused also to see the necessity of José's lessening dependence." After her death, Limón would occasionally invite friends and colleagues to rehearsals and ask for their comments. But he never found another Doris Humphrey. And critics pronounced many of his later dances long-winded.[19]

Doris Humphrey also served as choreographic adviser to Pauline Koner, who had deliberately sought her out. Koner made her debut as a solo dancer in 1930 and had enjoyed considerable success in the field, but by 1945 she felt that her career had arrived at a creative impasse. After a solo recital at New York's 92nd Street Y, she received a letter from Humphrey, who was then the director of the Y's dance education department. Humphrey offered praise, but her letter also contained some words of criticism that Koner found perceptive. Koner decided she needed what she called an "outside eye" to appraise her choreography, and Humphrey agreed to offer guidance. Thereafter, in choreographing new dances Koner would devise the steps, and Humphrey would scrutinize and comment on them.

When Beatrice Seckler left the Limón company, Humphrey asked Koner to appear as guest artist in one of Seckler's roles. Koner continued as what could be called a "permanent guest artist" until 1960. She never signed a contract with Limón. She simply worked with him and his dancers in a spirit of friendship and trust. Not the least unusual thing about Koner's arrangement with the company was the fact that, because she was an experienced choreographer, she was allowed to choreograph her own roles in the new works by Humphrey and Limón in which she was cast, including *Ruins and Visions* and *The Moor's Pavane*. Of course, the choreography she created would always be subject to the approval of Humphrey and Limón; nevertheless, it would be essentially her own.

Critics universally agreed that the association with Humphrey and Limón transformed Koner as an artist. John Martin even maintained that

> It is only in the years since she has been appearing with José Limón's company that she has arrived at her true fulfillment; and part of that fulfillment, indeed, lies in the very fact of her alliance with that company. For an independent solo artist of rank to join forces with another artist was an unheard-of proceeding when she did it. Far from being a gesture of debasement or defeat, however, it was an act of high artistic insight.[20]

The Limón company of the 1950s was an organization in which artists of different personalities and temperaments could work harmoniously together. "It was like a chamber music group," Koner says. The dancers were talented and enthusiastic, and they were supported by a devoted staff that included, perhaps most important of all, Pauline Lawrence and Simon Sadoff. Lawrence joined Denishawn as a dancer and rehearsal pianist in 1917 and left it with Doris Humphrey and Charles

Weidman in 1928. She married José Limón in 1941, and for his company was general organizer, business manager, tour booker, and costume and lighting designer. She was also, her colleagues recall, a splendid cook. Sadoff, who several times served as guest conductor for the New York City Ballet, was the company's pianist, conductor, and musical director. An amiable man and a thoroughly reliable professional, he eventually came to supervise all the summer musical operations at New London.[21]

Other than the dancers and staff members of the Limón company, the most artistically important person associated with the festival was surely Louis Horst. He was also what many of his students have called the festival's "resident ogre." Born in Kansas City and raised in California, Horst worked as a pianist for movie, vaudeville, and burlesque theaters until he was hired by Denishawn in 1915, supposedly as the accompanist for a two-week tour. Instead, he stayed with Denishawn for ten years. He was Martha Graham's accompanist and musical director from 1926 to 1948 and, at the same time, served as accompanist or conductor for such disparate choreographers as Doris Humphrey, Charles Weidman, Agnes de Mille, Helen Tamiris, Harald Kreutzberg, Ruth Page, and Tilly Losch. A composer in a spare, rhythmically crisp, and mildly dissonant style, he wrote thirty dance scores, eleven of them for Graham. Although neither a dancer nor a choreographer, he began teaching dance composition in 1928, eventually becoming one of the most important teachers of the subject. His only real rival as a composition teacher at the time was Doris Humphrey. In 1934 Horst founded *Dance Observer*, a magazine that championed modern dance and for which he was chief critic until his death in 1964. During the summers he also served as dance critic for the *New London Evening Day*. Horst knew just about everybody in the dance world. There were even times when it seemed as if just about everybody in the dance world had been his student at one time or another.

Despite the fact that everyone called him "Louie" and he hated being called "Mr. Horst," most people were slightly frightened of him. A heavyset, jowly, patriarchal figure with massive head, bushy eyebrows, and ice-blue eyes, Horst "looked a bit like Alfred Hitchcock," Paul Taylor says. A cigarette was always dangling from his lips, and, in class, he would sit at the piano and provide accompaniments for his students' composition assignments without ever seeming to look up at the dancers. Yet, somehow, he never missed a step, and he would deliver blistering criticisms in a voice that the critic Robert Sabin recalls could "coax like a child, with a petulant note, or snap like a whip." So severe were his comments that, according to Doris Hering, "when you finished studying with Louis, the harshest of professional reviews must have seemed like pure flattery."

In no conventional sense a handsome man, Horst nevertheless could exert a strange power over women. "At Connecticut, he could just blink at a girl, and she'd faint dead away," Paul Taylor says. Moreover, he appeared to relish making his female students blush, tremble, and weep. And no one quite knows how much of this classroom savagery was a matter of sheer perverse pleasure and how much was a deliberate attempt to prepare inexperienced, and possibly sheltered, young people for the grim realities of the professional theater. For whatever reason, Horst could be a tyrant, and one of the tasks of Doris Rudko, who for many years served as his teaching assistant, was to soothe shy students at Connecticut and make them feel secure about showing their assignments to him.[22]

Horst's composition classes forced students to analyze and organize choreographic materials. A determined antiromantic, he loathed mere "self-expression," particularly the sort of undisciplined and often semi-improvisatory "interpretive" works common during the early days of modern dance in which performers rushed soulfully hither and thither waving their arms about, but without actually communicating much of anything. Horst contemptuously dismissed such displays as "tree waving." Instead, says Theodora Wiesner, "Louis insisted that a dance should have a formal structure and a subject: it should be about something. He wanted you to get a theme, manipulate it, and develop it."

As might be expected of a professional musician with a scholarly knowledge of aesthetics, Horst borrowed much of his classroom terminology from the fields of music and art. He made a point of urging students to develop movement themes by means of the choreographic equivalents of such musical devices as inversion, augmentation, diminution, imitation, and rhythmic variation. But the musical form that he stressed most in working with neophytes was A-B-A. Horst regarded A-B-A as an inherently satisfying form because it had a beginning, a middle, and an end; a dance in A-B-A introduced a movement statement, offered a contrasting statement, then returned to the first statement and somehow resolved it. Horst was so adamant that students master A-B-A that some wits used to quip that "he taught the ABC's of A-B-A."

The two courses for which he was best known were those in what he called the preclassic and the modern dance forms, the preclassic course serving as his introduction to composition. In some ways, the course was misleadingly named. Although it made use of old court dances, it did not teach students how to perform them with scholarly authenticity or how to reconstruct them from notated manuscripts. Rather, because of their structural concision, he wished students to use the dances that flourished between the fifteenth and eighteenth centuries as formal models for compositions of their own. He assigned students pavanes and galliards the way the leader of a poetry workshop might assign sonnets and sestinas.

Occasionally, says Doris Rudko, if Horst were teaching at a school with very long academic terms, he would teach his students simplified versions of the authentic court dances before asking them to choreograph their own works. But more often—and especially at Connecticut College where the summer term was only six weeks—he would simply describe what the dances were like. The qualities that he stressed in his descriptions then had to turn up, in some contemporary way, in the students' works. Thus a galliard had to suggest gaiety; a courante had to be filled with running movements, and a pavane had to convey a sense of pride or power. Sometimes, as his own descriptions of his assignments in his book on preclassic forms indicate, he had very definite ideas about what sort of contemporary choreography best suited each of the old court dances. For instance, he declares of the minuet, "The best use to be made of this form by the student in dance composition is for the development of a delicate satiric vein, produced through the smallest possible movements." At times he suggested topical themes for the preclassic forms; thus it is not surprising that in 1937 he should write that the sarabande is "a grateful vehicle for choreographic ideas of serious, and also of social, import. The contemporary tragedy in Spain should supply much deeply felt subject matter."

Having mastered the preclassic forms, students progressed to the class in modern dance forms. Here, they had greater compositional freedom, yet they still had to concern themselves with structure. Assignments explored uses of space, the possibilities of asymmetry, and the influence upon modern art of art of other periods or styles, including primitive, archaic, and medieval art (but never art from the scorned Romantic period). Advanced students might then go on to a class in group forms.[23]

Horst's approach to teaching composition—an approach that seems both carefully thought out and wildly arbitrary—has prompted a wide range of reactions. Because Horst was not himself a choreographer, some dancers, particularly dancers who never studied with him, have questioned his qualifications for teaching composition. Yet many capable teachers of writing, though they may be good critics, are not necessarily also poets or novelists, and Nadia Boulanger, the twentieth-century's most famous teacher of musical composition, was not a composer.

A more serious objection is the charge that devising studies to fulfill the requirements of Horst's idiosyncratic assignments had little to do with the complexity of creating works for stage performance. As Pauline Koner puts it, "A-B-A is babytalk." Creating movement to meet Horst's demands has also been compared with solving puzzles.

Yet Horst did not really expect these little studies to find their way to the stage. After all, few exercises in canon and fugue by conservatory students are ever played by symphony orchestras. Horst's compositional formulas were not ends in themselves; they simply called attention to the necessity for disciplined movement invention. Doris Rudko says, "In Louis's classes you developed a sense of form, dance logic, and sequential ordering and manipulation of materials." Selma Jeanne Cohen agrees: "Louis's assignments, simply because they were so strict, forced you to ask yourself, can I do *this particular thing?*"

Paul Taylor says, "Louis taught me very early that the limitations you set up for yourself are a very important part of choreography. Louis taught you how to limit your movement palette. And if you know how to limit your palette for a section, or even for the entirety, of a piece, you'll be able to relate movements, and you can make a whole dance out of a minimum of material."

Jeanette Schlottmann adds that although Horst insisted upon the necessity of formal rules, he was often fascinated by the ways that choreographers who knew the rules might break them. Horst could be dogmatic in his attitudes and scathing in his criticisms, yet he never lost interest in what choreographers were up to. This is why even students who quarrelled with him violently can still speak of him with respect. One such former student is Trisha Brown, who had several courses with him at a time when she was eager to prove herself a choreographic maverick. Although this prompted classroom explosions, Brown is nevertheless now able to look back and say, "And yet I liked him very much. I really did."

By 1958 the Connecticut College School of the Dance and American Dance Festival were in many ways artistic successes. The school had a distinguished faculty; the festival offered works by some distinguished choreographers. Theory and practice, studio and stage, were united. Nevertheless, critics occasionally questioned whether things were really quite as successful as they seemed, and in 1956 John Martin wrote a long article in which he accused the festival's directorate of never really having decided what sort of event they wanted their festival to be. Martin said,

> There seem to be three possibilities to choose from. It may be truly a festival; that is, a presentation of great works of art, new or old or both, designed to regale and refresh the visitor, and sufficiently rare and notable to justify a pilgrimage from afar. Again, it may be a variety of "straw hat" theatre, without pretensions or particular policy, offering productions, as good as may be under the circumstances, to entertain the local public. Or still again, it may simply be the culminating event of a summer school, designed to allow its student body to get a glimpse of its instructors in action and generally to see in practice something of the theory it has presumably been learning.

Martin concluded that whereas the American Dance Festival may fit into the last two categories, "It must be pronounced a failure" in its attempt to fit into the first.

Martin then declared that the Connecticut organization should decide once and for all whether it was primarily a school or a festival: if a school, "then undoubtedly the performing sessions that come at its conclusion should be planned exclusively for the students, thus avoiding the serious risk of injury in the public mind to leaders in the modern dance field. That field is already weak enough." However, if the venture was primarily a festival, "then it needs a practical, theatrically minded, lively and vital director, who can not only plan a schedule of attractive, evocative and important programs, but can also arrange for the commissioning of a new work or two, and the proper artistic and financial atmosphere for the commissionee to work in."[24]

Martin's remarks, which could be considered merely impertinent or polemically inflammatory in 1956, became of urgent importance after 1958, when a new director—and that director's board—would have to make important decisions about festival policy.

IV

SEASON BY SEASON

1959–1968

———————————————— 1959 ————————————————

n 1959 Jeanette Schlottmann became director of the American Dance
Festival and its summer school. One of the first things she did in her
new post was to change the name of the school from Connecticut
College School of the Dance to what she considered to be the less
pompous-sounding Connecticut College School of Dance. For her "*the*
Dance" was much too fancy. That gesture was typical of her administrative style, and her colleagues found her unpretentious, warmhearted, and
thoroughly capable.

Schlottmann grew up in small towns near San Antonio, Texas, and
during her childhood, she says, "The dancing studios that existed were so
awful and taught such horrible things that most young girls were not
allowed to take dance. Instead, we all had music and elocution." She had
her first dancing lesson in 1936 when she was a student at Texas Woman's
University in Denton. After seeing an advertisement for the college's modern dance club in the campus newspaper, she decided to attend a session,
thinking she would learn the tango and fox-trot. Instead, she found a
teacher who had been to Bennington teaching a "modern" dance altogether
different from what she had expected. But it fascinated her enough to
make her join the dance club.

Shortly thereafter, Anne Schley Duggan came to head the college's
dance department. Duggan, who had studied at Teachers College, Colum-
bia University, and with many of the leading modern dancers in New
York, formed a modern dance group in Denton that regularly toured the
Southwest. Schlottmann became a member of the company, stayed on in
Denton to get an M.A., and was appointed to the college's dance faculty.

She taught there until 1950. "Then," she says, "I realized that, artistically speaking, I needed to be fed. I was feeding everyone else and no one was feeding me."

She went to New York and studied with José Limón, Martha Graham, and Louis Horst. Deciding to stay in the city, she found a teaching position at Barnard College. It was Doris Humphrey who told her in 1958 that, with Ruth Bloomer's retirement, Connecticut College needed someone to head its dance program in both the winter and summer. At first Schlottmann was reluctant to apply for what she feared would be a year-round job with no time for vacations or relaxation. Yet she liked Connecticut College. And the college officials decided they liked her.[1]

The 1959 festival was a tribute to Doris Humphrey. Its first concert, 13 August, included a performance of *Day on Earth*, Humphrey's allegorical account of the course of life, and the last concert, 16 August, was an all-Humphrey program, consisting of *Day on Earth*, *Lament for Ignacio Sánchez Mejías*, and *Ruins and Visions*. Choreographers presenting works as part of the regular festival series included Limón, Pauline Koner, Merce Cunningham, Sybil Shearer, Ruth Currier, Daniel Nagrin, and Helen Tamiris. In addition, a Little Concert Series offered lecture-demonstrations by Graham and Cunningham, an evening of dance films, a special performance of Erick Hawkins's *Here and Now with Watchers*, a children's program by the Merry-Go-Rounders, and a young choreographers' concert with dances by Juki Arkin, Jean Cébron, Harlan McCallum, Jack Moore, Carol Scothorn, and Annaliese Widman.

Once again, audiences interested in two different—and, for some of their partisans, antithetical—trends in modern dance could compare the new works of Limón and Cunningham. Of Limón's two premieres, *The Apostate* was the more favorably received. Concerning Julian the Apostate, it showed that fourth-century emperor torn between Christianity, represented by a figure called The Galilean (Lucas Hoving) and Greco-Roman polytheism, represented by a figure called The Olympian (Betty Jones). Louis Horst, who found the piece "short but exciting," particularly liked the "beautiful erotic duet" for Julian and The Olympian and the "violent duet of struggle with The Galilean." Doris Hering agreed that the work had "power and immediacy," and also suspected that it reflected some of the mixed emotions of a lapsed Catholic.[2]

Tenebrae—1914, inspired by the life of Edith Cavell, the British nurse who was executed by the Germans in Belgium for aiding wounded Allied soldiers in World War I, received generally less favorable notices.

However, for Horst, "the startling realism and the searing, relentless conclusion build to a cumulative dance-drama of tremendous impact." P. W. Manchester admired Ruth Currier as Edith Cavell, particularly in "the last moment when she stood, proudly immobile before the firing squad, her nurse's cloak falling about her in sculptural folds." Yet she complained that the work's "subject is not one that lends itself readily to dance form, and the goosestepping and thigh slapping of the helmeted soldiers, and the floor rolling histrionics of the wounded prisoners were clichés of the most embarrassing kind."[3]

Cunningham's plotless, but mysterious, new *Rune* also divided the critics. Hering was enthusiastic: "*Rune* transcends. It has a stillness and an agitation, a flow and a violence that seem to emanate from some secret, nonrevealable source. It is the very essence of drama without one stroke of dramatic action." Horst, too, was well-disposed toward it, although with a reservation: "*Rune* is a dignified work with fleeting moments of warmth that showed some concern with human relations. There was much fine movement. . . . All a pleasure to behold though still movement that overrides content." However, Manchester's combination of puzzlement over Cunningham's choreography and admiration for his dancers was perhaps typical of the reactions of many dancegoers of the time. Manchester thought *Rune* "as obscure as its title. What one admires is the marvelous coordination of these extraordinary dancers and the absorbed busyness with which they go about their traffic on the stage. Their contacts are as impersonal as their isolation; their physical beauty . . . is a constant delight to the eye though mind and heart remain disengaged."[4]

The 1959 festival featured two legendary modern dance choreographers in what would be their only association with New London, Sybil Shearer and Helen Tamiris. Shearer had a reputation for being willfully unconventional. A former member of the Humphrey-Weidman company, she had for many years lived in seclusion in a Chicago suburb. Shearer's concerts grew increasingly rare in frequency and rarefied in content. A nature mystic, she choreographed dances that were sometimes astonishing, sometimes only perplexing, and she did not concern herself much with the niceties of stage costuming and makeup.

At New London she offered a trilogy of dances called simply *Part I*, *Part II*, and *Part III*, the first two parts (a solo to Clementi and a jazz trio) being premieres. Much was expected of Shearer. Margaret Lloyd expresses what appears to have been the nearly unanimous critical reaction: "Noted for range of movement and loftiness of thought, she astonished everybody by descending from her accustomed heights to indulge in sweet and pretty stepping with Dalcroze effects. It was as if some philosopher of reputed profundity (and rather careless in dress) had come out on the lecture platform to chatter about trivialities." Hering compared Shearer with Cunningham: "Both are mystics. Both move as though chosen by the wind. But Miss Shearer's artistic development has not been nearly so constant as that of Mr. Cunningham—nor so cumulative in its sophistication. And at the present time she seems to be out of contact not only with her audience, but with herself."[5]

Helen Tamiris was the only major American modern dancer who had never been involved with Bennington. Now, at long last, she was associated with Bennington's successor. At New London she was in charge of the repertory group, a workshop in which students learned and performed dances by a major choreographer. In past years that choreographer had been Doris Humphrey.

Tamiris's students appeared during the festival in *Memoir*, a dance-drama about growing up in the slums as a member of an Orthodox Jewish family. *Memoir* was a revised version of *Chrysalis*, which Tamiris had choreographed in 1957 for students at the Perry-Mansfield Festival, a summer arts camp in Colorado. Seeing it then, Hering thought it remarkable because Tamiris had "welded a group of youngsters, most of whom had probably never seen a slum, into a covey of vicious, driven urchins." Hering was less pleased by the revised version. She found its characters "types, and not genuine people," and had reservations about its choreographic structure:

> She [Tamiris] makes fascinating movement statements, as in the street
> scene with its opposing groups and its solos like raindrops on water.
> But she rarely pursues a phrase to a satisfying conclusion. Instead
> she resorts to [an] eye-catching device (the favorite being to arrest the
> entire group and allow a soloist to move in opposition—or to halt
> the entire stage action). But when the dancing resumes, it does not
> develop a pattern already begun. Instead, something new and equally
> fragmentary is suggested.[6]

Other festival premieres were by Daniel Nagrin, Tamiris's husband, and Pauline Koner. Nagrin's *Theatre for Fools* was a commedia dell'arte suite about egocentricity during the course of which the characters revealed their true selves. Horst said it contained "a great deal of witty and satiric comment, most of it arising from flickering pantomime and choreography that gave off a spontaneous quality of improvisation." But, for Hering, it was "not really a dance. It was a pantomime bordering on dance."[7]

In *Tides* Koner combined dance with quotations from John Donne, read by Alexander Scourby, to examine the present-day disintegration of society and to express hope in the possibility of social renewal. Horst praised its ambitions but sadly concluded that "the probing intent of *Tides* was not fully realized; the choreography did not probe deeply enough." He also complained that the conclusion, in which Koner implied that love can conquer all, "was a too easy and surface solution."[8]

--- **1960** ---

Enrollment soared at the 1960 summer school to a recordbreaking 239 students (223 of them women) from thirty-two states and ten foreign countries.[9] That summer, memorials were established to two former faculty members. The Ruth Bloomer Loan Fund aided students in need of financial assistance, and the Doris Humphrey Fellowship was intended as an annual honor (although, in fact, it was not always awarded annually) that would provide a young choreographer, chosen by audition, with tuition, living and working space, and a choreographer's fee for a new dance.

Jack Moore was the winner of the first fellowship, which he used to create *Songs Remembered*, an emotionally charged duet to Alban Berg for himself and Nancy Lewis. Doris Hering summarized the action:

> The duet began with Mr. Moore running about with an attitude of listening. He reached and staggered and was then drawn back to running in a circle. The couple came together, not as though they were meeting, but as though she were an image of torment and recollection. After placing their palms on each other's faces they finished side by side, one kneeling and one standing.

Songs Remembered has prompted mixed reactions over the years. Seeing a Connecticut revival in 1968, P. W. Manchester called the dance "a heartbreaker, so simple in its means, so profound in its content." Hering was more guarded at the premiere: "Mr. Moore has sensitivity as a choreographer, but his movement style lacks definition, verging between the rough-hewn statements of prose and the finer threads of poetry—but with no palpable reason for the vacillation."[10]

The festival offered works by Limón, Merce Cunningham, Ruth Currier, Pearl Lang, Lucas Hoving, and Charles Weidman. The summer's equivalent of a Little Concert Series was a miscellaneous set of programs, including lecture-demonstrations by Limón, Weidman, and Martha Graham; a concert by festival musicians under the direction of Norman Lloyd; an evening of dances by Phyllis Lamhut and Beverly Schmidt; a program of dances from Korea, Argentina, Japan, Spain, Jamaica, and Haiti by foreign students at the festival, and a young choreographers' concert with works by Joan Hartshorne, Betty Jones, Joan Miller, Carol Anne Wallace, Rena Schenfeld, Lola Huth, and Jack Moore.

By a curious coincidence, two of the three festival premieres involved the use of elastic cords or bands. The dancers in Merce Cunningham's *Crises* wore such bands around the waist or arms and one performer could link up with another by slipping a hand through the band on that performer's costume. Despite its title, *Crises* was not a succession of dire events, but a rather mild-mannered, even fanciful piece, and Cunningham may have been using "crises" in the sense of meaning "turning points," the dance's specific turning points being those when the cast members linked or freed themselves. Louis Horst, who was entertained by *Crises*, said that, structurally, it consisted of "four consecutive nonchalant pas de deux performed by Mr. Cunningham in turn with each one of the four damsels" in the cast. Then in "the inevitable closing tableau . . . the four partners gang up on him to his complete embarrassment." As a former vaudeville musician, Horst appeared to relish what he called the dance's "most blatant score for player piano by Conlon Nancarrow that now and then brought a raucous spirit of carnival into this gentle field of Eros." Hering was also fascinated by the player piano music, which she said sounded "as though a hundred barroom doors had been thrown ajar to the wind."[11]

Dedicated to the memory of Margaret Lloyd, the late dance critic of the *Christian Science Monitor*, Pearl Lang's *Shira* took its title from the Hebrew word for "song" and was inspired by a complex Hassidic legend about how the mystical relationship between a spring and the heart of the world generates a spiritual life-force. During the course of the work, dancers held and manipulated long elastic cords, which were stretched across the stage to form what Don McDonagh has called "a shimmering web," the plucking of these strands symbolizing the song of creation. Walter Terry thought the use of the cords resulted in "images suggesting rippling streams, shimmering strips of clouds, pathways through space and the like." Entranced by the choreography, Hering said that the dancers "seemed to be responding not only to Miss Lang's summoning gestures, but to a stirring of seeds beneath the ground." *Shira*, she concluded, was an "ecstatic utterance."[12]

Like *Shira*, Ruth Currier's *Transfigured Season* was ritualistic and hard to explain: too hard to explain for Horst, who thought it required "more clarification of both idea and choreography." Hering speculated that its images of struggle "perhaps meant to symbolize the war of a human being against the passage of time, or even death"; whatever it meant, the choreography "had a wonderfully heroic quality and an intuitive sense of contrast and balance." And Terry was particularly struck by its images, for "in pictorial quality, it is rather as if Botticelli's La Primavera were suddenly invaded by figures from Goya paintings."[13]

1961

Summarizing the 1961 festival, Doris Hering wrote, "The statistics are impressive." Indeed they were. The festival featured works by nine choreographers (Doris Humphrey, José Limón, Merce Cunningham, Ruth Currier, Jack Moore, Paul Taylor, La Meri, Anna Sokolow, and David Wood), and there were six premieres. Limón and Sokolow could be taken as representing an emotionally intense and often dramatically explicit form of modern dance, whereas a newer, more abstract style was exemplified by Cunningham and Taylor. La Meri brought ethnic dance to the public festival programs for the first time. In addition, the Little Concert and Lecture Series presented a program of dances from Hawaii, Hungary, Okinawa, the Ukraine, Chile, Argentina, and India by festival students; a solo recital by Manja Chmiel, a German dancer; a concert of dances by Midi Garth and Robert Cohan, and a young choreographers' program with works by Carol Wallace, Jean Learey, James Payton, Meryl Whitman, Joseph Schlichter, Martha Wittman, and David Wood.

"Yes, the statistics are impressive. They may even represent some sort of record," said Hering. "But," she continued, "they bear a measure of tarnish. As the novelties were ticked off, we had the impression of seeing very little real dance—very little real theatre—and little in the way of skillful programming." P. W. Manchester agreed, calling the festival "a strange mixture of the exhilarating and the tedious, the hilarious and the solemnly pretentious."[14]

Many works that sounded fascinating in prospect turned out to be disappointing in actuality—for instance, the *Granada Suite* that La Meri designed for students in her class in Spanish dance. According to Louis Horst, "This four-part suite was well structured and contained many opportunities for the display of the fiery qualities of Spanish dancing. However, the student group was not very successful in the handling of this material."[15]

Nor did Limón's premieres arouse universal enthusiasm. *The Moirai* depicted an allegorical encounter between Man and the Moirai, the Three Fates of Greek mythology: Klotho, giver of life; Lachesis, the spinner of each person's allotted destiny; and Atropos, who severs the thread of life. Horst thought the piece "most satisfying." Other critics had reservations. Hering, for whom *The Moirai* was curiously lacking in impact, compared it as an allegory with George Balanchine's *Apollo* and noted that although Apollo is an abstraction, a symbol of man the artist, "he is also human and strangely lovable. One *cares* as he climbs the stairway-of-destiny, leading the muses behind him." But Man, in Limón's work, "does not stir a similar level of empathy. He never really becomes alive." Walter Terry also had trouble accepting the character of Man (danced by Chester Wolenski). In fact, he considered Man so weakly and dully characterized that "I found myself not caring what happened to the man and, indeed, wishing that the Fate with the shears would get on with it and snip off his life-thread."[16]

Sonata for Two Cellos, to a score by Meyer Kupferman, was a grueling virtuosic solo for Limón. It, too, divided the critics. Horst said, "It is a long work, but Mr. Limón and the beauty of his strong masculine movement were ever a joy to behold. At present a more lyric and placid section seems to be indicated for some moments of contrast." Hering disagreed: "Unbecomingly clad in yellow leotard and tights, he [Limón] turned and lunged and twisted and bowed, tiring himself mercilessly and to no discernible expressive purpose."[17]

Works by three younger choreographers also failed to achieve success. Hering dismissed David Wood's *The Initiate* because "Its conventional theme—a rite of initiation for a young girl—bore little surprise." Jack Moore's *Target*, which concerned problems of human beings struggling to reach one another, may also have possessed what was, for modern dance, a familiar theme, but Hering thought it of some interest, even though, finally, she pronounced it flawed: "Jack Moore creates movement that grows honestly and directly from himself and draws maximum identification from his dancers. But, often, the movement shapes do not adventure into space. It is as though he dropped stones into water and no ripples followed."[18]

Nobody appears to have liked Ruth Currier's *Resonances*. Nor were the critics sure just what it was supposed to be about. To Hering, it seemed to concern illicit love. Horst said it was specifically based upon the myth of Phaedra. Terry called it "a singularly soggy investigation of how miserable everyone onstage felt about something." An attempt to describe the action was made by Allen Hughes who, upon John Martin's retirement in 1962 would become the chief dance critic of the *New York Times*:

> It begins conventionally and clearly with four people obviously mixed up about love and mating. Later, though, when they strip down to leotards and begin wrapping themselves in gauze panels, pulled down from the set, everything becomes gray and meaningless to the innocent observer.
>
> At the end, the dancers become lumpy shapes under a gigantic piece of gray gauze that descends from overhead and the cause is truly lost.[19]

The premieres by Paul Taylor and Merce Cunningham aroused real controversy. Taylor, a former scholarship student at Connecticut, was now choreographing for the festival, and his presence on campus in 1961 suggested that, just as students who had gone to Bennington later developed into prominent choreographers, so New London was producing important choreographers of its own. Always eclectic and often surprising, Taylor baffled some critics of the late fifties and early sixties because of his fondness for the whimsical and the grotesque. One Taylor concert in 1957 had so befuddled his former teacher, Louis Horst, that Horst's review of it in *Dance Observer* consisted of nothing but an absolutely blank space on the page signed with the initials L.H.

Insects and Heroes, Taylor's first work for the festival, was in his grotesque vein. Its decor consisted of a set of doors, and the action was a series of encounters between people and a dancer costumed to resemble a black spiny creature, at once menacing and absurd, that some dancegoers have called a big bug, although Taylor himself says, "It's more like a sea urchin, really." The dance, which has moments of dark comedy as well as mystery, is now often interpreted as a work about courage and fear. But reviewers in 1961 were not quite sure what to think about it. Typically, Walter Terry conceded that the dance "had some marvelous movement

Elizabeth Keen, Elizabeth Walton, Paul Taylor, Linda Hodes, Dan Wagoner, and Maggie Newman in Taylor's *Insects and Heroes*, 1961. Photo, William Ship.

designs in it and also a good deal of humor (not always specific, but communicative); however, the title and the piece itself seemed to have nothing in common. There was one (not plural) creature who could possibly have been an insect (or so the costume suggested) and as for the heroes, I saw none." Horst took a stab at interpreting the dance very literally, concluding that it must be a depiction of "a fashionable beach resort. The basic idea of the dance seemed to be a war between the bathers and the persistent insects, represented by a master insect in a costume strongly suggesting the symbol of a primitive animistic ancestor. Some psychological relationship was no doubt present but it eluded this viewer."

To dancegoers and critics who have grown accustomed to choreography containing constantly shifting and emotionally evocative—but not necessarily dramatically literal—patterns, such a doggedly literal critical approach to *Insects and Heroes* seems surprising. One could even wonder whether this was a subtle way of damning the work. Taylor thinks not. Although he admits he had no intention of choreographing a dance about a beach resort, he nevertheless says, "If that's what Louis saw in it, that's what Louis saw in it. And I do think that there are what you could call 'little stories' in the dance: not long narratives, but dramatic situations that develop among the dancers." Taylor adds, "I don't think Louis was trying to be mean to me. Even when he wrote the blank review, I don't think he was trying to be *really* mean. I think he was always genuinely curious about what I was doing." Horst may well have been. But such reviews as Horst gave Taylor may have helped convince other young dancers that there was a widening aesthetic gulf between the sort of dance they were most interested in creating and that upheld by their teachers in what could be termed the modern dance "establishment."

However, at least one critic revealed that she was capable of enjoying Taylor's ambiguities without being intimidated by them. Hering's reactions to *Insects and Heroes* in 1961 seem much like those of audiences today at one of the dance's revivals. Commenting on the action, Hering wrote,

> The creature scuttled about—closing and opening the doors—leading a procession of dancers—tinkling a triangle—and at one point drawing forth from some body-aperture a checkered tablecloth. As for the other dancers . . . they glided about, sallied easily into the air, seemed completely impersonal and yet created a sense of contact with each other. It was not the contact of drama, but the contact of sharing an atmosphere. . . .
>
> What did it all mean? For some reason that was not important. It was a delicious dream. . . . And, after all, how often is one privileged to gaze upon a dream?

"It was not the contact of drama, but the contact of sharing an atmosphere": with those words Hering summarized an approach to dance-making that would come to dominate choreography for at least two decades.[20]

Whether one liked it or not, it was comparatively easy to classify *Insects and Heroes* as a piquant curiosity. But, for many dancegoers, Cunningham's *Aeon* was a total outrage. Often, in the ever-changing art of modern dance, a once-scorned trend or development will be, first, grudgingly tolerated and, then, thoroughly accepted, and reviews of previ-

Merce Cunningham, Steve Paxton, and Carolyn Brown in Cunningham's *Aeon*, 1961. Photo, Richard Rutledge.

ous works by the Cunningham company at the festival could have been interpreted as evidence that Cunningham's innovations were slowly being countenanced. *Aeon* changed all that.

Aeon's title referred to a long period of time and the piece lasted about forty minutes—rather a long time for a dance to last, considering the fact that the one-act dance and the mixed bill have established themselves as norms of twentieth-century dance programming. *Aeon*'s program note stated, "This is a dance of actions, a celebration of unfixity, in which the seasons pass, atmospheres dissolve, people come together and part. Its meaning is in the instant in the eye and ear, and its continuity is change." Terry dismissed this note as "puerile pomposity," yet the dance's ever-swirling action did seem in harmony with those statements. Designed by Robert Rauschenberg, *Aeon* possessed unusual scenic effects: magnesium flares went off, a mechanical contraption with a smoking wheel jerked its way across the stage, and in one sequence a man and woman wore flashing stroboscopic lights on their wrists.

But what caused the real fuss was John Cage's score. Cunningham had often danced to music that sounded odd to listeners. But this music was not only odd, but acutely painful. The score "ran its fingernails over our eardrums," Hering declared, and the audience at Palmer Auditorium was appalled.

Jeanette Schlottmann recalls,

> The sound was incredible. I had my fingers in my ears for 40 minutes. In many ways, it was a beautiful dance. But it was painful to be in the auditorium while it was going on. When it was over, a man came up to me in the lobby and he was livid and shaking. He said he was a scientist at the Underwater Sound Laboratory in Groton and he told me, "The sound level in that auditorium is dangerous for human ears!" Later, at a party, I asked Merce why John's music had to be so loud and he replied, "I think John will tell you that's the way the world will be in ten years and you'd better get used to it."

Since that statement was made, transistor radios have blared and rock-and-roll music has boomed on the streets. So it is possible to say that the prophecy came true. But whether the world is therefore a better place remains debatable.

Horst, who in past seasons had tried to come to terms with Cunningham, expressed his disapproval in journalistic terms almost as thunderous as Cage's music. *Aeon*, he wrote, went on and on for what seemed an endless and impertinent length of 45 or 50 minutes. One wonders for what eye the non sequitur movement was designed and for what ear the John Cage score, with its shattering and ear-splitting noise, was brought into monstrous birth. . . . We are apt to make Mr. Cage the Dennis the Menace of this work but Mr. Cunningham must also share the critical disapproval of many lovers of the arts who cannot be classified as fuddy-duddies.[21]

Yet the festival—and its new director—survived *Aeon*. Connecticut's students and faculty members were finding Schlottmann both efficient and charming. On 29 April 1961 she married Curtis Roosevelt, grandson of Franklin D. Roosevelt.[22] And even as she was receiving the kind wishes of her colleagues in New London, she was seriously wondering whether, now that she was married, it would be feasible for her to continue as a year-round member of the Connecticut faculty.

1962

The festival's fifteenth anniversary season was jubilant. Not only did it strive to be better than its predecessors, it was also, quite literally, bigger. Instead of clustering all public performances into the final weekend of the summer term, as had become the custom, there were performances scattered throughout the season; the last long weekend was shared by the companies of Martha Graham and José Limón, each group giving one matinee and two evening programs. Walter Terry had no doubt that this new programming format made the festival "theatrically stronger and more cumulative of interest than those in recent years." And, regarding the weekend by Graham and Limón, he could only exclaim, "What a rich fare."[23]

The printed programs for all festival performances contained a statement explaining the rationale for the anniversary season:

The programs scheduled for the eleven performances have been planned to give a cross section of the form of dance that emerged as an expression of the intellectual and artistic climate following World War I. In the three and one-half decades since its beginning, this art form—called variously modern American dance, contemporary dance, concert dance—has developed in many different directions. The thirteen artists presented in this Festival Season represent many of the diverse styles and forms which have enriched the entire field of movement expression through three generations of American choreographers.

The thirteen modern dance choreographers referred to were Graham, Limón, Erick Hawkins, Glen Tetley, Alvin Ailey, Ruth Currier, Lucas Hoving, Charles Weidman, Paul Taylor, Katherine Litz, Pearl Lang, Daniel Nagrin, and Carol Scothorn. In addition, there were performances by a fourteenth artist, the tap dancer Paul Draper.

These choreographers did indeed constitute a cross section of modern dance in the early sixties. But it should be noted that the list did not include either Merce Cunningham or Alwin Nikolais. And of the younger choreographers represented, only Taylor had a reputation for being really "controversial."

The programming format was not the only thing new about the festival. The Connecticut College School of Dance established its own new summer touring company, Dance Advance, in one of the festival's persistent attempts to arouse local interest in the art. Conceived by Jeanette Schlottmann and directed by Janet Mansfield Soares, Dance Advance offered works by student choreographers, and its hour-long programs included dance appreciation commentaries by Soares and question-and-answer sessions after the performances.

The anniversary summer was the last under the presidency of Rosemary Park, who had accepted an offer to become president of Barnard College. Her successor was Charles E. Shain, who came to Connecticut from Carleton College, where he had been professor of English and administrator of the American Studies program. Educated at Princeton, he had also taught at the University of Minnesota and Cornell University and at the Seminar in American Studies at Salzburg. From the time of his arrival until 1974, when he left Connecticut, Shain was a loyal friend of the American Dance Festival.[25]

The anniversary season was also the year when a Connecticut alumna returned to the campus to work in the college's publicity office. As the summer progressed she became increasingly excited about modern dance until one day, after seeing her go about her business, Curtis Roosevelt remarked to his wife, "She's hooked." He was right. The publicist was Marcia B. Siegel, today one of America's leading dance critics.

As might be expected at a choreographic birthday party, the season's premieres were almost entirely festive in nature. Graham's contribution to

Graham company in Graham's *Secular Games*, 1962. Robert Powell, center.
Photo, Martha Swope.

the first festival had been *Diversion of Angels*. Now, her company returned
to the fifteenth festival with another "diversion," *Secular Games*. Divided
into three parts (subtitled "Play with thought—on a Socratic island,"
"Play with dream—on a Utopian island," and "Play—on any island")
Secular Games was a joyous work that suggested that thinking, dreaming,
and loving could all be forms of play. As its title implied, said Doris
Hering, *Secular Games*

> was about people behaving like people. On one level it seemed to say
> that man's prime function lies in the exercise of intellect. This was
> represented by a Socratic ball game that occupied the first section and
> was briefly alluded to at the very end. But if one examined the
> symbolism of the props subsequently used (a ring, a serpent, and a

strip of red cloth), *Secular Games* took on a reverse meaning. . . .
Throughout, they played hard, these athletes of Eros.

Similarly, Allen Hughes wrote that "whether posing, playing ball, courting,
cavorting, or kidding ballet a little bit, the dancers seemed to be having
fun all the way," and he was happy that "nearly everything in the work is
touched with wit, and there is neither complication nor psychosis in any
part of it."

Amid the critical praise there was one resounding dissent. This came
from Jill Johnston, the recently appointed and almost immediately controversial dance critic of the *Village Voice.* Johnston detected in *Secular
Games* signs of choreographic deterioration and feared that Graham
technique, which had once been an expressive form of movement, was
turning into mere exhibitionism. Whereas Walter Terry thought that *Secular
Games* "contained some of the most brilliant movement that Miss Graham has ever designed for the men of her company," Johnston saw only
"narcissistic exertions" for "lovely teddy-bear boys." As for the piece as a
whole, she said, "It has plenty of big, husky movement, including some
ball-tossing and woman-juggling, and it demonstrates again how a technique loses its original vitality through degeneration to a purely physical
level of action." Later in her review, she became even harsher as she
specifically identified this "degeneration" as a "metamorphosis . . . from
emotion to vanity."[26]

Very clearly a new generation of dancers and dancegoers was arising
that did not regard its elders with total reverence. That very summer—on
6 July 1962—a band of rebellious choreographers rented New York
City's Judson Memorial Church and presented the first program of what
would come to be known as the Judson Dance Theater, a group that so
markedly influenced the course of American dance that some critics call
the dance that came after the Judson experiments "postmodern." To the
horror of many people in the dance establishment, Hughes praised that
first Judson concert in the *Times.* But the most enthusiastic critical partisan of Judson in its early years was Johnston in the *Voice.* Thus her attack
on Graham was ideological in nature. Yet it cannot simply be dismissed
as a polemical gesture, for, in years to come, other critics—including
critics basically sympathetic to Graham—began to complain that her
choreography was becoming increasingly decorative.

Jeanette Schlottmann remembers that when Paul Taylor arrived on

Elizabeth Walton, Dan Wagoner, and Sharon Kinney in Taylor's *Aureole,* 1962.
Photo, Fanny Helen Melcer.

campus in 1962 he told her, "Jeanette, I'm going to do a new dance
you're just going to *love!*" The resultant work was *Aureole,* a dance to
Handel that audiences have loved ever since. Just as *Insects and Heroes*
exemplified Taylor's fascination with the grotesque, so *Aureole* attested to
his equally strong love of lyricism. Yet Taylor says he was inspired to
choreograph *Aureole* out of a kind of orneriness: "Almost nobody in
modern dance in those days was dancing to Handel; they were all dancing
to Bartók or to someone else *moderne.* So I thought it kind of cheeky to
go up there and do Handel. Handel's music was considered too close to
ballet, and ballet was still a dirty word to some modern dancers."

Despite its similarities to ballet, *Aureole* is not entirely balletic.
Whereas trained ballet dancers often take lightness as a matter of course,
many sequences in *Aureole* could be said to depict weighted bodies achiev-
ing lightness, and the work's shifts of weight have puzzled ballet dancers
when Taylor has staged it for classical companies. Nevertheless, its élan

and its white costumes have led many critics to compare *Aureole* with ballet. Hughes called it a "white ballet." Using more flowery language, George Beiswanger termed it "a glowing declaration of dance's white simplicities." And Louis Horst renamed it "*Les Sylphides* 1962."

Hughes developed the comparison with ballet in his review and suggested that *Aureole* represented a new development in modern dance: "The 'white ballet,' after all, is a nineteenth-century classical ballet invention and, as such, typifies just about everything 'modern dance' has tried to do away with. But times are changing." *Aureole* disdained both the stormy narratives often associated with modern dance and the prankishness of much self-consciously "experimental" dance. Instead, said Hughes, "it's gracious movement for five dancers who danced like the liveliest barefoot angels one could imagine."

Horst's comments are also worth quoting. On the one hand, he praised *Aureole* because "its lyric, graceful and utterly cheerful phrases were most satisfying." Yet he suspected that "*Aureole* may not be or become his [Taylor's] most significant composition." Here, he was possibly in error. It may still be impossible to say whether or not *Aureole* is Taylor's *most* significant composition, but it is now almost universally regarded as a *very* significant one, and it has proved enduringly popular. But Horst's reservations about *Aureole*'s possible significance may have been conditioned by the fact that, as a proud spokesman for modern dance, he considered *Aureole* too similar to ballet and, therefore, not inherently serious enough.[27]

The anniversary festivities inspired José Limón to make one of his rare excursions into comedy. But *I, Odysseus* only confirmed the widely held view that comedy was not his forte. Critics pronounced the work stylistically confused. Terry said, "Mr. Limón vacillated between what conceivably may have been a satiric retelling of the wanderings of Odysseus and being deadly serious about it all." Certain characters in this choreographic *Odyssey* were played "straight." Yet much of the action took place in a modern nightclub, and, said Terry, "Circe was jazz-mad . . . Calypso was a tramp." In the role of Zeus, Simon Sadoff sat on stage at a piano, playing the score by Hugh Aitken while smoking cigarettes and giving orders to Louis Falco, as Hermes. It was, thought Horst, a "disjointed" effort; moreover, he considered the erotic duets so explicit that, though "marvelously choreographed and performed . . . they do call for some censorship."[28]

The festival's one serious new work was *The Lazarite*, the dramatic solo with a text based on Eugene O'Neill's *Lazarus Laughed* that Carol Scothorn had created as the summer's Doris Humphrey Fellow. It failed to arouse enthusiasm, and the remarks of Lillian Moore, at that time Terry's assistant critic at the *Herald Tribune*, typify the critical reception: "A pretentious affair which depended largely on the spoken word, it had a text dealing with the resurrection of Lazarus from the dead. The dance movement, which presumably was designed to illuminate this theme, would have been a good deal more appropriate in a production of 'West Side Story.'"[29]

Although she offered no premieres, Katherine Litz attracted attention for her fey, introverted, and often eccentric solos. Moore attempted to describe her style:

> Everything she does, from the consciously naive "Story of Love from Fear to Flight," with its fluttery hands and maidenly tremors, to the wry and sardonic "Fall of the Leaf," has about it an air of dilapidated gentility. This is true of the repressed and twitching lady of "Twilight of a Flower" (who always reminds me of a Tennessee Williams heroine, one of the battered aristocrats) and even of the genuinely moving "And No Birds Sing," where the repetition of a few aimless movements somehow adds up to an expression of deep despair.[30]

In general, the fifteenth anniversary festival was a great success. It was also the last festival to be directed by Jeanette Schlottmann. Deciding that because of her marriage she could no longer spend the year in New London, she resigned from Connecticut College, moved back to New York City, and was able to resume teaching at Barnard College (where, by coincidence, her college president was once again Rosemary Park).

A successor to Schlottmann had to be found before the 1963 season got under way. Theodora Wiesner, a member of the board, recalls that a meeting to choose a new director took place on a chilly windy day in Schlottmann's Greenwich Village apartment. Wiesner was suffering from a terrible cold and, ordinarily, would not have ventured outdoors at all. But the importance of the occasion forced her to go off, sniffling and sneezing, to the meeting. She was late. And when she arrived, her fellow board members welcomed her by saying that they wanted her to be the new director of the Connecticut College School of Dance and American Dance Festival. She says, "About all I could do then was sneeze and say yes."

---------------------------------- **1963** ----------------------------------

Theodora Wiesner, the festival's new director, grew up in Superior, Wisconsin. Fond of sports as a child, she decided to become a physical education teacher and enrolled as a "phys. ed." major at the University of Wisconsin in Madison. There, she discovered the innovative dance program that had been established by Margaret H'Doubler, and her love of sports gave way to a love of dance. After receiving an undergraduate degree in 1930, she moved to New York to do graduate work at New York University, then divided her time between graduate studies and teaching dance at various universities, including the University of Pennsylvania and the University of Chicago. She also attended all but two of the Bennington summer sessions.

She served as a lieutenant commander in the U.S. Navy women's reserve during World War II. With the coming of peace, she resumed work on a doctorate, which she received in 1952. From 1949 onward, she worked as an administrative assistant at the Connecticut College School of Dance, and in 1950 she became director of the dance program at Brooklyn College, retiring in 1975. Admired for her administrative capability, she soon found herself spending much of her time shuttling back and forth between Brooklyn and New London.[31]

Programs for Wiesner's first season as head of the Connecticut school and festival list Charles L. Reinhart as executive director. Although only a few years later Reinhart would return to the campus as the festival's actual director, the title he held in 1963, he says, was "just a fancy way of referring to the box-office manager and house manager."

The season was a varied one. In addition to modern dance works by José Limón, Donald McKayle, Paul Taylor, Merce Cunningham, Marion Scott, Doris Rudko, Lucas Hoving, and Ruth Currier, Jean-Leon Destiné presented examples of Haitian dance and Paul Draper offered tap solos. A special young choreographers' concert included dances by Janet Mansfield Soares, Gerda Zimmerman, and Margaret Beals; and the Merrymobile, a children's theater group, appeared in *Music, Please!*, a danced music appreciation show devised by John Wilson.

Destiné and Draper shared a program that included the premiere of Destiné's *Café Coumbite*, which Allen Hughes termed "a rather neutral if energetic opening group composition." Destiné himself was described by Walter Sorell as "a handsome man who knows how to capture his audience and how to create from the joyous and frightening moments in the life of his Caribbean compatriots an image which never goes shockingly deep and is always keyed to entertain." Sorell was even more impressed by Draper: "His shading of nuances, his phrasing and pacing, his lyricism and skill to give drama to contrast has remained unique in the history of tap dancing."

Hughes also enjoyed both performers. Yet he did slyly observe that whereas the festival had occasionally taken note of "ethnic" dance, this bastion of modern dance was still ignoring ballet.[32] He had a point. Ethnic dance—and, for that matter, tap—could offer modern dance no real competition: the dance forms arose out of totally different traditions. Programs of tap or ethnic dance could even remind modern dance students of how varied the art of dance can be. But ballet and modern dance were parallel—and, for some observers, rival—forms of serious Western theatrical dance. Moreover, in defiance of the claims of some of the early modern dancers that ballet was a decadent art that would soon wither away, ballet was gaining popularity: therefore, by ignoring ballet, was not the American Dance Festival ignoring an important aspect of American dance? However, in defense of the festival's directorate, it could be argued that if it began to include ballet among its regular offerings, the festival might conceivably lose much of its special character. The place of ballet on the festival stage and in the summer curriculum would continue to be debated for years to come.

The season's most important new work was Paul Taylor's *Scudorama*. Taylor's third premiere for the festival, it revealed yet another aspect of his choreographic personality. *Insects and Heroes* had been grotesque; *Aureole* had been lyrical. Now Taylor was returning to the grotesque. But whereas *Insects and Heroes* was whimsically grotesque, *Scudorama* was bleak, and Hughes remarked that if *Aureole* was Taylor's personal vision of a "white ballet," *Scudorama* was Taylor's Walpurgis Night.

Its title, containing an evocation of scudding storm clouds, was a word of Taylor's own invention. A choreographically stormy work, its printed program bore, as epigraph, a quotation from Dante's *Inferno*:

> What souls are these who run through this black haze?
> And he to me: "These are the nearly soulless
> Whose lives concluded neither blame nor praise."

Scudorama, which remained in Taylor's repertoire for many years, is usually interpreted as a depiction of "nearly soulless" modern man in the age of anxiety. At times, the cast wore such items of ordinary street clothes as sports jackets, sweaters, and raincoats. In one scene, dancers were pulled across the stage on beach towels and, at another point, towels were thrown at people. "The atmosphere is dark with suppressed feelings, veiled hostility, and indecision" (to quote Don McDonagh). And Marcia B. Siegel has said,

> Tortured and enigmatic, *Scudorama* was beautiful as only violence can be beautiful—a thunderstorm, a four-alarm fire, or Times Square on a rainy night. . . . With its strong, distorted movement, empty relationships, and shocking images—like a squirming pile of bodies on the floor—the dance gave an impression of the futility and isolation of modern life that was at once realistic and abstract.

A key to its tone lies in the fact that, when Taylor wished to begin rehearsals, Clarence Jackson's score was still unfinished; therefore Taylor started choreographing the work by putting Stravinsky's *Rite of Spring* on the phonograph. Jackson's score may have been jinxed. Though he sent a copy of it to Connecticut College, it never arrived, and the premiere was danced in silence. Ten years later, the music was found stored in the New London bus station.

Most discussions of *Scudorama* have tended to be similar to those of McDonagh and Siegel. Yet, reviewing its premiere, two critics came to somewhat different conclusions. Sorell was confused about the work's intent: "There is a great deal of creeping and crouching going on that looks very haphazardly done. Although, no doubt, this work has to do with relationships and their frustration on many levels, the subject matter never crystallizes." Doris Hering liked the piece. Yet, in contrast to all the critics who have found *Scudorama* a revelation of angst, she viewed it simply as an energy study: for her, it

> had to do with quickness. Like sails or clouds on a windy day, the dancers appeared, came together, and separated with a fleet, almost preoccupied urgency.
>
>   For contrast, the choreographer often introduced the device of crawling. And he gave it the same dignity that Balanchine, in *Ivesiana*, gave to people walking on their knees. There was humor, too, as the dancers wore crazily-patterned beach towels in which they ultimately converged to form a flower that looked as though each petal had come from a different part of the garden.[33]

Clarence Jackson also composed the score for another ambitious festival premiere, Donald McKayle's *Arena*, which evoked ancient Crete and the myth of the Minotaur in a set of choreographic struggles that could be interpreted as symbolizing opposing forces of light and darkness, goodness and evil. But Hering dismissed its ritualism as "second-hand Graham," and Hughes pronounced the symbolism "far-fetched."[34]

Lucas Hoving's new *Aubade* was received more favorably. Sorell thought this mood-piece had poetic beauty and that it seemed "to move on the threshold of the early morning when we lose track of our dreams." Writing in a similar vein, Hering said it concerned "three Giacometti-like figures" who "swayed and intertwined as though they were slowly emerging from a dream," and, though thin in choreographic texture, it nevertheless possessed "natural compassion and honesty of feeling."[35]

Marion Scott, the 1963 Doris Humphrey Fellow, presented *Aftermath*, a solo about a troubled woman that Sorell thought was "packed with emotional intensity"; yet its ending "may still need some editing." Walter Terry said, "It is not a very clear piece, for one cannot be sure what the 'math' was which led to the 'after,' but Miss Scott, a brilliant technician, danced it superbly."[36]

Ruth Currier had been scheduled to choreograph, and dance in, a new work, but she tore a cartilage in her leg. Instead of a premiere, her festival offering was a recently choreographed solo for Betty Jones that was new to the festival. *Diva Divested* proved something of a tour de force. Jones, the dancer who was occasionally required to sing, here portrayed a vain, aging prima donna, and, said Terry, the choreography for her ran "the gamut of stock operatic emotions — grandness, outraged femininity, demureness, terror, heroic self-righteousness and the like." Then, at her dressing table, the star "suddenly experiences the terror of loneliness, the panic of age as she desperately gathers up flowers from her fallen bouquet and, in a scene which is both hilarious and tragic, places them between her toes, her teeth and in her hair."[37] From reports, Jones did all this with a riveting intensity.

The festival moved briefly to New York in 1963, thanks to a cooperative arrangement made between Lincoln Center and the Connecticut College School of Dance. While other companies were performing in New London, three festival attractions appeared at Philharmonic Hall, as part of Lincoln Center's August Fanfare series. The companies of Paul Taylor and Donald McKayle shared a concert, 6 August, and the Merce Cunningham company danced 13 August. Then, after the Connecticut festival had closed, the Limón company appeared at Philharmonic Hall, 20 August. The hall, which had been designed for concerts, was not really suitable for dancing, yet the performances attracted much attention and were a truly festive finale to Wiesner's first season as director.[38]

--------------------------------- **1964** ---------------------------------

Louis Horst died 23 January 1964, less than two weeks after celebrating his eightieth birthday. Seeking to pay homage to him, the festival persuaded Martha Graham that three of her most famous dances with music by Horst ought to be revived: *Primitive Mysteries* (1931), *Frontier* (1935), and *El Penitente* (1940). All three works had been long out of her company's repertoire.

Graham was always reluctant to revive dances and preferred creating new works to restaging old successes. But she could hardly say no to a tribute to Horst. Nevertheless, she took no active part in the revivals. She went off to Israel to work with the Batsheva Dance Company, leaving the reconstructions in the hands of David Wood, the Graham company's regisseur, who assembled former company members who he hoped were blessed with good memories. Some of Graham's associates thought that Graham secretly wished that it would be impossible to complete the revivals and that the project would be abandoned. But the dancers persevered, and when Graham returned from Israel, "I think she was surprised," Sophie Maslow later told Don McDonagh. "First, I think she was surprised that anything had been put together. I think she was rather hoping it wouldn't be. And I think she was a little pleased, too. Probably surprised that it looked as good as it did."

The Horst memorial program was presented twice at New London —at a Sunday matinee, 16 August, and again that same evening—and it attracted large audiences of dancegoers who were eager, curious, and also a bit apprehensive, for if the stagings turned out to be flops, if the revivals were merely exhumations, the reputations of Graham and Horst alike might have plummeted disastrously. Instead, virtually everyone present agreed with Lillian Moore that "a more vital and exciting memorial would have been difficult to imagine, and impossible to devise." For P. W. Manchester, the program was "a rolling back of time into the historical beginnings of a vast area of dance. We marvel at the richness of Graham of 30 years ago as she permits us to see, for the first time, the start of her journey and the incredible distance she has traveled." And Doris Hering breathed a sigh of relief because the program "proved irrefutably that when a work of art is initially valid, it gains luster through time."

I paid my own first visit to the festival for the Horst memorial and, like many other dancegoers, was deeply impressed. Even Jill Johnston was mellowed by the program, though she did take care to inform her readers that she found the Connecticut festival's presentations slightly passé. Calling Limón and Graham the "King and Queen" of modern dance, she said, "Their dedicated Establishment flourishes at Juilliard in the winter and at New London in the summer, perpetuating the ideals of a tradition now defunct." But once she got beyond those snide comments, she had much to say in praise of the Horst memorial.[39]

The first of the three revivals on the program was *Frontier*, Graham's solo about a pioneer woman contemplating the American prairie and reacting to the vastness of the New World with both awe and courage. Like several other critics, Hering thought that Ethel Winter, who assumed Graham's role, "danced exquisitely and reverently. But by nature she possesses an untroubled demeanor, a lightly fleet way of moving . . . both just a trifle alien to Miss Graham's original image of gesture made firm through endurance." Nevertheless, the solo's choreographic merits were apparent, and Johnston said *Frontier* successfully conveyed "the sense of Whitmanesque grandeur and proud stability of pioneering woman."[40]

El Penitente was a choreographic version of the religious mystery plays about sin and forgiveness presented by members of flagellant sects in the American Southwest. Its choreography was deliberately stiff and severe, yet it also contained moments of sly erotic humor. The revival prompted divergent reactions. There were those who, like Hering, were disappointed, finding *El Penitente* "only a shadow of its former sweet, naive, solemn and faintly naughty self." But Allen Hughes considered the production essentially sound: "Its story patterns and symbolism are clear, and it needed only a more intense performance than that given . . . to make it take on the life that is inherent in it."[41]

The most eagerly awaited of the works—and the one that proved hardest to reconstruct—was *Primitive Mysteries*, a set of ceremonial dances inspired by rituals in honor of the Virgin Mary performed by Indian women of the Southwest. The austere work had the reputation of being one of Graham's early masterpieces. But no one had danced it in years, and there were no notated scores of it. Even Horst's musical score for flute, oboe, and piano was so lacking in tempo and dynamics markings that when Eugene Lester, the Graham company's pianist, tried to play it in rehearsals, he found it difficult to phrase.

Primitive Mysteries was painstakingly reconstructed by a group of former Graham dancers—"of all ages and physical conditions," Sophie Maslow recalls—who worked patiently in a studio, trying to fit their memories together. Possibly because *Primitive Mysteries* was the first dance she had been taught upon joining the Graham company in 1931— the year of the work's premiere—Maslow discovered that she remembered quite a bit and became responsible for the supervision of the revival.

Almost alone among the critics, Hughes was disappointed, calling *Primitive Mysteries* the only one of the Horst revivals "that looks like a period piece." Indeed, he thought that its "self-conscious and rigid stylizations" may have "given rise to the women's college dance style Mr. Horst is said to have called 'collegiate moderne.'"

For other critics *Primitive Mysteries* possessed an awesome grandeur. Hering praised Maslow for doing

> a masterful job of putting the work together and of imbuing today's lightweight, turned-out dancers with the straight-footed firmly treading style required in this instance. . . .
>
> One felt the selfless magic of ritual take over . . . everything the girls did, from their lashing circles to their quiet sitting on the floor, was absolutely clear, absolutely without sentimentality.

Johnston may have liked to sneer at the modern dance establishment, but she found nothing to sneer at in *Primitive Mysteries*, which she praised for "its spare formality of design" and for the way its choreography was "at once stiff and mobile." Moreover, she observed that, although its subject derived from the customs of Christianized American Indians, the dance also choreographically evoked "the stark Puritan posture of a people still hearing the Calvinist exhortations of Jonathan Edwards."

As the figure symbolizing the Virgin, a role created by Graham herself, Yuriko was much admired for what struck some reviewers, including Eugene Palatsky, as an almost mystical serenity: "Yuriko, primarily motionless, conveys an inner feeling of such adoration, anguish and awe—merely by raising her head to gaze at the invisible Crucifixion or by extending an arm to bless a suppliant—that a watcher is almost forcibly drawn into her soul to feel the thousand emotions that her mute face expresses."

Curiously, Graham's choreography received so much attention that many critics forgot to say much about the scores, although their composer was the reason for this program of revivals. However, most observers would probably have agreed with Walter Terry that "Mr. Horst's music—for all three pieces—retains its freshness and its miraculous identity with the rhythms, colors, moods and themes of the dances."[42]

Horst was not the only modern dance pioneer honored at that festival. Because the three Horst dances were too short to fill a program by themselves, the tribute included a performance of *Lament for Ignacio Sánchez Mejías*, as a memorial to its choreographer, Doris Humphrey. And Limón's new work, *A Choreographic Offering*, was also created in homage to Humphrey. Finding it eloquent and totally convincing, Manchester pronounced this dance to Bach's *Musical Offering* a "great work and a consciously beautiful memorial, offered by a man who, once a pupil, himself became a master and never forgot the debt to his teacher." Hering considered it less persuasive. One of its peculiarities was the way that Limón tried to weave fragments from fourteen works by Humphrey into the fabric of his own choreography. Hering found this attempt misguided:

> Like Rubens, Mr. Limón enjoys the challenge of a big, bold, fully peopled canvas. But a catalog is not a poem. A compendium is not a dance. In removing the dance fragments from their original contexts, Mr. Limón also deprived them of their emotional or dramatic moorings. In a sense this seemed like a violation of Doris Humphrey's basic esthetic that dance movement grows from human gesture.

Another peculiarity of the first performance involved casting: although he had designed the leading role for himself, a last-minute injury prevented Limón from dancing it; he therefore entrusted this role, conceived for a man, to a woman, Betty Jones.[43]

Other works performed that summer were by Ruth Currier, Paul Draper, Lucas Hoving, Matteo, Paul Taylor, Erick Hawkins, Pearl Lang, and Kazuko Hirabayashi. The premieres aroused only mild enthusiasm. The movements in Hawkins's *Geography of Noon* derived from those of butterflies, and Terry thought many of the patterns "most attractive." Yet, voicing an objection occasionally raised against Hawkins's choreography, he was troubled because too much of the choreography was "too much alike. There is, perhaps, a lyrical touch present but never a sense of rhythmic or even human urgency so that although patterns may vary, the colors remain much the same. In time, it palls." *To Everybody Out There*, Hawkins's second premiere, consisted of choreographic statements about human aloneness and togetherness. Hering thought the incidents varied considerably in quality, the best scene being one "in which the simple gesture of shaking hands was embellished upon." The worst was a sad-sack clown solo for Hawkins. "For some reason," sighed Hering, "he does not understand the way a clown should make an audience feel—the sad-happy effect. He merely makes one feel uncomfortable, as though one has arrived at a formal party in bare feet."[44]

Pearl Lang's *Shore Bourne* was admired for its windswept patterns. Yet Palatsky was troubled by the way its Vivaldi score was "misused by the dancers in something of a bacchanal, except when Miss Lang is dancing, channeling her tensions, accents and lyricism into the music."[45]

Kazuko Hirabayashi, the summer's Doris Humphrey Fellow, contributed *In a Dark Grove*, based upon the same Japanese novella that had inspired the film *Rashomon*. The very subject was a choreographic challenge because it required Hirabayashi to retell the story of a rape in several different ways, as if seen through the eyes of the victim, the criminal, and the victim's husband. Manchester said that "The choreography is a strikingly successful admixture of modern dance with traditional Japanese gestures, the two styles being perfectly assimilated." But, to Hering, "It vacillated between the ritualistic . . . and the naturalistic. . . . And the sequences of the action—past, present, and future—were not always clear."[46]

With a record-breaking enrollment of 282 students, age fourteen to sixty-four, from thirty-five states and six foreign countries, Connecticut College was, if nothing else, a busy place in 1964.[47] Yet it was not necessarily also an artistically lively place. Allen Hughes was worried that the festival was turning into a series of funeral rites. Not only was Horst memorialized that summer, there were also tributes to Humphrey. "The honoring of the dead has a proper place in the arts," Hughes conceded. However, "a concentration of memorial exercises does not make an altogether suitable climax for a public festival."[48]

Hughes may have been overstating his case: after all, it was only fitting and proper for a tribute to Horst to be presented in the summer after his death. Nevertheless, he was not the only member of the audience to feel that vitality was somehow slowly draining out of the festival: the charge would increasingly be made that the festival was living in the past.

1965

Although enrollment again was high at the summer school—253 students
—the 1965 performances offered little to allay the fears of those concerned about the festival's artistic health. The choreographers who participated included José Limón, Paul Taylor, Daniel Nagrin, Bertram Ross,
Ruth Currier, Erick Hawkins, Lucas Hoving, Paul Draper, and Yuriko. In
theory, they ought to have represented a fair range of dance styles. Yet
some people present found the festival's atmosphere stuffy,[49] and Doris
Hering was worried because "a good deal of this Eighteenth American
Dance Festival at Connecticut College seemed not really to be concerned
with dancing." Instead, she detected "a literary ponderosity" in many of
the works presented.[50] Some of her readers might have interpreted that
remark as symptomatic of a shift of taste in modern dance. Possibly
because audiences had been subjected to so many bad as well as good
examples of the genre, the dance based upon literature, history, or mythology was falling out of favor, to be replaced by a concern for what was
variously termed plotless, nonliteral, abstract, or "pure" dance.

However, most of that summer's premieres, whatever their strengths
or weaknesses may have been, could not really be termed "literary." Thus
Erick Hawkins's *Lords of Persia* was inspired by polo, and the members
of its all-male cast carried polo sticks. Because polo originated at the
Persian court, Hawkins gave the choreography an aristocratic and slightly
exotic air. Yet the piece was not literally about either polo or Persia.
Reviewing the festival shortly before Clive Barnes succeeded him as dance
critic of the *New York Times*, Allen Hughes observed that Hawkins's
premiere was "really about movement and sound," and he applauded the
result for being "stately, even ceremonial."[51]

Nor was Lucas Hoving's *Satiana* "literary" in the usual sense of that
term. Hoving set his lighthearted suite of dances to some of the whimsical
piano pieces of Erik Satie and to recitations of the nonsensical instructions or comments to performers Satie attached to his music. The spoken
statements included such phrases as "Like a nightingale with a toothache,"
"I'm out of cigarettes. Good thing I don't smoke," and "Don't tickle me,
lady, it makes me laugh." Hering called *Satiana* a "potentially nimble"
piece, but suggested that "further performances should ease the transition between movement and speech and add more fillip to the timing."[52]

Hoving also contributed a new dramatic dance, *The Tenants*, which,
said Hering, concerned "two melancholy men attracted to a radiant

woman. At the end each man was left with his own solitude, the men unchanged, the woman bereft of her radiance." Hering recalled that in previous dramatic works by Hoving "the dancing did not always take wing from the idea." But, here, "one found dance passages meaningful within themselves." Therefore she considered *The Tenants* "an appreciable step ahead" for Hoving.[53]

The season's two most ambitious premieres were also the most "literary." Neither was successful. Paul Draper's *Il Combattimento di Tancredi e Clorinda* was an attempt to devise a dance-drama from Monteverdi's "madrigal opera," based upon an episode from Tasso's *Jerusalem Delivered.* Tancredi, a Christian knight, fights a mysterious Saracen warrior in a duel; when the warrior is dying, Tancredi discovers that his opponent is really Clorinda, the Saracen woman he loves, disguised as a man.

The basic trouble with Draper's choreographic setting of this tale stemmed from the fact that he was a tap dancer venturing far outside his special field. Hughes declared that Draper's "career as a concert tap dancer has not given him a wide range of other movements and there is no tapping in this work. Almost all that Libby Nye and Daniel Nagrin, the dancers, had to do was to try to keep a rudimentary ballet sword battle going on for the better part of half an hour."[54]

If nothing else, one could at least smile indulgently at this ambitious attempt by a tap dancer to cope with Tasso and Monteverdi. But audiences did not know how to respond to Limón's new *My Son, My Enemy.* Nothing in Limón's career had quite prepared them for this dance about the struggle between Peter the Great and his son, Alexis. At times in the past Limón had been nobly tragic; at other times he had unflinchingly depicted human jealousy and treachery. But never before had he choreographed in such a violent and hysterical manner. *My Son, My Enemy* left its viewers aghast. Hughes called it "a work of brutality that is disquieting, to say the least," and he observed that "in terms of movement, the work is one of almost unrelieved hyperactivity."

Hering was scathing:

It is difficult to believe that beneath José Limón's habitually gracious and courtly exterior there could fester the rage, the frustration, the glint of sadism that turned up in his *My Son, My Enemy.* In theme, this large and long work had to do with Peter the Great's betrayal of his son, Alexis. But as one audience member commented, Limón's

Peter strongly resembled Ivan the Terrible.

Cracking whips against the floor, he stood, legs stiff, eyes blazing. Or he stomped around the spread-eagled figure of Louis Falco (Alexis). . . .

As for Louis Falco, he was tossed into the air like a member of a vaudeville adagio team . . . he was held upside down; he was sent crawling, running, rolling, tumbling. . . .

What was José Limón *really* saying in *My Son, My Enemy*? Was he commenting upon the Oedipal conflict between father and son? Was he voicing the resentment of the waning dancer against the young performer at the height of his physical powers? Was he trying to exorcise an unwanted aspect of his personality by killing it outwardly? Or did Louis Falco symbolize Doris Humphrey whose firm hand and uncompromising honesty must often in the past have prevented Limón from making cathartically revealing errors like this one?[55]

All artists, even the greatest, may produce disasters on occasion. However, it was especially unfortunate that this particular disaster came just at the time when Limón's choreographic preoccupations had started to seem outmoded to many members of a younger generation of dancers and dancegoers.

─────────────────────── **1966** ───────────────────────

The fare for the 1966 season seems remarkably skimpy. Limón, Ruth Currier, Lucas Hoving, Anna Sokolow, Paul Draper, and Martha Wittman were the only choreographers represented, and whatever their individual excellences may have been, they in no way served collectively as a representative sample of modern dance in the mid-sixties. There were only three premieres: a little dance by Draper, a big one by Limón, and a duet by Wittman, the summer's Doris Humphrey Fellow.

Draper's new solo, the curiously titled *Name-Who?, Number-What?, (Other)-(You), Address-Where?*, was something of an experiment. But unlike the previous summer's danced "madrigal-opera," it was an experiment within Draper's own tap idiom. Here, as Doris Hering observed, was an attempt to invest tap dancing—so often a jaunty dance form —with more somber emotional content:

There was no accompaniment except for Mr. Draper's eloquent feet. But it was not his use of tap rhythms (including a fierce barrage of sound at the end of the second section) which distinguished the dance. It was rather his attempt to reach a deeper emotional level. The inquisitional titles motivated him toward defiant stances, an introspective focus, despairing hand gestures, and a fall to his side with one arm up.

However, although the solo's emotional tone was unmistakable, Hering nevertheless admitted, "At this point the theme of the dance is not clear."[56]

Whatever its faults may have been, at least Limón's *The Winged* could not be accused of sadism, as *My Son, My Enemy* had been. *The Winged* was a study in choreographic ornithology, a suite of twenty-one vignettes all having to do with birds in some literal, metaphorical, or mythological way. Most of the piece was danced in silence. But breaking the silence from time to time would be brief flurries of percussion music by Hank Johnson. This interplay of sound and silence was one of the dance's most unusual features, and it was especially admired by P. W. Manchester, who declared, "No other work that I can recall has used silence so persuasively or so eloquently. Through it one seems to hear the beating and fluttering of wings."

The Winged was rich in movement invention. But, as Hering pointed out, its sheer choreographic abundance was both its principal virtue and its major fault: "It is so fertile in movement ideas and must have burst forth so freely from Limón's imagination that he either hasn't had the time or the artistic ruthlessness to cut it." Manchester, who termed it "a work of splendor," also considered it "too long at the moment." So did most other critics. Yet *The Winged* was never satisfactorily cut, and a year after its premiere Don McDonagh was sighing, "It really does seem that there is a good little dance lurking inside the infinities of this big and rather dull work."[57]

In *With Ancient Eyes* Martha Wittman turned to the story of Oedipus and the Sphinx, a story that Erick Hawkins had tackled at the first festival and which, over the years, has also inspired ballets by such choreographers as David Lichine and Glen Tetley. Hering thought that Wittman's version was particularly strong in its sense of characterization: "The styles for Miss Wittman as the destroyer with the marmoreal profile and for Reuben James Eddinger as the boyish victim were strongly defined and consistent." And Manchester praised the dance for its "sculptural, monolithic, eternal quality."[58]

But no one seems to have been excited by the festival as a whole.

─────────────────────── **1967** ───────────────────────

The festival's twentieth anniversary season was aided by a $15,000 match-ing grant from the National Council on the Arts. One innovation in the curriculum that summer was a course in critical writing, taught by Selma Jeanne Cohen. Out of this workshop an annual dance critics' conference would eventually develop.[59] Choreographers presenting works included José Limón, Martha Graham, Merce Cunningham, Paul Taylor, Lucas Hoving, Ruth Currier, Paul Draper, Pauline Koner, and Richard Kuch.

With *Agathe's Tale*, his fourth premiere for the festival, Paul Taylor once again revealed a new facet of his choreographic personality. What made this piece unusual was the fact that it told a story: it was a narrative dance at a time when many choreographers—some of them possibly inspired by the precedent of Taylor's own previous works—were explor-ing the possibilities of abstraction. It was also a somewhat peculiar narrative, for Taylor assigned himself two compositional problems (almost as if he were still a student in Louis Horst's classes): the characters had to remain on stage throughout, and the choreography had to evoke a medi-eval morality play. About this last stipulation, Taylor now says, "I read some books about medieval style, then I just went my merry choreo-graphic way." He asked Carlos Surinach to compose music that would sound like "a measly little street band." Instead, he got what he calls an "opulent" score. Yet, even if it was not quite what he had expected, it was a score that Taylor found usable.

Agathe's Tale showed Satan, disguised as a monk, contending with the Angel Raphael, disguised as a unicorn, over the fate of the fair Agathe; however, she is eventually claimed by Pan, Satan's ward. Whatever rela-tionship it might have had to an actual morality play, the piece was certainly moralistic. But just what was its moral? One could interpret its action in several ways. Looking back upon it in the context of Taylor's choreographic career as a whole, one can see it as one of several works (others being *Churchyard*, *American Genesis*, and *Big Bertha*) in which Taylor deplores extreme behavior of some kind—be it licentious or puritanical—and tries to find some moral "golden mean." Neither deprav-ity (the devil) nor austerity (the angel) conquers Agathe; instead, she is united with a lusty and life-loving, but not evil or debauched, figure from Greek mythology.

Over the years Taylor constantly fussed with details to clarify the action. At its premiere *Agathe's Tale* impressed Don McDonagh as "a moralistic tale full of childlike quirks and fancies embodying high moral purpose. It is, in a word, medieval." But Doris Hering thought that "Taylor has not quite decided between the gauche simplicity of a medieval mystery or some sophisticated context. . . . *Agathe's Tale* never works to a true climax." Nevertheless, as McDonagh pointed out, the work suggested that "more than ever, Taylor seems to be the meeting ground between the intensely dramatic thread in American dancing represented by Martha Graham and the abstract musical thread represented by George Balanchine."[60]

Limón's new *Psalm* was, in its way, as moralistic as *Agathe's Tale*. But, like all the festival's other premieres, it was somber in nature. Inspired by André Schwarz-Bart's *The Last of the Just* and conceived as a tribute to the suffering of the Jews throughout history, *Psalm* alternated tormented choreography for an eternal martyr—referred to as the Burden Bearer and danced by Louis Falco—with choreography for soloists, termed Expiatory Figures, and for a large ensemble. The action was supposed to be a danced meditation upon such matters as prayer, suffering, and compassion. But critics found the work structurally unsatisfactory. Hering said: "Stylistically and in mood, the three entities seemed to go their separate ways, as though prayer and suffering and compassion were unrelated. And yet this is surely not what Limón wanted to say." P. W. Manchester agreed: "As a majestic solo danced by the always magnificent Falco it would be enormously impressive. With each recurring intrusion of the other figures, and especially those of the ensemble, the work loses its hold."[61]

Paul Draper's *Help* was a brief mood study about a man seeking comfort, and it employed tap steps to suggest the man's melancholy; as England's *Ballet Today* observed, such use of tap made the solo "more akin to modern dance than to music hall."[62]

For Hering, Lucas Hoving's *Rough-In*, though tragic in intent, looked confused on stage: "Chase Robinson . . . appeared to be imprisoned by an unconquerable destiny. He encountered a man with a rope and girls carrying black flowers. . . . Finally the girls threw their flowers down; Robinson fell over, inert; and a single girl busily began to pick up the gloomy bouquets." But McDonagh wondered whether the dance's confusions might have been intentional, for he suspected Hoving was seeking "a combination of menace and humour."[63]

Ruth Currier's *Fantasies and Facades* aroused even less enthusiasm. Hering said,

> Like Lucas Hoving's *Rough-In*, Ruth Currier's new *Fantasies and Facades* seemed to have been born under a leaden sky of no-hope. Her figures alternated between life as they were living it and life as they wanted to live it. To accentuate the difference, Josef Wittman composed an electronic score which alternated with Beethoven "Bagatelles."
>
> In their neurotic existence the dancers struggled with masses of pliofilm, a ladder, a shopping bag, a garbage can . . . two girls had a tender duet, but the garbage can came between them. . . . all returned to their props.[64]

The Brood, by Richard Kuch, the summer's Humphrey Fellow, was as glum as most of the other premieres. But at least it had impact. Roughly based upon Brecht's *Mother Courage*, it was choreographed in an anguished style, both more expressionistically turbulent and less ironical than that of the play. The dance showed Mother Courage looking back upon the events of her life. As she did so, what Hering called "little currents" of choreographic activity "came alive—sometimes of defiance, sometimes of sharing, sometimes of innocent bravery." Yet Hering also thought that, eventually, "*The Brood* seemed to sag a little."

Perhaps the most astonishing thing about its premiere was Jane Dudley's interpretation of its central role. Dudley had been suffering from arthritis. Yet Kuch had been able to lure her out of retirement to dance Mother Courage, and her portrayal, said Hering, demonstrated that she remained "a great dance-actress." Since that time *The Brood* has been revived by both modern dance and ballet companies. But many dancegoers who remember the first production would still maintain that Dudley's interpretation remains unsurpassed.[65]

1968

Festival performances in 1968 were dedicated to the memory of Ruth St. Denis, who had died earlier that summer on 21 July. As someone who, early in the century, had attempted to create a meaningful dance idiom that owed little to the vitiated form of classical ballet common at the time, and as the founder, with her husband Ted Shawn, of the Denishawn school and company, out of which came such dancers as Martha Graham, Doris Humphrey, and Charles Weidman, St. Denis was one of the matriarchs of American dance, and it was altogether fitting that the 1968 festival should honor her.

Once again, the school's enrollment was high: 259 students (twentyfive of them male) from thirty-nine states and fifteen foreign countries and ranging in age from fourteen to forty-six.[66] That age range bothered some people, including Bonnie Bird, a member of the faculty.[67] Whereas in other years, students had included older, as well as young, dancers, and many faculty members had welcomed the opportunity to give the young dancers professional or preprofessional training, now some of the students were so young, so inexperienced and, most important, so unfocused in their ambitions that, says Bird, the school occasionally seemed a glorified summer camp.

The festival itself was not terribly festive. Modern dance was represented by the companies of José Limón and Paul Taylor. But only Limón offered premieres. There were two of them: one comic, one serious, and both of them attempts to be topical or "relevant," to use a favorite word of the troubled 1960s.

The comedy was called *Comedy*. An updated version of Aristophanes's *Lysistrata*, with the women in miniskirts and the men in Army fatigues, it was conceived as an eternally contemporary antiwar satire. Everyone who saw it agreed that *Comedy* was ribald and bawdy. But not everyone agreed that it was truly funny, as well. Limón, after all, was not known for his light touch. Anna Kisselgoff, who had become a critic at the *Times* that year, admitted that *Comedy*'s "frankness may not appeal to everyone, but its effect can only be termed compelling." She praised Limón's "use of the obvious but ingenious metaphor of animal behavior to signify the bestiality of men at war." To emphasize that point, sounds from the New London Zoo were incorporated into Josef Wittman's tape-collage score. All in all, thought Kisselgoff, Limón's utilization of "a jerky jazz idiom that is alien to him is clever and masterful."

Doris Hering was less pleased. *Comedy* made her reflect upon Limón's choreographic idiosyncrasies:

José Limón is a complex man. He is at once poet and peasant—an ascetic vulgarian wearing a halo trimmed with horns. Nowhere has this dichotomy been so evident as in his new *Comedy*, based on Aristophanes' *Lysistrata*. . . .

In updating it . . . Limón has made of it a long strung out dirty joke with here and there a flash of human insight or inspired movement.

Hering also described one comic episode—for Jennifer Muller and Louis Falco—that some viewers considered particularly offensive. She referred to it as "the world's longest titillation scene. One by one his [Falco's] socks and boots were removed and individually sprayed with deodorant. (A single use of this device would more than have made its point.)"[68]

Seasoned dancegoers who knew that Limón was seldom successful with comedy could overlook, or even forgive, his updated *Lysistrata*. But *Legend* posed another sort of problem. Dedicated "to the memory of black patriots and martyrs," *Legend* lashed out against racial oppression. It was undeniably high-minded. Yet, in it, Limón used hysterical and violent movement disturbingly akin to that of the ill-fated *My Son, My Enemy*. As a result, said Don McDonagh, *Legend* "is a poor piece that thematically is on the side of virtue, making it extremely painful to criticize."

Marcia Marks, one of Doris Hering's assistant critics at *Dance Magazine*, nevertheless made an attempt at serious analysis. She found the allegorical plot, in which a Slave, egged on by a Dark Angel, kills his Master and then is lynched by the Angel, "a confused progression of events," and, as a result of its confusion, *Legend* "falls tragically short of comprehending the black man and his struggle or of portraying it through dance."[69]

In addition to the Limón and Taylor companies, the festival schedule included performances by Lotte Goslar and Company and the First Chamber Dance Quartet. Their presence on the Connecticut College campus caused some faculty members and students to protest that they were not "modern" enough for this modern dance center. Although Goslar had studied modern dance with Mary Wigman and Gret Palucca in her native Germany, her specialty became a form of entertainment that combined miming with clowning. And although the members of the First Chamber Dance Quartet stressed choreographic eclecticism, their initial training had been in ballet—apparently still a suspect form to some "modernists." Nevertheless, Goslar charmed audiences with her gentle humor, and, among the dance quartet's offerings, Lois Bewley's *Visions Fugitives* was singled out for special praise by critics. Hering described it as a suite of ten vignettes that "darted on and off stage as briefly and as poignantly as fireflies." As they did so, they suggested that Bewley had "a tantalizing choreographic imagination—by turns macabre, funny, and adolescently sentimental."[70]

A special program billed *40 Amp. Mantis* by Kathryn Posin, the year's Doris Humphrey Fellow, with works created by three previous holders of the fellowship: Kazuko Hirabayashi's *In a Dark Grove*, Jack Moore's *Songs Remembered*, and Richard Kuch's *The Brood* (with Noemi Lapzeson in the role created by Jane Dudley). "Like the famed book on penguins," Marks said, Posin's dance "tells me more about 40 amp. mantises than I care to know." The dance whimsically combined natural history with science fiction: "Wearing lights on wrists and heads and goggly, antennaed costumes by David Krohn, the dancers come on in a *bug* cluster, break apart, bounce around, are drawn toward a strong light, and end up prone except for Miss Posin, who crouches on the back of one of the dancers in the guise of a preying (not praying, thank you) mantis."[71]

The Doris Humphrey Fellowship retrospective concert summed up eight years of trying to encourage young choreographers. Much of the entire festival was also retrospective. With its dedication to Ruth St. Denis, it could fit into the category of what Allen Hughes had termed "memorial exercises." Even the bickering over the aesthetic legitimacy of the First Chamber Dance Quartet recalled the ideological squabbles of an earlier era of modern dance. Yet if the festival found it easy to look back on the past, it was finding it increasingly difficult to live in the present. And Theodora Wiesner and her staff knew it, but they were not quite sure what to do.

All that summer the faculty and board met in committees to discuss ways of enlivening the festival and school. Bonnie Bird, one of the participants, says that these meetings involved no infighting between rival factions or cliques; nor were there any struggles between those who believed they wielded power and those who felt themselves powerless. Rather, everyone involved worked together for the good of the festival and its future.

Then Wiesner announced that, having been associated with the festival for so long, she felt exhausted and in need of a rest. Therefore she recommended that a new director be appointed, at least for the summer of 1969. After considering several candidates, the festival board and Connecticut College's administrative staff were most impressed by Charles

Reinhart, the young man who had held the grand, but misleading, title of "executive director" in 1963, and who had since become a successful manager of dance companies. Reinhart says, "I found myself being talked into accepting a new job." It is a job he still holds.

V

OVERVIEW 1959–1968

A STEADY, SECURE PLACE

B y the early 1960s the Connecticut College School of Dance and American Dance Festival had become what Selma Jeanne Cohen calls "a steady, secure place."[1] With the blessings of the Connecticut College administration, the venture had established itself as America's leading summer modern dance center. Based on sound foundations by Martha Hill and Ruth Bloomer, it continued to be soundly administered by Jeanette Schlottmann and Theodora Wiesner.

Its classes annually attracted more than two hundred students, and festival performances were regularly reviewed by New York dance critics. Various festival activities were significantly supported by grants during the sixties. A grant of $4,000 from the Lena Robbins Foundation in 1964 aided Helen Priest Rogers's dance-film project. A Rockefeller Foundation grant of $10,200 the following year went toward the commissioning of new works. A National Endowment for the Arts grant of $15,000 in 1967 helped support festival performances as a whole, and a second NEA grant, this time of $11,534, was awarded in 1968.[2]

A loyal audience developed. Members of the New York dance community repeatedly traveled up to Connecticut, usually by train, for weekends at New London. And because one so often saw the same people in the lobby of Palmer Auditorium that one saw at dance concerts in Manhattan, Allen Hughes termed the festival "a New York reunion transplanted to New London."[3] Yet people from the area also became modern dance fans. Sophie Maslow remembers a New London rabbi who read about *The Village I Knew* in newspapers and festival publicity releases. Curious about how this dance expressed Jewish traditions, he attended a performance and was so fascinated by what he saw that he became a regular dancegoer, walking a great distance from his home to campus, in respect for the Sabbath, when performances were scheduled on Friday nights.

Perhaps the most devoted of all the festival's fans was Nathan Clark, who now jokingly calls himself "the festival's oldest living inhabitant." Clark grew up in England where his family ran a well-known shoe company. (One of his cousins invented the Wallabee; Clark himself developed the shoe style known as the desert boot and personally cut the first pattern for it in 1948.) Clark came from a ballet-loving family, and he remembers seeing modern dance for the first time in the United States in the 1950s. But it was not until 1959 that he became virtually addicted to the art.

That summer he came to New London to visit a cousin of his mother who was on the Connecticut College board of trustees. Out of curiosity, he attended the American Dance Festival and liked what he saw. He therefore kept returning, attending all or part of every festival in New London (except for 1977, which he missed entirely) and in Durham. Although he says that he sometimes goes off to Madras to satisfy his craving for Indian dance, no other single cultural institution has captured his loyalties to the extent the American Dance Festival has.

One usually knew when Clark was in New London. He hosted parties for dancers, and, since he was as fascinated by automobiles as he was by dancing, he could often be seen driving around campus in an antique car. Yet the festival was more than a lark for him: Clark's concern for modern dance was serious indeed. Martha Hill once remarked, "Nathan has always been interested in the creative thrust of dance." And Clark has said, "I have felt it a great privilege to get to know so many distinguished teachers of modern dance and to be able to see students return as professional dancers or choreographers."

Other festival admirers could echo those sentiments. Nevertheless, though festival audiences were often enthusiastic, they were not always large. In fact, they could be "dismally small," as Doris Hering noted with alarm when she attended the 1968 festival. The size of the audience could significantly affect the atmosphere of a performance. Although Palmer Auditorium was adjacent to an attractive sculpture garden and boasted fine stage equipment, it was not a charmingly decorated theater. Therefore it could seem somewhat cheerless when empty.

Allen Hughes was not necessarily being complimentary when he pronounced the festival a transplanted "New York reunion." John Martin, his predecessor as dance critic of the *New York Times*, had recognized as far back as 1952 the importance of "trying to tie the local community into the dance community, instead of keeping the latter a kind of lonely importation." The festival tried hard to make New London dance-conscious. Through lecture-demonstrations and special dance classes in community centers, it kept on trying.

Sometimes the results were surprising. Jeanette Schlottmann recalls lecturing on the importance of dance as an art at a luncheon meeting of a civic club. To her astonishment, when she went to church the following Sunday she heard her lecture preached back to her, and the rest of the congregation, from the pulpit; the church's rector, a member of that civic club, had been so impressed by her ideas that he had incorporated them into his sermon. However, attempts to interest community leaders in dance could also be greeted with incomprehension. Thus, when Sophie Maslow lectured at a club's luncheon meeting, one of the first questions from the floor afterward was, "Is this modern dance you're talking about something like what Gypsy Rose Lee does?"[4]

Even as the festival was becoming "a steady, secure place," problems were developing. One involved the curriculum and student body. Hering complained in 1964 that increased enrollment meant ever more crowded classes, and she overheard one student say, "How can you learn to move, when there's no room to move in?" The content of some of those classes was also occasionally a matter for discussion. Typically, as the summer school's 1962 bulletin put it, technique classes were listed as "sections presenting the techniques of the artists listed below: José Limón, Martha Graham, Merce Cunningham, Lucas Hoving." However, some observers found it both misleading and restricting to give classes such labels as "Limón technique" or "Graham technique," since the choreographers associated with those techniques did not always teach all classes themselves, and good teachers can incorporate into their classes material they have learned from the various artists with whom they have worked throughout their careers.

Hering felt that the age range of students (fifteen to fifty in 1964) made structuring classes difficult, as did the different needs of the students. Classes attracted professional dancers, preprofessionals, teachers desiring to know what was new in their field, and people attracted to dancing primarily for avocational or recreational reasons. The growing number of very young students with no clearly formulated professional ambitions disturbed Bonnie Bird, who says that some advanced students may have stopped attending Connecticut College because they considered it no longer artistically challenging enough. And she suspects that some dance teachers may have stopped attending, first of all, because they did not wish to spend their summers with crowds of beginners young enough to be their students and, second, because they concluded that if summer dance programs now essentially attracted very young people, they would organize their own such programs in their own schools or communities. In the sixties, when interest in the arts grew rapidly and more money for the arts began to be available, that is exactly what many teachers did, Bird says.[5]

However, the most devastating charge that was raised against the festival was that it had grown stuffy. Stuffy! The charge rankled. Modern dance prided itself on being a modern art, and modern art, Louis Horst roundly declared, "is a free art and refuses to live within any boundaries." Nevertheless, Connecticut College—modern dance's summer home—was repeatedly accused of being stuffy. Don McDonagh certainly found it so in 1967 when he wrote, "What Bayreuth is to the true Wagnerian, Connecticut College is to the modern dance traditionalist." It was, he claimed, a place with "an unreconstructed '30s mentality, uninterested in the likes of Paul Taylor and Merce Cunningham." Rather, its leading lights were Graham and Limón, whose performances succeeded in "comforting those who want to believe that all is as it was, and that unrelated new dance things will go away if ignored."[6]

Taking these charges literally, it could be countered that McDonagh, a supporter of the Judson choreographers, overstated his case. Cunningham had danced at the festival as early as 1950, and, although no one could term it the festival's most favored attraction, his company had appeared there on several occasions and had offered five premieres. And the very year that McDonagh made his accusation Taylor presented *Agathe's Tale*—his fourth festival premiere—in New London. Nevertheless, the feeling remained: creative vitality was ebbing from the festival.

One of the first and, given the circumstances, most startling accusations of stuffiness came during the faculty meeting following the 1958 season when Doris Humphrey flabbergasted her colleagues by announcing that she would not return to teach at Connecticut in 1959. Instead, she would go to the West Coast to see what was choreographically happening there. According to her biographer, Selma Jeanne Cohen, Humphrey declared that the summer school "had become too much of a closed corporation; new people should be coming in to teach." Humphrey also said that her fellow faculty members were "all getting into a rut."[7] In part, Humphrey's speech was a gesture of bravado made by a courageous, strong-willed woman who was now desperately ill—not only with arthritis, but with cancer as well. Yet the content of her remarks could not be dismissed and her complaints would be voiced again and again in the decade following her death.

Several factors accounted for the stuffiness at Connecticut College. One of them was the directorial structure of the dance school and festival. As Jeanette Schlottmann puts it, the festival's director was "primarily a facilitator" and artistic decisions were essentially made by the board. Although the presence and authority of the board could conceivably serve as a stabilizing influence to prevent a director from pursuing madcap schemes, the board could also be too conservative in its attitudes, for decisions made by committees are often cautious ones. Moreover, in terms of its membership the board was certainly what Humphrey called a "closed corporation." Consisting of Connecticut College officials and important people from the dance world, it brought academia and bohemia harmoniously together. But, over the years its members may have become set in their ways.

The board could—and occasionally did—wield power over every aspect of the festival, as Trisha Brown discovered when one of her dances became something of a campus scandal. On Saturday mornings during the summer term, members of the composition classes would regularly show works at Palmer Auditorium, and the auditorium was also occasionally used for full-scale student concerts. One such concert was scheduled in 1962. Brown, a student at the school that term, wished to present a solo called *Trillium* and performed it at an audition presided over by members of the board.

Brown had received what could be called a traditional modern dance education and had taken several classes with Louis Horst. Yet she was also interested in new dance trends and became one of the important choreographers of the Judson Dance Theater. She says that *Trillium* showed traces of the concern for formal structure that she had developed in Horst's classes, yet was also influenced by the minimalist approach to choreography typical of many of the Judson experimenters. Looking back upon it, she describes the work as "a solo for a strikingly powerful, but inexperienced, performer who still didn't know quite what her choreographic edges were. It required intense concentration, plus raw energy and zeal, and contained some demanding and potentially dangerous sections, including repeated passages of going immediately from lying flat on the ground to jumping up in the air." If the movement was odd, *Trillium*'s accompaniment was even odder, for it was set to a tape of high-pitched wailing by Simone Forti.

The board rejected *Trillium* by a majority vote and, although several board members thought it should be presented, majority rule prevailed. However, some students had seen and liked *Trillium*, and they petitioned to have the solo included in the concert. That only made the board even more unbudgeable. Suddenly, Brown recalls, *Trillium* was a campus issue and everyone seemed to be asking, "Just what *is* this dance that has caused so much fuss?" To try to calm things down, the board said that Brown would be permitted to dance her solo if she scrapped the accompaniment. But now Brown had become adamant herself and refused to make any changes. At last the board relented, and *Trillium* was danced 7 August 1962 on a program along with works by Lenore Latimer, Karin Thulin, Rosalind Pierson, Margery Apsey, Janet Mansfield Soares, Pauline de Groot, and Diane Sherer.[8]

However knowledgeable the board members may have been, few possessed deep sympathy for the new choreographic developments that took place in the late fifties and early sixties. Young choreographers sensed this and resented it. Some may therefore even have taken special delight in shocking their elders. The elders, in turn, were often genuinely perplexed by what they saw about them. On the one hand, they knew that their own theories about modern dance committed them to supporting choreographic innovation. Yet they did not really like the innovations they encountered.

Louis Horst's attitudes toward the younger generation exemplify this ambivalence. Almost everybody seems to agree that, no matter how grouchy he could be, he never lost interest in what young choreographers were up to. Except when some element of a production outraged him —for instance, John Cage's score for *Aeon*—Horst wrote remarkably calm reviews and sincerely tried, though not always with success, to come to grips with what new choreographers were doing. Even the blank review of Paul Taylor, though presumably unfavorable in its intent, attracted so much attention and gave rise to so much merriment that, far from demolishing Taylor's reputation, it helped make him one of the most talked-about young choreographers in New York.

Horst, who in a review of Alwin Nikolais had placed himself in the camp of "us conservatives," revealed both his theoretical approval of innovation and his own actual conservatism in an interview with Walter Sorell. When Sorell asked him if he knew where modern dance was going, Horst replied, "What difference does it make where it goes? The main thing is it's going." However, in that same interview Horst exclaimed, "These kids take toilet-flushing for music and structureless immobility for dancing. To rebel, to be way out is fine. But they don't know how far they can go and still be with us!"[9]

Some people believe that, as he aged, Horst became increasingly rigid in his attitudes toward the assignments he gave his composition classes. Therefore rebellious students enjoyed devising dances that fulfilled the requirements of those assignments in whimsical or bizarre ways, even though they knew such choreographic pranks might arouse Horst's wrath. One student choreographer who annoyed Horst on several occasions was David Gordon. As a creator of dances, Gordon has always been fascinated by the ways structural rules can be made and broken. In this respect, he resembles Horst himself. But Horst never responded favorably to Gordon's impish sense of humor. Thus, in carrying out an A-B-A assignment, Gordon once created a solo that began with lots of jumping and shaking, continued with leg lifts, and then returned to further spasms of shaking. Horst was not amused to learn that the title of this opus was *The Spastic Cheerleader.*

However, a more serious dance by Gordon made Horst even more irate. This time, the assignment was to construct a duet in A-B-A form. In Gordon's duet the A section consisted of a solo for Valda Setterfield; she and Gordon danced together in the B section; then she left and the duet concluded with Gordon performing the same movements she had performed in the opening A section. Structurally, the dance was ingenious, and its action was rich in emotional implications. But when Gordon and Setterfield performed it, Horst objected at the outset, said it was not a duet at all, and thereafter never called upon Gordon again in class.

When this anecdote was related to Jeanette Schlottmann, she said, "That duet may have been fine choreography, and I have no idea how Louis would have reviewed it if it had been presented on a dance concert. But as a composition assignment, it was not what he would have considered a duet. For Louis, duets were dances in which two people moved together. And to succeed in Louis's classes, you had to give him exactly what he wanted."[10] Some students who tried to do so may have learned in the process how to limit their choreographic palette, to borrow Paul Taylor's phrase. But others might have been genuinely perplexed, offended, or even dismayed by Horst's dictatorial manner and habitual grumpiness.

The festival's programming, as well as the summer school's curriculum, received increasingly severe criticism. As early as 1955, Margaret Lloyd had identified what would eventually come to be the chief problem of festival scheduling. Speaking of that summer's attractions, she wrote, "The festival was, in fact, a fairly close [sic] corporation, for apart from Pearl Lang . . . the five programs represented individual concepts stemming from a single point of view."[11] The point of view to which she referred was that of the José Limón company as directly expressed in the dances of Limón and, by implication, in the choreographic precepts of his mentor, Doris Humphrey. If Humphrey had lived to see how securely the Limón company became enshrined at Connecticut, she might have been surprised or even grimly amused, for in the thirties Bennington, despite its self-proclaimed openness to all major trends in modern dance, had been considered Graham-oriented and, discussing Bennington in a letter to a friend, Humphrey had complained, "there is a permanent staff of Martha's Votaries, so anyone else is at a decided disadvantage."[12] Now, Connecticut College's festivals appeared to be celebrations by the votaries of Humphrey and Limón.

However, as Jeanette Schlottmann observes, this may have been only fair: "José was the company director who really committed himself to Connecticut College. So it was right that he got first priority." And Theodora Wiesner points out, "José was there from the start, and a lot of people came to the festival because they knew and liked his work."

Yet the Limón company did dominate the festival so much that even a critic like Doris Hering, who was basically sympathetic to Limón, could complain that such programming was bad aesthetic and pedagogical policy. In 1955 she declared, elaborating on the issues raised by Margaret Lloyd,

> this kind of concentration is indeed a tight interpretation of the term "American Dance." And although there were some fine discoveries among the new works and some interesting contrasts in the programs, the general feeling was one of sameness.

From a pedagogical point of view, it would probably be of more benefit for the Connecticut College students to see a broader range of modern dance. And from an artistic point of view it would be encouraging to find the college peppering its programs with more new works by young experimenters.[13]

Hering wrote her complaint during the directorial tenure of Martha Hill and Ruth Bloomer. However, for some critics, their successors did not do enough to correct this state of affairs. For Allen Hughes, the situation gradually worsened. In 1964 he said that the festival "has systematically, if subtly, focused attention upon one set of dance people at the expense of others who, though perhaps not part of a set, have been making equal (sometimes greater) contributions to the vitality of modern dance in America."[14] In another article that summer, Hughes protested because, at each year's festival, the Limón company always received "the prominent Saturday-night slot of the final weekend." (But, given Limón's importance to the festival, some viewers might think he deserved it.) Equally annoying, to Hughes, was the way the Limón company kept paying tribute to the memory of Humphrey, the 1964 season being a particularly irksome example. That year, even a program dedicated to Louis Horst also became a Humphrey memorial with the inclusion of *Lament for Ignacio Sánchez Mejías* on the bill. Given all this, claimed Hughes, a casual dancegoer who wandered in upon the festival only once or twice a season might conclude that New London was maintaining "some sort of perpetual wake" for Doris Humphrey.[15]

As Selma Jeanne Cohen says of José Limón and what he came to symbolize during the sixties, "The festival's saint became its scapegoat."

What was involved here was more than a matter of unbalanced programming. A shift of taste was occurring in modern dance. Walter Terry summed it up in a possibly oversimplified, but not totally inaccurate, form in 1961. Believing that modern dance now had an "old guard" and a "new guard," he said, "In general, the old guard looks upon modern dance as a way of communicating the inner passions, the psychological responses, the hidden dramas of man's heart and mind. The avant garde, in general, explores the formal relationships of bodies as they move through, or pause in, space and as they are guided (or not guided) by fixed or unfixed rhythms, sounds and colors."[16] Given this set of distinctions, Martha Graham, Doris Humphrey and José Limón would certainly qualify as members of the old guard; as for the new guard, Terry in that article identified two of its leaders as being Merce Cunningham and Paul Taylor.

Graham, Humphrey, and Limón choreographed dances in many different forms. But at least two types of dances they favored are worth noting here. One was a plotless or symbolical sort of dance that, despite the absence of conventional narrative, nevertheless managed to comment on aspects of the human condition or to celebrate noble aspirations. Several of these works, at least today, seem not all that different from some of the dances the new guard was then creating; what made them appear different may have been a matter of style and movement vocabulary, rather than of thematic intent. Thus both Humphrey's *Ruins and Visions* and Taylor's *Scudorama* deplore human indifference to suffering and, in their own ways, both Humphrey's *Passacaglia and Fugue in C Minor* and Taylor's *Aureole* affirm human dignity.

In addition, the old guard, especially from the 1940s onward, favored specifically thematic works drawing upon historical, legendary, mythological, or literary characters and situations. This type of dance was, for the most part, of no interest at all to the new guard. It was also a type of dance that Humphrey rarely attempted. But both Graham and Limón were very fond of it. By 1962, the year of the first dance concert at the Judson Church, Limón had choreographed works dealing with Othello, Cortés, Juarez, Don Juan, the Emperor Jones, Edith Cavell, Julian the Apostate, Odysseus, Adam and Eve, and Jesus Christ, while Graham's choreographic protagonists had included Emily Dickinson, the Brontë sisters, Medea, Ariadne, Jocasta, Judith, King Lear, Mary Stuart, Clytemnestra, Alcestis, Samson, Phaedra, Adam and Eve, and Joan of Arc. Sometimes in the arts new developments may occur simply because artists and audiences alike are tired of a certain form or style and are longing for something different. Given the prevalence of "literary" dance —and the fact that some of Limón's later works were both more long-winded and less interesting than his earlier creations—it may have been time for "something different" in modern dance. Doris Hering was not the only dancegoer to feel about a Limón-dominated festival that "Its relentless solemnity left one feeling leaden of foot and of heart," as she wrote in 1965.[17]

Yet little in the arts is totally unprecedented, and it could be argued that, in turning away from history and literature, choreographers were reaffirming one of the first principles of modern dance: a belief in the expressive powers of movement. In 1934, at the time of the founding of the Bennington festival, an unsigned article in the Springfield, Massachusetts, *Union Republican* asked and answered a fundamental question:

> What is the modern dance? . . . The dance is movement in space and in time. It is not the theater, acting, pantomime; it is not music, the transliteration of musical values into motion . . . it is not the pictorial arts, presenting a picture or an animated sculpture; it is not literature, telling a story. So generally the modern dance proclaims itself, its sole medium is movement, its sole intention is kinesthetic, it asks to be judged only in terms of itself.[18]

These sentiments could easily have been echoed by many of the "new guard" choreographers of the 1960s.

In retrospect, it is easy to conclude that the festival needed "something different" by the sixties. But in practical terms it was not necessarily easy at the time for the festival's staff and board to decide who was to provide it. The companies of Paul Taylor and Merce Cunningham already did make occasional festival visits; perhaps they should have been invited more often. Perhaps more use should have been made of the talents of such other innovators of the period as Alwin Nikolais, Murray Louis, and Erick Hawkins.

It might also be wondered why, after 1962, the festival did not offer works by the choreographers associated with the Judson Church. Among those who choreographed at Judson in the first five years of the Judson Dance Theater were Steve Paxton, David Gordon, Deborah Hay, Yvonne Rainer, Lucinda Childs, Trisha Brown, Judith Dunn, Rudy Perez, Elizabeth Keen, James Waring, Meredith Monk, Phoebe Neville, and Twyla Tharp. To exclude such artists from a major festival might now seem strange.

However, some remarks made in conversation by Theodora Wiesner deserve to be kept in mind. "I really wasn't all that impressed by what I had seen of the Judson people," she said. Although here she reveals her personal taste—something no festival director can be without—directors on occasion may include in their seasons works by artists not to their own liking yet of recognized importance. But it was more than personal taste that made Wiesner cautious of Judson. She said, "I wasn't sure what those Judson dancers would look like outside Judson. Often, choreography that looks interesting in some special milieu will not seem as interesting elsewhere." The Judson group included some experienced dancers and, in time, several of its choreographers became leading figures in American dance. But in the early and mid-sixties many of those same choreographers were scarcely more than beginners. And although the American Dance Festival did try to encourage new choreographers, presenting works by beginners—or by people the board might consider to be beginners —was not one of its principal functions.

In conversation Selma Jeanne Cohen has said that she thinks the festival ought to have taken radical action: it should not have asked the Limón company back for several seasons. "It was time for them to go," she says, "to go from Connecticut to someplace else for their own good and for the good of the festival. Then both the Limón company and the festival could have been able to find stimulation from new sources."

Instead, the festival kept on as before. There was even, Cohen thinks, a slight complacency in the attitude of its staff and board. She says, "It was as if they thought: we, as representatives of modern dance, are innovative by nature. Therefore we don't need to do anything else. But, finally, some of the students got restless and so, eventually, even the faculty did." And critics were increasingly complaining, as Marcia B. Siegel did in 1968, that "the American Dance Festival is already showing signs of tired blood. The ideas of the '60s find scant encouragement there."[19]

But 1968 was the year the festival itself acknowledged its "tired blood." The faculty met endlessly to discuss ways of improving the situation. According to Bonnie Bird, who was present at those meetings, the major problem that everyone recognized was that "there was no longer any thrust for innovation in either teaching or choreography at Connecticut."

Other issues also received serious attention: for instance, the ever-perplexing matter of how to make the local community interested in, and involved with, dance. Various "community outreach" programs were proposed. But the ones most likely to succeed were conceived on such a grand scale that their advocates suspected they would have to be administered not as a sideline to other festival activities, but as special projects with special staffs that might have to be in residence in New London all year long. Also discussed at faculty meetings were ways the festival could have some sort of impact in New York City. New York dance lovers regularly traveled to New London. Now the summer faculty began to wonder if it might somehow be possible for highlights of the festival to travel back to New York.

But, like the community outreach proposals, any scheme to bring performances to New York would have required a larger staff than the festival had at the time. A commitment to either project would have made the festival a more complex institution than it had ever been before. "But," says Bonnie Bird, "though we had lots of talk and hope, there was no one to organize things."

A feeling that the festival needed a strong organizer had already been voiced by Doris Hering in her review of the 1961 season. Scrutinizing that year's programming, she concluded that the lack of a single strong director to supervise scheduling made performances seem unfocused. Festival concerts tended to be catchalls of good and bad dances alike: "One feels the need of more discrimination in the choice and arrangement of repertoire. The ideal would be for the American Dance Festival to have an artistic director not on its teaching or administrative staff—an impartial person with the absolute authority to say 'yes'—and more important, the authority to say 'no.'"[20]

By appointing Charles L. Reinhart director, the festival acquired a strong organizer, a man who the dance writer Janice Berman has described as being both a "flagwaver" and a "cheerleader" for modern dance. Reinhart himself has admitted, "I was made for modern dance." Lovers of omens and portents might therefore find it prophetic that once, when he was a little boy and saw a woman rise on pointe in a movie, Reinhart had to close his eyes because the sight made his feet hurt. That, for certain choreographic mystics, might be interpreted as a sure sign that Reinhart's destiny was to be modern dance rather than classical ballet.

But the only "modern" dancing this native of Summit, New Jersey, did as a boy was of an altogether different sort: he was the jitterbug champion of Chatham, New Jersey, High School—class of 1948. After attending Newark College of Rutgers University and serving in the army during the Korean War, he decided to go to New York University Law School with the aid of the GI Bill. To earn extra money, he also worked as an "office temporary." One of his assignments was to the office of the theatrical publicists Isadora Bennett and Richard Pleasant. Bennett, known as "Izzy" to her colleagues, had been a reporter for the Chicago *Daily News* in the 1920s. But from the thirties onward she was one of New York's most respected press representatives. Dance was her great love, and she handled publicity for such artists as Martha Graham and José Limón, as well as for Ballet Theatre and, later, the Joffrey Ballet. By her avoidance of cheap publicity stunts and her insistence upon honesty in press releases, Bennett, as many who knew her have remarked, helped transform the field of theatrical publicity from a racket into a profession. Pleasant, her partner, had been one of the founders and, in 1940, the first director of Ballet Theatre (now American Ballet Theatre).

Reinhart found the atmosphere in the Bennett-Pleasant office congenial and his duties there stimulating. His employers also found him bright and eager and offered him a permanent position. Yet Reinhart was restless and became curious to visit Europe. Therefore in 1956 he left on a boat bound for Denmark. He chose Denmark, he says, largely because "the boat was going there." He lived for much of the time in Copenhagen until 1962, when he returned permanently to the United States. To support himself abroad, he picked up money in a variety of ways: he wrote about the Royal Danish Ballet (Bennett was the company's American publicist), taught basketball, acted in Danish films, worked for a Danish wire service, did news reports for NBC's "Monitor" program, and guided foreigners on tours sponsored by the Danish tourist office. Until his GI Bill ran out, he studied at the graduate school of the University of Copenhagen and became involved in a research project on the attitude toward foreign policy of six Danish political parties.

Ted Shawn, director of the Jacob's Pillow Dance Festival, came to Copenhagen to be knighted by King Frederick IX for having introduced Danish ballet to America at his festival. After meeting Reinhart during that visit, Shawn asked him to handle publicity at Jacob's Pillow for the summers of 1960 and 1961. Reinhart also worked again for Bennett, helping her to locate and to book in Europe dancers for the Asia Society's performing arts series, and in 1963 he was on the American Dance Festival staff.

At "the Pillow," dancers had started to come to him with booking and management problems. Therefore, in 1962, Reinhart opened his own management office. Paul Taylor was one of his first major clients. Taylor had told Bennett that he needed a manager; she, in turn, recommended Reinhart, and when Taylor showed Reinhart *Aureole* as an example of his choreography, Reinhart was so overwhelmed by it that he literally fell out of his chair. By 1969, when Walter Terry wrote an article about him for the *Dance Magazine Annual*, Reinhart's attractions, as advertised in that annual, included the companies of Taylor, Lucas Hoving, Don Redlich, Shanta Rao, Donald McKayle, and Glen Tetley. Reinhart was also married to one of Taylor's dancers, Molly Moore, from 1966 to 1974. His present wife, Stephanie Singer Reinhart, had worked eight years with the dance and education program of the National Endowment for the Arts before becoming associated with the festival. She married Reinhart in 1977, and, she says, they spent their honeymoon at the ADF.

In 1966 Reinhart had helped establish the NEA's Dance Touring Program, and he ran it for ten years. Possessing a thorough knowledge of modern dance, Reinhart has an amazing ability to get things done in a field in which rugged individualism can often seem to threaten chaos. "I'm not really sure what religion is," he once told dance critic Nancy Vreeland, "but the closest thing I have to it is modern dance."[21]

When he took over the American Dance Festival, Reinhart vowed to make significant changes in both the performance schedule and the curriculum. Charles Shain introduced him to Martha Myers, and, giving her the title of dean, Reinhart placed her in charge of the summer school. A teacher, dancer, choreographer, film producer, television performer, and writer, Myers completed her undergraduate work at Virginia Commonwealth University and received an M.S. degree from Smith College. She studied modern dance at various New York studios and, in 1952, at Connecticut College. Married to a professor of philosophy, Gerald Myers, who, with Stephanie Reinhart, now directs the festival's humanities programs, she has been active as a teacher in the dance departments of several colleges and universities, including Smith College and the University of Wisconsin at Milwaukee. She has also served as director of women's news for WBNS-TV (CBS) in Columbus, Ohio, and was coproducer, writer, and narrator for nine dance appreciation programs called "A Time to Dance" that were initially distributed to educational television stations under the auspices of the NET Council during the 1960–61 season and which have been used ever since by colleges and universities.

Myers came to Connecticut College as a full-time faculty member in 1968 when Charles Shain expressed a desire to strengthen the college's regular winter dance curriculum. She now holds the title of Henry B. Plant Professor of Dance at Connecticut.[22]

With the appointments of Reinhart and Myers, the festival was, in a sense, renewing itself. The American Dance Festival had been founded by choreographers and teachers who had been associated with Bennington. Gradually, it began to develop its own choreographers—notably Paul Taylor. Now it sought a change of direction. Yet to guide that change it hired a former festival employee and a former summer school student. However fierce its growing pains may have been, the American Dance Festival was developing by a process of evolution.

But reforms were needed and Reinhart was determined to institute them. At a meeting of the board he outlined his plans. However, the board objected to his proposal that Twyla Tharp be named the next Doris Humphrey Fellow. Tharp was still too controversial a choreographer for some board members, and one of them suggested that, if he wished, Reinhart should offer Tharp a festival residency without giving her the title of Doris Humphrey Fellow. Since then, the festival has aided many young choreographers, but it has never again awarded the Humphrey fellowship.

Reinhart discarded the institution's cumbersome dual name of Connecticut College School of Dance and American Dance Festival, settling upon American Dance Festival at Connecticut College, which is what many members of the general public had long called it. Then, to show Reinhart that he fully backed the idea of getting the festival off to a fresh start, Charles Shain allowed the board to be dissolved.[23]

VI

SEASON BY SEASON

1969–1977

1969

The American Dance Festival's first season with Charles Reinhart as director and Martha Myers as dean was, in many ways, both chaotic and invigorating. Looking back, one person familiar with the festival under all its directorial regimes remarks, "That summer was a real mess. It seemed as if Charley and Martha were so eager to prove how innovative they were that they decided to do nothing the way it had been done before. But that meant they couldn't even get through something as cut-and-dried as registration without turning it into an absolute shambles."[1] Both Reinhart and Myers deny that they made changes merely to be "different." Nevertheless, Reinhart has said, "Everyone knew that changes were necessary. But I had to decide whether to make changes gradually or to come in with a bang. I decided to come in with a bang."[2]

The festival commissioned works from Paul Taylor, Alvin Ailey, Yvonne Rainer, Twyla Tharp, James Cunningham, and Talley Beatty—five choreographers who could be viewed as representatives of a variety of important contemporary dance styles. But for the first time in the festival's history there were no performances by the José Limón company. As usual, the curriculum featured courses in modern dance techniques and composition. But the courses offered also included such things as eurhythmics, "the Tao of movement," and, for the first time, ballet (taught by James Clouser) and jazz (taught by Talley Beatty). The innovations, which attracted 320 students, were for the most part applauded, although some critics did voice reservations.

Thus Doris Hering complained that students were not auditioned for placement in classes, and, consequently, near-professionals and fumbling beginners might find themselves side by side in the same studio. As a way of providing an alternative to the compositional theories of Louis Horst and his associates, which had been branded as dogmatic in some circles, the composition classes for 1969 stressed improvisation. Unfortunately, perhaps too much emphasis may have been placed upon it, for before the summer was over Hering heard students sigh, "Gee, we're tired of all that improvisation." Yet, despite the complaints, there was excitement in the air. As one faculty member told Hering, "Our administration is all confused and nobody knows what is going on. But apparently when people do manage to find something it turns out to be interesting."[3]

In some ways it was virtually a whole new festival. Writing for the *Christian Science Monitor*, Kathleen Cannell declared that whereas for the past ten years almost every face in the festival audience had been familiar to her, now she recognized only one or two people other than her journalistic colleagues. Cannell was fascinated by the hair and whisker styles of what appeared to be an unusually young audience, and both she and *Dance Magazine*'s Stephen Smoliar reported that during some curtain calls screaming young women would rise up from their seats, throw off their shoes, and dance in the aisles, pelting the stage with flowers.[4] The "flower children" of the sixties had discovered the American Dance Festival.

Other aspects of the festival also were typical of that freewheeling decade. Students staged a "happening" at a nearby supermarket and a sound-and-movement event on the campus lawn. Even some of the official festival presentations took place outdoors, although Palmer Auditorium was now air-conditioned for the first time. The new spirit of the festival was symbolized by its opening attraction: a program, 19 July, shared by two experimental choreographers, Twyla Tharp and Yvonne Rainer. Neither used the auditorium, and both augmented their own companies with what seemed to be hordes of student dancers. Both in response to the era's love of egalitarian "togetherness" and as a way of giving students a chance to work directly with professional choreographers, festival attractions for several seasons to come would draw upon the student body.[5]

Tharp's *Medley* took place in the early evening, while it was still light, on the lawn in front of the college's Lyman Allyn Museum. As spectators arrived at the performance space, two women, one in pointe shoes, were already dancing on a small board. Four other women from

Sarah Rudner in Tharp's *Medley*, 1969. Photo, Leonard Knyper.

Tharp's company joined them in sequences that included imitations of gestures they saw being made by members of the audience. Suddenly, thirty-three student dancers, who had been placed in the audience rushed into the performing area and they and the members of Tharp's company divided into large groups. Then the entire cast scattered across the lawn, some dancers stopping close to the spectators, others posting themselves about as far away as the eye could see, and everyone began to perform an adagio that was so slow that the dancers barely appeared to be moving at all. Gradually, dancers dropped out until only one was left.

Tharp had a reputation for being a mathematically precise, forbiddingly austere choreographer, and some critics who had not liked her work in the past did not like *Medley*. Thus Cannell declared that Tharp "specializes in cybernetics to make her dancers ungainly in the extreme." But other critics considered *Medley* choreographically rich and even emotionally warm. For Don McDonagh, it displayed Tharp's "newly apparent concern with dancer personalities, an element that has heretofore been rigorously subservient in the computer-correct format of her choreography." Smoliar found *Medley* fascinating and slightly perplexing:

> The actual progression across the vast area was a somewhat strange experience. There would be long, seemingly redundant passages which would undergo subtle changes and then transform into something radically different with no apparent motivation other than the scheduling of the timetable. It was somewhat like watching the Lincoln Center fountain run through all its phases.

Everyone who liked *Medley* thought the final adagio astonishing in its effects of slow motion. Here, Tharp played perception games for, as Smoliar observed, the dancers "moved so gradually that they appeared to be static; but if one looked at something else and then looked back, it was apparent they had moved."

Formally, *Medley* was a dance without apparent beginning or end. When the audience arrived, it had already started. And when only one dancer was left in the adagio, she was replaced at half-hour intervals by another member of Tharp's company until all six of her dancers had performed the solo sequence. Because of mosquitoes, the last dancer was permitted to complete her solo indoors. Meanwhile, the audience had moved to a nearby student center for Rainer's *Connecticut Composite*. Thus Tharp's soloists were performing without spectators to watch them and for purely conceptual reasons.[6]

Like *Medley*, Rainer's work played games with time and space. *Connecticut Composite* was a sort of living museum with exhibits and activities (including pieces of both new and old choreography) on view simultaneously in several areas of the student center. Members of the audience were provided with a map of the space and a timetable of events and were free to wander as they pleased. Films were shown in a lounge. People who ventured into one of the building's dance studios could listen to a taped lecture by Rainer; if they wished to look at something while they listened, they could contemplate a dangling skeleton with no right leg and a disjointed right shoulder. In another studio twenty-eight students performed *Trio A*, an essay in complex, but uninflected movement that had become Rainer's most famous single composition. Rainer's own group kept itself busy in a gymnasium with *Continuous Project—Altered Daily*, improvised variations on a set of movement themes. Marching back and forth through the gymnasium—and blocking and opening up areas of the space to spectators as they came and went—was a line of linked dancers called the *People Wall*, which, said Marcia B. Siegel, was "as inevitable as a juggernaut, although an amiable one." For Smoliar, *Connecticut Composite* was "a five-ring circus," while Siegel thought it had "the clangor and conviviality of a Horn and Hardart" cafeteria.

The entire program by Tharp and Rainer brought "a joyous spirit of adventure back" to the festival, said McDonagh: "One would have to return to the dewy days of the 22-year-old festival to duplicate the feeling of this opening concert." Siegel agreed, marveling at "an evening that had been so vivid and so full of ideas." Reinhart's tenure as festival director had opened auspiciously indeed.[7]

There was other choreography of interest to be seen among the premieres. But many of them were not really in finished form when they were put on the stage, and some were frankly labeled as "works-in-progress." Like that year's summer school, the festival ran cheerfully, but not always smoothly.

Stephen Smoliar, a young critic invited by Doris Hering to review the festival for *Dance Magazine*, summarized the summer's productions. The first work in an unequivocally balletic idiom to have its premiere at the festival was James Clouser's *The Kiss of the Mome Rath: A Febrile Farad.* Though it may have been purely classical in its technique, it was facetious in its intent. A set of movement non sequiturs, it was termed "balletic jabberwocky" by Smoliar, who pronounced it "self-indulgent in its nonsense" and "rather discouraging" as an example of ballet. Clouser, who had been trained in both ballet and modern dance, also offered another new work, *Lovely in the Dances*, to songs by his wife, Sonja Zarek, a singer and guitarist. Choreographed in an idiom that fused ballet, modern dance, folk dance, and mime, it celebrated love, joy, and religious solace. Smoliar found it, too, self-indulgent, "this time on the mushy, lyric side."

Clouser was not the only choreographer to employ comic non sequiturs. James Cunningham, a young choreographer who virtually specialized in them, devised his own bit of jabberwocky, *The Zoo at Night*, which received, said Smoliar, "a riotous performance" that the predominantly youthful audience greeted with "a tremendous ovation, complete with screaming flower-throwers and dancing in the aisles."

Al Huang attempted to fuse aspects of Oriental dance with Western modern dance in *The Monkey and the Moon* and *Owari*. In the former, a solo, Huang portrayed a monkey who, after seeing the reflection of the moon below him, jumped for it (in this case, into the orchestra pit) and emerged soaking wet. Smoliar was neither amused nor edified: "The work was described as a Zen koan which, according to Huang's notes, 'is used in Zen study to break through intellectual abstractions, in order to return to intuitive realizations of simple everyday truth.' Indeed." *Owari* was a psychedelic fantasy that combined sinuous dance movements with the flashings of blinking lights in cagelike constructions. But Smoliar was disappointed because "there seemed to be no relationship between the dancers and the vagaries of the dominating contraptions."

Talley Beatty's passionate *Bring My Servant Home* was dedicated to the memory of Dr. Martin Luther King, Jr. However, although Smoliar thought it "had much of the same impact" of many earlier dances by Beatty, it was a work-in-progress that seemed to be "clearly in an unfinished state."

An even more fragmentary effort—indeed, "the most unfinished piece in the festival," according to Smoliar—was something by Paul Taylor set to medieval music called *Work in Progress: Duets*, a series of duets for Carolyn Adams and Daniel Williams. It was never completed. Yet, says Taylor, some of the choreography it contained found its way into *Churchyard*, choreographed later that year.

Another work, Alvin Ailey's *Masekela Langage* eventually was polished to become one of Ailey's most powerful compositions. It depicted the lethargic habitués of a seedy bar on a hot, sweltering day and their reactions when a fatally wounded man staggered into their midst. Since the man was presumably the victim of racist bigotry and the action occurred to music by the South African trumpeter, Hugh Masekela, the dance could be interpreted as an attack upon apartheid. Smoliar called the work-in-progress version seen at the festival "intense" and "seething." And critics have used similar adjectives to describe the final version.[8]

Except for the works in the concert shared by Tharp and Rainer, many of the summer's attractions were in a somewhat disheveled state. Yet there was an undeniable excitement about the performances, and, said McDonagh, "The festival proved one thing and that was that modern dance was exactly what choreographers wanted it to be and not what anyone thought it ought to be."[9]

———————————————————— **1970** ————————————————————

The excitement of 1969 prevailed again in 1970. Indeed, that year the festival sponsored an almost bewildering profusion of events, and all festivals since then have been similarly crowded with activities. The official festival—the performances for the general public—included dances by Martha Graham, Lucas Hoving, James Cunningham, Meredith Monk, Ray Cook, June Lewis, Martha Myers, Richard Englund, Peter Saul, and Dorothy Vislocky. But just as the American Dance Festival used to have a Little Concert Series—and the Edinburgh Festival has a "fringe" festival along with its main attractions—so in 1970 there were many special performances, including a concert by Kaleidoscope (a company directed by Seamus Murphy and Libby Nye), another concert shared by Murphy and Eugene Harris, a demonstration of choreographic and musical improvisation by Gwendolyn Watson and Joel Press, a solo concert by Margaret Beals, and a jazz dance evening by Hoving and Paul Knopf.

A festival event also took place off campus. Erin Martin staged her *Beach Piece* outdoors at twilight at Harkness State Park in Waterford, Connecticut. A cast of thirty-five students used a garden, an open field, and a beach as sites for dance events, and the movement ranged from formal patterns in the garden to a frolic on the beach. Don McDonagh reported that "the movement invention was slight but the varying locales were sensitively chosen to enhance the situations."[10]

The summer's school activities included at least two important innovations. Selma Jeanne Cohen, who had taught dance writing on campus since 1967, had long dreamed of establishing a workshop for professional dance critics. Now, with the aid of a $10,000 grant from the National Endowment for the Arts and matching funds from the ADF (as the American Dance Festival increasingly referred to itself), she was able to organize the first Dance Critics' Conference: a four-week—in subsequent years, a three-week—seminar to which five working critics received full scholarships. Sessions were devoted to writing style, dance history, problems relating to dance in the critics' communities, and movement analysis. Participants were assigned to write about festival activities and then discussed one another's reviews. That year's faculty was headed by Cohen and George Beiswanger, who were in residence for the entire four weeks, and there were visits for shorter periods of time by Deborah Jowitt, Marcia B. Siegel, Walter Terry, Arlene Croce, and myself. Doris Hering, who was also to have been on the faculty, was prevented from attending by illness. The critics' conference, directed in later years by Deborah Jowitt, Nancy Goldner, Camille Hardy, and Don McDonagh, has remained a regular feature of the festival.[11]

A second innovation addressed that old and ever-vexing problem of how to involve the New London community with dance. An ambitious Community Outreach program was established, directed by Dora Sanders. There were special on-campus lunchtime classes for children and their mothers and daily classes for local high school students. Festival students and teachers also worked with emotionally disturbed children, the blind, and the elderly and staged events at a local shopping mall, including a ballet demonstration by Gage Bush and a performance by the Lucas Hoving Dance Company.[12] Like previous efforts of this sort, such events called attention to the festival's presence, but no one could ever determine what long-range effects they had upon the community.

Just as the choreographic sensations of 1969 had been dances by two experimentalists, Twyla Tharp and Yvonne Rainer, so the sensation of 1970 was a new work by another experimentalist, Meredith Monk. A former student at the festival, Monk by the late sixties had become the exponent of a hard-to-label, mixed-media form that has variously been called movement-theater and multimedia-theater. (She herself in conversation once jokingly referred to it as "mixed pickles.") Monk based her new, and cryptically titled *Needle-Brain Lloyd and the Systems Kid* on the theme of a quest or voyage, and, because she wished to make it panoramic in scale, she used much of the Connecticut College campus as her stage.

The action began late in the afternoon beside a lake in the college arboretum, then shifted to the campus lawn. After a dinner break, the piece resumed in twilight on the lawn and concluded in darkness back in the arboretum. The first image the audience beheld in the afternoon was a couple rowing across the lake in a boat; and the final image was the same couple rowing back into the night. Between these two moments came a phantasmagoria of images involving galloping horses, speeding motorcycles, questing figures in red-dyed costumes that reminded some viewers of the "reddlemen" in Thomas Hardy's Wessex novels, eighteenth-century aristocrats, genteel lawn party croquet players, and Western pioneers.

Discussing the spectacle, McDonagh said, "The piece had a mosaic charm and it was enlightened of the American Dance Festival to allow Miss Monk to space her artistic concerns outside of the somewhat inhibiting proscenium stage." But, though certainly true, that sober statement

Meredith Monk's *Needlebrain Lloyd & the Systems Kid*, 1970. Photo, © 1970 Peter Moore.

fails to capture the piece's giddy excitement. A better sense of what *Needle-Brain Lloyd* was like can be found in a review by John Mueller, a critic from Rochester, New York, who was attending the Dance Critics' Conference. Left astonished by the extravaganza, Mueller wrote,

> When swarms of characters scream and sweep across a field, once following a group of mounted horses, once at seeming crosspaths with a group of roaring motorcycles; when lights in a darkened build-ing suddenly flash on revealing at the windows grotesque characters in contorted poses; when a group of people in Victorian dress playing croquet and laughing far across a field seem to have materialized from nothing in broad daylight (because one's attention has been diverted elsewhere)—when these images are projected, the effect is impossible to forget.
>
> Meredith Monk's art is striking and original, beautiful and perplexing.[13]

None of the other premieres was on so grand a scale. Peter Saul's *Simple Fractions* presented twenty-two dancers in patterns that McDonagh said ranged from "cockeyed military formations" to "shapeless crowds," and it did all this with "a bright and sharp-edged sense of timing and direction." Clearly, McDonagh had a better time at *Simple Fractions* than Kathleen Cannell, who complained, "Weak as I am in fractions, I must beg to be excused for not understanding the problem."[14]

Dorothy Vislocky's *Suite of Things* consisted of humorous tableaux on and around two clusters of white cubes, and the action literally involved a lot of things: toy horses, trains, vacuum cleaners, and television sets, to name only a few. In one section of the work, slide pictures of fields and flowers were projected onto the dancers' white leotards, thereby turning them into human flowers; in another episode of this romp "the dancers mimed amusingly erotic passages that quoted extensively from the dance clichés of the 1930's" (said McDonagh).[15]

Lucas Hoving's *Reflections*, a dance-drama about the Prodigal Son and his brother, received mixed notices, Cannell pronouncing it "subtle, richly sinuous and sensuous." But to McDonagh it looked dated, and the anxieties it depicted "have simply lost their currency." He concluded, "No one really worries that way anymore."[16]

Ray Cook freely reinterpreted another biblical tale in his *Genesis 3*, to music by Kazimierz Serocki. According to Laura Shapiro of the *Boston Phoenix*, this choreographic creation myth began with a "primeval jungle-like effect" of "bodies leaping suddenly about in the dimness." After rituals of hunting, capture, sacrifice, and worship, an Eve figure was created. But this proved to be accompanied by such aggressive movement for the male dancers that Shapiro was forced to declare that she felt Serocki's music was "terribly melodramatic" and Cook's choreography was "terribly manly" in a most unpleasant way.[17]

Shapiro found June Lewis's *If I Am I* no more profound, but considerably more palatable. The piece began with Lewis and two men hanging on ropes. "Once on the ground," said Shapiro, "they run through an evenly paced set of not quite predictable duets and trios. Miss Lewis never quite makes it back to her rope but I'm sure there's no message involved. It's a pleasing number and quite short."[18]

Other than Monk's mixed-media event the festival's most elaborate premiere was James Cunningham's *The Junior Birdmen*, which was staged in the gymnasium with a cast that included seventy students informally clad in jeans. Like many of Cunningham's creations, this one was a choreographic crazy quilt of movement jokes. There were comments on sexual role-playing, spoofs of sports events, and parodies of dance styles.

Thus, in Cunningham's antic restaging of a scene from *Swan Lake*, dancers rushed around with a squirt gun and insect repellant, and Rothbart, the evil sorcerer, made an entrance in a solid gold G-string. Shapiro reported, "The piece ended with a mass frolic, in which the audience was urged to participate."[19] The fact that many spectators accepted the invitation says much about the "hip" spirit of those times—and about the American Dance Festival.

--------------------------------- **1971** ---------------------------------

Certain aspects of the 1971 festival disturbed Doris Hering. For her, there was so much "self-indulgent choreographic junk disguised by pretentious categories like 'structured improvisation,' 'unstructured improvisation,' and 'intercommunal workshop'" that she feared choreographers were forgetting the difference between dance as a theatrical art and dance as a form of physical or psychological therapy. Although she admitted that dance-as-therapy could be of value to a choreographer—"It's a good idea to know yourself before you try to know others"—she pointed out that "therapy is essentially personal" and therapeutic dance is not necessarily "much fun for an audience, especially when the performers are technically mediocre. In the classroom, okay. In the theatre, *pourquoi?*"[20]

Her remarks were surely prompted by the presence at the festival of Ann Halprin and her San Francisco Dancers' Workshop, a group that aroused enormous controversy and even managed to alienate many of the dancegoers who had applauded Tharp, Rainer, and Monk. Halprin's concerns turned out to be fundamentally different from those of the other innovators Charles Reinhart had invited to the festival.

Yet her background was totally respectable. She had attended the University of Wisconsin, had studied at Bennington in the summers of 1938 and 1939, and had danced on Broadway in 1944 in the musical *Sing Out, Sweet Land*, choreographed by Doris Humphrey. After she married the landscape architect Lawrence Halprin, she and her husband moved to San Francisco, where she established a company in collaboration with Welland Lathrop. Then, in 1955, she founded her own Dancers' Workshop.

Halprin's presentations over the years became increasingly experimental until by the early 1960s they were occasionally compared with "happenings." In 1967 her company made its New York debut in *Parades and Changes*, which created an uproar both because of its inventiveness and because of its nude scene. Yet, although *Parades and Changes* was strikingly theatrical, Halprin about this time developed a preoccupation with dance as a therapeutic tool to promote personal growth and social harmony. For some of her former admirers, the conflicting claims of theater and therapy kept pulling her choreography in two entirely differ-ent directions. This conflict was almost blatantly apparent in *West/East Stereo*, her festival premiere.

Whatever one thought of the merits of *West/East Stereo*, no one could brand it a slapdash effort. Halprin sent assistants to Connecticut six weeks before the premiere to work with festival students who wished to be in the production. Then Halprin and her regular company arrived, having spent the same period of time rehearsing material in California. Once on campus, Halprin allowed herself to be interviewed, explained her theories in detail, and gave public lecture-demonstrations in which she had her dancers pretend to be animals—usually, quarrelsome ones.

At last the actual performance arrived. What the audience saw were rituals and structured group improvisations based upon animal behavior. There was much chattering, chirping, and fighting. Animals made love, protected their mates, gave birth, and killed other creatures for food. The sight of all this made Marcia B. Siegel declare, "Ann Halprin's *West/East Stereo* defies analysis. I'm not even sure it should be reviewed." Neverthe-less, several critics made a stab at reviewing it, and at least one, Frances Alenikoff of *Dance News*, was decidedly enthusiastic. Alenikoff found the experience

> a dive into the collective unconscious from which I for one emerged refreshed by recognitions—sensory and psychic. Loaded with echoes of African tribal rites, universal myths and a clear identification (in the animal transformations that are the matter and heart of the piece) with the primitive ethos which Cassirer calls "the consanguin-ity of all living things," it is a time-out-of-mind ritual: of being, becoming, catharsis, exorcism and community affirmation.
>
> Key figures and themes are all there: the scapegoat who dies to be reborn, a priest-exorcist, silent witnesses who sit, black shrouded, watching throughout (like ancient death archetypes), bush ancestor souls, ranged up a totem pole like a chattering clan of monkeys, even a "Voice in the wilderness," goading the ritual doers into self-searching by his questions.

Siegel, however, referred to this figure as a kind of stage manager and said that when he asked participants how they felt about the animal rituals, they could only shuffle and shrug and mumble a phrase like, "Man, I feel good." Such incidents explain why most critics were either dumfounded by, or actively hostile to, *West/East Stereo*: they found it inarticulate; if it meant something to the participants, they could not communicate that significance to the onlooker. And when meanings did arise, they were sometimes unpleasant in their implications. Thus Hering, like several other critics, was disturbed because the action seemed so "belligerent," and "Often the imitations of wings and other animal and bird appendages made them [the dancers] resemble maimed people."

"I felt vaguely sad," Hering concluded about the performance. "Much of it had bored me. So much had been made of the *process* of art that little was left for the result." Siegel raised yet another issue: "Ann Halprin seems to be caught somewhere between art and therapy. . . . *West/East Stereo* made me wonder if the artist has the right to expose a real therapeutic situation to an audience." With time, Halprin may have resolved this problem. Now calling herself Anna Halprin, she devotes herself almost exclusively to workshops, communal rituals, and what some people have termed choreographic encounter sessions; by so doing, she may have left the theater behind her.

A member of the audience at *West/East Stereo* was a visiting British critic who wrote as James Monahan for *The Dancing Times* and as James Kennedy for the *Guardian*. In *The Dancing Times* he took an urbane above-it-all attitude toward the proceedings, calling the production "Little therapy, I thought, and less art, but thoroughly (if not quite intentionally) entertaining." But he was much more blunt in the *Guardian*: expressing alarm at the increasing pluralism of American dance, he proclaimed, "The present abundance, which finds room for Ann Halprin's multiracial San Franciscans playing at being lions and bunny rabbits . . . is not so much a promise of brave new developments as evidence of a breakdown."[21] Few other critics would ever reach so drastic a conclusion, yet the extreme eclecticism of the festival in seasons to come did occasionally cause observers to wonder about what artistic principles were operative in program planning.

The eclecticism of 1971 permitted Connecticut audiences to see works by another major California choreographer, Bella Lewitzky of Los Angeles, whose choreography had never before been presented in the East. Lewitzky had first achieved acclaim as a leading dancer of the company organized by Lester Horton, one of the pioneers of modern dance in California. Then she had gone on to found her own company. But whereas Horton's dances were often flamboyantly theatrical, Lewitzky favored a cooler approach to composition. As Alenikoff pointed out:

> Her dances are sturdy in composition, adhering to conventional notions about patterning, juxtapositions and progressions. There is an emphasis on cool precision—both a strength and a weakness: the first in that it produces clarity and lucidity, the second because it tends to rob movement of that element of spontaneity which opens dances up, making them kinetically exciting.

As for the kinds of steps Lewitzky employed, Alenikoff said, "Stylistically, she likes to play with internal body rhythms, pitting one part of herself against another, hands, head and shoulders explored in articulations, percussive accents, fluid gestures, shifts, halts and pauses, all underpinned by a suspended, elongated torso." But Lewitzky's meticulousness and analytical powers could occasionally give the effect of constriction. Thus Deborah Jowitt observed of her dancers that

> curiously, almost all of them are tight in the head-neck-shoulders-upper back area. It may also be tension that frequently causes them to withhold their weight from the movement—of working neither to avoid the pull of gravity, not [sic] to comply with it, nor to play with it, nor to affirm it. Sometimes they seem to be skittering over the surface of a dance.

Nancy Mason, a young critic who, along with Doris Hering, covered festival events for *Dance Magazine* that summer, attended Lewitzky's classes and demonstrations and found them impressive for their excitement and sense of creative spontaneity. Therefore she was puzzled by the fact that, in her company's concerts, Lewitzky's choreographic "clean style bordered on the antiseptic and . . . I missed differences in tension and movement quality." *Pietas*, Lewitzky's premiere, was a Holocaust memorial and one of her most intense efforts, requiring the dancers, said Jowitt, to "plunge, gesture frantically or pleadingly, collapse, contort, rise again"—yet to surprisingly little avail, for "lacking extremes of collapse or out-of-control movement, it is more a litany of oppression than a drama of combating it."[22]

No one was aware of its importance at the time—nor could anyone not clairvoyant have been aware of it—but one concert at the 1971 festival included a performance by someone, then virtually unknown, who has since become one of the most controversial figures in modern dance. Lucas Hoving invited a young German dancer who had been studying in America to appear in his new *Zip Code* and to choreograph her own role in the production. As a result, festival audiences saw a bit of early choreography by Pina Bausch who within a decade would, as director of the Wuppertaler Tanz Theater, virtually revitalize European modern dance.

Zip Code was described by Alenikoff as containing "an assortment of bizarre inhabitants, denizens of a nether world in a surreal ambiance, caught in the grip of private deliriums." Hering described some of the incidents: "three couples, dressed as though newly emerged from their baths, played at mate swapping until the men crawled away and the women strode off in deep knee bends. A couple embraced in an overhead light while a violin and a woodwind labored away at a waltz. Men alternated between carrying girls and crouching and twitching with them on the floor." Hering's conclusion about all this was, "Lots of contrivance here."

But both Alenikoff and Hering admired Pina Bausch's solo. Alenikoff said, "Pina Bausch, her face sombre, masklike, peers into the dark, a haunted, predatory creature stalking in deep crouches, spiralling turns and angled, disjointed poses." Hering also likened her to a nonhuman creature; for Hering, Bausch "stretched and curved like a mythological serpent, more beautiful than fearsome."[23]

Rudy Perez's new *Annual* introduced festival audiences to an American choreographer who was attracting attention for dances in which severe, almost minimalist formal patterns were nevertheless often charged with comic or intensely serious dramatic meanings. Alenikoff called Perez's perception of space "essentially geometric." She continued, "He characteristically locks his muscle structure in upright stances, feet close together, arms at side. Tension is released sporadically, in bursts, convulsive jumps with arms suddenly flailing, or sudden runs coming to equally sudden halts." Alenikoff admitted that she had always found it "difficult to respond with more than minimal interest to his minimal, retentive aesthetic, with its emphasis on withdrawal, repetitions and confined movement." Yet she was amiably surprised because *Annual* suggested Perez was expanding his choreographic range: "The materials are the familiar ones, but they occur in more frequent bursts and juxtapositions. There are hints of pleasure in kinetic impetus and increased leaning toward lightness and humor." She deplored some of this humor for being "annoyingly childish." However, Kathleen Marner in *Dance Magazine* found all the humor "deliciously comic."[24]

A totally comic work in a summer of predominantly serious premieres was Paul Taylor's *Book of Beasts*. For this whimsical bestiary set to familiar, even hackneyed, pieces of classical music (including Saint-Saëns's "The Swan"), Taylor devised portraits of real or mythological animals. Alenikoff described it all as "a grand ceremony of spoof, a super-camp frolic in a medieval court setting." Yet, though a bit of nonsense, *Book of Beasts* was meticulously constructed, and, said Jowitt, "Some of the group sections are very exciting. I liked the combination of almost hectic speed and energy with print-neat floor patterns." One of the few critics who neither admired nor laughed at *Book of Beasts* was James Monahan: the piece, he said, merely "confirmed my previous, unpopular view that his [Taylor's] dance vocabulary is meagre and that his own dancing is feeble, a (to me) distasteful blend of bigness and softness."[25] But, finally, this visiting British critic appears to have been bewildered by American modern dance in general.

--------------------------------- **1972** ---------------------------------

When Charles Reinhart took over as director, the American Dance Festival began to make a determined effort to prove how up-to-date it was. But in 1972 the festival deliberately took a look backward, for 1972 was its twenty-fifth anniversary, and the celebration emphasized the achievement of modern dance.

Festival participants included the companies of Louis Falco, Don Redlich, Murray Louis, Alvin Ailey, and, for the first time since Reinhart became director, José Limón. There were also some "fringe" events, including performances of works by June Lewis and Walter Nicks, a marathon concert of student works, an event staged by Margaret Beals in the city's Veterans' Park, and another outdoor event by Redlich, *She Often Goes for a Walk Just After Sunset*, which used parts of the campus lawn and sculpture court. In 1972 the festival also hosted for the first time meetings of the National Endowment for the Arts Artists-in-Schools Dance Component.

But the festival's highlights were performances by the new Repertory Company, directed by Charles Reinhart and Martha Myers, organized to celebrate the silver anniversary by performing revivals of what were termed "dance classics" by Martha Graham, Doris Humphrey, Charles Weidman, and José Limón, as well as a new work by Rudy Perez. Aided by grants amounting to a total of $130,000 from the National Endowment for the Arts, the Rockefeller Foundation, and the Ford Foundation for the filming and notating of its productions, the Repertory Company consisted of eighteen dancers chosen from 175 applicants at open auditions in New York City. One such audition, on 15 April 1972, was presided over by Weidman, Myers, Martha Hill, Theodora Wiesner, Bertram Ross, Patricia Birch, and Daniel Lewis and, as Anna Kisselgoff reported in the *New York Times*, it drew a crowd of eager dancers. But it turned out that at least two of them were there by mistake, for one young woman complained, "The notice was misleading. I thought dance classics meant classical ballet." And her companion sniffed, "I'm a ballet dancer. I'm not going to dance without shoes."

The festival made much of its Repertory Company. But Doris Hering could not see the point of all the self-congratulation: "I wonder why performing a work by Limón, one by Humphrey and another by Perez on the same program becomes a rare challenge. Should works by these people not be within the compass of any decently trained dancer?"[26] Although she had long sympathetically viewed the modern dance scene, Hering, who in 1972 became the executive director of the National Association for Regional Ballet, here displays what could be termed a balletic viewpoint.

Ballet companies usually perform works by several choreographers, and no one thinks it unusual that they do so. But in modern dance, as Hering surely knew, the situation was somewhat different. Although there are exceptions (such as Alvin Ailey's company), modern dance groups tend to be one-choreographer companies. Moreover, in the early days of modern dance, some choreographers wielded charismatic power over their dancers and discouraged them from working with representatives of other styles and techniques. Increasingly, however, dancers began to acquaint themselves with many techniques, and versatility became prized. Thus when Martha Hill established the dance department at Juilliard she insisted that all dance students take classes in both ballet and modern dance, and that school's continued emphasis upon versatility may help explain why eleven of the Repertory Company's eighteen members were Juilliard-trained.

Most previous attempts at organizing repertory companies had failed: somehow, the rugged individualists of modern dance just could not manage to work successfully and happily together for any long period of time.

The festival's new company deliberately made no plans for the future, as it was scheduled to self-destruct at the end of the summer. But that very fact raises the issue of how good a company it was or ever could have been: did it really have enough time to become the truly first-rate, stylistically eclectic organization it hoped to be? That problem troubled the critics, for though they wished the group well, they did not find it in any way extraordinary. Deborah Jowitt said, "The company has some very good dancers in it. They all look excited and brave on opening night, yet understandably tense. It's hard to become an instant ensemble." And Clive Barnes concluded in the *New York Times*, "It tried energetically, but it did not look much better than a talented group of students"[27]—which, to some extent, was exactly what it was.

The only premieres of the entire festival were two works by Rudy Perez, both related in some way to the anniversary celebrations. *Salute to the 25th* was the overall title given to a suite of dances presented both indoors and outdoors. It got under way inside Palmer Auditorium with "Salute," in which dancers lined behind Perez and tied a placard about him reading "25." Subsequent episodes took place on a lawn and in one of the campus parking lots. "Steeple People" and "Lot Piece/Lawn 1971" emphasized movements and formations for large groups of people. But Perez's most unusual creation was "Thank You, General Motors," a set of choreographed traffic patterns for one bicycle, six cars, and two motorcycles, to music by the Surfers, a local marching band. Don McDonagh commented, "The formation work of the cars was particularly fine, like a group of mammoth elephants on wheels."[28]

Like most of his works, *Asparagus Beach*, Perez's premiere for the Repertory Company, set groups of people moving through carefully devised patterns that occasionally took on emotional colorations. Some of these activities were disorderly, while others, said Jowitt, were "as neat as print" or reminiscent of "a bold, cursive script." The dance reminded Hering of the way people run and group themselves and huddle together in streets during a rainstorm. For the most part, said Hering, Perez "used everyday movement. Now and then it exploded into a series of jetés or a solo for a girl doing repeated falls that conveyed the momentary pressure of tragedy." The dance was enhanced by Thomas Skelton's lighting effects that made the dancers cast shadows on the auditorium walls, creating the illusion that solid human beings had turned immaterial when they left the stage.

Clive Barnes loathed *Asparagus Beach*: "It takes triviality, facetiousness and camp to their most inconsiderable lengths. It is neither fresh nor original, merely the sophomoric ramblings of an overaged sophomore." But other critics were genuinely pleased by it. Hering particularly praised the movement jokes and the way Perez "doesn't *make* humor. He discovers it and pins it down with the light touch of a lepidopterist." Several critics were fascinated by the woman's solo with repeated falls that Hering thought brought a hint of tragedy to the piece. Alenikoff observed that the anguished action, repeated many times, "suddenly humanizes the dance, cracking its noncommital surface by its injection of the personal, unexpected projection of agony." And Jowitt wondered, "Is it by coincidence that she [the dancer] looked like a Vietnamese village girl?"[29]

Whether one liked it or not, *Asparagus Beach* demonstrated that the Repertory Company was able to perform a dance of today. But what audiences were most curious about was how well it could dance the choreography of yesterday. In most cases, its performances were considered conscientious. But they were not always compelling. Speaking of the Repertory Company in Graham's *El Penitente*, Hering said that the work "has fooled a lot of performers. . . . It looks utterly naive. . . . But it is the naiveté of true sophistication. . . . These nuances have yet to manifest themselves in the three participants."[30]

In staging José Limón's *Emperor Jones*, the company took a great risk, for this adaptation of Eugene O'Neill's play, choreographed in 1956, had originally been acclaimed not so much for the ingenuity or expressiveness of its formal design (which could be preserved in a revival) as for the powerful performances of Limón, as the self-appointed ruler of a Caribbean island, and Lucas Hoving, as the White Man, his adversary. Such performances could not easily be duplicated by a young cast. Remembering the original production, Hering said she vividly recalled "the massiveness and misery of Limón's own gestures for Jones and Lucas Hoving's dry, decadent rapacious gait as the White Man. Their complementary strengths made one overlook occasional moments of muddled choreography." Although scarcely equal to Limón and Hoving, those roles' new interpreters, for Hering, possessed many virtues. Thus she liked Clay Taliaferro (as Jones) for the way "he combined the ignominiousness of a newspaper headline gangster" with "the tragedy of any human being living without values." And concerning Edward DeSoto (the White Man), she said, "I was fascinated by the way his body slithered on and off like a silent oil slick." But, she added, "some of the incidental punctuation in hands and head had been lost in translation or not yet learned." Barnes, who had also seen the 1956 cast, summed up the opinion of many critics: "The work as a whole did not seem to have the sharp impact of the original."[31]

Nor did the revival of Charles Weidman's *Flickers*, a parody of silent movies created in 1941. The characters in this spoof included such figures associated with the silent screen as a villainous landlord seeking to claim both a homestead and a virtuous maiden, a femme fatale (in more than the metaphorical sense) who has just escaped from a leper colony, a Valentino-like sheik, and a family of stalwart pioneers. The choreographic style tried to duplicate the running of film through a projector, the dancers occasionally jerking as if the film were about to go out of control.

Few critics thought the revival very funny, and a number of theories can be advanced to account for this. Audiences of 1941 might have looked down upon silent films as "primitive" and inferior to the more recent invention of the sound film; therefore, for such people, a spoof of silent films would have been almost automatically amusing. But by 1972 many of those once-derided films had attained the status of cinematic "classics." Moreover, Hering thought that the dancers of 1972 had no real sense of Weidman's comic style. These dancers simply treated the piece, she said, like "a charade."[32]

The Repertory Company's most ambitious revivals were Doris Humphrey's *New Dance* and *With My Red Fires*, two parts of the so-called "*New Dance* trilogy," choreographed in 1935 and 1936. Here, in three independent, yet thematically related, works, Humphrey concerned herself with a vision of an ideal society and with the depiction of forces inimical to the establishment of such a society. *Theatre Piece* (which, apparently, is now unrevivable) castigates the rat race of competition. In *With My Red Fires* a formidable matriarch tries to thwart her daughter's romantic desires: a portrait of what has come to be called "smother love," the dance is an attack upon the way one domineering person may blight the lives of others. Finally, in a work that was simply called *New Dance*, Humphrey offered a vision of individuals and groups moving harmoniously together.

The concluding section of this utopian piece had been notated and was occasionally revived with success by college dance groups. But the remaining sections of *New Dance* had to be reconstructed from memory by former members of the Humphrey-Weidman company, under Weidman's direction. Perhaps expecting an aesthetic experience equal to that provided by the revival of *Primitive Mysteries* in 1964, dancegoers eagerly awaited *New Dance*. But many would agree with Anna Kisselgoff that what they saw was a "real disappointment."

Both its movement style and the way that style expressed Humphrey's themes seemed naive. "To me," said Hering (who pointed out that she had never seen the Humphrey-Weidman company), the dance's "upraised arms, palms flat forward" and the dance's "deliberate adherence to the Wallingford Riegger score took on the didactic appearance of a sermon about brotherhood." Kisselgoff found *New Dance* both "limited in its vocabulary and deadened by its formality. There were marvelously inventive moments of atomizing the dancers as units and rearranging them in imposing formations. But these were few, and there was a certain naive beatitude in the barely discernible brotherhood theme." *New Dance*, Hering concluded along with many of her colleagues, "looked strangely wooden, strangely predictable."[33]

The surprise of the season was *With My Red Fires*, with Dalienne Majors as the matriarch and Nina Watt and Raymond Johnson as the young lovers. Here was a dance that, for many viewers, genuinely deserved revival. "A strange, ambiguous hybrid," as Alenikoff termed it, "*With My Red Fires* blends private drama with public ritual; meshing the universal and the particular in an allegory on possessive love and the relentless, crushing weight of authoritarian society on individual lives." The way Humphrey made the domineering mother become a symbol for dictatorship was considered most ingenious, and Jowitt saw in the dance references to "many aspects of dictatorship, public and private, and several kinds of ritualized societies. It is the curious, almost imperceptible way in which these layers dissolve in and out of the texture of the work which gives it the ambiguity that is so fascinating." Jowitt found the movement itself interesting: "The movement is full of angles—flexed feet, sharp turns at wrist and elbow and knee. Executed in steadily pulsing or pounding rhythms, it looks elemental and extraordinary at the same time. The spareness of incidental gestures is wonderful: the Matriarch lifts a leg only twice, and it becomes an extension of her pointing, accusatory fingers."[34] Thus the Repertory Company had at least one real success, and audiences interested in dance history could return home happy to have seen at least a bit of the past come vividly to life. As had been planned, all the company's productions were filmed. And then, also according to plan, the company disbanded.

───────────────────────── **1973** ─────────────────────────

José Limón died 2 December 1972, and with his passing the American Dance Festival lost yet another of the key figures associated with its development. The 1973 season, which attracted three hundred students, was dedicated to Limón's memory and a permanent scholarship was established in his name.[35] The Limón company performed at the festival, and, that summer, Ruth Currier was appointed Limón's successor as director. As a tribute to his memory, Carla Maxwell, a member of the company (and Currier's successor as director), created *A Suite of Psalms*, a duet for herself and Jennifer Scanlon that Don McDonagh said was "like a choreographic letter from an admirer to an artist, commenting on his work and offering a small-scale replica of it."[36]

A Dance/Television Workshop was established in 1973[37] for the purpose of exploring new techniques for televising dance. However, from the point of view of the general public, the festival's most unusual aspect was what was billed as a Mélange Weekend, a weekend crowded with performances—both during the day and at night, and both in Palmer Auditorium and outdoors—by several young choreographers. Participants included the Rudy Perez Dance Theatre, Marjorie Gamso's Dance Concoctions, Pilobolus Dance Theatre, Bruce Becker and Jane Kosminsky's 5 by 2 Company, and Nora Guthrie and Ted Rotante. Similar "mélanges," although not always billed under that title, would be features of many festivals in the summers to come.

This first mélange was uneven in quality and only a mixed success. A major miscalculation in programming was the scheduling of a multitude of dance events by Marjorie Gamso throughout the weekend. A minimalist and seemingly indefatigable choreographer, Gamso staged her works in such locations as a dance studio, the college arboretum, the Sculpture Court, a lawn, a student lounge, and a swimming pool. The audience that loyally turned up to watch her company soon found its curiosity turning to annoyance. It was a very hot weekend, and indoor and outdoor sites alike were uncomfortable. Thus *Delicate Negotiations*, a premiere, was performed in the airless East Studio, and, as described by Deborah Jowitt, the circumstances of its presentation prevented it from being a pleasure to watch: "Someone turns the fan off. At least half the audience wilts, grits its teeth, prepares to hate Marjorie Gamso." The dance consisted of steps performed "with minimal intensity and fluidity. Over and over." By the end, said Jowitt of the dancers, "I feel like killing them."

Gamso's style was not one capable of charming people made testy by the weather. Jowitt reported, "The Gamso dancers do have an ungainly look." And, formally, said Anna Kisselgoff, the dancers "were given a number of set movements or poses . . . which they appeared free to perform or repeat at will and at their own rate," and "while the governing ideas may be clear in her own mind, their execution is less impressive." Kisselgoff thought Gamso's best effort was *Decination*, performed in a lakeside clearing: "The gimmick here—and one that worked—involved a dancer's pointing a finger upon finishing a dance phrase. This was a signal for a man to plant a stalk of grain on the spot. A musical ensemble, the sylvan setting and the sight of more and more stalks rising from the ground—all this made "Decination" . . . the loveliest part of the Gamso opus."[38]

Like Gamso, Rudy Perez had his dancers perform in several locales, scheduling events in Palmer Auditorium and on the lawn. *Americana Plaid* and *Walla Walla*, his premieres, were in his usual—and to regular festival audiences, his familiar—style, which Jowitt described by saying that "the drill-team aspect is important; so is the contrast between the playful look of individuals—the springy runs and jumps—and the severe formations they usually end up in."[39]

Two "mélange" attractions, the Kosminsky-Becker 5 by 2 and Guthrie and Rotante, were programs of solos and duets by various choreographers. Kosminsky and Becker sought to present concerts that would encapsulate the history of modern dance. Kisselgoff praised them for their ambition and pointed out their weaknesses: "Both are very fine dancers. Yet in striking out on their own now to present a historical and repertory view of modern dance, they might benefit from some coaching." In particular, she thought that some excerpts from Limón's *There Is a Time* were "totally lacking in spiritual quality."

Becker, who was Helen Tamiris's nephew, attracted attention by dancing *Negro Spirituals*, a suite consisting of some of the solos to spirituals that Tamiris had choreographed between 1928 and 1942. Tamiris was one of the first white choreographers to take black culture seriously—to regard it as something more than exotic or piquant—and her solos created a stir when they were new.

Revived in 1972, they created another kind of stir. To begin with, these solos created by a woman for herself were now performed by a man. Nothing in the choreography makes explicit references to sexuality; nevertheless, some observers thought it strange to see a man dancing them. Others in the audience felt uneasy about seeing spirituals danced by a white person, male or female, and so would have been made equally uneasy had they been able to see Tamiris herself in the solos. Jowitt commented upon both the solos and some of the reactions to them:

> The dances are austere, deliberately repetitive, but rich in invention and dynamic shading. I think Tamiris was moved by the simple eloquence, naive sweetness and humor that spirituals share with most kinds of folk music. Her dance looks nothing like black dance today; some young black students in the audience are outraged, not giving a damn about how radical and sympathetic Tamiris' creation of these dances was back in the '30s, both artistically and politically.[40]

Corporate Images, a new work by Rotante, was part of his program with Guthrie. Unlike Kosminsky and Becker, Guthrie and Rotante did not attempt a historical overview of modern dance. Instead, they offered what Kisselgoff found to be good entertainment, and she called Guthrie and Rotante "well-trained dancers who are sharply tuned in to the values and humor of their own generation"; in fact, they "showed the timing and presence of an excellent vaudeville team."[41]

The real hit among the "mélange" attractions was the Pilobolus Dance Theatre. Named after a fungus and founded in 1971 by some Dartmouth College students, Pilobolus created a small sensation in New York when it appeared at the Space, an art center run by Alwin Nikolais and Murray Louis. The group's whimsical and grotesque dances were unusual in many ways: they were collaboratively choreographed, they derived from acrobatic movement rather than from conventional modern dance technique, and they were performed by an all-male company. As Kisselgoff noted in her review of the Connecticut performance, Pilobolus exemplified "a healthy attitude toward body contact . . . that would have been impossible on stage among men more than five years ago. Pilobolus's men have no hangups, and their ability to enjoy themselves has a contagious effect."

The invitation to perform in New London could be taken as a sign that Pilobolus was being regarded not just as a stunt by clever pranksters, but as an accepted part of the dance community. Moreover, although it still favored collaborative choreography, the company now included two women, and these women were professional dancers, not athletic students turned dancers. If some observers feared that Pilobolus was thereby in danger of losing its undergraduate charm, Kisselgoff was happy to find that "the group gains from the women's professionalism, and the women's dance orientation fits comfortably into a men's style in a work in progress."[42] This new piece, unnamed at its first showing, eventually acquired the title of *Ciona*, and Pilobolus made many return visits to the festival.

In addition to the "mélange" choreographers and the Limón company, festival participants included the companies of Alwin Nikolais and Erick Hawkins, the Inner City Dance Company, and Dance Theatre of Harlem. The Inner City company had been organized by Donald McKayle in Los Angeles, but Don McDonagh noted that McKayle was not listed as either director or resident choreographer on festival programs. Considering this a symptom of the group's lack of firm direction, McDonagh said, "This is a company with great energy but little finesse, and one longed to see the artistic hand of a knowing and autocratic director." Reviewing the season in *Dance Magazine*, Ernestine Stodelle agreed with McDonagh about the company's energy, but thought it entirely the wrong sort, for "the show on the whole was too Hollywood-geared for even recently innovative Connecticut College."

The problem of undirected, or misdirected, energy plagued Inner City's premiere, Talley Beatty's *Caravanserai*, which, said McDonagh, "wandered boundingly all over the stage. The endlessly repeated crossover jumps and turns began to have a numbing sameness." And Stodelle declared that such an emphasis upon glittering virtuosity made "short shrift of whatever structural forms the choreographer had in mind."[43]

George Balanchine's neoclassical balletic choreography came to the citadel of modern dance when Dance Theatre of Harlem presented his *Agon*, to Stravinsky, on a program that also included Milko Sparemblek's *Ancient Voices of Children* and Walter Raines's new *Haiku—A Dream for Brown Eyes*. Stodelle found the premiere "over-elaborate," and Balanchine's masterpiece dominated the bill. However, Dorothy Stowe, of the *Hartford Times*, thought that Raines's work, a set of seventeen vignettes akin to visual haiku, was "hauntingly beautiful" because of the mysterious way "the company drifted through a series of almost disembodied episodes, as if viewed under water."[44]

Choros of the Daughters of Okeanos, Erick Hawkins's premiere, was only an excerpt from a longer work-in-progress, *Greek Dreams With Flute*, a suite of dances on Hellenic themes. Yet many reviewers found that this delicate ceremonial piece for laurel-crowned women in filmy chiffon costumes was thoroughly satisfying in itself. Leslie Pfeil of the *Groton News* considered it "all very reminiscent of the chorus in classical

Greek tragedy. The flowing costumes accentuated the graceful lines of the nearly nude bodies underneath, and the flute accompaniment [by Matsudaira] helped to create an atmosphere of peace and serenity."[45]

─────────────────────── 1974 ───────────────────────

Writing about the 1974 festival for *Dance Magazine*, Rose Anne Thom titled her review "Innovation or Inundation?" Visiting Connecticut College for the first time, Thom, a young New York critic, was overwhelmed by the sheer quantity of performances: on some occasions, several events occurred, one after the other, on a single evening, the last of them scheduled for as late as 11 P.M. The festival had mushroomed to such an extent that it was now virtually impossible for any single individual to take it all in. If this meant that dancegoers had lots to choose from and that there was something for everybody, one could also fear that such a profusion of activities might prevent the festival from having any real focus.

The year's most startling innovation brought theater as well as dance to the Connecticut campus. Festival residencies by seven experimental theater companies—all of them members of the organization known as A Bunch of Experimental Theatres of New York Inc.—were arranged in association with the Eugene O'Neill National Theatre Center/National Playwrights' Conference (which had its headquarters in nearby Waterbury, Connecticut) and the Theatre Communications Group. Mercedes Gregory served as project director, and the participants included the Performance Group, the Ontological-Hysteric Theatre, the Ridiculous Theatrical Company, the Manhattan Project, Section Ten, the Mabou Mines, and Meredith Monk/The House. There were two new productions: *Lulu* by Section Ten, and Wallace Shawn's *Our Late Night* by the Manhattan Project. Justifying such theatrical programming, Charles Reinhart declared, "The wall which used to exist between theater and dance no longer does." He may have had a point, for one of the companies among the theater groups, Meredith Monk's multimedia The House, had appeared at the festival in 1970 as a dance attraction.

Once again there were "mélange" performances, this time billed as programs by "Emerging Generation" choreographers. And there were concerts by established companies, as well. Thus festival audiences had opportunities to see works by Kathryn Posin, Paul Taylor, Trisha Brown, Alwin Nikolais, Nora Guthrie and Ted Rotante, the Multigravitational Experiment Group, Sara and Jerry Pearson, Daniel Nagrin (who offered a retrospective concert of his solos since 1948), Louis Falco, Pilobolus, and Laura Dean. Nor was that all. Another innovative special program brought four choreographers and four composers together to collaborate on new works that were performed with the St. Paul Chamber Orchestra, which also presented a day-long "Bach Blast" of its own, conducted by Dennis Russell Davies. A benefit concert for the festival's scholarship program became an international event, for it contained African and Afro-American dances by the Chuck Davis Dance Company, Indian dances by Ritha Devi, and balletic pas de deux by Anna Aragno and George de la Peña and Lynne Charles and Victor Barbee.

Classes and workshops were equally eclectic. A second Dance/Television Workshop was directed by Roger Englander. Jeannette Stoner taught a dance-composition class for deaf students and gave demonstrations of their work. An expanded Community Outreach Program was directed by Walter Nicks, while Meryl Green supervised a Campus Community Classes Program that offered on-campus dance classes for children and teenagers, as well as special mother-and-child classes. In addition, a Dance Educators' Workshop was organized by Bonnie Bird and Marion North for dance teachers or movement specialists working with school-aged children.[46]

One might have thought that all these activities would be enough to keep Reinhart busy. Yet, in that busiest of summers, Reinhart was also running another festival. For the first time in their histories, the country's two major dance festivals, the American Dance Festival and the Jacob's Pillow Dance Festival, near Lee, Massachusetts, were under the same direction. Ted Shawn, for many years the director of Jacob's Pillow, had died in 1972. The 1973 season—a glamorous and star-studded, but financially troubled, festival—had been organized by Walter Terry, who resigned as director when his board declared that it did not wish to operate with such a high deficit. Therefore Reinhart, who was known for his efficiency and organizational abilities, was appointed acting director of Jacob's Pillow for 1974. Guiding two festivals appeared to pose neither practical nor artistic problems for him. The festivals, he told the press, "are not in competition. . . . The geography is too big. One is in the Berkshires, the other is on the shore. As for operations, I believe in delegation of authority. I have excellent staffs at both places."[47]

A development that would significantly affect the future of the American Dance Festival was the naming of Oakes Ames as president of Connecticut College, replacing Charles Shain. Ames had taught physics at Princeton University (1958–66) and, since 1966, at the State University of New York at Stony Brook, where he also headed the physics department. Reinhart says he remembers that Shain assured him that, even though Ames's background was in science, he believed in supporting the arts, and, therefore, the dance festival's future seemed assured at Connecticut College.[48]

All festival premieres in 1974 were works either by young choreographers or by the experienced choreographers chosen to participate in the special collaborations with composers. That venture, Project: Music and Dance (MAD, for short), resulted in new works by Bella Lewitzky (music: Max Lifchitz), Jennifer Muller (music: Charles O. B. Curtis-Smith), Manuel Alum (music: Ira Taxin), and Nancy Meehan (music: Rocco di Pietro).

The project was admirable in its ambitions. Yet Rose Anne Thom concluded that it was "difficult to measure" how successful it truly was. She said, "I sensed a certain tentativeness in the total performance, as though neither composers nor choreographers felt completely comfortable in the venture. The choreographers appeared limited to their familiar territory rather than challenged."

Of the collaborations, Thom thought that Meehan's *Yellow Point* "probably worked the best," in part because di Pietro's score "was similar to the kind of music she [Meehan] usually chooses to accompany her work. It was not bound by a tight thematic structure, but formed a textural atmosphere for the dance." Yet Thom also felt that "both the score and the dance rambled amiably without ever reaching, or trying to reach, a particular intensity."

For Thom, Lewitzky's *Five* also displayed a real "affinity between the dance and the music." This work contrasted "sharp, forced phrases of music" and "choppy" movements for dancers confined behind screens with lyrical music and fluid movements when the screens were lifted. Like *Five*, Muller's *Winter Pieces* contained a hint of dramatic or thematic significance. A study in alienation, *Winter Pieces* was, choreographically, a "mysteriously bleak landscape"; however, its music eventually became "too elaborate and dramatic. It was as if the music and the choreography took off in different directions and both for too long." Finally, Alum's *Yemaya* seemed "unfinished rather than unsuccessful," for, said Thom, in this ceremonial tribute to a goddess of the sea, "it was only in the final image of the dance that a compelling sense of the ritual was conveyed."[49]

The festival's other premieres included some very unusual dances. Laura Dean's *Changing*, presented in the arboretum, was a study in slow motion that many viewers found spellbinding. The three women in its cast were costumed to resemble highborn ladies who might have stepped out of a Gainsborough painting, and they somehow managed to move so slowly that it was virtually impossible to tell that they were advancing; nor, once one realized that they were indeed doing so, could one really be sure just how they were doing it. As Deborah Jowitt said, "You couldn't see the women's feet moving, nor did their bodies betray them with the slight side-to-side sway a walk usually engenders. They weren't *walking*, they were simply coming towards us — sailing very slowly and by infinitesimal degrees. Chess figures moved by a hidden hand." When they reached a stairway leading to a pond of water, the women seemed to float down it. Because the audience could not see the entire length of the stairway, the dancers were able to leave the space without anyone knowing exactly where they had gone. The effect was that of a magical disappearance. "They had sunken into the earth," said Jowitt. "Several small children ran to look for them."[50]

Trisha Brown's *Pamplona Stones*, a duet for Brown and Sylvia Whitman, involved the manipulation of two stones, two armchairs, a mattress, and a piece of fabric; and the dancers were required to converse as they moved. Contributing to the fun of the zany piece were the puns and wordplays of these conversations. Thus Jowitt remembers a moment when one woman told the other, "Now I have you cornered," as she herself walked into a corner.[51]

Stephanie Evanitsky's Multigravitational Experiment Group was one of several companies at the time to combine dancing with some form of acrobatics or gymnastics. The group also sought to defy or transcend the dancegoer's customary awareness of gravity by placing all action above ground on specially built constructions that would either seem to impose new laws of gravity or declare old laws of gravity inoperative. The construction designed for Evanitsky's enigmatically titled *Buff Her Blind — to Open the Light of the Body* involved three tiers of ropes, from which dancers hung and on which they walked and crawled. The apparatus was set up outdoors, and the dance was repeated at various times of day (including once, said Thom, at 4:30 A.M.). Its mood was gentle, with many dreamy crossings and fixed stares into space. "The piece was beautiful," Jowitt declared, "but very nebulous."[52]

The productions by the husband-and-wife teams of Sara and Jerry Pearson and Nora Guthrie and Ted Rotante were more modest in scale. In *Exposure* the Pearsons remained in the center of the Palmer Auditorium stage and never budged from the spot. Instead, said Jowitt, "he kept

Alison Chase, Robby Barnett, Martha Clarke, Moses Pendleton, Michael Tracy, and Jonathan Wolken in Pilobolus's *Monkshood's Farewell*, 1974. Photo, © 1974 Herbert Migdoll.

curled up, or in some way secret, through almost the whole dance, while she very beautifully and deliberately examined the space from safe perches on his crouched-over back or stood on his lying-down body and quietly pulled his limbs into fences around herself." Because they never looked at each other, Jowitt pronounced the dance "strangely dispassionate." Guthrie and Rotante were more lively in their *Learn To* (which was also referred to as *Success* in festival announcements), a study of various kinds of dancing, beginning with an exhibition waltz, continuing through scenes in a dance studio, and culminating in the depiction of an unsuccessful attempt to win a gold trophy in a competition. Jowitt found it "a small, casually serious dance."[53]

One of the year's greatest successes was the work by Pilobolus now known as *Monkshood's Farewell*, but which was listed as *Monkshood's Delight* on festival programs. Here, Pilobolus made its acrobatic tricks take on a medieval coloration, complete with a scene reminiscent of a joust, so that the viewer beheld what Jowitt called "a world of medieval grotesquery, both sinister and comical." Thom found the piece intriguing because it seemed to indicate that "the group might venture beyond the 'acrobatic-shape' stage. Though the literary references of this work escaped me, I sensed a medieval atmosphere and I was aware of individuals expressing personalities rather than anonymous creatures."[54]

With so many different things going on, 1974 might very well be called a season of both innovation and inundation. But it could also have made some observers wonder if *too much* might be going on at the festival.

1975

The inundation continued. The 1975 festival included works by Raymond Johnson, Ze'eva Cohen, Dance Theatre of Harlem, Elizabeth Keen, Pauline Koner, Bhaskar, Iolani Luahine, the Alvin Ailey Junior Company, Twyla Tharp, Chuck Davis, Trisha Brown, Nora Guthrie and Ted Rotante, Nancy Meehan, Pilobolus, and Kathryn Posin. In addition, Violette Verdy and Helgi Tomasson of the New York City Ballet danced classical pas de deux, Kirk Nurock presented a concert of his music, and performance artist Robert Wilson staged what he termed a "conversation" between himself and Christopher Knowles. Knowles also led a student workshop. The alliance between the festival and A Bunch of Experimental Theatres was maintained with performances by Section Ten, the Ridiculous Theatrical Company, the Manhattan Project, the Performance Group, and the Mabou Mines (which staged the premiere of *The Saint and the Football Players*). Members of those companies conducted classes and workshops. Among the summer school's special offerings were a workshop in music and dance collaboration led by Sheldon Soffer, a dance therapy workshop led by Linni Silberman, and a Total Theatre Project, involving people from the fields of dance, drama, music, design, and television who pooled their talents to create a fifteen-minute work for television.[55]

Bhaskar, an Indian dancer, and Iolani Luahine, a Hawaiian dancer, represented two major non-Western dance forms. Iolani Luahine was awaited with special interest, for she was considered an authority on the authentic and uncommercialized hula. Accompanied by her niece, Hoakaklei Kamauu, who narrated, sang, and played coconut tree and gourd drums, she proved to be, said Deborah Jowitt, "a small, fierce, merry old lady. Her hips sway, her hands slice gentle gestures in the air, her eyes snap."[56]

The return to the festival of Twyla Tharp's company made some dancegoers astonished at the development Tharp's choreography had undergone since her first visit in 1969. Since then, she had achieved great popular success with her works to eighteenth-century music, ragtime, jazz, and old pop tunes, and she had even choreographed pieces for the Joffrey Ballet. As Robb Baker, of *Dance Magazine*, put it, she had become "a kind of cult figure, a distinction which it would seem she herself has coveted." Since the late sixties, said Baker, Tharp had developed "one of the few truly distinctive and creative movement vocabularies in all of contemporary dance." Nevertheless, Baker was forced to conclude that her work "has also become repetitive, self-satisfied, even a bit coy."

Tharp's New London programs included the American premiere of *Ocean's Motion*, a romp—vaguely reminiscent of *Deuce Coupe*, her hit for the Joffrey to music by the Beach Boys—that examined the behavior and dance styles of certain teenagers of the 1950s. "Dressed in satiny greys and pinks," reported Baker, "five Tharp dancers spiraled, flailed their arms, clenched their fists, toyed with balance, chewed bubblegum, walked nonchalantly on and off the stage and struck assorted would-be macho poses (both the men and women alike). . . ." All this struck Jowitt as pleasantly "sassy and aggressive." But *Ocean's Motion* deeply disappointed Baker: "It is simply *Deuce Coupe* revisited (to Chuck Berry, instead of the Beach Boys) . . . the new work is a rather pale carbon of that earlier classic."[57]

Audiences in search of something more truly novel, though perhaps equally gimmicky, found it in Pilobolus's deliberately untitled *Untitled*, which began innocuously enough by showing two women in fancy nineteenth-century dresses braiding each other's hair. Then, as if they were characters from *Alice In Wonderland*, they magically grew to enormous heights, hairy masculine legs extended from beneath their skirts, and they appeared to give birth to two nude men. Although the sexual symbolism of such sequences was provocative, Laura Shapiro nevertheless thought that in addition to being untitled, the piece "also looks unfinished and, except for the stunning idea it's based on, untidy. . . . Such a startling and curious concept really calls for more than it receives here." Shapiro was also bothered because Pilobolus appeared to be settling too easily for gimmickry: "They're pretty good gimmicks, to be sure: the dances are full of provocative images, they just lack any movement ideas to connect them."[58] Shapiro's reservations prefigure complaints that would increasingly be made about Pilobolus.

Pauline Koner made a choreographic return to the festival with her new *Solitary Songs*, a study of human isolation. Calling it "gripping" and "definitive," Patricia Mandell, of the *New London Day*, described the action: "At first, the dancers can make only harsh, disharmonious movements of opposition and chaos. There is no strength and unity among them. . . ." However, when they are struck down, "a bond forms among them and they seek the strength that unity brings."[59] Once again, Koner —like her mentor, Doris Humphrey—recognized human weaknesses, yet refused to succumb to despair.

Also returning to the festival that year was Kathryn Posin, who had been the last young choreographer to receive the Doris Humphrey Fellowship. *Waves*, Posin's premiere of 1975, soon established itself as one of the most popular items in her company's repertoire. Mandell described it as "a peacefully slow dance of undulating movements, giving the eerie feeling of being underwater and the difficulty of moving underwater. . . . The seven dancers twine around each other . . . and follow each other symmetrically in what must be very disorienting steps to execute. But all is accomplished with perfect grace."[60]

Two other attractions that season were a little dance and a big one. Jowitt called Elizabeth Keen's *Line Drawing*, the little dance, "crisp and forthright. In one prominent part, the six dancers, all dressed in black and white, do a lot of stamping. As if they were planning to type the dance instead of to do it. When a softly luscious Fauré song is heard, they seem to be tracing its outline and no more."[61]

With its cast of forty, Ted Rotante's *Going to the Sun Road* was one of the "people pieces" for which the festival became known in the 1970s. Since it began in the gymnasium and progressed across campus to a green near Palmer Auditorium, it exemplified yet another popular form of the period: the environmental dance. A *Hartford Courant* critic who wrote both under the pen name of Dinovelli and under her full name of Donna Dinovelli particularly liked the opening episode: "Seen from the gym balcony, the dancers seemed to take on the quality of musical notes, floating across the bare gym floor." Dinovelli also liked the way the dancers, after moving to the green, vanished over an embankment. The attractively designed Connecticut College campus had stimulated the imaginations of several choreographers since Charles Reinhart took over as director. But although audiences responded warmly to these environmental spectacles, Reinhart now says he suspects certain college officials regarded them as nuisances because they made it difficult to keep buildings and grounds in proper order.[62]

By the mid-seventies, it seemed as if the festival had virtually taken over the entire campus. Such growth could be interpreted as a sign that the festival was booming. Yet Anna Kisselgoff looked beyond the euphoria and wrote, "One question that needs to be asked is whether the festival has outgrown its campus setting."[63]

1976

Anna Kisselgoff's speculation of 1975 became an urgent issue in 1976. That year, the festival was formally incorporated as American Dance Festival, Inc., the Internal Revenue Service granting the corporation tax-exempt nonprofit status. Reinhart says his principal reason at the time for seeking incorporation was to increase the festival's eligibility for funds from arts councils, among them the Connecticut Commission on the Arts. Such councils, he points out, insist upon dealing with clearly—and legally—defined organizations, rather than with, say, some legally nebulous project that seems to have ambiguous connections with a college. But Kisselgoff found potential significance of another sort in the incorporation: "This means that Reinhart can pick up the festival and take it elsewhere."[64]

And Reinhart threatened to do just that. Ordinarily affable, optimistic, and even ebullient in his public statements, Reinhart in 1976 startled the festival's home community and the dance community in general by charging that New London's habitual indifference to the festival had become a genuine scandal. He drew up a whole list of complaints: "There is no support from the local area in ticket buying or in financial support from business. Businessmen won't advertise in our programs. . . . In New London, we have a town that doesn't care about its cultural facilities." These charges led the *New London Day* to editorialize that, if the festival moved, the area might annually lose $3 million generated by the presence of students, performers, and audiences, almost all of whom patronized local businesses and restaurants.

Reinhart's statement of discontent had one unexpected result. Mayor Humphrey J. Donnelly of Newport, Rhode Island, announced that if New London did not appreciate its dance festival, he was ready to "hijack" it to his own town. What is more, he did—for at least part of the summer. After a season of classes and performances as usual in New London, 28 June–7 August, the American Dance Festival held its first festival away from Connecticut by scheduling performances in Newport, 22–27 August.

Reinhart speculated that, in seasons to come, the festival might offer events concurrently in the two cities, and he said he thought that, unlike New London, Newport was capable of attracting a steady stream of visitors who could be induced to attend dance performances.[65]

He was right. A seacoast city, Newport was long a vacation spot for the wealthy, and its palatial mansions were considered objects of both architectural and sociological curiosity. A major jazz festival was held in Newport from 1954 to 1971. Although Newport's popularity as a resort had declined somewhat, in the mid-seventies it was starting to perk up again with newfound civic pride, and extensive restoration and historical preservation work was being done. Dancegoers crowded Rogers High School Auditorium for the festival's week of performances by Pilobolus, Paul Taylor, and the debut of the American Dance Machine, with Judith Jamison as guest artist in *Cry*, Alvin Ailey's tribute to black women. In some ways, it was all the festival could have hoped for: the theater was full and the audiences were happy.

Unfortunately, as Amanda Smith reported in *Dance Magazine*, Rogers High School Auditorium was cavernous and unappealing, and Paul Taylor remembers that its lack of proper stage equipment made his company's engagement there "a nightmare." The theater lacked a pit, and placing the orchestra on the auditorium floor, as had been initially proposed, would have made it impossible for many members of the audience to see over the musicians' heads and instruments. Finally, the problem was solved—but in a manner neither attractive nor comfortable—by crowding the musicians onto a small platform built at one side of the proscenium arch.[66]

Nevertheless, Pilobolus and Taylor were as popular as ever, and Taylor staged the premiere of an unusual work. With a setting by Alex Katz that consisted of an enormous cube, *Polaris* consisted of two renditions of the same dance. Yet, while the choreography remained unaltered, each rendition was for a different cast to different music by Donald York and with different lighting effects. Taylor says it was intended to be "an exercise in looking" to make spectators aware of how much music and dancers' personalities can affect responses to choreography. York's score was light in texture for the first version of the dance, darker in quality for the second. Since the choreography was always the same, these extreme musical contrasts troubled Smith: "What I think is the biggest flaw in the work is the discrepancy in this first rendering between the mood of the music, which was light and playful, and the mood of the dance, which had an

Victoria Uris, Carolyn Adams, Linda Kent, Elie Chaib, and Christopher Gillis in Taylor's *Polaris*, 1976.

overall darker quality to it. It seemed, simply, the wrong music with the right dance. The second section, with lights lowered and starker music, seemed the truer version."[67]

American Dance Machine had been founded by Lee Theodore in the belief that musical comedies often contained first-rate choreography —choreography of genuine interest for its own sake, quite apart from the context of the show in which it occurred; yet this choreography usually vanished into oblivion when the show closed. American Dance Machine sought to preserve significant examples of such choreography, and its Newport offering was a tribute to the Broadway and Hollywood choreographer Jack Cole. Though it contained film clips of Cole's dances, demonstrations of his technical vocabulary, and reconstructions of excerpts from his musicals, Smith considered the program "not always very carefully but together," and she said that "the dancers gave the impression of being more a pick-up group than a real company."[68]

Earlier, in New London, the festival's main season had included works by Bill Evans, Annabelle Gamson, Pauline Koner, Chuck Davis, the Metropolitan Opera Ballet Ensemble, Alwin Nikolais, Bella Lewitzky, Nora Guthrie and Ted Rotante, Murray Louis, Nancy Meehan, and Walter Nicks. There were also theatrical presentations by Mabou Mines and concerts by Kirk Nurock and Natural Sound.

That, as usual, was a lot. But the festival now had its own tradition of creative abundance to live up to. And, for at least one critic, this festival had choreographic abundance without also having much choreographic creativity. Writing in *Dance Magazine*, Jackie Coleman sighed because "the great days of the Festival seem really to be only memories: this summer the dances there were often likable, but disappointingly unexceptional."[69]

One new dance that many viewers found likable was Pauline Koner's *A Time of Crickets*, a lyrical piece that Doris Hering found praiseworthy for its moods "of celebration, of oneness, of hope."[70] Another attractive celebration was Bella Lewitzky's *Greening*. The dancers in this ode to youth and innocence often reminded Coleman of "saplings growing." Yet she added, "Much about this was lovely, but the central idea of 'Greening' was disturbingly hazy."[71]

Still another cheery piece was Murray Louis's *Glances*, to a score by jazz composer Dave Brubeck that was played live at its premiere by a combo headed by the composer's son, Darius Brubeck. Choreographer and composer worked well together, yet managed to maintain their independence. First, Louis choreographed the dance in silence and sent a videotape of it to Brubeck, who proceeded to write a score for it. Then, after hearing Brubeck's music, Louis made a few adjustments to his choreography so that music and dance would be in harmony. The result was what Anna Kisselgoff termed "a fruitful collaboration" that was a credit to the festival's Music and Dance project, which had commissioned the work. *Glances* kept alternating between lyricism and liveliness. The lyrical passages, for Kisselgoff, possessed "the serenity of the eternal," whereas in the lively sections, the choreography matched the score, which sounded like "a sophisticated gloss on Broadway show tunes."[72]

Audiences seeking sterner stuff might have found it in Bill Evans's new *Dallas Blues*, a depiction of an urban demimonde that included a sadomasochistic homosexual pas de deux and scenes involving the confusion of sexual identities. Coleman remained unconvinced and unenlightened: "There was a kinky appeal to all this which the choreographer seemed to enjoy, and the dancers were nicely slinky, but the piece was hard to believe and simplistically crafted."[73]

Nora Guthrie's *The Five Boons of Life* was inspired by a fairy tale for adults by Mark Twain. But whereas Twain's original story is wry, Guthrie's choreography merely showed an encounter between a young man (Ted Rotante) and a well-meaning Good Fairy, who presented him with dancers symbolizing pleasure, love, fame, and riches. Guthrie herself was the Good Fairy and, said Hartford critic Donna Dinovelli, the piece "was best when Guthrie was on stage. At other times the dancers surrounding Rotante seemed to be part of a crowd scene just filling space."[74]

Ballet made one of its sporadic—and not always warmly welcomed —appearances at the festival when the Metropolitan Opera Ballet Ensemble offered a program that ranged from *Carnaval*, Michel Fokine's delicate fantasy of 1910, to Bob Fosse's "Rich Man's Frug" from the musical *Sweet Charity*. There were also three works by Norbert Vesak, the troupe's director: *Die Fledermaus Variations*, *Belong*, and *Once for the Birth of . . . .* The ensemble was made up of dancers from the Metropolitan Opera and attempted to provide them with opportunities to dance on their own outside the demands of the operatic repertoire. But Coleman did not consider it an impressive company. She found the dancers insufficiently adept in Fosse's musical comedy style; she thought the revival of *Carnaval* looked insubstantial, and, using a phrase she also used for Evans, she called Vesak's choreography surprisingly "simplistic."[75]

If 1976 was the year in which Reinhart shocked the community by accusing it of providing insufficient support for the festival, so it was also the year in which the festival received a shock of its own. That autumn, Connecticut College's new president, Oakes Ames, after acknowledging that "we have made every possible effort to accommodate the needs of the Festival within the constraints of our budget," went on to declare that, because of economic limitations, "we feel we must ask everyone using the campus to share in its operational expense." Therefore Connecticut College now proposed to charge the American Dance Festival an annual rental fee of $15,000. Announcing the proposal to the press, Reinhart said, "This represents a radical change in the College's policy toward the Festival," and he added that "due to a breakdown in negotiations with Connecticut College, the Festival plans to begin a search for a new home."[76] Reinhart committed the festival to staying at least one more year in New London, and some observers hoped for a rapprochement. But Reinhart also made it clear that when he talked about picking up the festival and moving it, he was not making idle threats.

────────────────────────── **1977** ──────────────────────────

Relations between Connecticut College and the American Dance Festival had not improved by 1977. Yet a busy season was offered and, once again, after the usual session in New London, 25 June–6 August, the festival moved to Newport, this time giving nine performances, 19–27 August, the Newport attractions including Dance Theatre of Harlem, Annabelle Gamson, Don Redlich Dance Company, Carmen de Lavallade and Company, and Pilobolus. Among the special features of the New London season was a conference of the National Endowment for the Arts Artists-in-Schools Dance Component, which brought together four hundred dance teachers, administrators, and representatives of dance companies and state arts agencies. A special emphasis appears to have been placed upon dance education, for, in addition to community classes and workshops in New London, similar activities were scheduled in Newport and in scattered locations throughout southern Connecticut.[77]

It was also what could be called an international summer, and two great forms of dance outside the ballet and modern dance tradition were featured. Maria Benitez and Luis Rivera gave a concert of Spanish dance, and both artists were praised by Don McDonagh:

> Miss Benitez showed her strong footwork in a crackling display of temperament and discipline. She has a forthright manner that makes little use of ruffles and flourishes and emphasizes a direct attack on movement. . . . Mr. Rivera has a highly developed sense of pictorial correctness, and he made a nice frame for her in their duets as well as a sharp impression in his solos.

The dances of India were represented by Lakshmi, who offered a recital of traditional Bharata Natyam dancing. One of the unusual features of what McDonagh called "an impressive program" was the fact that Lakshmi's accompanying singer was her mother, Balasaraswati, by universal agreement one of this century's greatest Indian dancers and teachers.[78]

The American debut of the London Contemporary Dance Theatre gave New London audiences a look at a major modern dance company from abroad. Directed by Robert Cohan, a former dancer with Martha Graham, it was an outgrowth of the London School of Contemporary

Dance, which had been founded in 1966 by Robin Howard, a London restaurateur and patron of the arts who had been so impressed by the Graham company that he vowed to make modern dance flourish in Britain. At first, many of the London group's productions were heavily derivative of Graham. But, in time, the company developed its own style, choreographers, and repertoire.

There were those who feared that bringing British modern dance to the ADF would be a matter of carrying coals to New London. Yet in the first of two articles she wrote about the London Contemporary Dance Theatre Anna Kisselgoff was delighted to find that "the results are remarkable. Mr. Cohan has not created a copy of the Graham company but a group that has its own character and uses any choreographic idiom it pleases." In her second review she wrote, "Several aspects of the company stand out. One is the commitment that the troupe's 17 members bring to their dancing. They have the ensemble spirit of a young artistic organization that is still fervent about itself." The repertoire included works by Cohan, Siobhan Davies, and Robert North, and Kisselgoff was particularly pleased by Cohan's elegiac *Stabat Mater* and his *Cell*, a study of trapped people.[79]

Continuing to encourage new choreographers, the festival offered premieres by three "Emerging Generation" choreographers: Danny Williams Grossman (who had danced with Paul Taylor's company as Daniel Williams), Senta Driver, and Douglas Dunn. Beginning as a three-part canon and ending with an icon-like image of Christ, Grossman's *Ecce Homo* was, according to Clive Barnes, "an odd work, musical and passionate, that combined a quirky, lively imagination with a sensitive visual sensibility." *Bella*, a collaboration between Grossman and Judy Jarvis, was a set of children's games involving the two choreographers and a toy horse. The games were set to excerpts from Puccini's *La Bohème* and *Madame Butterfly*; but, said Barnes, they bore "no emotional link to the music. However, the huge toy horse is a joy in itself, and the contrasts between the performers and the recorded dramatics does evoke something of that odd poignancy you notice with the children playing games oblivious to murder in Alban Berg's 'Wozzeck.'" Summing up his work, Barnes said that Grossman had "a diversity of styles, yet no choreographic signature at present."[80]

Like Grossman, Senta Driver had danced with Paul Taylor's company. But, since leaving it, she had developed an unusual—and, to some

Senta Driver and Timothy Knowles in Driver's *Sudden Death,* 1977. Photo, Johan Elbers.

dancegoers, a disconcerting—personal style. Believing that modern dance's earlier concern for effort and weightedness had given way to an almost balletic lightness, she began to emphasize weighted steps and the pull of gravity. Her dances were often made up of strenuous, and almost grotesque, activities. Barnes said of her style, "Miss Driver is fond of walking or running and particularly fond of parachute rolls. She favors images of corpses and embryos." He described her new *Sudden Death* in the following way:

A man (Timothy Knowles) and Miss Driver are first seen with their legs astraddle a yellow line. A sound—a tank, perhaps—twice approaches and twice recedes, while the performers graphically demonstrate various degrees of shivering, gibbering panic. At the end, the woman grabs the man and kisses him passionately. Miss Driver is an intellectual, so possibly she was taking the phrase "Sudden Death" in its Elizabethan sense.

The choreography suggested to Barnes that Miss Driver possessed "a questing mind and a willingness to experiment with space and juggle with an audience's expectations."[81]

Douglas Dunn, the third "Emerging" choreographer, contributed *Celeste*, which Joyce Mariani of the *Norwich Bulletin* thought was "perhaps best termed an exercise in attention." Formally, it was an environmental piece of a sort now familiar to New London audiences: after performing patterned movements outside on the green, the cast moved into Palmer Auditorium, where the work concluded. Yet it did contain surprises: two parachutists landed among the dancers outside, and the activities inside the auditorium occurred to a showing of scenes from the film *National Velvet*.[82]

Pilobolus offered its old familiar gymnastic tricks and several new pieces. But Barnes considered them to be in the nature of sketches. *Shizen*, a duet for Alison Chase and Moses Pendleton, was a living-statue essay with "graceful contortions" and "serpentine gymnastics." The mystifyingly titled *Renelagh on the Randon* turned out to be a mimetic and, to Barnes, somewhat feeble solo in which Jonathan Wolken portrayed a swordsman fencing in time to music. In *Harvest*, a solo for Martha Clarke that was also known as *Wakefield* and that was billed as a work-in-progress, Clarke sat by rows of bundles resembling cabbages. She stabbed some, seemed to give birth to some, and harvested others. Trying to find some significance in this, Barnes speculated, "It seems she might be hinting at the self-destructive nature of birth as a function of the life cycle. On the other hand, it may just be about someone who stabs cabbages in place of kings."

Whereas Barnes was slightly disappointed by the sketchiness of many works by Pilobolus that season, I found the company more satisfying in its shorter works than in its longer efforts. One of the troupe's problems, I wrote in *The Dancing Times*,

> involves continuity. Most of the choreography . . . consists of surprise effects. But that means the dancers must always find some satisfactory way of going from one effect to another. In brief pieces, this is easily managed: the piece features one type of movement or gymnastic trick, and when its possibilities are exhausted the dance ends. However . . . longer compositions . . . are grab-bags of tricks, and so many tricks following each other without respite may exhaust viewers.[83]

Don Redlich's new *Finisterre* seemed cryptic to some viewers. Yet it was clearly a serious effort. In this melancholy mood piece, said McDonagh, a choreographer with a "normally ebullient sensibility" adopted "a more somber tonality" in order to create a work in which the dancers "inhabited a world that appeared beyond conflict, where the sense of leave-taking dominated all else."[84]

Untitled, Arthur Mitchell's work-in-progress for Dance Theatre of Harlem, was presumably equally serious in its intent. But McDonagh pointed out that *Untitled* is what many choreographers like to call dances with which they are still struggling; at its festival showing, Mitchell's work was nothing but a collection of bits and pieces, and "it has a long way to go before it settles in to have a local habitation and a proper name."[85]

A novel by Camus was the inspiration for Daniel Nagrin's *The Fall*, which Ernestine Stodelle called "a penetrating study of an egocentric intellectual who is incapable of forming natural, healthy relationships." Although the solo combined movement and text, there was no dancing in the conventional sense because, said Stodelle, "such a man could never dance." Yet, through an adroit use of gesture, Nagrin offered "a Goyaesque delineation of the true imprisonment of a man's ego."[86]

The list of festival attractions may suggest that in 1977 it was creativity as usual at Connecticut College. Yet there was also a strange mood of uncertainty on campus. The festival staff was finding college officials increasingly unsympathetic. Some of these officials, in turn, were regarding the festival as a sort of cultural monster that annually threatened to swallow up their college. While students were taking classes and choreographers were rehearsing dances, serious discussions were being made by a panel organized by Reinhart to consider the possibilities of moving from New London. Its members included June Batten Arey, an arts consultant; Marilyn Grossman, president of New London Friends of the Festival; Rhoda Grauer, executive director of the Twyla Tharp Dance Foundation; Stuart Hodes, chairman of the New York University dance department; Robert Joffrey, director of the Joffrey Ballet; and Peter Zeisler, director of the Theatre Communications Group.

After months of soul-searching and fact-finding, a decision was made that autumn: the American Dance Festival's new home would be on the campus of Duke University in Durham, North Carolina.[87]

VII

OVERVIEW 1969–1977

A NEW BEGINNING

With Charles L. Reinhart as director and Martha Myers as dean, the American Dance Festival entered upon a period of unprecedented growth. Reinhart did more than introduce unfamiliar choreographers to Connecticut College audiences. He combined change with development, and, in many instances, development involved the inauguration of new projects or the steady expansion of existing activities. Reinhart also found ways of obtaining financial support for these activities. During the first four years of his tenure as festival director, he obtained grants from the National Endowment for the Arts, the Connecticut Commission on the Arts, and the Ford and Rockefeller foundations, and in some years one or more of these agencies awarded the festival several grants, each going to a different summer project.

By holding special seminars, conferences, and institutes in fields as varied as television, therapy, and criticism, the festival began to appeal to members of the dance community other than performers, technique teachers, and choreographers. Moreover, the summer school's traditional basic curriculum was enlarged so that in addition to classes in modern dance technique and composition, students could study ballet, jazz, African dance, Indian dance, improvisation, anatomy, and therapeutic massage.

At times Reinhart could be almost gleeful when he spoke of these myriad activities, as if he found the very process of expansion exhilarating for its own sake. Thus, announcing the 1974 season, he declared, "Here's this big pot . . . let's pour all this into it and see what comes out." Ferment was valued, and whatever individuals may have thought of the festivals after 1969, almost no one found them totally dull. Visiting Connecticut College in 1971, the British critic who wrote under the names of both James Monahan and James Kennedy was thunderstruck by an abundance of "activity, diversity, and American earnestness," and he concluded that the festival was most un-British because "Americans are, perhaps, more addicted than we are to congregations and to worrying, in congregation, a subject to death—or to life."[1]

Attending Reinhart's first festival in 1969, Doris Hering was so struck by its diversity that she termed it a "smorgasbord."[2] That term caught on, and, as the festival continued its eclectic policies, many other writers compared the summer sessions with smorgasbords. These comparisons were not always intended to be favorable.

Whereas commentators on the festival in the mid-1960s complained that the New London seasons suffered from a sameness of programming and a cut-and-dried curriculum, now there was what Anna Kisselgoff in 1975 characterized as a bewildering array of events. However, as far as performances were concerned, quantity did not necessarily guarantee quality. A look at programs from 1948 to 1968 will readily show that many performances included inconsequential works by minor choreographers; yet programs after 1969 contained their own inconsequentialities: the choreographers responsible for them simply were different, and audiences soon discovered that an awkwardly constructed abstraction in the minimalist mode could be just as stultifying as a clumsy retelling of a Greek myth.

In her 1975 article[3] Kisselgoff noted that, given the range of festival activities, critics could not be expected to see and review every performance. The more the festival grew, the harder it became to appraise as a whole. During the festival's earlier years such critics as John Martin, Walter Terry, Doris Hering, Margaret Lloyd, P. W. Manchester, and Walter Sorell usually devoted at least part of their summers to New London, and, by choosing their dates carefully, they could manage to see most, or all, of the performances and also have time to observe classes. Thus, by reading certain critics, one could obtain a clear idea of the festival's development from season to season.

By the early 1970s this was no longer possible, and not simply because some of those older critics had died and others had retired or moved on to other occupations. Whereas earlier festivals were often confined to a weekend or two near the end of the term, there were now performances throughout the entire six-week season. Therefore few, if any, critics could be expected to stay long in New London—especially since the New York summer dance season was also expanding. Some publications sent several reviewers to Connecticut during a single season. Yet many events received only scanty coverage, at best. And readers of such reports did not necessarily get an overall view of festival seasons.

For most observers this was an unavoidable annoyance and one they were willing to forgive, especially since the New London campus was now livelier than it had been in years. Yet there were those who considered the festival's eclecticism a sign of decadence.

Erick Hawkins has warned that such eclecticism may lead to the vitiation of modern dance as an art form. "You can't have eclecticism and have power," he declares. "That's why Connecticut [American Dance Festival] is going downhill. It's going down the drain like a gurgle out of your bath, because there's no vision." Hawkins does not believe that the process of attrition began with Reinhart. Rather, he has specifically charged, in an interview with Sali Ann Kriegsman, that Martha Hill "destroyed modern dance when she brought ballet into Juilliard" back in 1951.

Hill justifies her policies by pointing out that Juilliard's dance division was expressly founded to provide students with professional training, and, given the contemporary dance scene, young dancers—even those who do not intend to join a classical company—should have at least some knowledge of ballet. Critics and aestheticians may complain, and with justice, that modern dance has grown too balletic or that purely classical ballet technique can be distorted by the influence of modern dance. But only a fanatic would discourage a student of one dance genre from being inquisitive enough to learn about other genres. The presence of ballet—or, for that matter, non-Western dance—in the curriculum of both Juilliard and the American Dance Festival helps make students aware of the manifold possibilities of the art to which they are devoting themselves.[4]

Other criticisms of the festival's eclecticism were made in articles by James Monahan (Kennedy). Writing as James Kennedy in the *Manchester Guardian Weekly*, he conceded that "Americans are, of course, stimulated —so was I in Connecticut—by the variety of styles and theories which now abound." Then he somberly added that "Americans with a longish memory of the subject would, I think, agree that this is, indeed, a time of decadence in their 'modern dance.'" However, Kennedy failed to identify the specific Americans "with a longish memory" who shared that view.

His conclusions about decadence appear to derive from a love of tidiness and from the notion implicit in some of his writing that at any particular time only one style can be dominant in each of the arts. On the basis of similar theories, other observers have attacked the pluralism that has developed in all the American arts since the 1960s. Pluralistic tolerance, they fear, may lead to an abdication of aesthetic standards and to a dissipation of creative energy. Yet it could be argued in reply that pluralism may reflect a healthy distrust of dogma—including aesthetic dogma—and that pluralism may be inevitable in a society in which the mass media can easily acquaint audiences with a multitude of art forms from around the world: thus pluralism may even be a sign of cultural abundance. Nevertheless, writing as James Monahan in *The Dancing Times*, the British critic foresaw only "a break-up (and break-down) of genuine creative energy."[5]

Critics may have argued over whether it was a virtue or a fault. But no one could deny that, as Anna Kisselgoff put it, "Flux . . . has become the policy of the festival . . . there is a deliberate attempt at lack of focus." Reinhart himself expressed this view in a profusion of metaphors: "Our main job is to make sure this doesn't become a fixed institution. We must keep the doors open so new ideas can be born, come forth, blossom. It is so easy to be comfortable and sit back, but that's the beginning of death."[6] Reinhart could bound like a grasshopper from idea to idea and project to project, and if this at times could be perplexing or disconcerting, he managed to get things done. Thus, for years, Selma Jeanne Cohen had tried to organize a dance critics' conference at New London because, she says, she wished to call attention to criticism "as an important activity that took diligence, intelligence, and hard work." Theodora Wiesner had always told her that the summer budget would not permit such a conference. But Reinhart helped bring the first critics' conference into existence in 1970. Reinhart also made sure that the festival maintained its admirable record of commissioning works, and with its Project: Music and Dance, supervised by Sheldon Soffer, choreographers and composers were brought into collaboration.

Reinhart's concern for Community Outreach activities has been equally strong, and in his support of such programs he exemplifies what could be called one of the blessed paradoxes of modern dance. The advocates of modern dance have always insisted that it is an art of the

utmost seriousness—hence their distrust of ballet's supposed frivolity
—yet, at the same time, modern dancers have thought of their art as one
capable of attracting and holding a large audience, if only people could
somehow be enticed to see it. Reinhart is a populist in this tradition.
Especially after the well-meaning but consistently unsuccessful attempts of
his directorial predecessors to take dance into the community, he could
easily have confined himself exclusively to events on campus. Instead, he
insisted upon outreach, and he appears to have been motivated by both
practicality (outreach might eventually win new friends and supporters
for the festival) and pure idealism (dance was a wonderful art that deserved
to be widely known and loved). Under the direction of Walter Nicks,
Community Outreach programs were instituted in 1969. By 1974 Nicks
and members of his company were offering dance classes not only in New
London, but also in nearby towns, and Reinhart insisted, "These are not
workshops for dancers. They're also for shlubs like me."[7] Summing up his
attitude toward such programs as they developed in New London and,
later, in Durham, he said, "If we want the arts to take root, we must get
really down to the community to make it [art] a higher priority in people's
lives, not a one-time thing. We're determined to make the arts a familiar,
not a foreign substance in their life. And if you're responsible to the
community, it will be responsible to you."[8]

Will it always? During the mid-1970s, Reinhart may have asked himself
that question increasingly often. Dance classes and workshops may have
somehow enriched the lives of children and inquisitive adults, yet there
was little increase in support for the festival by local businessmen, and in
1976 the New London City Council rejected a request that the festival
receive $7,500 from community development funds.[9] Nor were audiences
necessarily flocking to dance concerts. Over the years the festival had had
its share of sold-out performances. Yet, more often, one could buy a ticket
right up to the rise of curtain, and in 1976 it was estimated that of Palmer
Auditorium's 1,330 seats, between 700 and 800 were usually filled at
each performance. It was not only New London residents who were
indifferent to the festival. Certain nearby communities along the Connecticut shore annually attracted affluent and well-educated vacationers. Such
people would almost certainly attend plays or concerts in winter. But
nothing could draw them to modern dance in summer.[10]

For Reinhart and everyone else associated with the festival, lack of
community support, though a serious problem, was not a new one. Mar-

tha Hill, Jeanette Schlottmann, and Theodora Wiesner could have told Reinhart sad stories about their own efforts to make New London dance-conscious. What came as a rude surprise in the mid-1970s was what Reinhart and his staff regarded as a significant shift in the attitude of Connecticut College's administration. To a great extent, the festival had been lucky. Because two presidents of the college—Rosemary Park and Charles Shain—had supported the festival enthusiastically, Reinhart simply assumed that Oakes Ames would be equally supportive. The festival's existence on campus during the presidencies of Park and Shain could even be described as idyllic. However, stonyhearted lawyers or businessmen might have called the festival a legal and financial mess. For one thing, its exact relationship to Connecticut College had never really been defined. As Reinhart has said in conversation,

> The festival just existed. There was a very nice woman in the account-ing office who handled financial matters for the festival—and that was it! A little pot of money—from any surpluses that had accumu-lated in previous years—was kept aside, and it was dipped into when necessary. The relationship between festival and college was, at best, strange. Yet it was one I was used to, for I'd never had a formal contract with any of the artists I'd worked with. I never remember even thinking about our official relationship to the college. I just felt we were all in this field together trying to make the light shine.

In fact, the festival might never have been incorporated if such a step had not been found necessary in order to obtain arts council funds.

When Shain retired, he assured Reinhart that his successor was a lover of the arts. But Reinhart was perhaps too quick to assume that Ames would therefore prize dance above the other arts. Reinhart may also have been unwilling or unable to realize that, as the festival grew, it threatened to make more and more of the campus unavailable for other summer activities. Then in 1976 Ames declared that everyone using the campus should share in its operational expenses. That October he pro-posed that the festival make a cash contribution of $27,400; the follow-ing month, he modified his request, asking for $15,000 rent.[11]

It soon turned out that this $15,000 was to be regarded only as "a base figure." Ames wrote Reinhart on 3 August 1977, "Inflation in costs will require the College to increase that fee for the 1978 season and in subsequent years." Ames also clarified his own ideas of a summer arts program:

we want to continue the summer dance program at the College as part of a more extensive effort in the arts. The Committee [College Committee on the Arts] envisions a program encompassing all of the arts which are taught at the College during the academic year, and which would be an extension of these programs. In addition to dance, there would be music, theater, and studio art. . . . However, if the college is to develop summer activities in music, theater, and art, in addition to dance, we are likely to be faced with some difficult space problems. . . . We think that such adjustments can be made, but only if the dance program stays at about the present size.[12]

Reinhart's response to all such proposals was, "We're not a cute little thing anymore. The festival would begin to die if its growth didn't continue."[13] Reinhart's exasperation is understandable. Yet, in its own way, so is Ames's fear that the festival might be taking over the campus. The statements of Reinhart and Ames exemplify two opposing attitudes regarding a college's cultural policies. Ames's is that of an educator and a practical administrator. He sees the arts as a necessary and valuable part of his college's curriculum, and because he wishes to have a balanced curriculum he tries to insure that no single art takes precedence over the others. In contrast, Reinhart's attitudes suggest that he is one of those thinkers who believe that, in democratic America, a college or university may serve as an equivalent of a Renaissance patron by sheltering and promoting artistic projects and organizations that may benefit not only the student body, but the entire community. By nurturing such projects and organizations, a college may gain acclaim and distinction, just as a Renaissance prince achieved fame as a supporter of artists. The dance festival had regarded Connecticut College as its Medicis. And now the Medicis were charging rent.

Once the issue of rent had arisen, other grievances started being aired. Some members of the buildings-and-grounds staff fretted because students trampled lawns and flowerbeds when they staged outdoor events. The college had long discovered that, although dancers can seem sylph-like on stage, dance classes can be rough-and-tumble sessions that subject floors and walls to considerable wear and tear. Martha Myers points out that any time students gather temporarily at a college other than the one they attend the rest of the year, they may be more lax in their standards of campus behavior than they would be at their home schools. A few even indulge in petty theft—stealing books from libraries, or silverware from the cafeteria—sometimes virtually for the sheer thrill of it. Thus it may have been understandable that, after more than a quarter-century of dance on campus every summer, some Connecticut College staff members may have grown weary of the festival. A longtime observer of the festival also wonders if certain officials might have found the festival a troublesome presence for still another reason: Connecticut College was now emphasizing that it was a coeducational institution, but to these officials dance may have had the reputation of being primarily a "woman's art."

Fortunately, if Connecticut College was unsure just how much it wanted the festival, other communities sought to lure it. In 1976—the year the festival first held performances in Newport—two ski associations in Killington, Vermont, expressed interest in having the festival relocate there.[14] Newport and Killington were found unsuitable, and the festival's advisory panel got down to work. After giving serious consideration to eleven possible sites, the panelists selected three final candidates: Duke University, the University of Massachusetts at Amherst, and the University of Wisconsin at Milwaukee. Questionnaires were sent to these institutions, containing such queries as these:

> What would be the feeling of the University and the community about profanity and nudity in performance?
>
> Is there someone the Festival can identify who would help bypass the bureaucratic system of the University when necessary?
>
> Are the studio spaces, living spaces, theater and cafeteria located in close proximity to one another . . . ?

Duke continued to impress Reinhart and his panel. Therefore they directed another question specifically to that university: "The Panel . . . felt that the American Dance Festival must continue to maintain its independent entity in residence at Duke University. Would this status present a problem regarding the 'rules and regulations' of the University . . . ?"[15] The reply must have proved satisfactory, for the festival chose Duke.

The origins of Duke University go back to 1838 when Brown's Schoolhouse, a one-room log school in Randolph County, in central North Carolina, was rebuilt and renamed Union Institute. In 1851 it became Normal College, a teacher training school, and in 1859 it was reorganized yet again as Trinity College, a liberal arts college under the auspices of the Methodist Church. Some years later, however, Trinity's faculty and staff began to feel they were languishing in rural isolation, and when a chance came to relocate the college, the opportunity was seized.

A Baptist women's college had thought of establishing itself in Durham, then decided not to on the grounds that Durham was a factory town totally unsuitable for young ladies. Whether or not it may have been an unsuitable town, Durham was incontrovertibly a "factory town" and a "tobacco town," a town that had the reputation of being a less desirable place to live than two other nearby cities: Chapel Hill, site of the University of North Carolina, and Raleigh, the state capital. For much of its history, Durham has suffered from a kind of civic inferiority complex, and its citizens have been quick to take offense at slights against their community. They have also, on occasion, been quick to take action to upgrade it, socially and culturally. The Baptists' rejection of Durham enraged many residents, among them Washington Duke, whose family after the Civil War had established a financial empire based upon tobacco products. Hearing that Trinity College wished to move, he offered to donate money to it if it would come to Durham, which it did in 1892. Historians fond of drawing parallels might well liken this acquisition of a new civic treasure in the 1890s to Durham's wooing of the American Dance Festival in the 1970s.

Just as Connecticut College was originally associated with the "New Woman," so Trinity in its early years in Durham became involved with several controversial issues. In 1896 Washington Duke offered Trinity $100,000 if it would admit women students on equal terms with men. A potentially more inflammatory incident occurred in 1903 when John Spencer Bassett, a professor of history at Trinity, published an editorial in the *South Atlantic Quarterly* in which he suggested that the two greatest Southerners were Robert E. Lee and Booker T. Washington—a linking of names sufficient in itself to make diehard racists seethe—and then proceeded to deplore the treatment of blacks. Many influential citizens demanded his dismissal, yet Bassett was given full support by Trinity's faculty and administration.

Trinity College was transformed in 1924, when James Buchanan Duke, son of Washington Duke, signed a $40,000,000 endowment to create Duke University, in honor of his father. Extensive building was undertaken, and the university acquired the distinctive look it still retains. Duke University consists of two campuses a mile apart, separated by a wooded tract: the West Campus in the Gothic Style and the East Campus in the Georgian style. The American Dance Festival's advisory panel must surely have felt encouraged by the fact that the West Campus contained Page Auditorium, a 1,507-seat theater adjacent to the university's cathedral-scaled chapel. Moreover, there was studio space on the East Campus, which at that time was often unused in summer. Equally encouraging to the committee was the enormous enthusiasm of certain Durham residents, who were determined to bring the festival to North Carolina. And Terry Sanford, who was named president of Duke University in 1969, was known for his commitment to the arts. As governor of North Carolina from 1961 to 1965, he had overseen the establishment of the prestigious North Carolina School of the Arts in Winston-Salem, and he liked to refer to North Carolina as "the state of the arts." Sanford has even said in conversation that "the golden thread in North Carolina's history is its support for the arts."[16]

Euphoria seems to have brought the festival to Durham. Some of that euphoria was generated by Vicky Patton, a personal assistant and social secretary to Sanford who was often placed in charge of special projects —including special summer projects—at the university. Her interest in dance increased after she became a friend of Suzanne Manning, a North Carolina dancer and choreographer, and her husband David Manning, a novelist who later served as media director for the festival's first season in Durham. In 1976 Patton organized Summerdance, a series of dance classes on Duke's East Campus, and Loblolly, an organization designed to promote summer dance, music, and drama. She sought advice from Nancy Hanks, at that time the head of the National Endowment for the Arts and a member of Duke's board of trustees. Hanks, in turn, suggested that she study the programs developed by Charles Reinhart in New London.

She therefore paid a visit to Connecticut College and promptly fell in love with the festival. "It was the most magnificent thing I'd ever seen," she says. A few months later, she was surprised to learn that the festival was thinking of moving. "So," she remembers, "I thought to myself: why not bring it here? Yet, at first, the very idea of the ADF at Duke sounded preposterous." Nevertheless, she was encouraged in her attempts to lure the festival to Durham by her husband Robert Chapman, the Mannings, and some of their like-minded friends, and she was able to persuade Terry Sanford of the festival's importance.

However, for a long time she was unable to make Reinhart think seriously about Durham. "He was just not interested in the South," she says. "Finally, I asked him if I could get him down here in a private jet, would he come? He said yes to that. But now I had the problem of finding a jet!"

Euphoria again prevailed. The Durham supporters of the festival had managed to arouse the interest of several officials of the Liggett Group, a Durham-based conglomerate that produced such varied goods as liquor, tobacco, pet food, and athletic equipment. Liggett provided a jet for Reinhart, and Reinhart got his first taste of Durham euphoria.[17]

Several factors may have convinced Reinhart that Durham had more than enthusiasm to offer. Durham was part of a metropolitan area, with a population of more than a half-million people, known as the Durham–Raleigh–Chapel Hill Triangle. All three cities were university towns, and between them was Research Triangle Park, a center for government and corporate research. As a result, the Triangle area had the highest per capita concentration of Ph.D.s in America. That fact alone suggested that an educated audience might exist for the dance festival.[17]

Under the agreement that was eventually made between Duke and the festival, the festival would pay the university $14,000 rent. Since that was only $1,000 less than the rent Connecticut College proposed to charge, one might wonder what advantage there was in relocating. But Duke was to be more than a landlord. The Duke University Office of Development and the Liggett Group pledged to coordinate a campaign to establish a million-dollar trust fund for the festival. To facilitate the move to North Carolina, Reinhart appointed June Batten Arey, an arts consultant, as the festival's North Carolina consultant for programming and development, and while he commuted between New York and North Carolina, she was in Durham developing community interest, planning subscription drives, and negotiating the arrangements with Duke. The American Dance Festival had long been considered modern dance's Mecca. Now Mecca was moving South.

The move was made with trepidation as well as anticipation, and even some of the festival's greatest enthusiasts in Durham were uncertain how modern dance would fare in their community. However, Reinhart points out, "We had one thing in our favor. Much to our surprise, the ADF's struggles in Connecticut were written up as stories not only in the dance publications, as you might expect, but in the daily papers as well. The ADF was suddenly hot news. So if Durham didn't know just what it was getting, it certainly knew it was getting something big."

VIII

SEASON BY SEASON

1978–1985

1978

With the American Dance Festival's move to the Duke University campus, Durham became a lively place for dancegoers to visit in the summer.[1] Audiences flocked to performances, and the festival aroused considerable local interest. Cultural organizations turned over their mailing lists to the festival without charge. Volunteers from church groups and senior citizen clubs addressed festival flyers. Committees to support the festival were organized in Durham, Raleigh, and Chapel Hill. The region's bookshops began to stock dance books.

Once the festival got under way, the sight of dancers crossing the campus often made Duke University employees drop their work and rush to the windows, just to see what the dancers were up to. Discovering that, in addition to being physically attractive, dancers were usually also mentally alert and socially charming, prominent citizens vied with one another in giving parties and receptions for members of companies appearing at the festival, and Anna Kisselgoff assured readers of the *New York Times* that Southern hospitality was not a myth.

The Arthur Hall Afro-American Dance Ensemble went from the campus into the town to give free performances and classes at churches, schools, and community centers. Barbara Roan staged a parade through the city streets featuring dancers, clowns, a juggler, a drum major, a fire engine, National Guard trucks, and people distributing handbills advertising the festival. As his own contribution to the summer's excitement, Daniel Nagrin organized an old-fashioned cakewalk competition that became an annual event for summer students. Dance came to Durham and conquered.

The press releases and ceremonial speeches of that summer contained many noble sentiments and flowery phrases, at least two of which deserve close examination. Advertising brochures celebrated "A Rich Heritage Since 1934." That date is significant for, with the move to Durham, Reinhart and his staff more than ever stressed the American Dance Festival's links to the Bennington festival. By emphasizing this association with Bennington, the festival in 1984 was able to hold a fiftieth anniversary season only twelve years after it had celebrated its twenty-fifth anniversary in New London. An argument could be made against such constant harking back to Bennington because during World War II there had been no Bennington festivals, and the festival that opened in Connecticut in 1948 could therefore be considered a new venture. Yet that Connecticut festival was unquestionably an outgrowth of Bennington, and its guiding spirits included some of the people responsible for Bennington.

There were also practical advantages in calling attention to Bennington. To be able to point to "A Rich Heritage Since 1934" might help convince potential donors that far from being a newly established and possibly fly-by-night outfit, the festival was a stable institution. And to be able to point out that a project founded at Bennington had then been transplanted to New London and was now in Durham helped make it clear that the festival was an independent entity, rather than an offshoot of any specific college or community.

There were similar implications in a second remark that merits attention. Greeting the audience at the opening performance, Duke's president Terry Sanford declared, "We have never pretended this is a Duke University project. I welcome you to a North Carolina project."[2] Several levels of meaning can be discerned in this statement. First of all, it reflects Sanford's commitment to the arts of his state. Yet it, too, calls attention to the essential autonomy of the festival as an organization *at* Duke and working *with* Duke, without being totally *of* Duke.

The dancers seemed happy that summer. So did most of the audiences. Yet there were some objections to the season's programming. Linda Small said in *Dance Magazine* that the festival began in its new home "on a cautious note—with an eye to pleasing its new hosts and paying its bills." Similar conclusions were reached by Deborah Jowitt in the *Village Voice*. She said, "By cannily presenting proven successes by brilliant choreographers . . . and nothing too difficult, too experimental, the festival has probably secured a loyal audience for the seasons to come."[3] Such critics had a point. Yet one should avoid belaboring it, for at no time in its history since 1948 did the festival function primarily as a showcase for the avant-garde.

The 1978 season opened on 17 June with a gala celebrating the history of modern dance. There were speeches by Terry Sanford and Governor James B. Hunt, Jr. Annabelle Gamson performed her reconstructions of solos by Isadora Duncan and Mary Wigman. A filmed interview with Charles Weidman was shown. The José Limón Company's performance of *The Moor's Pavane* was introduced by Pauline Koner, Betty Jones, and Lucas Hoving, all of them members of the original cast and all on the faculty for 1978. And the diversity of contemporary dance was exemplified by Paul Taylor's *Aureole* and Pilobolus's *Ciona*.[4] Subsequent performances were by the Taylor company, Pilobolus, Jane Goldberg and Charles Cook: Jazz Tap, Eliot Feld Ballet, José Greco, North Carolina Dance Theatre, Pauline Koner Dance Consort, Lakshmi Shanmukham, Twyla Tharp Dance Foundation, Arthur Hall Afro-American Dance Ensemble, American Dance Machine, Senta Driver's Harry, Daniel Nagrin, and the Don Redlich Dance Company. The Taylor company immediately became a festival favorite, and audiences also enjoyed the witty acrobatics of Pilobolus.

If the critics who accused the festival of being cautious could charge that there was nothing controversial about most of these attractions, no one could deny that they were varied in style. Nor could anyone deny that the Duke campus was exciting that summer. Thus, in the same article in which she gently chided the festival for its conservatism, Small declared that the season's most stimulating activity occurred in classrooms, studios, and student lounges where people representing different aspects of dance were able to get together and exchange ideas.

An innovation in the curriculum that summer was an outgrowth of MAD (Music and Dance) called MAD Jr.: Choreographers and Composers Workshop for Young Professionals, directed by Sheldon Soffer. Here, the emphasis was not upon producing a body of finished work, but upon investigating the process of collaboration.[5]

Ironically, one of the season's attractions that could be cited as representing an unabashed appeal to popular taste turned out to be one of the festival's greatest disappointments. The American Dance Machine had been asked to stage one of its programs of dances from old Broadway musicals. But, because of conflicting contractual agreements, the Dance Machine's main company proved unavailable, and Lee Theodore, the director, had to form a second company for Durham. This hastily assem-

Alison Chase, Moses Pendleton, Jonathan Wolken, and Robby Barnett in
Pilobolus's *Molly's Not Dead*, 1978. Photo, © 1978 Herbert Migdoll.

bled troupe was billed as the Bravo Team—"a misnomer if there ever was
one," wrote Giora Manor, an Israeli critic reviewing the festival for *Dance
News*, who felt that all the Dance Machine was able to provide was "a
rather weak copy of its Broadway successes."[6]

Two premieres were decidedly lighthearted in tone. Possibly to com-
memorate the festival's move to the south, Pilobolus set *Molly's Not
Dead* to country music. Choreographically, it was what Jowitt called "a
hillbilly bash": the cast divided up into feuding clans, and when dancers
announced that someone named Molly had died, bodies were lifted in
acrobatic variations upon a country funeral. The choreography was also
studded with bawdy jokes on a fraternity-house level of humor—among
them, a sequence in which three men glued to one another like Siamese
triplets went off in amorous pursuit of a young lady. Such jokes caused
Small to complain of "a disturbingly nasty sexuality" in the piece. And
Jowitt concluded that *Molly's Not Dead* "doesn't seem quite fully formed":
it was nothing more than "a series of jokes."[7]

Don Redlich's *One Guiding Life* was a spoof on the snarled personal affairs of characters in soap operas. "Everyone screws everyone else with the speed and glazed fervor of wind-up rabbits," Jowitt noted. But many of the jokes were obvious, and Jowitt said that after a few minutes of laughing, "I suddenly stopped caring."[8]

In two new solos Daniel Nagrin looked back upon his career. Such retrospection was probably occasioned by the fact that Nagrin had recently undergone knee surgery and was only beginning to be able to dance again. The premieres turned up on a program of older solos, originally choreographed by Nagrin for himself but revived on this occasion by other dancers. *Time Writes Notes on Us*, danced by Marcus Schulkind, was a little anthology of gestural patterns from Nagrin's choreography that, for Jowitt, "seemed to be Nagrin's way of acknowledging that all his fierce solos spring from a single sensibility." Nagrin himself appeared in *Getting Well*, and the solo depicted his process of convalescence. Each stage of recovery was set to a different piece of music. But that, for Jowitt, was the trouble with the piece: instead of making "his own organic time," Nagrin had to tailor his episodes to fit the music, and "all the new musical beginnings make the dance feel very, very long." Nevertheless, the dance as a whole impressed her as deeply felt.[9]

Another premiere in a serious vein was Pauline Koner's *Cantigas*. Subtitled "A Medieval Masque," it contrasted merry scenes for dancers resembling strolling players with somber episodes, all containing references to death. The dance's fascination lay in these emotional juxtapositions. Nevertheless, I found the dance's appeal primarily intellectual, and, writing in the *New York Times*, I speculated that this may have been because the "characters never seemed individualized human beings. They remained allegorical figures in a rigorously structured medieval sermon."[10]

The season's most unusual new work was Senta Driver's *On Doing*. Set to a text by Tom Johnson that enumerated a number of ways in which a step might be performed, the choreography demonstrated some of these possibilities. Driver's variations included hardly doing a step, overdoing it, and not doing it at all. Like many of Driver's dances, *On Doing* mixed methodology with mischief, and—also like many of her dances—it delighted some viewers and annoyed others. Small was not amused: "Sincere or not, it comes off more of a cerebral exercise than a dance, an irritatingly arch lecture-demonstration." But Manor liked the way the piece "explored the very nature of performing itself. The message, clear and crisp, was that body language is much more precise, lucid and compact than spoken language."[11]

The season ended with almost everyone concerned with the festival rejoicing. Yet, as the applause faded, certain problems began to loom. The festival's budget, which had been $636,000 at New London and Newport in 1977, had risen to $861,000 in Durham, and though ticket sales in Durham brought in $134,000, the festival had a $84,351 deficit at the summer's end. Moreover, Kisselgoff and other critics began to wonder in print just when, if ever, that much-talked-about million dollar trust fund would become a reality. Nevertheless, there was no question about leaving Durham: a concerted fund-raising campaign began on local and national levels, and the festival announced that in 1979 it would collaborate with the Brooklyn Academy of Music in commissioning a new work by Laura Dean.

Meanwhile, Connecticut College, not wishing to be idle as a dance center, sponsored a summer dance program of its own, coordinated by Laurie Cameron and Carolyn Coles, as part of a summer arts session. But some observers found the summer project disappointing, and, after 1978, although dance continued to be part of its regular winter curriculum, Connecticut College no longer offered special summer dance activities.[12]

1979

Before the 1979 season opened, the Liggett Group, which had been expected to provide the festival with much moral and financial support, announced that it was moving from North Carolina to Montvale, New Jersey. Although, as Charles Reinhart points out, it has continued to contribute generously to the festival, geography now made it seem a well-wisher from afar, rather than a visible force in the Durham community.[13] Instead, it was the festival itself that now seemed a part of Durham. To emphasize its ties to the area, it opened its second Durham season, 19 June, with a program by local exponents of traditional forms of folk and country dancing and country fiddling.[14]

An innovation of 1979 was a Town Hall discussion series, in which critics and philosophers discussed aesthetic issues. The scholarly papers that were read and the critics' responses to them were later collected in *Philosophical Essays on Dance*, an anthology edited by Gordon Fancher and Gerald Myers.[15] Festival programs included performances by the Dancers of Bali, Pilobolus, and the companies of Alvin Ailey, Kathryn

Felix Blaska, Martha Clarke, and Robby Barnett in Clarke's *Haiku*, 1979.

Posin, José Limón, Arthur Hall, Laura Dean, Merce Cunningham, and Paul Taylor, as well as the debut of Crowsnest.

Crowsnest was the first of several subsidiary groups that were to develop out of Pilobolus, each of these separate organizations putting the parent company's acrobatics to new uses. A choreographic collaboration like Pilobolus, Crowsnest was the brainchild of Martha Clarke and Robert Barnett, of Pilobolus, and Felix Blaska, a Russian-born dancer who had been trained in France and who had achieved acclaim on the Continent as a choreographer for both ballet and modern dance companies. Crowsnest specialized in vignettes on grotesque, even bizarre, themes. Reviewing the troupe's debut for *Ballet News*, Susan Reiter acknowledged that its pieces possessed "a strong dramatic sense," yet she was disturbed

Laura Dean company in Dean's *Music*, 1979. Photo, Larry Craven.

because so many were "concerned with a type of deformity." Therefore, she decided, "The unvaried debut program was a continuously dark, uneasy odyssey with no real destination in sight."[16]

The closing night of the festival, 28 July, brought the festival out of Durham and into living rooms across the nation, for the premiere of Paul Taylor's *Profiles* was telecast live by the Public Broadcasting Service. Always on the lookout for new scores, Taylor had asked to hear some of the music composed for the previous year's workshop for young choreographers and composers. Taylor was so impressed with a piece by Jan Radzynski, a Polish-born emigrant to Israel, that he decided to use it for his new dance. Robert Greskovic of *Ballet News* thought Taylor must have created at least part of the choreography for *Profiles* with television in mind, for he found that much of the abstract dance for two couples "moves in a relatively shallow space and concentrates on sculptural forms," and that the "flattened frieze-like angle of view . . . presents easily read, maximal forms." Such concern for visually striking forms resulted in a dance that "looked compelling, even reduced to the tube."[17]

The critics who charged in 1978 that, possibly to attract a new audience, the festival was avoiding controversy could not have made such a complaint in 1979. In addition to the grotesqueries of Crowsnest and Taylor's experiment with television, there were premieres by two controversial choreographers, Laura Dean and Merce Cunningham.

Dean's *Music* was the jointly commissioned work that the festival and the Brooklyn Academy of Music had announced the previous season. As she had done for many of her previous works, Dean provided both the choreography and the score, and the choreography—again as in many of her previous works—emphasized repetitions of, and variations upon, units of activity, including the spinning movements that had become Dean's choreographic trademark. Whereas some choreographers disturbed viewers by their urgency, it was Dean's very refusal to hurry that made the sixty-five-minute piece bothersome to certain members of the audience. Yet those who could adjust to the pace of *Music* found it satisfying.

Reiter, who admired it very much, described its action in detail. *Music* began with a "leisurely but never lethargic" sequence. Speaking of the dancers, Reiter said, "The relaxed, lilting energy of their gently shaped arm and leg movements makes them look dreamy. They give the impression of moving through vapor." Eventually, the tempo picked up in passages of spinning, yet "there is no sweat flying, no sense of strain, just pure energy carried by the driving music." The dance then swept along to the end. However, Reiter observed, "Rather than a feeling of finality, there remains an exhilarating sense of nearly intoxicating energy."[18]

If the first performance by the Cunningham company in Durham prompted furrowed brows and nervous titters, it also generated fierce discussions in lobbies during intermissions and warm applause. Cunningham was in an impish mood in his new *Roadrunners*, to a score by Yasanao Tone that combined electronically modified sounds for piano and viola with the recitation of fantastic legends from an ancient Chinese encyclopedia. The choreography had nothing literally to do with China. Instead, as I reported in the *New York Times*,

"Roadrunners" abounded with swift but very brief phrases—squiggles or doodles of movement, one might call them—that came to sudden stops in which everyone stood motionless in some peculiar pose. There was such a constant alternation of stops and starts that sometimes one had the illusion of seeing photographs of the dance at the same time that one was seeing the dance itself. . . .

"Roadrunners" was a comic dance—an abstract comic dance, to be exact. It was funny, not because it retold a funny story about

Merce Cunningham and Meg Eginton in Cunningham's *Roadrunners*, 1979.
Photo, Lois Greenfield.

real life, but because its movements were incongruously juxtaposed so that the choreography seemed intrinsically witty.[19]

Other new works were by Kathryn Posin and Pilobolus. As its title suggested, Posin's *Windowsill* was dominated by a large window frame inside which dancers were posed. The premiere gave Charles Horton of the *Chapel Hill Newspaper* an opportunity to discuss the strengths and weaknesses of Posin's style in general:

What has evolved from her work is a combination of neo-classic elements of ballet, the acrobatics of modern dance and the spontaneity of jazz.

What has also evolved is an indecision about just where some of the body lines and movements are going and a lack of a clear architectonic concept of some of her works as a whole piece. . . .

Each section of the new work opened with something of a tableau in which a body was frozen in some rather ominous pose inside a windowsill. From this static beginning the dancers immediately moved into a work that was exceptionally intense and frugal in pattern and movement. The work is extremely classic in its economy of space and movement. . . .

The ending of "Windowsill" is consistent with the style of conclusions that has almost become a trademark with Posin—the work doesn't seem to end, it simply stops.[20]

According to the *Chapel Hill Newspaper*, Pilobolus's *The Detail of Phoebe Strickland* was offered incomplete as a work-in-progress. But, as a company, Pilobolus once again astonished audiences and caused Roy Dicks of the *Spectator* to say, "I'm throwing off my critic's mantle of reserve and balance and am simply going to rave: Pilobolus is fabulous!"[21] Whatever reservations some critics might have about its works, Pilobolus never failed to win adherents to the cause of modern dance.

---------------------------------- **1980** ----------------------------------

The American Dance Festival's increasing concern with dance therapy was apparent during the 1980 season when the summer school's offerings included Dance Therapy Workshops, directed by Arlynne Stark and Dianne Dulicai, as well as the First National Body Therapy Workshop, which was devoted to discussions of the therapeutic value of several approaches to the study of the human body. A continuing commitment to dance forms other than modern dance was reflected in a program of jazz and jazz dance, 23 June, with Dizzy Gillespie, Scoby Stroman, Honi Coles, and the Rutgers/Livingston Jazz Professors, and by the fact that the festival's opening night gala, 17 June, was "A Salute to Vaudeville Dance" that paid tribute to authentic vaudeville dance, to the modern dance pioneers who had performed in vaudeville, and to contemporary dance in the vaudeville tradition. Joe Roth, an eighty-four-year-old veteran of vaudeville, presented a comic mime act with a recalcitrant deck chair as his prop. Jay Marshall appeared as a magician and ventriloquist. Sandman Sims did some expert tap dancing. Catherine Coplin and François Szony were teamed in an adagio act. Elisa Monte danced reconstructions of solos by Ruth St. Denis. And Michael Tracy, of Pilobolus, offered a solo which, because it involved balancing precariously on contantly shifting paper rolls, could be called a modern-day vaudeville routine.[22]

Two of the premieres could only be described as mishaps. Erick Hawkins's *Avanti* scarcely existed at all, for less than five minutes after the curtain rose upon eight skipping and leaping dancers, it came down again—and stayed down, leaving viewers unsure whether they had just seen a fragment from a longer composition or a dance that, like a Japanese haiku, was intended to be a miniature. *Avanti*, it turned out, was a fragment: Hawkins had been unable to finish his choreography in time for the premiere. But, although he can be a persuasive speaker, he missed the opportunity to step before the audience and explain the situation. Therefore the result was befuddlement.[23]

If *Avanti* was not enough of a work to make an impression, Pilobolus's *Black and Blue* struck some observers as being "too much!" A kinky "dark comedy" to a score combining punk rock with blues, *Black and Blue* concerned a mobster's decision that a certain woman he encountered had to be rubbed out. Some dancegoers detected in the choreography references to gangster ballets ranging from George Balanchine's *Slaughter on Tenth Avenue* to Paul Taylor's version of *Le Sacre du Printemps*. Yet there were critics who found the piece more repellent than amusing. Thus, in *Ballet News*, Charles Horton wrote, "The choreography consists of jerky and spasmodic movements and seemingly endless slinking and cliché sexy posing. . . . *Black and Blue* is unusual, unfunny, uninspired and unfortunate. The new wave of funkiness is definitely not the garden path Pilobolus needs to be led down."[24]

In contrast, Crowsnest, which had seemed shrill and grotesque the previous summer, was in a restrained mood in its new work, *The Garden of Villandry*. Set in a garden that could have come from an Impressionist painting, the dance depicted the shifting emotional relationships of two men and a woman. I wrote in the *New York Times* that its fascination derived from the fact that, although these three people looked like proper Victorians, one soon knew that all was not right with them—yet one could never quite tell just what was wrong with them.[25]

In the fourth of the summer's premieres, *Light, Part 15 (The Second Windfield)*, Kei Takei, a Japanese-born dancer, devoted herself to one of the themes with which she has been obsessed throughout her choreographic career: the struggle between man and the environment. For Horton, the theme had not lost its power to inspire Takei to create memorable dance, and he reported that *Light, Part 15* "moves to a metaphysical plane of almost hypnotic drama."[26]

However, the big news of 1980 had nothing to do with premieres. Rather, it was an announcement made by Charles Reinhart after the season had ended. According to Reinhart, the American Dance Festival was planning to operate as a year-round dance institute, and he hoped it would be able to move to headquarters in some former tobacco warehouses that would be remodeled specifically to serve as the festival's new home. Moreover, plans were being made to restore the Carolina Theater in downtown Durham as a theater suitable for dance performances. Reinhart also declared that the festival intended both to encourage young choreographers and to establish an award honoring lifetime achievement in choreography.[27]

1981

The plans for restoring and renovating Durham buildings to serve as a new home for the festival have remained visionary schemes. But in 1981 Reinhart kept his promise to acknowledge achievement and encourage promise. That summer saw the presentation of the first Samuel H. Scripps American Dance Festival Award, an honor established at the festival by Samuel H. Scripps, a member of the family of newspaper publishers and the founder and former president of the American Society for Eastern Arts. Designed to be presented annually to a choreographer who has made a significant lifetime contribution to dance, the award carries with it the sum of $25,000, and, in terms of money, it is believed to be the largest annual award in the performing arts. The first recipient, selected by an advisory panel, was Martha Graham—and surely no one in the dance community could have doubted the wisdom of that choice.[28]

Another long-term achievement was honored when the festival dedicated the 1981 season to Lisa Booth. A member of the festival staff for a decade, Booth now held the title of administrative director and had decided to leave the organization to pursue independent projects.[29]

It was more than a summer of commemorations. The season included performances by five young choreographers—Johanna Boyce, Molissa Fenley, Bill T. Jones, Charles Moulton, and Marleen Pennison—who had been chosen by a panel from fifty applicants as examples of what was billed as the "Emerging Generation" of choreographers. For these performances, the festival expanded beyond the Duke campus—indeed, out of Durham itself—to North Carolina State University in Raleigh, scheduling the "Emerging Generation" concerts in that university's Stewart Theater and gymnasium. The move from Duke represented one way in which Reinhart hoped to make the festival serve the entire region and to emphasize that it was not necessarily tied to a single campus.

An entire week was reserved for "Emerging Generation" programs. Each choreographer presented old works and new, and there were several performances daily. The final Saturday was a real marathon, for it included a concert in the morning, two in the afternoon, and one in the evening. As I wrote in the *New York Times*, "After all that dancing, one's eyes might have been dazzled and one's brain might have been boggled. But one would have gone away enlightened."

By journalistic coincidence, the "Emerging Generation" week was covered by two critics who are poets: I was one; the other was J. D. Reed, who is also a novelist and sportswriter. Reed's command of imagery and experience in describing sports movement surely helped him in his discussions of choreography. However, he was a newcomer to dance criticism. Commenting on the festival for *Time*, but not reviewing every specific work presented, Reed appeared to be bothered by the lack of explicit thematic content in many of the dances and by what struck him as a fondness for difficult, but mechanized, movement on the part of certain choreographers.

Reviewing Fenley's *Gentle Desire*, he said, "Stabbing the air, twisting in undefined space, these expressionless dancers—blankness being a hallmark of new wave productions—fail to establish their point." Like Reed, I certainly thought the dance "went licketysplit." Yet, far from being intimidated by it, I was fascinated by its "bewildering array of shrugs and shakes and whirls and jumps."

Moulton also disturbed Reed. Moulton had become noted for gamelike dances in which dancers passed balls back and forth in a variety of tempos and patternings. Such ball-passing occurred in the works he presented in Raleigh, including his new *Expanded Ball Passing*. That dance also incorporated the ball-passing into passages that resembled sprints and dashes and fantastic games of tag. I was pleased by the breezy, rough-and-tumble character of the choreography and by the deft way Moulton made the act of ball-passing a part of his personal dance technique, just as other choreographers might employ jumps and turns as part of their own techniques. But, for Reed, Moulton's dancers simply resembled "robots playing an electronic game. . . . Moulton's vision, like Fenley's, occurs in a hyperspace between the mind and the heart. Neither triumphs, and only motion itself, divorced from experience, is explored to its banal extreme."

However we may have disagreed about the season's "pure dance" works, Reed and I probably would have concurred that the most interesting of the "Emerging Generation" dances were those concerned with drama, as well as dexterity. Pennison's *Free Way* consisted of bittersweet vignettes about small-town boys who dreamed of cars and girls and who grew up to get married and, in some cases, divorced. I found *Free Way* interesting for its choreographic eclecticism: "There was much realistic nondance gesture. Yet an auto race was indicated by virtuosic runs and turns. For Miss Pennison, the important thing was not whether her movements fitted conventional definitions of dance, but whether they were dramatically appropriate."

Jones's *Social Intercourse* was a complex four-part composition, and its separate segments could either be joined together to form a single long work or presented as independent entities on a program with other dances. Choreographically, the four parts all featured repetitive movements performed with great force. But one soon realized that this was more than a study in dynamics. Rather, the harsh, insistent choreography came to symbolize the anxiety and frustration of American blacks, and it built to a mighty crescendo. Similarly impressed by Jones's choreographic energy, Reed said, "His considerable talent lies in choreographing street reality with a raw vitality, evident in the most exhilarating soul-handshake in theater and the use of a 'ghetto blaster' portable radio."

The strangest work to be seen in Raleigh was Boyce's new *Waterbodies* presented, to the accompaniment of harp music, in the swimming pool of the university's gym. The dancers' splashings and paddlings were combined with films of dancers moving underwater. It was a sweet, clever piece. Yet, for me, it also contained a measure of social commentary: "As Miss Boyce's dances on land have done in the past, this aquatic piece presented ordinary people at their attractive best. Because they all appeared to be good friends, we in the audience started wishing we could be their friends, too."[30]

It was a lively season in Durham, as well as in Raleigh. The festival again paid tribute to American popular dance with a jazz program (featuring the Johnny Griffin Quartet, Scoby Stroman, and Jafar Abdallah) and a vaudeville program with Elisa Monte, Joe Roth, Betsy Baytos, Sandman Sims, François Szony and Toni Ann Gardella, and Michael Tracy. And there were performances by Pilobolus, Dance Theatre of Harlem, North Carolina Dance Theatre, and the companies of May O'Donnell, Laura Dean, Paul Taylor, and Chuck Davis.

North Carolina Dance Theatre opened the season, 18 June, with a notable premiere commissioned by the festival, Senta Driver's *Resettings*, in which members of Driver's company, Harry, joined the dancers of Robert Lindgren's troupe from Winston-Salem. The professional company attached to the North Carolina School of the Arts, North Carolina Dance Theatre had established a reputation for both the versatility of its dancers and the eclecticism of its repertoire. All its members were classically trained. Yet, as Lindgren once said, "We are not strictly a ballet company, but a contemporary dance theater." The company had made a favorable impression during the festival's first season in Durham with a program that included ballets by George Balanchine and Antony Tudor. It created an even greater stir in 1981. In addition to Driver's piece, it offered Balanchine's *Square Dance*; Oscar Araiz's *Women*, to songs of Grace Slick; and Salvatore Aiello's *Piano Concerto No. 1*, to a score by the rock composer Keith Emerson. The well-rehearsed performance pleased the audience mightily, and Charles Reinhart remarked afterward, "This really was North Carolina's night."

In *Resettings* Driver mingled ballet and modern dance styles and steps, and the choreography reflected her ongoing concerns with gravity, weight, and dance as an activity requiring effort. There were sequences of groveling and rolling, passages of shoeless pointe work, and moments when Driver deliberately flaunted conventions: thus spectators gasped

Rebecca McLain, Gwendolyn Leonard, Traci Owens, Richard Prewitt, and Rick Michalek of the North Carolina Dance Theatre in Driver's *Resettings*, 1981.

audibly when a woman lifted a man. Yet, as Dee Dee Hooker noted in the *Raleigh News and Observer*, humor as well as hard labor made *Resettings* slyly hilarious. It has proved to be more than a one-time-only experiment. Without the presence — and not really requiring the presence — of Driver's own dancers, it remained a popular item in North Carolina Dance Theatre's repertoire, and it has also been successfully staged by the Pennsylvania Ballet.[31]

Just as *Resettings* exemplified some of Driver's creative obsessions, so *Tympani* contained many of the choreographic trademarks of Laura Dean. The prospect of seeing still further examples of geometric pattern- ing and spinning steps might have made some dancegoers worry about whether Dean was becoming a prisoner of her own distinctive style. *Tympani* certainly looked as if it were "typically Laura Dean." Yet Charles Horton, in *Ballet News*, rejoiced that it "was fortunately not another whirl premiere." Instead of being merely a repetition of her previous dances, he regarded it as a culmination of several years of creative activity: "It synthesizes and crystallizes in one work elements of pattern and repetition that have been seen only in whole, separate dances of hers in the past."[32]

Pilobolus was not so lucky. It still managed to amaze. Yet some dancegoers found that repeated viewings made its choreographic tricks less amazing than they had seemed at first glance and that its new dances were not always as successful as its old. Pilobolus offered two premieres. *Untitled II*, conceived and performed by Alison Chase, was an exploration of the kinds of patterns of light that could be created by a dancer manipulating two flashlights. For Horton, these explorations never really got anywhere, and although this was essentially a "lightweight, unrealized and undeveloped" choreographic idea, the piece was nevertheless so long that it occupied one-third of the evening's program. Therefore he was forced to describe it as "totally self-indulgent."

Day Two, the other premiere, was an exuberant romp, which, said Susan Broili in the *Durham Sun*, "captured that feeling of wild abandonment which sometimes prompts members of the human race to go dancing in the rain." It even ended with Pilobolus's dancers sliding across a stage covered with water. But whereas Broili found the piece "fun to watch," Elizabeth Lee thought that its choreographic "structures seemed to have no meaning or unifying force. They fell one into the next with a kind of randomness."[33]

Chuck Davis scored a success with his *Rites of Passage*, a ritualistic dance celebrating the passage of two youths into manhood. Horton found the regal and ecstatic choreography "another of Davis's contagiously disarming tributes to life and man's close ties to nature." As director of the festival's Community Services Program, Davis had demonstrated that he could be an unusually persuasive missionary for the cause of dance. Here, he was choreographically persuasive, as well, and he emphasized the communal nature of *Rites of Passage* by including members of the Durham community—among them, his eighty-two-year-old father—in the cast.[34]

1982

Merce Cunningham received the Scripps ADF Award in 1982, which was a year of growth for the festival and its school. A new student center opened at Duke, and its Reynolds Industries Theater was made available for summer dance, thus giving the festival two proscenium theaters on campus. Another innovation was a Dance Medicine Seminar, organized in association with the Duke University Medical Center's Physical Therapy Department.

The festival received important new grants. A $30,000 challenge grant from the Liggett Group carried with it several stipulations, yet they were intended to help the festival win additional support in its own region: thus the festival was required to meet $5,000 of the award with an equal amount from Durham County residents, and the remaining $25,000 had to be met with $50,000 from companies doing business in North Carolina.

"Emergency grants" to cut the deficit the festival faced at the beginning of the summer came from the Z. Smith Reynolds and the Hanes foundations. The Exxon Corporation contributed $60,000 to several aspects of the festival's National Choreography Project to assist new choreographers. Funds going to the Young Companies in Residence Project enabled choreographers Danny Buraczeski, Jim Self, and Charlie Vernon to collaborate with composers in workshops led by Lucas Hoving and Morton Subotnick. Funds to the Ascending Generation Project aided choreographers Johanna Boyce, Charles Moulton, and Kei Takei. Leonard Fleischer, senior adviser on Exxon's arts program, told the *New York Times* when the grant was announced that "This is the largest grant we've made in the field of modern dance, not including our public-television dance programs."[35]

The grants made possible several new dances. Three turned up on the program offered by the Young Choreographers in Residence, which I reviewed for the *New York Times*. Charlie Vernon's *Dances of Identity* consisted of restless, repetitive movement to a score by David Felder that combined music with the sounds of recorded voices telling stories over and over. Sometimes the same stories were told by both men and women, and, in addition to the stories, the script included remarks about how we all keep on telling the same stories in our lives. Although the piece was interesting, it was nevertheless bothersome that the movement was usually much more bland than the spoken text.

The high speed and constant shifts of movement quality in Jim Self's *Perpetrator* showed the influence of Merce Cunningham, with whose company Self had danced, and Frankie Mann's electronic score—which sometimes sounded as if someone were fussing with the dials on a radio —also could have served to accompany a work by Cunningham. Yet the constant changes of *Perpetrator* had their own vitality. So did the propulsive leaps and whirls of Danny Buraczeski's jazz-inspired, but choreographically eclectic *On the Side of Light*, to music by Eric Valinsky, which celebrated the joys of being alive and in motion.[36]

However, at least one Durham critic, Elizabeth Lee, was disturbed because, in her opinion, such young choreographers as Self and Charles Moulton "have substituted a look at themselves for a look at the world." Into this group she also placed Johanna Boyce, who offered a new work called *Kinscope*. With its ritualized ball-passing movements, it seemed indebted to Moulton's pieces in this genre: "glancing sideways" at other people's dances was how Lee characterized it. And although many of Boyce's previous works contained explicit social commentary, Lee felt it necessary to chide her—and Moulton, as well—in 1982 for their refusal to "look up from their own self-contemplation." Moulton offered the premiere of *Motor Party*, which consisted of sharp phrases performed to the rhythms of tango, waltz, and polka. According to Lee, "Gestures seemed to indicate references to social dance, but nothing specific emerged. Danced with vigor but not sureness, the work looked under-rehearsed." *Motor Party* may have been still a work-in-progress. Yet Lee found herself wondering, "Are Charles Moulton's motor motions taking us for a ride somewhere or are we really standing still?"[37]

Like Boyce and Moulton, Kei Takei used game movement in her new *Light, Part 17, Dreamcatcher's Diary*. But, unlike Boyce and Moulton, Takei, for Lee, managed to invest those movements with significance. Much of the dance was devoted to a kind of relay race in which dancers kept donning clothes until they could scarcely waddle. Lee thought the opening of the first bundle of clothes suggested a "Pandora's box of greed and competition" and that in the piece as a whole Takei had examined the "very American ritual of game-playing with humor and insight."[38]

However, the performances that made 1982 a special festival were those of four Japanese modern dance troupes: Dai Rakuda Kan and the companies of Miyako Kato, Bonjin Atsugi, and Shigeka Hanayagi. Over the years several foreign companies had appeared at the festival. But never before had the festival made a concerted effort to present a cross section of another country's modern dance. Now, with the aid of funding from the Japan-U.S. Friendship Commission, the Japan Foundation, and the International Communications Agency, American audiences were able to have a look at Japanese modern dance.

The visiting companies aroused curiosity. It was known that modern

Kai Takei's repertory class in performance of Takei's *Light Part 18 (The Wheat Field)*, 1982. Photo, Jay Anderson.

dance was a thriving art in Japan. American companies had toured there with great success. Japanese dancers who had studied in America and who had joined American companies proved to be well-trained, sensitive performers. Works by several Japanese choreographers had been favorably received at the festival in the past. Yet Americans knew little about Japanese modern dance as a whole and did not know what to expect from the visitors.

When one studies some of the reviews that the festival's Japanese venture received, it seems prophetic that, before the Durham performances began, Miyabi Ichikawa, a Japanese critic, had warned readers of the *New York Times* that these dancers might not "fulfill the expectation of the American audience of seeing something 'Japanese.' But their work is the result of global modernization. Tokyo, New York, Paris—all the metropolitan cities—have more in common with each other than with rural areas in their own countries." Ichikawa issued a further caution: "Also, remember that originality is not an important aspect of our culture, as it is in America."

Elizabeth Lee found much to admire in the Japanese works, and she was particularly impressed by the way all the choreographers were able to

Dai Rakuda Kan company in Maro's *Sea-Dappled Horse*, 1982. Photo, Jay
Anderson.

invest physically demanding movement with a sense of serenity. "At best:
awesome. At least: lovely and warm," she concluded. However, the issues
that Ichikawa raised were seized upon by Annalyn Swan, in *Newsweek*,
and Anna Kisselgoff, in the *New York Times*. Thus Swan thought that, of
the companies, "the least impressive are those that seem less Japanese
than sleekly international." And Kisselgoff considered too many works
derivative of such abstract choreographers as Merce Cunningham (who
was himself influenced by Zen) and the minimalists. Swan's comments on
Miyako Kato are typical of the criticism that was directed against several
of the presentations: "In 'Arabesque,' Miyako Kato, an obviously talented
young choreographer, piles together so many ideas, all of them acceptably
'post-modern,' that the piece quickly loses a controlling sensibility." And
while the bravura of Bonjin Atsugi's *Tearing Sign 8*—a minimalist and
repetitive trio—was impressive, Swan still felt as if the Japanese dances
were often "too much like gifted copies."

Given this sort of response to other choreographers, it was probably
not surprising that Swan was more sympathetic to Shigeka Hanayagi, for

Hanayagi was an "updated traditionalist . . . who has taken Kabuki movement and abstracted it into a new dance form all its own." Swan particularly admired *A Poem: Forest*, which was danced in kimonos: "As in
Kabuki, one is constantly reminded of nature—in the way the women
snap their fans together like the beating of a bird's wings, in the butterfly
flutter of their sleeves, in their hummingbird darts across the stage.
Hanayagi's works are a delicately beautiful new hybrid." Kisselgoff was
less impressed by Hanayagi's *Snow Won't Be Stopping*, an encounter
between a man and a woman in falling snow: "The hidden story is too
hidden and suggests the risk in combining highly symbolic and straightforward art forms." Summing up Hanayagi, Kato, and Atsugi, Kisselgoff
concluded that what these choreographers "had in common was a middle-
level respectability, lacking a true creative spark but earnest in their attempt
to keep up with an all-purpose modern-dance formalist approach. The
fact that there were no surprises is in itself no surprise."

But there was a surprise—a big one. No one in Durham had been
prepared for Akaji Maro's *Sea-Dappled Horse*, as performed by the
company known as Dai Rakuda Kan. With a name that means "great
camel battleship" in Japanese, Dai Rakuda Kan provided American
audiences with their first glimpse of *butoh* (or "dark soul") dance, a
form of violently Expressionistic—and self-consciously post-Hiroshima
—dance that had arisen in the 1960s. Dai Rakuda Kan specialized in
what Swan called "living nightmares." *Sea-Dappled Horse* began, she
said, with "a vision of some primordial bog" filled with writhing men and
women wearing nothing but G-strings, their bodies covered with white
paint. Maro proceeded to offer savage comments upon both Oriental and
Occidental culture with images of Japanese courtesans accompanied by
"a filthy and autistic samurai" and a chorus line of Western women
"dressed in long formal gowns, whose mouths gape open in silent screams
and whose eyes stare madly at the audience." The Durham audience stared
back in a mixture of horror and fascination, for, as Swan pointed out,
"Maro's images are often startlingly beautiful."[39]

———————————————— **1983** ————————————————

The festival looked to France and Africa in 1983. Yet it also emphasized
that its roots were now in North Carolina by transferring its main office
from New York City to Durham.[40]

Although the Japanese companies of 1983 did not receive universally favorable reviews, they nevertheless attracted much attention, and Reinhart was encouraged to bring to Durham significant examples of work from another nation that had recently developed an interest in modern dance: France. Persuaded by Susan Buirge, an American choreographer who had settled in France, that French modern dance was worth looking at, Reinhart made two trips to France, saw forty-two companies, and selected five to appear in what was a joint project of the American Dance Festival and the Festival of Dance of Aix-en-Provence. Buirge, an adviser for the Aix festival, helped make arrangements for the French dancers' American visit.

The groups that came to Durham were Ballet Théâtre de l'Arche, Compagnie de Danse l'Esquisse, Compagnie Karine Saporta, Compagnie Dominique Bagouet, and Caroline Marcadé et Compagnie. The most pleasant surprise about these companies was that, despite the enormous success such American choreographers as Merce Cunningham and Alwin Nikolais had had in France, the festival's French groups—unlike some of the Japanese groups the previous year—did not appear obviously derivative. Far from being minimalist or abstract, their works often possessed strong dramatic implications and could be said to concern what Anna Kisselgoff referred to in the *New York Times* as The Human Condition. Yet when she raised this point in a panel discussion with the choreographers, they bristled at the suggestion and insisted that they were primarily concerned with movement problems rather than with dramatic ideas. Apparently, a formalist aesthetic remained still fashionable in France, even though these dancers' actual choreographic practice was more free-wheeling than their theories might imply. On the other hand, Caroline Marcadé, one of the choreographers, told Jim Wise, of the *Durham Morning Herald*, that French modern dance was "pure emotion" and totally unlike currently fashionable American styles. Moreover, she recalled being "sad and furious" when Nikolais saw one of her works and told her to take the emotion out of it.

All the French choreographers kept emotion in their dances, several of which were quite intense. In fact, the movement in the productions of Karine Saporta and Joëlle Bouvier and Régis Obadia (directors of Compagnie de Danse l'Esquisse) often turned violent. Saporta's *Escale 1* was an enigmatic encounter for two strangers in a strange place, and in her *Hypnotic Circus*, for three dancers and a mattress, the human performers, who kept bounding up from squatting positions, were virtually treated as coiled springs. *Terre Battue*, by Bouvier and Obadia, abounded with anguished risings from the floor; their *Clay Wedding* was

Ballet Théâtre de l'Arche in Marin's *May B,* 1983. Photo, Jay Anderson.

a mating dance of curious bouncing movements, and their *Tête Close* was a particularly grueling piece for people who seemed both childlike and ancient as they discovered the brutalities of existence. "They are not easy to watch, but fascinate," said Elizabeth Lee in *Ballet News.*

Lee was less pleased with Dominique Bagouet's *Insaisies* (*Indiscernible Things*). She thought, "The most indiscernible thing was the reason for making this dance" of "frozen poses, random exits and entrances, and meandering solos." She much preferred Caroline Marcadé's *Pierre Robert*, which began with Marcadé sitting on stage while Dominique Petit stared up at her from the pit. A dance of searching gestures, it called attention to human frailty, yet also contained "wide, flamboyant patterns" and "sudden stops, surprising lifts, and changes of direction."

The most ambitious, and for some viewers the most successful, of the French attractions was *May B*, the tribute to Samuel Beckett that Maguy Marin choreographed for Ballet Théâtre de l'Arche. The ninety-minute work neither introduced specific characters nor retold specific incidents from any of Beckett's plays or novels. Instead, said Kisselgoff, "What Miss Marin has succeeded in doing is capturing a sensibility essential to Beckett and translating it in movement terms of her own. Moreover, she has done so with a restricted vocabulary that is congenial to Beckett's own laconic visions." The result was a dance filled with hunched-up, woebegone figures who shuffled about like tramps, cripples, or blind men. Many dancegoers already familiar with Beckett found *May B* eloquent at times. Yet it mystified those who did not know Beckett's writings, and it was also the only French work to provoke heated discussion for more than purely aesthetic reasons. A scene suggesting masturbation disquieted some people, and a reporter for the *North Carolina Leader* heard one disgruntled spectator complain, "It was gross, just gross."

"French contemporary dance is young yet, still wet behind the ears," is how Lee summed up the French season. Susan Broili of the *Durham Sun* was more severe in her judgments, finding that "most of these companies have a long way to go." Yet she did concede that "French modern dance has emerged with original dance, not just copies of American modern dance."[41]

Chuck Davis brought Africa to the festival. Davis organized Festival Africa, three nights of African dance and music. The first major festival of its kind in the Southeast, it featured performances by American companies specializing in African dance and by African-born dancers now living in the United States. The participants included Kombo Omolara, Olukose Wiles, Art of Black Dance and Music, Chuck Davis Dance Company, Calabash Dance Company, Weaver Street Dancers, the Cultural Movement, and Dinizulu and His African Dancers, Drummers, and Singers. Among the attractions was Davis's company in its first performance of *Fonki*, an all-male dance from Guinea that young men perform before their elders in order to demonstrate their physical prowess. The festival culminated with the premiere of *Drum Awakening*, an evening-long piece, devised by Chuck Davis, Ayanna Frederick, Yao Odoni, Deama Battle, and Olukose Wiles, that brought together all the companies. It concerned some modern-minded members of a Gambian village who refused to participate in a traditional ceremony to appease the spirits. The spirits then caused two people to fall into a trance, from which they could be released only through ritual dancing. For Broili, the dancing was not only exciting, it also provided one with a view into another culture: "there was a sense of being an onlooker at the clearing's edge."[42]

The season also offered performances by Pilobolus, Eiko and Koma, and the companies of Maria Benitez, Charles Moulton, Kei Takei, Lar Lubovitch, José Limón, and Paul Taylor (who received the Scripps ADF

Mackie Boblette, Bill McKinley, Claire Porter, and LeAnn Schmidt in Porter's *Panel*, 1983. Photo, Jay Anderson.

Award), and there was a program of new works by three young choreographers: Claire Porter, Gina Buntz, and Catlin Cobb.

The program's hit was Porter's *Panel*, a mimetic comedy about members of a panel trying to reach a decision. The choreography was based upon exaggerations of natural gestures, and, during the course of the piece, pencils were tapped, brows were furrowed, and legs were crossed and recrossed until the rules of order were tossed aside and the panelists gave vent to their real feelings of rage or frustration.

Buntz's *Chorines* was a trio for women who seemed equally unable to stay together or remain apart. Cobb's *Blanca* explored ways of folding and manipulating white sheets, and the choreographer treated the sheets both as elements in a formal design and as metaphors for the tasks of daily life. Lee termed the Young Choreographers' program "light at heart, but not lightweight." But, for me, it was decidedly slight, and in the *New York Times* I said I found it neither as ambitious nor as imaginative as previous concerts of its sort had been.[43]

There were three other premieres. Charles Moulton's *Fireworks*, offered on the Fourth of July, was a choreographic fireworks display in which three women repeatedly burst out of stillness into explosive fragments of movement. These pyrotechnics pleased Allison Adams of the *Durham Sun*, who was fascinated by the way the dancers "shook their heads from side to side, leaped, twirled and shook their entire bodies." But Lee was disappointed because the choreography was "all very small, the explosions truncated, sparse. Absent were the growing blaze and the lingering, floating, falling finish of the real thing." Lee also admitted to feeling increasingly disturbed by Moulton's fondness for tightly controlled movements. Thus she was led to wonder: "Has motor madness mechanized Moulton at last?"[44]

Like most of her pieces, Kei Takei's *Daikon Field Solo* was a study in repetition, and, like many of her pieces, this solo in which Takei placed daikons (Japanese white radishes) on the ground concerned relationships between man and nature. Lee found other implications in it: the radishes resembled nuclear weapons; yet they were funny-looking, as well. "Our world is full of contradictions," she concluded, "and Ms. Takei's work makes us aware of them and gives us positive ways to respond."[45]

Eiko and Koma's *Beam* was equally rich in implications. It was set on and around a dune. Yet that dune could have been Mt. Everest, for the dance was filled with images of struggling uphill and slipping down. Even as it showed how such struggles could be wearisome, *Beam* affirmed the dignity of effort, and, although its title remained unexplained, I considered the dance "as sturdy as a beam of wood and as intense as a beam of light."[46]

1984

By considering the Bennington summer of 1934 as its first season, the American Dance Festival was able to celebrate its fiftieth anniversary only twelve years after it had celebrated its twenty-fifth anniversary in New London. Using another system of counting, Charles Reinhart also planned a tenth anniversary season for 1987 in honor of its tenth year in Durham. Some choreographers and teachers who had been associated with Bennington and New London smiled at this juggling with figures. But the smiles were indulgent ones, and everyone agreed that the 1984 season was ambitious in scope and joyous in atmosphere.

Lisa Giobbi and Robert Faust (standing) in Pilobolus's *Return to Maria La Baja*, 1984. Photo, Jay Anderson.

Joy Hintz (center) and Nikolais company in Nikolais' *Graph,* 1984. Photo, Jay Anderson.

As always, there was an emphasis upon new American choreography. Eight works were commissioned, four of them specifically designated as "golden premieres." There was also another Young Choreographers program. But the festival did more than encourage American choreography. Over the years—and particularly with its importation of Japanese and French troupes in 1982 and 1983—it had made several attempts to acquaint American audiences with the contemporary dance of other countries. It did so again during the Golden Anniversary by presenting what was billed as the world's First International Modern Dance Festival, which included an international choreographers workshop and dance attractions chosen by Charles and Stephanie Reinhart during a world tour financed by the U.S. Information Agency in exchange for lectures by the Reinharts on arts administration and American dance. Following the close of the season in Durham, the festival moved to Japan to offer classes during August. Thus, for the first time, the festival scheduled activities in a foreign country. Also in Japan, Laura Dean offered the premiere of *Trio.*

John Carrafa and Shelley Washington in Tharp's *Sorrow Floats,* 1984. Photo, Jay Anderson.

Hanya Holm received the Scripps ADF Award and a new Humanities Program sponsored a photographic exhibition chronicling the history of modern dance and a set of panel discussions and demonstrations involving scholars and choreographers. Special features of the summer school ranged from a workshop for young dancers between thirteen and sixteen to the third annual Dance Medicine Seminar, this one concentrating upon injuries of the foot and ankle. Funding for the Golden Anniversary included grants of $50,000 from the National Endowment for the Arts, AT&T, Grand Met USA, Inc. (owners of the Liggett Group), and the Ford Foundation. In 1984 the festival was in the third year of a grant from the Mellon Foundation, and the Humanities Program was aided by grants from the National Endowment for the Humanities and the North Carolina Humanities Committee.[47]

A new work by Pilobolus—one of the "Golden Premieres"—gave rise to consternation among members of the audience and the press alike. When the curtain fell on *Return to Maria La Baja,* a man in the theater shouted, "Racist! Sexist!" Jennifer Dunning, of the *New York Times*, who was also present, wrote that she found the charge of racism hard to understand. The charge of "sexism" was less easily dismissed.

An unusually dark, violent work, inspired by a story by Gabriel García Márquez, *Return to Maria La Baja* told a Gothic tale involving rape and systematic dehumanization. During the course of it, a man turned into an evil old woman who tortured a ward who was eventually rescued by an androgynous hero. Throughout, said Dunning, there were choreographic references to gender confusion and lethal sexuality. However, far from glorifying unsavory behavior, Dunning thought the piece created "such a feeling of horror in the viewer that it has the sense of being a brief against brutality." It also had "the look of an unfinished work," and its unusual effects were "not strong enough to support it to the end."[48]

Of the other Golden Premieres, Alwin Nikolais's *Graph* was similarly dark in emotional tone, although nowhere near as controversial. Rope graphs controlled the dancers and windowpanes imprisoned them. Dancers could not even get together, for a strobe light kept splitting the flow of their movements into fragments. In *Graph*, said Elizabeth Lee, Nikolais created "a suspiciously dangerous environment." Merce Cunningham's *Doubles* was more benign. Consisting of sets of contrasting images—for instance, the women often moved coolly, while the male choreography emphasized sharp bursts of activity—*Doubles* was pronounced "Friendly, unpredictable, honed to simplicity," by Lee. However, Twyla Tharp's *Sorrow Floats* was jinxed. For one thing, it ended unexpectedly early when its accompanying tape stopped functioning. A dancer who was alone on the stage at the time bravely continued to move until the curtain fell. Many in the audience cheered, yet the piece was booed by a heckler—identified by Anne Levin of the *Oak Ridger* as Mark Morris, one of the summer's Young Choreographers, who also shouted after Tharp's emotionally stormy *Nine Sinatra Songs*, "No more rape!" Given the circumstances, it may have been hard to assess the merits of *Sorrow Floats* on its opening night. Nevertheless, Lee was impressed by a unison duet in it; because Tharp was noted for her choreographic fidgets and tangles, this clear, direct sequence was "something so rare in Tharp that its simple pleasure was moving."[49]

Two other premieres concerned struggles. Telling a story about Louisianians during the hurricane of 1957, Marleen Pennison's *The Hurricane: Dedans l'Année de Cinquante-Sept* depicted a struggle with forces of nature. According to La Fleur Paysour of the *Charlotte Observer*, "The

Eiko in *Elegy,* 1984. Photo, Jay Anderson.

Koma in *Elegy,* 1984. Photo, Jay Anderson.

Ruby Shang & Co. in Shang's *The Small Wall Project*, 1984. Photo, Jay Anderson.

work is light on dance, heavy on theater. She [Pennison] took a risk building a dance on such simple movement, but she won and left a reminder of the fragility of security and passing of danger." The struggles in Eiko and Koma's *Elegy* were certainly physical, but they also had several layers of thematic implications. Both dancers were naked and each was discovered standing in a pool of water at the curtain's rise. Linda Belans said in *Spectator*, "They struggle in uncomfortably slow time with their faces lifted, not in spiritually motivated expression, but in an emotionally painful configuration. Where in time and space have we encountered them? On their way up or down; trying to escape the water's powerful pull or attempting to give in to it?"[50]

New works by Ruby Shang and Chuck Davis recalled some of the extravaganzas with enormous casts that used to be popular at Connecticut College during the 1970s. Shang's *The Small Wall Project* used the entire East Campus, and its cast of two hundred included Charles Reinhart as well as thirty-six women who appeared like dryads among the trees, forty participants in choreographic tennis games, and thirty dancers who leaped across the lawn in a manner reminiscent of photographs of students at the old Bennington festivals. According to Lee, "The work was

Dance Indonesia from the Jakarta Institute of the Arts in Daud and Hasan's
Hhhhhuuuuu, 1984. Photo, Jay Anderson.

splendid, nostalgic, humorous and in true community spirit." Members
of the Durham community were part of the cast of Davis's *War of the
Guardians*, a protest against bigotry. Belans conceded that the piece lacked
sophistication, but thought this was because it was "Davis' desire to make
his message easily accessible to everyone."[51]

Shang was not the only choreographer that summer to refer back to
an earlier period of modern dance. The patterns of Mark Morris's *Forty
Arms, Twenty Necks, One Writhing*, presented on the Young Choreographers program, reminded Dunning of Bennington and Lee of Denishawn.
Yet whereas Shang was celebratory, Morris created a dance that Lee
thought interesting for its "moody loneliness." The other Young Choreographers were impish. In Pooh Kaye's rough-and-tumble *Wild-Fields*, said
Lee, six dancers "knocked each other into ingenious new shapes and
jerked inconceivably upward from impossible postures." Stephanie Skura's
Climbing the Waltz was equally odd. If anything, it was too self-consciously
so. Skura set her series of blackout sketches to squawkings that Lee said
could be regarded as "components of a waltz no one could dance to. Nor

Cecile Sicango and Brandon Miranda of Ballet Philippines in Miranda's *Awakening*, 1984. Photo, Jay Anderson.

did the dancers want to, for they entered with a reluctance and pleased themselves by exiting as often as possible."[52]

The International Season of companies from foreign countries was fascinating for the way it showed the influence of modern dance upon other dance forms. Lee concluded that this "cross-fertilization appears to be a liberating aesthetic force, but, especially in the cultures with strong classical traditions, more a passage out of the limitations of the past than a comfortable fundamental source of expression."[53]

Uday Shankar was one of this century's pioneers in the revitalization of traditional Indian dance; as early as the 1920s and 1930s, he had attempted to blend classical Indian forms with elements of Western ballet and modern dance. Therefore it was appropriate for the festival to include

London Contemporary Dance Theatre in Jobe's *Run Like Thunder,* 1984. Photo, Jay Anderson.

performances by the Uday Shankar India Cultural Center Dance Company, directed since its founder's death in 1977 by Shankar's widow, Amala Shankar. One of the works by Shankar that remained in the troupe's repertoire was *Harmony*, a dance-drama showing the effects of mechanization upon rural society. Astad Deboo and Bharat Sharma, the Indian soloists who shared a festival program, could be said to carry on the trend inaugurated by Shankar, for in their pieces, which Lee termed "fantastic concoctions," they not only combined Indian dance with modern dance styles apparently derived from such diverse sources as Martha Graham, Pina Bausch, and Pilobolus, but they also borrowed from jazz and Japanese dance.[54]

Dance Indonesia simultaneously managed to preserve some of its country's dance traditions and to appear surprisingly up-to-date. Among the things that made it seem contemporary was the way its dancers would establish, repeat, and develop sets of basic choreographic patterns. Tem-

Thaddeus Bennett (left) and The Chuck Davis African-American Dance Ensemble in Davis's *Drought*, 1985. Photo, Jay Anderson.

Gloria Muldrow, Ivy Burch, and Venita Ashford (front row, left) with Jimi Williams in Davis's *Saturday Night/Sunday Morning*, 1985. Photo, Jay Anderson.

Jean Christophe Pare of G.R.C.O.P. (Groupe de Recherche Choréographique de l'Opéra de Paris) in his *La Couleur du Secret,* 1985. Photo, Jay Anderson.

pos would be established, and then the dance would steadily accelerate, the participants accompanying themselves as they moved with hand clappings, finger snappings, and smackings of their hands against their chests. All this, to some viewers, made the Indonesians unexpectedly akin to certain Western "minimalist" dancers. Lee called their rhythmically mesmerizing style "definitely contagious. But you will thoroughly enjoy catching it."[55]

Trained by Alice Reyes, the members of Ballet Philippines in many ways resembled Western modern dancers. Yet Belans thought they retained characteristics of their own Philippine culture, including "highly stylized hands and arms . . . erect proud torsos reflective of Asian influence," and, in their differentiation between masculine and feminine ways of moving, a sense of "machismo personalities living in a matriarchal society." The company's presentations were not confined to Philippine themes, and one of the best-liked works was Denisa Reyes's *Muybridge/Frames*, inspired by the motion studies of Eadweard Muybridge, the nineteenth-century photographer.[56]

European modern dance was exemplified by the London Contemporary Dance Theatre, the Susan Buirge Project of Paris, and Groupe Emile Dubois of Grenoble. The Londoners were once again praised for their choreographic craftsmanship and finely honed dancing, which Kisselgoff thought looked particularly impressive in Robert Cohan's *Songs, Lamentations and Praises*, a work containing fleeting biblical allusions that had been created for a "Bible in Dance" seminar in 1979. Both French groups offered scenically elaborate ninety-minute pieces that often were of more visual than kinetic interest. The designs for Buirge's *Des Sites* included video images and a striking set consisting of scaffolding and mirrors. However, the choreographic action, which attempted to depict the emotional relationships of two women, was extremely ambiguous, and Belans found the choreography "too repetitive and uninteresting, while the 'plot' becomes murkier." Jean-Claude Gallotta's *Ulysse*, for Groupe Emile Dubois, was also pronounced murky. Its choreographic images were inspired by the myth of Ulysses and his journey home. But what many spectators thought most interesting about the piece was its all-white set and the fact that its cast included a white turkey. The pleasure of *Ulysse*, said Lee, was "the sheer pleasure of preplexity."[57]

Once the Durham season closed, the festival offered classes taught by Betty Jones, Bella Lewitzky, Ralf Haze, Kei Takei, Ruby Shang, and Martha Myers in three Japanese locations: Shikoku, Osaka, and Tokyo. There were also performances by Crowsnest and Laura Dean's company. With its fiftieth anniversary celebrations and first venture abroad, the 1984 festival was a memorable one. It was also a successful one: attendance rose from 23,326 in 1983 to 26,580; subscription ticket sales rose from 1,465 to 1,892, and memberships in the Association for the American Dance Festival brought in $36,331, compared to $25,486 the previous year.

As a delighted Charles Reinhart put it, "Life begins at 50."[58]

1985

Reinhart, in conversation, said something else about being fifty: "Fifty is sexy; 51 isn't." By this he meant that he knew it would be harder to attract financial support for a fifty-first season than for something that sounded as grand and alluring as a golden anniversary. Yet there was a fifty-first season and, when it ended, plans were being made for a fifty-second.

Alwin Nikolais received the 1985 Scripps ADF Award and offered the premiere of *Crucible*. Like most works by Nikolais, it abounded in multimedia effects: in this case, effects created by mirrors placed about the stage. But, unlike many works by Nikolais, it also contained overtly sensual and sexual images. Praising its ingenuity, Linda Belans remarked, "The most extraordinary aspect of the dance is that we never see the dancers' legs or feet."[59]

Crucible was not the only unusual production that summer. Chuck Davis's community-based African-American Dance Ensemble, a group of dancers who performed avocationally in their free time, staged the premiere of *Saturday Night/Sunday Morning*, an attack upon money-hungry preachers that, given its subject matter, could be regarded as a somewhat daring work to be presented in the "Bible Belt."[60] Martha Clarke offered *The Garden of Earthly Delights*, her mixed-media fantasy inspired by the paintings of Hieronymus Bosch. Festival audiences were introduced to Robert Desrosiers, a Canadian experimentalist, and to G.R.C.O.P. (Groupe de Recherche Chorégraphique de l'Opéra de Paris), the Paris Opéra Ballet's experimental unit. There were performances by Pilobolus, Eiko and Koma, and the companies of David Gordon, Pooh Kaye, and Paul Taylor. And the festival looked back upon modern dance history by presenting the

Martha Clarke and company in Clarke's *The Garden of Earthly Delights*, 1985.
Photo, Jay Anderson.

Deborah Carr Theatre Dance Ensemble in a program of works by Charles Weidman. As Anna Kisselgoff put it, it was a season of "rampant diversity."[61] Few admirers of either modern dance or the American Dance Festival would have quarreled with that designation. The festival may have been fifty-one, but it was showing no signs of seeming old.

IX

SINCE 1978

A NEW HOME

E very summer since 1978 Durham has witnessed what one resident
has called "the invasion of the posture people." The coming of June
signals the arrival of the American Dance Festival's performers,
teachers, and students—all of them seemingly blessed with
unquenchable vigor and impeccable posture.

Although the dancers have done much to enliven Durham, Terry
Sanford likes to point out that in summers before the festival moved to
North Carolina Durham played host to many civic, cultural, and educational projects. And he is literally correct. Yet visitors to Durham in those
years might have received another impression of the city in summertime.
For them, Durham could easily seem a hot, lazy little city—not necessarily an unpleasant place, but by no means a lively one. The festival has not
been able to do anything about the heat. But it has brought excitement.

The stir the first Durham festival created was understandable: the
festival was a novelty, a new cultural toy. One could not expect so tumultu-
ous a reaction every year. Nevertheless, what is remarkable is the enthusiasm that remains. Summing up the festival's history in 1983, Charles
Reinhart declared that "there's a definite dividing line: B.D. and
A.D.—before Durham and after Durham. It's something our artists felt
immediately. The first thing that hit them was the quality of the response,
not to mention the size. The word spread throughout the dance world
that, hey, this is something special."

In turn, Durham residents regard the festival as "something special,"
and some fans have become so excited about dance that they are willing
to do volunteer work for the festival. In 1983 the *Raleigh Times* reported

that Bruce Elledge, a retired violinist of New Bern, North Carolina, had been able to accompany festival classes; consequently, he said, he felt like "a bee in clover." And Tony Johnson, ordinarily an admissions officer at the Duke Medical Center, spends part of his summers distributing festival flyers. For him, the coming of the festival is "like spring opening up. . . . You can see people bloom."[1]

If Durham is interested in the festival, the festival has tried to show that it is interested in Durham. The festival's main office is no longer in New York, but in Durham. And the festival's community services programs, under the direction of, first, Arthur Hall, and, later, Chuck Davis, have taken dance into the community all year long by means of classes, demonstrations, and workshops. Davis has also developed the Weaver Street Dancers, a young people's group, and the African-American Dance Ensemble. By working in Durham, Davis has returned to—and has shown a commitment to—the area in which he was born, for his hometown is nearby Raleigh.[2]

Although most observers regard the festival's move to North Carolina as an artistic success, its presence in Durham has not been without problems, and several criticisms have been leveled against it. Some can probably be dismissed as minor.

Thus just as, earlier, the buildings and grounds department at Connecticut College had been surprised at the capacity of dancers for breaking things, so a few Duke custodians have discovered that dancers can leave the part of the campus where they have lived and worked looking untidy. But Sanford minimizes the havoc dancers wreak: "I don't think the festival does as much harm to campus equipment as a fraternity party could do on a Saturday night."

Other complaints—and, fortunately, they are rare—have come from members of the Durham community who are disturbed by the festival's moral tone. There have been protests against nudity, particularly in certain works by Pilobolus and Johanna Boyce, and in 1981 a Durham clergyman, the Rev. Jerry Hooper, director of a group called Concerned Christians for Good Government, opposed municipal funds for the festival and kept asking city council members, "How many of you are going to be righteous and how many are going to be wicked on this issue?" Yet no further fuss appears to have been made on the matter, and Reinhart pointed out to the press that, in moving to Durham, "we were told we wouldn't have to worry about our artistic license."[3]

Sound consultant David Meschter and composer John Cage recording air-conditioner sounds for Cunningham performance, 1984. Photo, Jay Anderson.

But it is not only people who believe dance to be devilish who have questioned aspects of the festival. Certain dance lovers have raised their own objections. Once again, in Durham as in New London, there have been complaints that the festival has grown too complex in its organizational structure and too broad in its school curriculum. The term "smorgasbord" continues to be used, and the fear remains that students may do little more during the summers than sample course after course without receiving in-depth training in any single area of dance. To such objections, Reinhart invariably replies, "Look, we have only six weeks. In six weeks you can't make a student an expert in any technique. So what can you do? We believe that you can make students aware of the sheer range of dance. Many of our students come from colleges that have only two or three dance teachers at most. The festival attempts to show them the breadth and width of dance. And that's something that few institutions anywhere can do." And, commenting on the charge that the festival is a "smorgasbord," he has said, "Well, we may be a smorgasbord. But we may also be the only smorgasbord around."[4]

The sheer range of dance is indeed what the festival emphasizes. Selma Jeanne Cohen says that Reinhart's "vision of dance is unusually wide and he has shown more enterprise than the directors who preceded him. The other directors would probably not have brought in the Japanese or the French dance groups. Or, if they had thought of doing it, they might not have known how to go about it. But Reinhart can combine artistic curiosity with practicality."

The relocation of the festival in North Carolina made some observers wonder whether, in his attempts to attract a new audience, Reinhart might grow increasingly cautious in his choice of attractions. Certainly, modern dance has been augmented by programs of ballet, jazz, and vaudeville dance. Yet modern dance performances remain the festival's principal attractions, and, ironically, when the festival did seem to be making an obvious effort to please the general public by offering the American Dance Machine in its musical comedy dances, the attempt was a failure.

Deborah Jowitt has raised a more subtle charge against the summer programming. She is disturbed that several works commissioned by the festival have been nothing more than "useful additions to the touring repertory of whatever company was presenting them," rather than "brave new statements hatched during the comparative leisure of a hot summer,

Merce Cunningham and company rehearsing, 1982. Photo, Jay Anderson.

as was the case in the festival's lean old days at Bennington during the '30s."[5]

In reply, it could be pointed out that, since 1948, the festival has never been the sort of cloistered creative workshop that Bennington epitomized. The very decision to establish the American Dance Festival in a town directly on one of the major railroad lines out of New York suggests that the festival's organizers intended it to be very much in the eye of the general theatergoing public. Presumably, after World War II, Martha Hill thought that modern dance could now appeal to such a public. If, as it turned out, that public did not always flock to New London, a new public is now attending performances in Durham, and, without substantially altering the content of its programs, the festival seems to be turning many members of that public into serious dance lovers.

For all its eclecticism, Reinhart's programming is not totally unfocused or capricious. Rather, it reflects both Reinhart's own taste and his shrewd assessment of the taste of the time. No single company now dominates the festival in the way that the José Limón company once did. Nevertheless,

Betty Jones (center) with technique class, Durham, 1982. Photo, Jay Anderson.

just as the Limón company could be regarded as a prime example of certain important choreographic trends of the 1940s and 1950s, so two groups that keep returning to Durham can be said to represent American dance since the late 1960s: the Paul Taylor Dance Company and Pilobolus.

If American dance can now be best described as pluralistic, then one of the finest exemplars of that pluralism is Taylor. His choreographic output is so diverse that it is hard to generalize about it, and as soon as one starts formulating rules about his approach to composition, he may break those rules in his next work. He himself has said about composition, "There are no rules; just decisions."

Taylor began by rejecting—and, in practice, he continues to show little concern for—the grandiloquent modern dance choreography associated with both Martha Graham and José Limón. His works may often be serious, but they are seldom solemn. Rather, they can be sweet or sour, sad or joyful, frivolous or noble, or, occasionally, several of these qualities simultaneously. Even individual phrases of movement may contain their own contradictions. Deborah Jowitt has noted that, quite early in Taylor's

Paul Taylor (far right) and the Taylor company at rehearsal of *Arden Court,* 1981.
Photo, Jay Anderson.

choreographic career, "He developed an unusual way of moving, using
the floor as if it were spongy, the air as if it were thick."

Given all this, Taylor may be what the philosopher Isaiah Berlin
would call "a fox," an image borrowed from one of the mysterious fragments left behind by the ancient writer Archilochus: "The fox knows
many things, but the hedgehog knows one big thing." According to Berlin's
personal interpretation of that statement, "hedgehogs" are people who
relate everything in life to one central, overriding vision, whereas "foxes"
may pursue many, even seemingly contradictory, ends. Taylor is surely a
fox, just as José Limón, with his preoccupation with human agonies and
ecstasies, was most likely a hedgehog.

Yet if Taylor's works may be considered representative examples of
American modern dance in the 1980s, Taylor does not wield the sort of
influence over the American Dance Festival that Limón once did. Nor, he
says, does he believe it possible for him to do so because the festival is
now broader in its programming than it once was, and though his com-

pany may make repeated visits to Durham it is never in residence there throughout the summer, as Limón's company always was in New London. Modern dance's pluralism may have helped Taylor to achieve acclaim. Yet it has not required him to play the role of artistic guru.[6]

Whereas Taylor's creations exemplify the diversity of contemporary dance, Pilobolus is a group made possible by one particular form of choreographic experimentation. At least since the time of the first dance concert at the Judson Church in 1962, certain choreographers have been asking, "What kinds of movement may serve as a dance movement?" And because they have asked a question that might not even occur to choreographers satisfied with traditional dance techniques, their answer inevitably is, "Any sort of movement may serve as a dance movement." As a result, there have been rigorous experiments with everyday movements, game movements, work movements, and task-generated movements.

Yet, although choreographers may disdain the frills of classical ballet or the convolutions of Graham technique, it may be neither possible nor theatrically desirable to banish spectacle entirely from dance productions. Consequently, some choreographers have taken new delight in movement display, but without returning either to ballet or to any established modern dance technique. Instead, they have often borrowed movements from sports, athletics, and gymnastics.

When some Dartmouth College students formed a choreographic collective called Pilobolus in 1971, they were, in a sense, the inheritors of at least a decade of movement exploration, and, through their own wit, cleverness, and athletic skills, they demonstrated that they knew how to raise serious aesthetic questions in a palatable, even entertaining manner. Each of their gymnastic dances does indeed ask—and gives the expected experimentalist answer to—the question, "What is dance movement?" But few people who enjoy Pilobolus bother with aesthetic arguments. Rather, they applaud the surprising ways bodies in a dance by Pilobolus may link, entwine, and wrap around one another and the way kinetic images may suddenly pop up in sharp clarity of outline, only to metamorphose oozily into totally different images.

However, one problem faced by many artists who deliberately restrict themselves to certain specialized aspects of their art form is how to continue producing works that seem fresh. The artist may exhaust the possibilities of a given style. Or the artist's audience may tire of that style, even though that style continues to absorb the artist. Just how can the next all-black painting be made to appear as interesting as the last? And at what point does one gymnastic dance start looking well-nigh indistinguishable from all other gymnastic dances?

Pilobolus was initially applauded for its cheeky athleticism. If it was a dance group with a gimmick, that gimmick worked wonderfully. Yet the members of Pilobolus must soon have sensed a need to widen their artistic horizons. Women were admitted to the company. And whereas the group's earliest dances tended to be studies in eccentric shapes, later dances were enigmatic narratives.

However, such dramatic content began to bother critics. If assuming weird shapes in dances involved a distortion of the natural line of the body, nobody seemed to mind this in works that resembled animated abstract paintings. But when bodily distortion was combined with a predilection for grotesque drama, then some viewers became disturbed. Thus at a Brooklyn concert in 1976, Deborah Jowitt heard a member of the audience say of Pilobolus, "If they weren't so young and beautiful, it would be *gross*." Two years later Jowitt acknowledged that there was a "cheerful raunchiness" about Pilobolus, then confessed that she felt uneasy about the company because "sometimes the games with sex, deformity, idiocy, and death miss being Rabelaisian and end as sick jokes."[7] And in 1984 a new work by Pilobolus occasioned an angry outcry at its festival premiere.

Pilobolus has done much to delight audiences. But Pilobolus may also constantly have to ask itself, "Where do we go from here?"

The entire American Dance Festival has often had to ponder such a question. It could be argued that, by moving to Durham, the festival has become more "American" in the broadest sense than it ever had been. The festival had always attracted students from many parts of the country. Yet in New London it remained, in a sense, an extension of the New York dance scene. Now the situation has changed. Although a few festival devotees—including Nathan Clark—have paid visits to Durham, most New York dancegoers are unlikely to think of spending a weekend by attending performances in North Carolina. In terms of travel time, Durham is really not all that remote: whereas it takes approximately two-and-a-half hours to go from New York to New London by train, it takes only about an hour-and-twenty-minutes to fly from New York to Durham. Nevertheless, psychologically, for many people (particularly urbanites) a train ride can seem like a commuter's trip, whereas, even in this day of frequent jet travel, a plane trip can seem something of a major undertaking. Thus, with the move to Durham, the festival could no longer expect performances to be regularly attended by large contingents of New Yorkers. It would have to develop its own audience in its own community. And this, fortunately, it is apparently succeeding in doing.

Remoteness from New York may also have affected the sort of journalistic coverage the festival receives. New York critics who, because of the Manhattan "dance boom," found it increasingly difficult to devote a block of time to the festival's last seasons in New London, may be finding it even harder to spend much time in North Carolina. Indeed, given the scope of the festival, few newspapers or magazines from around the country can hope to report on it in its entirety. Just about the only papers who can do so are those in the Durham area. Therefore, because they are able to keep a journalistic record of the festival, for a few weeks each summer the North Carolina critics become some of the most important dance critics in America.

Now that the festival has committed itself to North Carolina, it is impossible to predict what may happen next. No one now talks about the hypothetical million-dollar trust fund that helped lure the festival to the South in the first place. Yet sources of funds must constantly be sought since, according to a report by Dee Dee Hooker in 1983, it costs more than $1 million annually to mount the festival, with major companies receiving between $30,000 and $50,000 for a residency. In comparison, the 1977 budget for the festival's last season in New London and Newport was $636,000.[8]

However, although Reinhart must always worry about money, he insists that he does not worry about the loss of the million-dollar endowment. Referring to the support he has received, he says, "North Carolina's overall effort to keep us going is more important. If you really look at the bottom line, everybody's lived up to their promises, even though there are specific things that haven't been lived up to." He takes a similarly pragmatic attitude toward such schemes as moving the festival off campus to a renovated warehouse or a restored Carolina Theater or any other hypothetical location. The festival's options remain open.

Yet one thing seems clear. The American Dance Festival has found a real home in North Carolina. According to Terry Sanford, "The arts exert a civilizing influence upon any community, large or small." If he is correct, then the festival is certainly exerting such an influence in Durham.

X

A SUMMING UP

George Beiswanger once called the American Dance Festival "a multi-purpose and many-splendored affair."[1] Most dancegoers would probably still agree with him. Yet the festival has not defined its purposes or attained its splendor in isolation. Throughout its history, it has been a microcosm of American modern dance as a whole, and both its achievements and its problems have been symptomatic of those of modern dance across the nation.

To some extent, modern dance was born out of both a vision and a misapprehension. Its founding figures and the venturesome choreographers who came after them made it a tenet of their aesthetic creed that dance could be a great art of the utmost moral, social, and spiritual significance. But no extant dance form seemed as grand or as noble as they wished dance to be. Ballet, the most historically important of Western theatrical dance forms, seemed particularly sterile to them. Therefore they concluded it was moribund and had to be supplanted. Here, they were in error. At the very moment that some of the modern dance pioneers were fulminating against ballet, the innovative choreographers of Sergei Diaghilev's Ballets Russes were revitalizing the art. However, having little direct contact with this rejuvenation, the modern dancers invented a whole new dance form of their own, a form that from its inception emphasized personal creativity.

Believing that dance was good for body and soul alike and that the dance experience should be available to anyone desiring to investigate the art, many modern dancers and dance teachers sought support from colleges and universities.[2] In fact, modern dance became so closely associated with colleges that, today, when Charles Reinhart talks of possibly moving the American Dance Festival to some site off the Duke University campus, he occasionally bewilders dance lovers who cannot imagine the festival apart from a college setting.

In the early years of modern dance not even the most sympathetic college administrators were daring enough to establish autonomous departments of dance at their schools. Nor, in many cases, were already existing departments of theater or music willing to welcome dance into their folds. Therefore, because it could easily be demonstrated that dancing promoted fitness, dance took root in departments of physical education. But, always, there were zealots who insisted that dance was more than a system of exercises: it was an art. One such crusader was Martha Hill, and every dance project she has founded has emphasized art as well as education, performance as well as pedagogy. To a great extent, Bennington's summer programs existed to train teachers.[3] But those teachers were made to realize that they were participating in an art form. And, combining high seriousness with crusading zeal, they attempted to bring it to as many people as possible.

By the 1950s, modern dance was no longer a maverick art. It had acquired its own establishment, and, increasingly, the American Dance Festival was regarded as that establishment's creative center. Yet some of the festival's own guiding figures were perceptive enough to realize that the festival was no longer reflecting all important trends in modern dance. A new directorate therefore assumed power in what was a benign and bloodless revolution. This new directorate responded to the economic as well as the aesthetic changes that had occurred in dance. During the 1960s the National Endowment for the Arts came into being, and state and municipal arts councils and philanthropic foundations began to show interest in supporting dancers and dance companies. As a result, American dance experienced one of its recurrent "booms." Today, both American dance in general and the American Dance Festival in particular are aesthetically pluralistic and economically something of a big business.

This state of affairs disturbs some people. Among them are dance lovers nostalgic for the good old days when the dance scene was smaller and simpler than it has become. There was a time—and it was not so long ago—when one could get to know virtually every important modern dancer, teacher, and choreographer in the country: modern dance, for all its occasional internecine squabbling, could seem a cozy little community of kindred spirits. Now, not only has the number of dancers and choreographers increased, but the range of dance styles has also widened. Therefore, in its eclecticism, the American Dance Festival is an accurate reflection of contemporary dance. The festival—like dance in general —may be lacking in focus. Nevertheless, the proliferation of companies and styles can be taken as a sign of growth, rather than disintegration. As Paul Taylor says, "The trend today is that there are so many different trends."[4]

The American Dance Festival's continuing ability to stimulate dancers and audiences is one reason why it remains a major force. It has acted as a sort of magnet, drawing together divergent dance companies, styles, theories, and methods of training. Whereas for most of the year modern dance activities are spread across the country, for six weeks in summer a single festival serves as the focal point of the art.

To students desiring professional careers, this can have practical benefits. Studying at the festival can be a way of getting one's self known to prominent teachers and choreographers. Students still unsure about the dance style in which they wish to specialize can see several dance companies perform at the festival, and some students have been able to audition for the directors of those companies. Similarly, audiences can acquaint themselves with current dance styles, and teachers from schools across the country can return home after a festival with a sense of what is vital in dance.

Just as Bennington students grew up to become influential dancers, teachers, and choreographers, so American Dance Festival students have also matured to become leaders of the dance world. A look at old class rosters or cast lists for student presentations can be instructive and even surprising: sometimes it seems as if many of the important people in modern dance were students at the American Dance Festival at one time or another.

Thus in 1952 Martha Myers presented a dance called *Complaint* in Louis Horst's modern forms class; that same year, a demonstration of "Variations on 7-7-10 Rhythm" was presented by members of Doris Humphrey's intermediate and advanced composition class, and the cast included Paul Taylor. In 1956 Dan Wagoner offered a solo called *Frolic* as an example of a galliard in Horst's class in preclassic forms. Two years later, for the same course, Steve Paxton choreographed *Power*, a pavane. The student roster for 1959 included David Gordon (who later became an important member of the Judson Dance Theater), Valda Setterfield (who

married Gordon and danced with Merce Cunningham), and Renee Kimball
(who joined Paul Taylor's company). Kimball was back on campus in
1960, and so were Sharon Kinney (who also became a Taylor dancer),
Margaret Jenkins (today one of San Francisco's leading modern dancers),
and David McLain (who became director of the Cincinnati Ballet). Among
the students of 1961 who developed into successful choreographers were
Trisha Brown, Lucinda Childs, Deborah Hay, Jennifer Muller, Marcia
Plevin, and Kathryn Posin. In 1962 Senta Driver was a member of Bessie
Schönberg's composition class. The next year, Margaret Beals and Meredith Monk were festival students. Very probably two decades from now a
historian examining the records of more recent seasons will find the
names there of still other dancers and choreographers who went on to
achieve acclaim.

Not all former students at the festival became dancers; some are now
distinguished figures in other dance-related fields. For instance, two of
America's finest lighting designers once studied dance at the festival.
Thomas Skelton choreographed a courante called *Mosquito Hunt* for
Horst in 1951, and, in 1953, Jennifer Tipton created *Hymn to the Sun* for
Nona Schurman's elementary composition class.

Listings of prominent festival alumni could be extended for many
more pages. And they would be of more than nostalgic or anecdotal
interest. Such listings reveal much about the nature of modern dance and
how it manages to survive and develop. To some observers, it has always
been a most peculiar art, for, as José Limón once put it, modern dance is
"in essence non-academic; in principal, experimental; in practice, eclectic
and inclusive."[5] But, for those very reasons, hostile viewers have charged
that modern dance is rootless; that, unlike ballet, which has developed
a jealously guarded, yet steadily evolving technique, modern dance
movement is often closely associated with the stage presence of a few
charismatic individuals and so may be incapable of being developed by
anyone else in the future. Because of this, it is charged, modern dance is
inherently fragmentary, transitory, and incapable of surviving. Such a
staunch classicist as Lincoln Kirstein, for whom modern dance is ana-
thema, has gone so far as to compare ballet tradition with the Christian
concept of apostolic succession, and he condemns modern dance as
"pernicious heresy."[6]

But a consideration of the American Dance Festival's history may
suggest that modern dance is not as rootless as its detractors allege, even
though it is the art that Paul Taylor once defined by saying, "To me,

modern dance is a license to do what I feel is worth doing, without somebody saying that I can't do it because it does not fit into a category."[7] Modern dance may indeed emphasize individual creativity and countenance iconoclasm. Yet it manages to pass on its creative discoveries by precept and example, each new generation of dancers learning, absorbing, and then accepting, modifying, or rejecting the work of the previous generation.

If ballet develops according to a kind of apostolic succession, then modern dance's development may be epitomized by a secular, but almost equally venerable, principle: apprenticeship. After examining the field as a whole, fledgling dancers, in a sense, apprentice themselves to master craftsmen by studying with a particular teacher or by joining a particular choreographer's company. In time, these young artists may wish to organize companies of their own and do their own choreographic work. Many factors influence a student's choice of choreographic masters, and students often switch from studio to studio. However, the sampling of styles and techniques that a student receives at the American Dance Festival may help make artistic choices carefully considered decisions, rather than rash impulses.

Modern dance, then, is a self-renewing art. Like the phoenix, it may burn in glory and then seem to burn out, only to rise triumphant from its own ashes. This process of rebirth can be seen in miniature in the American Dance Festival where, at various times, creative vitality has flared up, subsided, and blazed forth anew.

In 1953 John Martin compared the festival with a place of pilgrimage. So, twenty-five years later, did Charles Reinhart who, when asked why he bothered to keep the festival going, looked dumfounded and then replied, "Even when we were having our greatest difficulties, we never once thought of stopping. The American Dance Festival really means something. It is as holy a Mecca as one can find in the dance world."[8]

FESTIVAL CHRONICLE

In company repertoire lists, unless a choreographic credit is given in parentheses, all works are by that company's director. Unless separate credits are given, the "designs" credit includes both scenery and costumes. An asterisk indicates that a work was commissioned by the festival. The listings of "teaching staff" include both faculty members and teaching assistants, when the assistants' names were included in festival bulletins. Names of companies are listed as they were on festival programs.

1948
---

13 July–24 August 1948

Administrative officials: Rosemary Park, president, Connecticut College; Ernest O. Melby, dean, School of Education, New York University; John F. Moore, chairman, administrative board for Connecticut College

Administrative board: Martha Hill, chairman; John F. Moore, chairman for Connecticut College; Ruth Bloomer, Ernest O. Melby, Jay B. Nash, Rosemary Park, Ralph E. Pickett, Francis C. Rosecrance, Mary Josephine Shelly, Ruth Stanwood, Ruth Thomas

Festival executive committee: Martha Hill, chairman; John Moore, Mary Josephine Shelly, Norman Lloyd, Doug Hudelson

Teaching staff: William Bales, Ben Belitt, Ruth Bloomer, Jane Dudley, Joseph Gifford, Martha Graham, Harriette Anne Gray, Erick Hawkins, Martha Hill, Louis Horst, Doug Hudelson, Doris Humphrey, Delia Hussey, Billie Kirpich, Pearl Lang, Arch Lauterer, José Limón, Norman Lloyd, Ruth Lloyd, Muriel Manings, Sophie Maslow, Carl Miller, Natanya Neumann, Miriam Pandor, Helen Priest Rogers, Jo Van Fleet, Betty Walberg, Shirley Wimmer, Ethel Winter, Yuriko

Repertoire

Martha Graham: *Appalachian Spring, Night Journey, Herodiade, Dark Meadow, Errand into the Maze, Cave of the Heart*
Jane Dudley, Sophie Maslow, William Bales and Company: *Folksay* (Maslow), *Spanish Suite*

(Dudley, Maslow), *The Lonely Ones* (Dudley), *Peon Portraits* (Bales), *Harmonica Breakdown* (Dudley), *Champion* (Maslow), *Suite* (Dudley, Maslow, Bales), *Song for a Child* (Dudley), *Soliloquy* (Bales), *Dust Bowl Ballads* (Maslow), *Partisan Journey* (Maslow), *Short Story* (Dudley), *New World a'Comin'* (Dudley)

José Limón and Company: *Concerto in D Minor, Day on Earth* (Doris Humphrey), *Story of Mankind* (Humphrey), *Lament for Ignacio Sánchez Mejías* (Humphrey), *Chaconne in D Minor, Voice in the Wilderness* (Pauline Koner), *Sonata*

Premieres

Wilderness Stair (Diversion of Angels), 13 August 1948. choreography: Martha Graham; music: Norman Dello Joio; setting: Isamu Noguchi; cast: Pearl Lang, Helen McGehee, Natanya Neumann, Dorothea Douglas, Joan Skinner, Dorothy Berea, Dale Sehnert, Mark Ryder, Robert Cohan, Stuart Hodes

Corybantic, 18 August 1948. choreography: Doris Humphrey; music: Bartok; costumes: Pauline Lawrence; cast: The Defender: José Limón; The Antagonist: Miriam Pandor; The Innocent: Betty Jones; The Fatalist: Pauline Koner; The Compassionate: Letitia Ide

The Strangler, 22 August 1948. choreography: Erick Hawkins; poetry: Robert Fitzgerald; music: Bohuslav Martinu; designs: Arch Lauterer; cast: Oidipous: Erick Hawkins; Sphinx: Anne Meacham; chorus: Joseph Wiseman

--------------------------------- **1949** ---------------------------------

11 July–21 August 1949

Administrative board of the School of the Dance: Ruth Bloomer, Martha Hill, cochairmen; Rosemary Park, Ernest O. Melby, Louis Horst, Doris Humphrey, Jay B. Nash, Ralph E. Pickett, Francis C. Rosecrance, Mary Josephine Shelly, Ruth Stanwood

Festival committee: Rosemary Park, chairman; Ruth Bloomer, Martha Hill, Louis Horst, Ruth Stanwood

Teaching staff: William Bales, Ben Belitt, Valerie Bettis, Ruth Bloomer, Nancy Brock, Eva Desca, Jane Dudley, Doris Goodwin, Els Grelinger, Martha Hill, Louis Horst, Doris Humphrey, Delia Hussey, Hazel Johnson, Betty Jones, Pauline Lawrence, José Limón, Sophie Maslow, Carl Miller, Duncan Noble, Miriam Pandor, Jo Van Fleet, Betty Walberg, Theodora Wiesner

Repertoire

Dudley-Maslow-Bales Trio and New Dance Group Company: *Folksay* (Maslow), *Suite* (Dudley, Maslow, Bales), *Song for a Child* (Dudley), *New World a'Comin'* (Dudley), *Dust Bowl Ballads* (Maslow), *The Lonely Ones* (Dudley), *Short Story* (Dudley), *Champion* (Maslow), *Peon Portraits* (Bales)

Valerie Bettis and Company: *Yerma, As I Lay Dying, The Desperate Heart, The Earth Shall Bear Again*

José Limón and Company: *Lament for Ignacio Sánchez Mejías* (Doris Humphrey), *La Malinche, Corybantic* (Humphrey), *Story of Mankind* (Humphrey)

Premieres

Invention, 13 August 1949. choreography: Doris Humphrey; music: Norman Lloyd; costumes: Pauline Lawrence; cast: José Limón, Betty Jones, Ruth Currier

Judith, 13 August 1949. choreography: William Bales; music: Hazel Johnson; setting: Charles Hyman, William Sherman; cast: Israelites: Nina Caiserman, Andora Hodgin, Muriel Manings, Anneliese Widman, Ronne Aul, Irving Burton, Normand Maxon; Elder: Donald McKayle; Judith: Sophie Maslow; Her Handmaiden: Lili Mann; Cup Bearer: Normand Maxon; Wrestlers: Ronne Aul, Irving Burton; Holofernes: William Bales

Out of the Cradle Endlessly Rocking, 13 August 1949. choreography: Jane Dudley; music: Beethoven; setting: Charles Hyman, William Sherman; a solo for Dudley

Domino Furioso, 14 August 1949. choreography: Valerie Bettis; script: John Malcolm Brinnin; music: Bernardo Segall; costumes: Consuelo Gana, Helen Rosenthal; cast: The Author: Robert Foster; The Pierrot: J. C. McCord; The Harlequin: Richard Reed; Second Pierrot: Duncan Noble; Second Harlequin: George Reich; The Columbine: Valerie Bettis; Second Columbine: Barbara Ferguson

Vagary, 16 August 1949. choreography: Jane Dudley; music: Bartok; costume: Eileen Holding; a solo for Dudley

Festival (later incorporated into *The Village I Knew*), 16 August 1949. choreography: Sophie Maslow; music: Gregory Tucker, Samuel Matlowsky; costumes: Eileen Holding; cast: Orphan Girl: Muriel Manings; A Boy and Two Young Girls: Ronne Aul, Andora Hodgin, Anneliese Widman; Rabbi: Normand Maxon; Merrymakers: William Bales, Donald McKayle, Irving Burton; Three Women: Nina Caiserman, Lili Mann, Sophie Maslow

The Moor's Pavane, 17 August 1949. choreography: José Limón; music: Purcell, arr. Simon Sadoff; costumes: Pauline Lawrence; cast: The Moor: José Limón; His Friend: Lucas Hoving; The Moor's Wife: Betty Jones; His Friend's Wife: Pauline Koner

It Is Always Farewell, 18 August 1949. choreography: Valerie Bettis; music: Irwin Bazelon; costumes: Consuelo Gana; cast: Valerie Bettis, Duncan Noble, Doris Goodwin, J. C. McCord, Richard Reed, George Reich

--- **1950** ---

10 July–20 August 1950

Administrative board: Ruth Bloomer and Martha Hill, cochairmen; Louis Horst, Doris Humphrey, Ernest O. Melby, Jay B. Nash, Rosemary Park, Ralph E. Pickett, Francis C. Rosecrance, Mary Jo Shelly, Ruth Stanwood

Festival committee: Rosemary Park, chairman; Ruth Bloomer, Martha Hill, Louis Horst, Allen B. Lambdin

Teaching staff: William Bales, Ruth Bloomer, Nancy Brock, Jane Dudley, Martha Hill, Louis Horst, Doris Humphrey, Delia Hussey, Hazel Johnson, Pauline Lawrence, José Limón, Ruth Lloyd, Sophie Maslow, Jo Van Fleet, Betty Walberg, Theodora Wiesner, Drusa Wilker

Repertoire

Dudley, Maslow, Bales and Company: *Bach Suite* (Dudley, Maslow, Bales), *Lonely Ones* (Dudley), *Folksay* (Maslow), *Vagary* (Dudley), *Champion* (Maslow), *Dust Bowl Ballads* (Maslow), *Peon Portraits* (Bales), *Harmonica Breakdown* (Dudley)

José Limón and Company: *Invention* (Doris Humphrey), *Lament for Ignacio Sánchez Mejías* (Humphrey), *Chaconne in D minor*, *Day on Earth* (Humphrey), *The Moor's Pavane*, *La Malinche*

Pauline Koner Company: *Concerto in D Major*, *The Visit*

Merce Cunningham: *Two Step*, *Root of an Unfocus*, *The Monkey Dances*, *Before Dawn*

Katherine Litz: *Suite for a Woman*, *Twilight of a Flower*, *Fire in the Snow*, *Daughter of Virtue*

Nina Fonaroff: *Mr. Puppet*

Pearl Primus and Company: *Fanga*, *Spirituals*, *Prayer*, *Shouters of Sobo*, *Chants of Africa*, *Drum Rhythms*

Premieres

Impromptu, 5 August 1950. choreography: William Bales; music: Satie; costume: Eleanor De Vito; a solo for Bales

The Exiles, 11 August 1950. choreography: José Limón; music: Schoenberg, arr. Simon Sadoff; setting: Anita Weschler; costumes: Pauline Lawrence; cast: José Limón, Letitia Ide

Passional, 12 August 1950. choreography: Jane Dudley; music: Bartok; costumes: Eleanor De Vito; cast: Jane Dudley, Sophie Maslow, William Bales, Anneliese Widman, Donald McKayle, Ronne Aul, Alvin Beam, Irving Burton, Nina Caiserman, Billie Kirpich, Muriel Manings

The Village I Knew, 18 August 1950. choreography: Sophie Maslow; music: Gregory Tucker and Samuel Matlowsky; costumes: Eileen Holding; cast: Rabbi: Alvin Beam; Housewife: Jane Dudley; Orphan Girl: Muriel Manings; A Boy and Two Girls: Ronne Aul, Sophie Maslow, Anneliese Widman; Merrymakers: William Bales, Donald McKayle, Irving Burton; Two Women: Nina Caiserman, Billie Kirpich; Mother: Nina Caiserman; Daughter: Anneliese Widman; Fiddler: Ronne Aul

Concert, 19 August 1950. choreography: José Limón; music: Bach; costumes: Pauline Lawrence; cast: José Limón, Pauline Koner, Lucas Hoving, Betty Jones, Ruth Currier

----------------------------------- **1951** -----------------------------------

9 July–19 August 1951

Administration: Rosemary Park, president, Connecticut College; Ruth Bloomer, Martha Hill, codirectors; Margaret Hazlewood, administrative assistant

Festival committee: Ruth Bloomer, Martha Hill, Louis Horst, Allen Lambdin, Rosemary Park

Teaching staff: William Bales, Ruth Bloomer, Jane Dudley, Els Grelinger, Martha Hill, Louis Horst, Doris Humphrey, Delia Hussey, José Limón, Ruth Lloyd, Sophie Maslow, Theodora Wiesner

Repertoire

José Limón and Company: *The Exiles, Tonantzintla, Dialogues, La Malinche, The Moor's Pavane*
Repertory Class: *Passacaglia and Fugue in C Minor* (Humphrey)

Premieres

Amorous Adventure, 16 August 1951. choreography: Pauline Koner; music: Freda Miller; story and designs: Abner Dean; cast: A Kind of Wife: Pauline Koner; A Sort of Husband: Charles Weidman; A Man with a Predictable Future, Inevitable Present, and Contrived Past: Lucas Hoving

Four Sonnets, 16 August 1951. choreography: Sophie Maslow; music: Schumann; costumes: Charlotte Trowbridge; cast: Jane Dudley, Sophie Maslow, William Bales

Quartet No. 1 (Night Spell), 16 August 1951. choreography: Doris Humphrey; music: Priaulx Rainier; costumes: Pauline Lawrence; setting: Thomas Skelton; cast: First Figure: José Limón; Three Figures: Lucas Hoving, Betty Jones, Ruth Currier

A Song for You, 18 August 1951. choreography: Charles Weidman; music: Brazilian songs recorded by Elsie Houston; a solo for Weidman

The Haunted Ones, 18 August 1951. choreography: William Bales; music: Leon Kirchner; costumes: Charlotte Trowbridge; cast: The Daughter: Jane Dudley; The Mother: Sophie Maslow; The Son: William Bales

---

1952

---

14 July–24 August 1952

Administration: Rosemary Park, president; Ruth Bloomer, Martha Hill, codirectors

Festival committee: Rosemary Park, chairman; Ruth Bloomer, Martha Hill, Louis Horst, Allen Lambdin

Teaching staff: William Bales, Ruth Bloomer, Jane Dudley, Ruth Ferguson, Martha Graham, Els Grelinger, Martha Hill, Louis Horst, Doris Humphrey, Hazel Johnson, Pauline Koner, José Limón, Sophie Maslow, Theodora Wiesner

Repertoire

José Limón and Dance Company: *Day on Earth* (Humphrey), *Concerto Grosso, Story of Mankind* (Humphrey), *Variations and Conclusion from "New Dance"* (Humphrey)
Dudley-Maslow-Bales and Company: *Sonata* (Dudley), *Sonnets* (Maslow), *The Village I Knew* (Maslow)
Ronne Aul: *Street Musician, The Possible Hunter, Caller of the Wind, Movement Dance*
Emily Frankel and Mark Ryder: *And Jacob Loved Rachel, The Misfits, Biography of Fear*
Pearl Lang and Company: *Song of Deborah, Legend, Moonsung, Windsung*
Repertory Class: *Song of the West* (Humphrey)

Premieres

The Queen's Epicedium, 21 August 1952. choreography: José Limón; music: Purcell;

costumes: Pauline Lawrence; cast: Letitia Ide, Ruth Currier, Lavina Nielsen, Betty Jones

Mostly Like Flight, 21 August 1952. choreography: Ronne Aul; music: Stravinsky; a solo for Aul

Family Portrait, 22 August 1952. choreography: Jane Dudley; music: Meyer Kupferman; setting: Milton Wynne; costumes: Harriet Winters; cast: The Boy: Ronne Aul; The Mother: Sophie Maslow; The Father: William Bales; The Cat: Anneliese Widman; Tina: Muriel Manings; The Grandmother: Billie Kirpich; A Present, the Jacket: David Wood; The Older Cousin: Charles Czarny; Another Present, the Rifle: Irving Burton

Snow Queen, 22 August 1952. choreography: Sophie Maslow; music: Prokofieff; costumes: Harriet Winters; cast: North Wind: Jane Dudley; Snow Queen: Sophie Maslow; The Youth and Girl: David Wood, Muriel Manings; Lovers: Anneliese Widman, William Bales; Companions: Billie Kirpich, Charles Czarny, Irving Burton; Young Man: Ronne Aul

Fantasy and Fugue in C Major and Fugue in C Minor, 23 August 1952. choreography: Doris Humphrey; music: Mozart; costumes: Pauline Lawrence; cast: Betty Jones, José Limón, Lavina Nielsen, Lucas Hoving, Pauline Koner, Ruth Currier

The Visitation, 23 August 1952. choreography: José Limón; music: Schoenberg; costumes: Pauline Lawrence; cast: The Man: José Limón; His Wife: Pauline Koner; The Stranger: Lucas Hoving

---

1953

13 July–23 August, 1953

Administration: Rosemary Park, president; Ruth Bloomer, Martha Hill (advisory), codirectors

Festival committee: Rosemary Park, chairman; Ruth Bloomer, Martha Hill, Louis Horst, Allen Lambdin

Teaching staff: Ruth Bloomer, Robert Cohan, Ruth Currier, Margret Dietz, Ruth Ferguson, Martha Graham, Louis Horst, Lucas Hoving, Doris Humphrey, Delia Hussey, Hazel Johnson, Betty Jones, Pauline Koner, José Limón, Sophie Maslow, Ruth Murray, Natanya Neumann, Helen Priest Rogers, Nona Schurman

Repertoire

José Limón and Dance Company: *Invention* (Humphrey), *Night Spell* (Humphrey), *The Moor's Pavane*, *Ritmo Jondo* (Humphrey)

Sophie Maslow and Dance Company: *Dust Bowl Ballads*, *The Village I Knew*, *The Wall*

Ronne Aul: *The Possible Hunter*

John Butler Dance Company: *Masque of the Wildman*

Repertory class: *With My Red Fires*, excerpts (Humphrey)

Premieres

Cassandra, 20 August 1953. choreography: Pauline Koner; music: Copland; a solo for Koner

Ruins and Visions, 20 August 1953. choreography: Doris Humphrey; music: Britten; setting:

Paul Trautvetter; costumes: Pauline Lawrence; cast: The Mother: Pauline Koner; The Son: Lucas Hoving; The Actress: Lavina Nielsen; The Actor: José Limón; Another Actor: Crandall Diehl; Newsboy: Charles Czarny; Two Girls: Betty Jones, Ruth Currier; The Bride: Lavina Nielsen; Young Man: Crandall Diehl

Malocchio, 20 August 1953. choreography: John Butler; music: Aldo Provenzano; designs: Paul Barnes; cast: The One with the Evil Eye: Felisa Conde; The Stranger: Glen Tetley; Children: Violet Ortiz, Paul Rena, Rosemary Weekley, Gardiner Meade

Perilous Flight, 21 August 1953. choreography: Lucas Hoving, Lavina Nielsen; music: Bartok; costumes: Consuelo Gana; cast: Lavina Nielsen, Lucas Hoving

Suite: Manhattan Transfer, 21 August 1953. choreography: Sophie Maslow; music: Pine Top Smith, Jimmy Yancy, Pete Johnson; cast: Sophie Maslow, Ronne Aul, Charles Czarny, Alvin Schulman, Anneliese Widman

30th at 3rd, 22 August 1953. choreography: Ronne Aul; music: Albeniz, Laparra, Falla; a solo for Aul

Sonata for Dancer and Piano, 22 August 1953. choreography: Ronne Aul; music: Sam Raphling; a solo for Aul

Satyros: Spring, 22 August 1953. choreography: Lucas Hoving; music: Poulenc; cast: Lavina Nielsen, Lucas Hoving

Don Juan Fantasia, 22 August 1953. choreography: José Limón; music: Liszt; costumes: Pauline Lawrence; cast: Don Juan: José Limón; Don Gonzalo: Lucas Hoving; The Ladies: Betty Jones, Ruth Currier, Lavina Nielsen

---

1954

12 July–22 August 1954

Administration: Rosemary Park, president; Ruth Bloomer, Martha Hill (on leave), codirectors

Festival committee: Rosemary Park, chairman; Ruth Bloomer, Martha Hill, Louis Horst, Allen Lambdin

Teaching staff: Ruth Bloomer, Valerie Bettis, Ruth Currier, Margret Dietz, Ruth Ferguson, Martha Graham, Martha Hill, Louis Horst, Lucas Hoving, Doris Humphrey, Delia Hussey, Hazel Johnson, Betty Jones, Pauline Koner, José Limón, Ruth and Norman Lloyd, Ruth L. Murray, Natanya Neumann, Helen Priest Rogers, Lucy Venable, Thomas Watson, Theodora Wiesner, Yuriko

Repertoire

José Limón and Dance Company: *Ritmo Jondo* (Humphrey), *Variations and Conclusion from "New Dance"* (Humphrey), *The Visitation, Chaconne in D minor*

Daniel Nagrin: *Man of Action, Strange Hero, Spanish Dance, Dance in the Sun*

Pauline Koner: *Cassandra*

Charles Weidman and Theatre Dance Company: *James Thurber's "The War Between Men and Women," Flickers*

Yuriko: *Tale of Seizure, The Gift*

Repertory class: *Soaring* (Humphrey and Ruth St. Denis), *Water Study* (Humphrey)

Premieres

*The Traitor, 19 August 1954. choreography: José Limón; music: Gunther Schuller; setting: Paul Trautvetter; costumes: Pauline Lawrence; cast: The Leader: Lucas Hoving; His Followers: Charles Czarny, Richard Fitz-Gerald, Michael Hollander, Alvin Schulman, Otis Bigelow, John Coyle; The Traitor: José Limón

Four Windows, 19 August 1954. choreography: Yuriko; music: Bartok; cast: Yuriko, John Coyle

. . . where the roads . . . , 19 August 1954. choreography: Yuriko; music: Eugene Lester; cast: Twins: Yuriko, Alice Uchida; Man: Alvin Schulman

Man Dancing, 20 August 1954. choreography: Daniel Nagrin; music: Bartok; a solo for Nagrin

A Dream, 21 August 1954. choreography: Margret Dietz; music: Ulrich Kessler; a solo for Dietz

Felipe el Loco, 21 August 1954. choreography: Doris Humphrey; music: traditional Spanish guitar; setting: Paul Trautvetter; costumes: Pauline Lawrence; cast: Felipe: José Limón; Imaginary Dancer: Pauline Koner; Ensemble: Lucas Hoving, Betty Jones, Ruth Currier, Lavina Nielsen, Charles Czarny

--------------------------- **1955** ---------------------------

11 July–21 August 1955

Administration: Rosemary Park, president; Ruth Bloomer, Martha Hill (on leave), codirectors

Festival committee: Rosemary Park, chairman; Ruth Bloomer, Martha Hill, Louis Horst, Allen Lambdin

Teaching staff: George and Barbara Beiswanger, Ruth Bloomer, Margret Dietz, Ruth Ferguson, Virginia Freeman, Martha Graham, Louis Horst, Lucas Hoving, Doris Humphrey, Hazel Johnson, Pauline Koner, José Limón, Ruth and Norman Lloyd, Michael Lopuszanski, Helen Priest Rogers, Lucy Venable, Thomas Watson, Theodora Wiesner

Repertoire

José Limón and Dance Company: *La Malinche, Night Spell* (Humphrey), *The Traitor, The Moor's Pavane, Ruins and Visions* (Humphrey)
Pearl Lang: *Moonsung, Windsung, And Joy Is My Witness, Rites*
Lucas Hoving and Lavina Nielsen: *Ballad*
Repertory class: *The Shakers* (Humphrey)

Premieres

*Airs and Graces, 18 August 1955. choreography: Doris Humphrey; music: Locatelli; setting: Paul Trautvetter; costumes: Pauline Lawrence; cast: The Music Lover: Lucas Hoving; The Graces: Ruth Currier, Betty Jones, Lavina Nielsen

Symphony for Strings, 19 August 1955. choreography: José Limón; music: William Schuman; costumes: Pauline Lawrence; cast: José Limón, Pauline Koner, Lucas Hoving, Betty Jones, Ruth Currier, Lavina Nielsen

Scherzo, 19 August 1955. choreography: José Limón; music: Hazel Johnson; costumes:

Pauline Lawrence; cast: Richard Fitz-Gerald, Michael Hollander, Harlan McCallum, John Barber

Idyl, 20 August 1955. choreography: Ruth Currier; music: Bartok; costumes: Lavina Nielsen; cast: Ruth Currier, Richard Fitz-Gerald

The Antagonists, 20 August 1955. choreography: Ruth Currier; music: Stravinsky; costumes: Lavina Nielsen; cast: Ruth Currier, Betty Jones

Satyros: Summer, Autumn, 20 August 1955. choreography: Lucas Hoving, Lavina Nielsen; music: Poulenc; setting: Paul Trauvetter; cast: Lucas Hoving, Lavina Nielsen

Concertino in A Major, 20 August 1955. choreography: Pauline Koner; music: Pergolesi; costumes: Consuelo Gana; cast: Pauline Koner, Lucy Venable, Elizabeth Harris

--------------------------------- **1956** ---------------------------------

9 July–19 August 1956

Administration: Rosemary Park, president; Ruth Bloomer, Martha Hill (on leave), codirectors

Festival committee: Rosemary Park, chairman; Ruth Bloomer, Martha Hill, Louis Horst, Allen Lambdin

Teaching staff: George Beiswanger, Ruth Bloomer, Ruth Currier, Margret Dietz, Ruth Ferguson, Virginia Freeman, Martha Graham, Patricia Heigel, Martha Hill, Michael Hollander, Louis Horst, Lucas Hoving, Doris Humphrey, Hazel Johnson, Betty Jones, Pauline Koner, José Limón, Norman and Ruth Lloyd, Murray Louis, Lavina Nielsen, Alwin Nikolais, Helen Priest Rogers, Doris Rudko, Anna Sokolow, Lucy Venable, Thomas Watson, Theodora Wiesner

Repertoire

José Limón and Dance Company: *Symphony for Strings, There Is a Time, Scherzo, Ritmo Jondo* (Humphrey), *The Exiles, Theatre Piece No. 2* (Humphrey)
Ruth Currier and Dance Group: *Becoming, Triplicity*
Pauline Koner and Dance Company: *Concertino in A Major*
Henry St. Playhouse Dance Company (Alwin Nikolais): *Kaleidoscope*
Theatre Dance Company (Anna Sokolow): *Rooms, Lyric Suite*
Repertory class: *Song of the West* (Humphrey)

Premieres

The Shining Dark, 16 August 1956. choreography: Pauline Koner; artistic adviser: Doris Humphrey; music: Leon Kirchner; cast: One in Silence and Darkness: Pauline Koner; One Who Comes to Teach: Lucy Venable; One Who Comes to Help: Elizabeth Harris

Winter, 18 August 1956. choreography: Birgit Akesson; music: Vivaldi; a solo for Akesson

Music for Strings, Percussion, and Celeste, 18 August 1956. choreography: Birgit Akesson; music: Bartok; a solo for Akesson

Persephone Dance, 18 August 1956. choreography: Birgit Akesson; music: Karl-Birger Blomdahl; a solo for Akesson

Of Burden and of Mercy, 18 August 1956. choreography: Margret Dietz; music: Ben Johnston; a solo for Dietz

——————————————————— **1957** ———————————————————

8 July–18 August 1957

Administration: Rosemary Park, president; Ruth Bloomer, Martha Hill (on leave), codirectors

Festival committee: Rosemary Park, chairman; Ruth Bloomer, Martha Hill, Louis Horst, Allen Lambdin

Teaching staff: George Beiswanger, Ruth Bloomer, Ruth Currier, Margret Dietz, Ruth Ferguson, Virginia Freeman, Martha Graham, Faith Gulick, Michael Hollander, Louis Horst, Lucas Hoving, Doris Humphrey, Delia Hussey, Hazel Johnson, Betty Jones, Pauline Koner, José Limón, Norman and Ruth Lloyd, Evelyn Lohoefer, Murray Louis, Alwin Nikolais, Helen Priest Rogers, Doris Rudko, Lucy Venable, Thomas Watson, Theodora Wiesner, Ethel Winter, David Wood

Repertoire

Festival Concerts
José Limón and Dance Company: *Night Spell* (Humphrey), *La Malinche*, *Emperor Jones*, *Scherzo*, *Ritmo Jondo* (Humphrey), *Ruins and Visions* (Humphrey), *The Moor's Pavane*
Pauline Koner: *Cassandra*
Daniel Nagrin: *Strange Hero, Man of Action*
Mary Anthony Dance Theatre: *Threnody*
Ruth Currier with Betty Jones: *The Antagonists*
Repertory class: *Passacaglia and Fugue in C Minor* (Humphrey)

Little Concert Series
Beverly Schmidt: *Rite, Droll Figure, Two Characters, Caprice, Mobile, Premonitions*
Murray Louis: *Antechamber, Man in Chair, Belonging to the Moon, Reflections, Improvisation, Quartet, Corida*
Michael Hollander: *Two Dances (In Retrospect and Anticipation)*
David Wood: *Episodes, Country Style*
Diane Quitzow: *The Golden Sphere*
Durevol Quitzow: *Flowers Trains Trunks and Things*
Dance Quartet (Virginia Freeman, Meriam Rosen, Patricia Wityk, William Hug): *Opening Suite* (Wityk, Rosen, Hug), *Murdered Sleep* (Rosen), *Five Portraits* (Rosen), *In One Is Contained* (Freeman), *Celebration* (Freeman), *Rhythm Ritual* (Hug)
Dore Hoyer: *Signal, Between Yesterday and Today, Dynamic, Revolving Dance, Indian Elegy (From Silence to Silence), Holiday Eve, Ruth the Reaper Meets Boas, Potiphar's Wife Tempts and Denounces Joseph*

Premieres

*Dance Overture, 15 August 1957. choreography: Doris Humphrey; music: Paul Creston; costumes: Pauline Lawrence; cast: Lola Huth, Vol Quitzow, Lucy Venable, Chester Wolenski, Lavina Nielsen, Ronald Chase, Harlan McCallum, Betty Jones, Michael Hollander, Ruth Currier, Pauline Koner, Lucas Hoving, José Limón
Blue Roses, 16 August 1957. choreography: José Limón; music: William Lorin, based on themes of Paul Bowles; costumes: Pauline Lawrence; cast: The Son: Lucas Hoving; The

Mother: Lavina Nielsen; The Daughter: Betty Jones; A Friend of the Son: José Limón; Gentleman Callers: Michael Hollander, Harlan McCallum, Chester Wolenski, Ronald Chase, Vol Quitzow, Kenneth Bartness

Runic Canto, 16 August 1957. choreography and music: Alwin Nikolais; color design: George Constant; cast: Gladys Bailin, Murray Louis, and festival students

Indeterminate Figure, 17 August 1957. choreography: Daniel Nagrin; music: Robert Starer; a solo for Nagrin

The Great Song, 18 August 1957. choreography: Dore Hoyer; music: Dimitri Wiatowitsch; a solo for Hoyer

---

1958

7 July–17 August 1958

Administration: Rosemary Park, president; Ruth Bloomer, Martha Hill (on leave), codirectors; Theodora Wiesner, administrative assistant

Festival committee: Rosemary Park, chairman; Ruth Bloomer, Martha Hill, Louis Horst, Allen Lambdin, Norman Lloyd, Thomas Watson, Theodora Wiesner

Teaching staff: George Beiswanger, Ruth Bloomer, Ruth Currier, Ruth Ferguson, Virginia Freeman, Martha Graham, Michael Hollander, Louis Horst, Lucas Hoving, Doris Humphrey, Hazel Johnson, Betty Jones, Pauline Koner, José Limón, Norman and Ruth Lloyd, Evelyn Lohoefer, Helen Priest Rogers, Doris Rudko, Lucy Venable, Thomas Watson, Theodora Wiesner, David Wood

Repertoire

Festival concerts
José Limón and Dance Company: *Ritmo Jondo* (Humphrey) *There Is a Time*, *The Traitor*
Merce Cunningham and Dance Company: *Nocturnes*, *Changeling*
Pearl Lang and Dance Company: *Nightflight*, *Once Upon a Wish*, *Falls the Shadow*
Pauline Koner and Dance Company: *Concertino in A Major*, *The Shining Dark*
Inga Weiss: *Etudes*, *Twelve Variations*
Ruth Currier and Dance Company: *The Antagonists*
Repertory class: *Life of the Bee* (Humphrey)

Little Concert Series
William Hug: *Dancers Count*, *Rhythm Ritual*, *Conversations*, *Regulations*, *Moods*
Vol Quitzow: *Short Story*
Diane Quitzow: *Fly*
Connie Keyse: *Red*, *Primeval Encounter*
Pola Nirenska: *Vigil by the Sea*, *The Eternal Fool*
Michael Hollander: *Eight Inventions*, *Icarus With a Ladder*
Jack Moore: *The Geek*, *Cry of the Phoenix*, *The Act*
Doris Rudko: *The Time Between*, *Field of Torment*
Marion Scott: *The Tenderling*, *Animal Courtship*

Premieres

Antic Meet, 14 August 1958. choreography: Merce Cunningham; music: John Cage; designs: Robert Rauschenberg; cast: Merce Cunningham, Carolyn Brown, Viola Farber, Cynthia Stone, Marilyn Wood, Remy Charlip

Serenata, 14 August 1958. choreography: José Limón; music: Paul Bowles; setting: Thomas Watson; costumes: Pauline Lawrence; cast: The Lover: José Limón; His Lady: Pauline Koner; The Lady's Voice: Betty Jones; The Lover's Voice: Chester Wolenski

Dances, 15 August 1958. choreography: José Limón; music: Chopin; costumes: Lavina Nielsen; cast: Lola Huth, Chester Wolenski, Betty Jones, Harlan McCallum, Michael Hollander, Ruth Currier, Lucy Venable

Summerspace, 17 August 1958. choreography: Merce Cunningham; music: Morton Feldman; designs: Robert Rauschenberg; cast: Merce Cunningham, Carolyn Brown, Viola Farber, Cynthia Stone, Marilyn Wood, Remy Charlip

---

1959

6 July–16 August 1959

Administration: Rosemary Park, president; Ruth Bloomer, adviser; Jeanette Schlottmann, director (Ruth Bloomer died 17 April 1959)

Advisory board for the School of Dance: Rosemary Park, chairman; Ruth Bloomer, Martha Hill, Louis Horst, José Limón, Pauline Lawrence Limón, Norman Lloyd, Ruth Lloyd, Jeanette Schlottmann, Theodora Wiesner

American Dance Festival committee: Rosemary Park, chairman; Martha Hill, Louis Horst, Allen Lambdin, Norman Lloyd, Jeanette Schlottmann, Thomas Watson, Theodora Wiesner

Teaching staff: James Baird, Carolyn Brown, Ruth Burke, Merce Cunningham, Martha Graham, Louis Horst, Lucas Hoving, Lola Huth, Hazel Johnson, Betty Jones, Pauline Koner, José Limón, Norman and Ruth Lloyd, Evelyn Lohoefer, Douglas Maddox, Harlan McCallum, Daniel Nagrin, Joan Phillips, Helen Priest Rogers, Doris Rudko, Eleanor Schick, Jeanette Schlottmann, Bessie Schönberg, Helen Tamiris, Virginia Tanner, Lucy Venable, Christine Walton, Thomas Watson, David Wood

Repertoire

Festival concerts
José Limón Company: *Day on Earth* (Humphrey), *Lament for Ignacio Sánchez Mejías* (Humphrey), *Ruins and Visions* (Humphrey)
Daniel Nagrin: *Dance in the Sun, Indeterminate Figure*
Merce Cunningham: *Antic Meet*
Sybil Shearer: *Part III*
Ruth Currier: *Dangerous World*

Other events
Erick Hawkins: *Here and Now with Watchers*
Young choreographers program: *Theme As of Revelation* (Harlan McCallum), *Of the Land*

(Carol Scothorn), *Wild Horse* (Jean Cébron), *Poem* (Cébron), *Model for a Mobile* (Cébron), *Aquatic Vision* (Cébron), *Area Disabled* (Jack Moore), *Figure '59* (Moore), *First Song* (Anneliese Widman), *Pantomime in Movement* (Juki Arkin)

Premieres

Tenebrae 1914, 13 August 1959. choreography: José Limón; music: John Wilson; setting: Ming Cho Lee; costumes: Pauline Lawrence; cast: Ruth Currier, Harlan McCallum, Chester Wolenski, Robert Powell, James Payton, Stephen Paxton

Tides, 14 August 1959. choreography: Pauline Koner; music: Villa-Lobos, Jimmy Giuffre, Harold Farberman; text: John Donne; narrator: Alexander Scourby; cast: Pauline Koner, Lucy Venable, Harlan McCallum, Jan Stockman, Rima Berg, Stephen Paxton

Rune, 14 August 1959. choreography: Merce Cunningham; music: Christian Wolff; costumes: Robert Rauschenberg; cast: Merce Cunningham, Carolyn Brown, Viola Farber, Marilyn Wood, Judith Dunn, Remy Charlip

Part I, 14 August 1959. choreography: Sybil Shearer; music: Clementi; a solo for Shearer

Part II, 14 August 1959. choreography: Sybil Shearer; music: Owen Haynes; costumes: Joe Kaminski; cast: Sybil Shearer, Paul Berna, Mel Spinney

Memoir, 15 August 1959. choreography: Helen Tamiris; music: Chavez; setting: Howard Bay; costumes: Anna Hill Johnstone; cast: Orphan Girl: Eleanor Schick; A Crazy One: Linda Call; A Wild One: Anneliese Widman; A Leader: Daniel Nagrin; Father: Daniel Nagrin; Mother: Anneliese Widman; Aunts: Linda Call, Carol Scothorn; Uncles: Gilberto Motta, James Payton, Stephen Paxton, Robert Powell; Cousins: Ann Amter, Chris Walton; Children: festival students

Theatre for Fools, 15 August 1959. choreography and designs: Daniel Nagrin; music: Bartok; cast: With a Cape: Daniel Nagrin; In Blue: David Wood; In Flesh Tights: Marni Thomas; In Lavender: Gail Ewert

The Apostate, 15 August 1959. choreography: José Limón; music: Ernst Krenek; The Apostate: José Limón; The Galilean: Lucas Hoving; The Olympian: Betty Jones

---

1960

---

11 July–21 August 1960

Advisory board for the School of Dance: Rosemary Park, chairman; Martha Hill, Louis Horst, José Limón, Pauline Lawrence Limón, Norman and Ruth Lloyd, Jeanette Schlottmann (director), Theodora Wiesner

American Dance Festival committee: Rosemary Park, chairman; Martha Hill, Louis Horst, Allen Lambdin, Norman Lloyd, Jeanette Schlottmann, Thomas Watson, Theodora Wiesner

Teaching staff: Loretta Abbott, George Beiswanger, Carolyn Brown, Ruth Burke, Merce Cunningham, Ruth Currier, Ralph Davis, Bettie de Jong, Viola Farber, Martha Graham, Louis Horst, Lucas Hoving, Lola Huth, Hazel Johnson, Betty Jones, Pauline Koner, José Limón, Norman and Ruth Lloyd, Evelyn Lohoefer, Anne McKinley, Helen Priest Rogers, Doris Rudko, Bessie Schönberg, Jan Stockman, Virginia Tanner, Marnie Thomas, Lucy Venable, Thomas Watson, Charles Weidman, Theodora Wiesner, Martha Wittman, Chester Wolenski, David Wood

Repertoire

Festival concerts

José Limón and Dance Company: *The Traitor, Passacaglia and Fugue in C Minor* (Humphrey), *Toccanta* (Ruth Currier), *Ritmo Jondo* (Humphrey), *Night Spell* (Humphrey), *Missa Brevis, The Moor's Pavane*

Merce Cunningham and Dance Company: *Night Wandering, Septet, Rune, Suite for Five*

Pearl Lang and Dance Company: *Black Marigolds*

Lucas Hoving and Dance Company: *Wall of Silence*

Charles Weidman Repertory Group: *Atavisms: Lynchtown, Bargain Counter*

Doris Humphrey Fellow: Jack Moore (*Songs Remembered*)

Little Concert Series

Martha Graham: lecture-demonstration

Beverly Schmidt: *9 Points in Time*

Phyllis Lamhut: *Herald, Pastel, Portrait, Hands, March*

Charles Weidman: *Classroom Modern Style, Dance of the Streets, The Moth and the Star*

José Limón: open rehearsal of *Passacaglia and Fugue in C Minor* (Humphrey), *Barren Sceptre* (Limón and Pauline Koner), *The Moor's Pavane, Missa Brevis*

Joan Hartshorne: *Escape for Five*

Betty Jones: *The Snare*

Joan Miller: *Protest*

Carol Anne Wallace: *Sketches of Gauchette*

Rena Schenfeld: *El Barco Negro*

Lola Huth: *The Keeper of the Moon*

Jack Moore: *Intaglios*

Dances by students from Korea, Argentina, Japan, Spain, Jamaica, and Haiti

Premieres

*Transfigured Season, 18 August 1960. choreography: Ruth Currier; music: Jack Behrens; cast: Figure in Time: Martha Wittman; Premonitory Figure: Ruth Currier; The Changing Ones: Julie Arenal, Joan Miller, Tryntje Ostrander, Jan Stockman, Dimitra Sundeen, Ann Vachon

*Shira, 19 August 1960. choreography and costumes: Pearl Lang; music: Hovhaness; setting: Thomas Watson; cast: Pearl Lang, Dale Sehnert, Bruce Marks, Patricia Christopher, Paul Berensohn, Bettie de Jong, Victor Melnick, Koert Stuyf, Rina Schenfeld, Tryntje Ostrander, Jennifer Muller

*Crises, 19 August 1960. choreography: Merce Cunningham; music: Conlon Nancarrow; costumes: Robert Rauschenberg; cast: Merce Cunningham, Carolyn Brown, Viola Farber, Marilyn Wood, Judith Dunn

───────────────────── **1961** ─────────────────────

10 July–20 August 1961

Advisory board for the School of Dance: Rosemary Park, chairman; Martha Hill, Louis Horst, José Limón, Pauline Lawrence Limón, Norman and Ruth Lloyd, Jeanette Schlottmann (director), Theodora Wiesner

American Dance Festival committee: Rosemary Park, chairman; Martha Hill, Louis Horst, Allen Lambdin, Norman Lloyd, Jeanette Schlottmann, Thomas Skelton, Theodora Wiesner

Teaching staff: Susan Babel, William Bales, George Beiswanger, Carolyn Brown, Ruth Burke, Marsha Cheaskin, Merce Cunningham, Ruth Currier, Viola Farber, June Gebelein, Martha Graham, Louis Horst, Hazel Johnson, Betty Jones, Jean Learey, Nancy Lewis, José Limón, Norman and Ruth Lloyd, La Meri, Ann McKinley, Jack Moore, Carol Newman, Helen Priest Rogers, Doris Rudko, Bessie Schönberg, Thomas Skelton, Virginia Tanner, Marnie Thomas, Lucy Venable, Christine Walton, Martha Wittman, Chester Wolenski, David Wood

Repertoire

Festival concerts
José Limón and Dance Company: *Performance, The Moor's Pavane*
Merce Cunningham and Dance Company: *Crises*
Paul Taylor and Dance Company: *Fibers, 3 Epitaphs*
David Wood and Dance Company: *The Initiate*
Anna Sokolow Dance Company: *Dreams*
Repertory class: *Brandenberg Concerto No. 4* (Ruth Currier and Doris Humphrey)

Little Concert Series
Carol Wallace: *Theme and Variations*
Jean Learey: *Mirage*
James Payton: *Sinister Ritual, Out and Beyond*
Meryl Whitman: *The He and the She of It*
Joseph Schlichter: *Ekstasis*
Martha Wittman: *Journey to a Clear Place*
David Wood: *Danza*
Manja Chmiel: *Suite in Gray, Moved from Outside, Colored Suite*
Midi Garth: *Ricadanza, Voices, Time and Memory, Sea Change, Anonymous, Double Image*
Robert Cohan: *The Eclipse, The Pass*
Dances by students from Hawaii, Hungary, Okinawa, the Ukraine, Chile, Argentina, and India

Premieres

Aeon, 17 August 1961. choreography: Merce Cunningham; music: John Cage; designs: Robert Rauschenberg; cast: Merce Cunningham, Carolyn Brown, Remy Charlip, Judith Dunn, Viola Farber, Marilyn Wood, Shareen Blair, Steve Paxton, Valda Setterfield

Resonances, 18 August 1961. choreography: Ruth Currier; music: Ernst Krenek, Vladimir Ussachevsky, Jack Behrens; setting: Thomas Skelton; costumes: Lavina Nielsen; cast: Ruth Currier, Jack Moore, Martha Wittman, James Payton

*The Moirai, 18 August 1961. choreography: José Limón; music: Hugh Aitken; costumes: Pauline Lawrence; cast: Klotho: Betty Jones; Lachesis: Lola Huth; Atropos: Ruth Currier; Man: Chester Wolenski

Insects and Heroes, 18 August 1961. choreography: Paul Taylor; music: John Herbert

McDowell; designs: Rouben Ter-Arutunian; cast: Paul Taylor, Linda Hodes, Dan Wagoner, Maggie Newman, Elizabeth Walton, Elizabeth Keen, Sharon Kinney, Renee Kimball, Daniel Lewis

Granada Suite, 19 August 1961. choreography and costumes: La Meri; music: Joaquín Turina; cast: Erika Rehm, June Schwartz, Sue Ellen Swerdlin, Carole Weinstein, Junko Hamakawa, Marcia Halmers, Carol Mable, Christine Walton, Louis Falco, Jean Learey, Carol Wallace, Harriette Brouden, Lucinda Childs, Marcia Dunbar-Soule, Juliette Fisher, Marcia Holmes, Renee Kimball, Virginia Olney, Katherine Wyly, Louise Grinberg, Kathleen Joyce, Robin Leeger, Susie Watts

Sonata for Two Cellos, 19 August 1961. choreography: José Limón; music: Meyer Kupferman; costume: Pauline Lawrence; a solo for Limón

Target, 20 August 1961. choreography: Jack Moore; music: Evelyn Lohoefer, Keter Betts; cast: Jean Learey, Nancy Lewis, Chester Wolenski, Jack Moore

1962

9 July–19 August 1962

Advisory board for the School of Dance: Rosemary Park, chairman; Martha Hill, Louis Horst, José Limón, Pauline Lawrence Limón, Norman and Ruth Lloyd, Jeanette Schlottmann (director), Theodora Wiesner

Festival committee: Rosemary Park, chairman; Martha Hill, Louis Horst, Norman Lloyd, Jeanette Schlottmann, Theodora Wiesner

Teaching staff: Alvin Ailey, William Bales, George Beiswanger, Bonnie Bird, Carolyn Brown, Patricia Christopher, Merce Cunningham, Ruth Currier, Robert Dunn, Viola Farber, June Gebelein, Martha Graham, Louis Horst, Lucas Hoving, Hazel Johnson, Betty Jones, José Limón, Evelyn Lohoefer, Chase Robinson, Helen Priest Rogers, Doris Rudko, Bessie Schönberg, Thomas Skelton, Ineke Sluiter, Marnie Thomas, Thomas Watson, Theodora Wiesner, Martha Wittman, Chester Wolenski, David Wood

Repertoire

José Limón and Company: *Night Spell* (Humphrey), *Emperor Jones, Missa Brevis, La Malinche, Brandenburg Concerto No. 4* (Humphrey and Currier), *The Traitor*

Martha Graham and Her Dance Company: *A Look at Lightning, Phaedra, Diversion of Angels, Samson Agonistes, Alcestis, Seraphic Dialogue, Acrobats of God*

Erick Hawkins, with Barbara Tucker, Kelly Holt: *Early Floating, Here and Now with Watchers*

Alvin Ailey Dance Theater: *Gillespiana, Hermit Songs, Revelations*

Charles Weidman and His Theater Dance Company: *Three Thurber Fables*

Ruth Currier and Dance Company: *Quartet, The Antagonists*

Lucas Hoving and Company: *Wall of Silence, Strange to Wish Wishes No Longer*

Glen Tetley, with Linda Hodes, Robert Powell: *Pierrot Lunaire*

Paul Draper: *Informal, Solfeggietto, Sonata for Tap Dancer, Tea for Two, Ad Lib*

Katherine Litz: *The Story of Love from Fear to Flight, And No Birds Sing, Twilight of a Flower, The Fall of the Leaf*

Paul Taylor Dance Company: *Meridian, Tablet, 3 Epitaphs*
Pearl Lang and Company: *Shira, Apasionado*
Daniel Nagrin: *With My Hand and With My Eye, Indeterminate Figure*
Young choreographers program: *Coplas* (Lenore Latimer), *Tears and Laughter* (Karin Thulin),
   Trillium (Trisha Brown), *The Return* (Rosalind Pierson), *Faces in the Fire* (Pierson), *No
   Nato* (Margery Apso*), Eccentric Convention* (Janet Soares), *Canticle No. 1* (Pauline de
   Groot), *Teach Us to Care and Not to Care* (Diane Sherer)

Premieres

Aureole, 4 August 1962. choreography: Paul Taylor; music: Handel; cast: Paul Taylor,
   Elizabeth Walton, Dan Wagoner, Sharon Kinney, Renee Kimball
The Lazarite, 11 August 1962. choreography: Carol Scothorn; music: Daniel Jahn; a solo
   for Scothorn (Doris Humphrey Fellow)
Secular Games, 17 August 1962. choreography: Martha Graham; music: Robert Starer;
   setting: Jean Rosenthal; properties: Marion Kinsella; cast: Robert Powell, David Wood,
   Richard Kuch, Richard Gain, Clive Thompson, Dudley Williams, Peter Randazzo,
   Helen McGehee, Lois Schlossberg, Juliet Fisher, Phyllis Gutelius, Takako Asakawa,
   Mabel Robinson, Carol Fried

I, Odysseus, 18 August 1962. choreography: José Limón; music: Hugh Aitken; properties:
   Thomas Watson, William McIver; cast: Zeus: Simon Sadoff; Athena: Betty Jones;
   Circe: Ruth Currier; Poseidon: Harlan McCallum; Calypso: Lola Huth; Hermes: Louis
   Falco; Odysseus: José Limón; Penelope: Lucy Venable; Companions of Odysseus:
   David Wynne, Joseph Schlichter, Donato Capozzoli, Chase Robinson; Sirens: Betty
   Jones, Ruth Currier, Lola Huth, Sally Stackhouse, Lenore Latimer

-- **1963** --

8 July–18 August 1963

Advisory board for the School of Dance: Charles E. Shain, chairman; Martha Hill, Louis
   Horst, José Limón, Pauline Lawrence Limón, Norman and Ruth Lloyd, Jeanette
   Schlottmann, Theodora Wiesner (director)

Festival committee: Charles E. Shain, chairman; Martha Hill, Louis Horst, Norman Lloyd,
   Rosemary Park, Jeanette Schlottmann, Theodora Wiesner

Teaching staff: William Bales, Orville Ballard, Bonnie Bird, Patricia Christopher, Selma
   Jeanne Cohen, Ruth Currier, Jean-Léon Destiné, Martha Graham, Louis Horst, Lucas
   Hoving, Hazel Johnson, Betty Jones, José Limón, Ruth Lloyd, Evelyn Lohoefer, Donald
   McKayle, Claire Mallardi, Emerante de Pradines, Helen Priest Rogers, Doris Rudko,
   Ineke Sluiter, Walter Sorell, Sally Stackhouse, Marnie Thomas, Jennifer Tipton, Lucy
   Venable, Thomas Watson, Theodora Wiesner, Martha Wittman, David Wood

Repertoire

Festival concerts

José Limón and Dance Company: *Missa Brevis, Concerto Grosso in D Minor, Passacaglia and Fugue in C Minor* (Humphrey), *There Is a Time, The Traitor*

Paul Draper: *Chorale and Chorale Prelude, Sonata for Tap Dancer, Tea for Two, A Politician Making a Speech, Ad Lib*

Jean-Léon Destiné and Company: *Yoruba Bakas, Bal Champêtre, Jaiba, La Legende de l'Assotor*

Donald McKayle and Company, with Carmen de Lavallade: *Nocturne, Blood of the Lamb, Rainbow 'Round My Shoulder*

Paul Taylor and Company: *Aureole, Piece Period*

Ruth Currier, with Betty Jones and Juan Carlos Bellini: *Diva Divested*

Merce Cunningham and Dance Company: *Collage III, Story, Night Wandering, Antic Meet*

Lucas Hoving, with Patricia Christopher and Chase Robinson: *Has the Last Train Left?*

Special concerts

A Program of Dances by Young Choreographers: *Dance* (Marcia Thayer), *Partita* (Rosalind Pierson), *At the Threshold* (Alice Condodina), *Transformation* (Gerda Zimmermann), *The Players* (Louise Reichlin), *Declaration* (Janet Mansfield Soares), *Millay Moments* (Margaret Beals), *To Set Astir* (Vicki Blaine)

A Special Dance Program: *The Sealed Room* (Lynn Rawlins), *Ritual* (Therese Brancale), *The Spectator* (Janet Wynn), *Preview* (Vicki Blaine), *Patterns of Soliloquies* (Doris Rudko), *Passacaglia and Fugue in C Minor* (Humphrey), *Shakers* (Humphrey), *Aftermath*

Doris Humphrey Fellow: *Aftermath*, 17 August 1963 ("A Special Dance Program"). choreography: Marion Scott; music: Varèse; a solo for Scott

Premieres

Café Coumbite, 27 July 1963. choreography: Jean-Léon Destiné; music: traditional; costumes: Ellie Antoine; cast: Shawneequa Baker, Eddy Walrond, Audrey Mason, Shirley Spiceur, Leroi Fentresse, Marianne Marvellia, Miguel Rios, Emerante de Pradines

*Arena, 3 August 1963. choreography: Donald McKayle; music: Clarence Jackson; designs: Normand Maxon; cast: Maid of Light: Sylvia Waters; Bull Ring Team: Claire Mallardi, Esta McKayle, Raymond Sawyer, Dudley Williams; Leaper: Louis Falco; Liege of Darkness: Donald McKayle

*Scudorama, 10 August 1963. choreography: Paul Taylor; music: Clarence Jackson; designs: Alex Katz; cast: Paul Taylor, Elizabeth Walton, Dan Wagoner, Bettie de Jong, Sharon Kinney, Renee Kimball, Twyla Young (Tharp), Geulah Abrahams

Aubade, 18 August 1963. choreography: Lucas Hoving; music: Karl-Birger Blomdahl; costumes: Lavina Nielsen; cast: Lucas Hoving, Patricia Christopher, Chase Robinson

—————————————————— **1964** ——————————————————

5 July–16 August 1964

Advisory board: Charles E. Shain, chairman; Charlotte A. K. Durham, Martha Hill, José Limón, Pauline Lawrence Limón, Norman and Ruth Lloyd, Rosemary Park, Jeanette Schlottmann Roosevelt, Theodora Wiesner (director)

Festival committee: Charles E. Shain, chairman; Warrine Eastburn, Martha Hill, Rosemary Park, Jeanette Schlottmann Roosevelt, Theodora Wiesner

Teaching staff: William Bales, Orville Ballard, Bonnie Bird, Sue Hawes Broadhead, Patricia Christopher, Ruth Currier, Vivian Fine, Martha Graham, Faith Gulick, Lucas Hoving, Hazel Johnson, Pearl Lang, José Limón, Evelyn Lohoefer, John Martin, Matteo, Joan Miller, Michael Rabbit, Chase Robinson, Helen Priest Rogers, Doris Rudko, Bessie Schönberg, Marion Scott, Janet Soares, Sally Stackhouse, Marnie Thomas, Ann Vachon, Lucy Venable, Theodora Wiesner, Martha Wittman, Carl Wolz, David Wood

Repertoire

Ruth Currier and Dance Company: *Quartet, The Antagonists, The Night Before Tomorrow*
Paul Draper: *Alcina Suite, Sonata for Tap Dancer, Time Out, Blues, Ad Lib*
Lucas Hoving, with Patricia Christopher and Chase Robinson: *Aubade, Icarus, Incidental Passage*
Matteo: Dances of Spain, India, and Japan
Paul Taylor Dance Company: *Party Mix, Tracer, Scudorama, Piece Period*
Erick Hawkins and Dance Company: *Early Floating, Cantilever*
Pearl Lang and Dance Company: *Apasionada, Dichotomy (Broken Dialogues)*

Premieres

Geography of Noon, 13 August 1964. choreography: Erick Hawkins; music: Lucia Dlugoszewski; designs: Ralph Dorazio; cast: Eastern Tailed Blue: Nancy Meehan; Cloudless Sulphur: James Tyler; Spring Azure: Pauline de Groot; Variegated Fritillary: Erick Hawkins
To Everybody Out There, 13 August 1964. choreography: Erick Hawkins; music: Lucia Dlugoszewski; designs: Ralph Dorazio; cast: Nancy Meehan, Pauline de Groot, Beverly Hirschfeld, Ellen Sue Marshall, Marilyn Patton, James Tyler, Erick Hawkins
Shore Bourne, 14 August 1964. choreography: Pearl Lang; music: Vivaldi; cast: Paula Kelly, Patricia Beatty, Ellen Tittler, Melinda Williams, Wesley Fata, Cliff Keuter, Lar Lubovitch, Larry Richardson, Micheline Wilkinson, Pearl Lang, Raymond Sawyer
A Choreographic Offering, 15 August 1964: choreography: José Limón; music: Bach; costumes: Pauline Lawrence; cast: Betty Jones, Libby Nye, Michael Uthoff, Jennifer Muller, Fritz Ludin, Alice Condodina, Daniel Lewis, Sally Stackhouse, John Parks, Kelly Hogan, Laura Glenn, Louis Falco, Margaret Beals, Karen Craig, Selina Croll, Brenda Dixon, Edward Effron, Laurie Freedman, Mary Ellen Freese, Margaret Goettelmann, Michal Ann Goldman, Vep Martinson, Mimi Mason, Judith Offard, Lynn Ramsbottom, Jacqueline Rice, Dora Sanders, Nancy Topf, Kay Uemura, Jody Zirul

Special Events

Doris Humphrey Fellow: *In a Dark Grove*, 15 August 1964: choreography: Kazuko Hirabayashi; music: Lawrence Rosenthal; cast: Wife: Kazuko Hirabayashi; Bandit: Stanley Berke; Husband: Richard Kuch

Louis Horst Memorial, 16 August 1964
José Limón Dance Company: *Lament for Ignacio Sánchez Mejías*. Choreography: Doris

Humphrey; music: Norman Lloyd; setting: Michael Czaja; costumes: Pauline Lawrence; cast: The Bullfighter: Louis Falco; Figure of Destiny: Letitia Ide; Figure of a Woman: Patricia Hammock

Martha Graham Dance Company: *Frontier*. Choreography and costume: Martha Graham; music: Louis Horst; setting: Isamu Noguchi; a solo by Ethel Winter

El Penitente. Choreography: Martha Graham; music: Louis Horst; setting: Isamu Noguchi; cast: Penitent: David Wood; Christ Figure: Gene McDonald; Mary Figure: Marnie Thomas

Primitive Mysteries. Choreography: Martha Graham; music: Louis Horst; cast: Yuriko, Takaka Asakawa, Carol Fried, Juliet Fisher, Phyllis Gutelius, Noemi Lapzeson, Janet Aaron, Priscilla Frank, Diane Gray, Kazuko Hirabayashi, Marcia Lerner, Molly Moore, Jeanne Nuchtern

---

1965

6 July–15 August 1965

Advisory board: Charles E. Shain, chairman; Charlotte A. Durham, Emily Genauer, Martha Hill, José Limón, Pauline Lawrence Limón, Rosemary Park, Vincent Persichetti, Jeanette Schlottmann Roosevelt, Theodora Wiesner

Festival committee: Charles E. Shain, chairman; Warrine Eastburn, Martha Hill, Rosemary Park, Jeanette Schlottmann Roosevelt, Theodora Wiesner (director)

Teaching staff: William Bales, Sid Bennett, Harriet Berg, Lawrence D. Berger, Cynthia Berrol, Odette Blum, Patricia Christopher, Ruth Currier, Norma Dalby, Paul Draper, Martha Graham, Linda Grandy, Faith Gulick, Lucas Hoving, Hazel Johnson, Betty Jones, Richard Kuch, José Limón, Evelyn Lohoefer, John Martin, Donald McKayle, Lavina Nielsen, Chase Robinson, Helen Priest Rogers, Doris Rudko, Marion Scott, Sally Stackhouse, Clive Thompson, Irma Topper, Marian Van Tuyl, Theodora Wiesner, Carl Wolz, Yuriko

Repertoire

José Limón and Company: *A Choreographic Offering, Missa Brevis*
Daniel Nagrin: *Path, A Gratitude, In the Dusk, Not Me But Him, Indeterminate Figure*
Bertram Ross and Dance Company: *If Only, Untitled*
Ruth Currier and Dance Company: *A Triangle of Strangers, Of Meetings and Partings*
Erick Hawkins and Dance Company: *Cantilever, Geography of Noon*
Lucas Hoving, with Patricia Christopher and Chase Robinson: *Icarus*
Yuriko and Company: *Three Dances, . . . and the wind, Forgotten One, Wanderers, Wind Drum*
Paul Taylor Dance Company: *Junction, 3 Epitaphs, Duet, Post Meridian, Aureole*

Premieres

*Lords of Persia, 31 July 1965. choreography: Erick Hawkins; music: Lucia Dlugoszewski; designs: Ralph Dorazio; cast: Kelly Holt, James Tyler, Rod Rodgers, Erick Hawkins

Il Combattimento di Tancredi e Clorinda, 7 August 1965. choreography: Paul Draper; music: Monteverdi; cast: Tancredi: Daniel Nagrin; Clorinda: Libby Nye

The Tenants, 7 August 1965. choreography: Lucas Hoving; music: George Riedel; cast: Patricia Christopher, Lucas Hoving, Chase Robinson

Satiana, 7 August 1965. choreography: Lucas Hoving; music: Satie; costumes: Lavina Nielsen; cast: Chase Robinson, Patricia Christopher, Lucas Hoving

My Son, My Enemy, 14 August 1965. choreography: José Limón; music: Vivian Fine; costumes: Pauline Lawrence, Charles D. Tomlinson; cast: Father: José Limón; Son: Louis Falco; Venus: Jennifer Muller; Visions, Fantasies, Judgment, and Vengeance: Alice Condodina, Ann Vachon, Lenore Latimer, Daniel Lewis, Jennifer Scanlon, Kelly Hogan, Laura Glenn, Fritz Ludin, John Parks, Peter Randazzo, Clyde Morgan, David Krohn, Sarah Ford, Tamara Woshakiwsky, Carla Maxwell, Avner Vered, David Earle

———————————————— **1966** ————————————————

10 July–21 August 1966

Advisory board: Charles E. Shain, chairman; Charlotte A. Durham, Emily Genauer, Martha Hill, José Limón, Pauline Lawrence Limón, Rosemary Park, Vincent Persichetti, Jeanette Schlottmann Roosevelt, Theodora Wiesner (director)

Festival committee: Charles E. Shain, chairman; Warrine Eastburn, Martha Hill, Rosemary Park, Jeanette Schlottmann Roosevelt, Theodora Wiesner

Teaching staff: William Bales, Barbara and George Beiswanger, Harriet Berg, Vicki Blaine, Ruth Currier, Norma Dalby, Paul Draper, Martha Graham, Linda Grandy, Faith Gulick, Gary Harris, Charlotte Honda, Lucas Hoving, Hazel Johnson, Betty Jones, Michael Judson, Pauline Koner, Richard Kuch, José Limón, Fritz Ludin, Lauren Persichetti, Chase Robinson, Helen Priest Rogers, Doris Rudko, Carol Sandvik, Bessie Schönberg, Tryntje Shapli, Sally Stackhouse, Marnie Thomas, Marian Van Tuyl, Lucy Venable, Theodora Wiesner, John Wilson, David Wood

Repertoire

Festival concerts
José Limón and Company: *Chaconne, The Exiles*
Ruth Currier and Dance Company: *Toccanta, The Night Before Tomorrow, Some Idols*
Lucas Hoving, with Nancy Lewis and Chase Robinson: *Variations on the Theme of Electra, Icarus, Satiana*
Anna Sokolow Dance Company: *Lyric Suite, Session for Six, Dreams*
Paul Draper: *Chorale and Chorale Prelude, Jig, Tea for Two, Political Speech*

Special concerts
Al Huang and Suzanne Pierce: *Kites, Cicada Song, A Cloud Passed, O, Vaporous Heart!, Butterfly Dream, Dandelions and Sunflowers, Yin and Yang*
Advanced Studies Class: *Concerto Grosso in D Minor* (Limón), *There Is a Time* (Limón)
Doris Humphrey Fellow: *With Ancient Eyes*, 20 August 1966. choreography: Martha Wittman; music: Armin Schibler; cast: Martha Wittman, Reuben James Edinger

Premieres

The Winged, 20 August 1966: choreography: José Limón; music: Hank Johnson; costumes: Pauline Lawrence; cast: José Limón, Louis Falco, Betty Jones, Sally Stackhouse, Jennifer Muller, Lenore Latimer, Jennifer Scanlon, Laura Glenn, Carla Maxwell, Sarah Ford, Tamara Woshakiwsky, Diane Mohrmann, Daniel Lewis, Fritz Ludin, John Parks, Clyde Morgan, Avner Vered, Jim May, Edward De Soto

Name-Who?, Number-What?, (Other)-(You), Address-Where?, 21 August 1966. a solo by Paul Draper

---

1967

9 July–20 August 1967

Advisory board: Charles E. Shain, chairman; Emily Genauer, Martha Hill, José Limón, Pauline Lawrence Limón, Mary Anna L. Meyer, Rosemary Park, Vincent Persichetti, Jeanette Schlottmann Roosevelt, Theodora Wiesner (director)

Festival committee: Charles E. Shain, chairman; Warrine Eastburn, Martha Hill, Rosemary Park, Jeanette Schlottmann Roosevelt, Theodora Wiesner

Teaching staff: William Bales, Bonnie Bird, Selma Jeanne Cohen, Ray Cook, Ruth Currier, Evelyn Lohoefer de Boeck, Paul Draper, Laurie Freedman, Linda G. Grandy, Lucas Hoving, Lavina Nielsen Hovinga, Hazel Johnson, Betty Jones, Dick Kuch, José Limón, Fritz Ludin, Muriel Manings, Adinah Margolis, Jennifer Muller, Michael Rabbit, Chase Robinson, Carolyn Rosenfield, Doris Rudko, Bessie Schönberg, Sally Stackhouse, Naomi Stamelman, Marnie Thomas, Ann Vachon, Thomas Watson, Theodora Wiesner, John Wilson, David Wood

Repertoire

José Limón and Company: *The Moor's Pavane, The Winged*

Martha Graham and Dance Company: *Seraphic Dialogue, Secular Games, Diversion of Angels, Dancing Ground, Appalachian Spring*

Merce Cunningham and Dance Company: *Scramble, Winterbranch, How to Pass, Kick, Fall, and Run, Collage III, Field Dances, Place*

Lucas Hoving and Company: *Icarus*

Ruth Currier and Dance Company: *Brandenburg Concerto No. 4* (Humphrey and Currier)

Paul Draper: *Gigue from Partita in B-Flat, Sonata for Tap Dancer, Tea for Two, Political Speech, Ad Lib*

Paul Taylor Dance Company: *Duet, Post Meridian, Aureole, Orbs*

Pauline Koner: *The Farewell*

Doris Humphrey Fellow: *The Brood*, 19 August 1967. choreography: Richard Kuch; music: Pierre Schaeffer; costumes: François Barbeau; cast: Jane Dudley, Richard Gain, Yuriko Kimura, Reuben James Edinger

Premieres

*Rough-In, 6 August 1967. choreography: Lucas Hoving; music: Hank Johnson; setting: Thomas Watson; costumes: Lavina Nielsen; cast: Chase Robinson, Nancy Lewis, Chris-

topher Lyall, Marcia Lerner, Karen Brydenthal, Deborah Darr

Fantasies and Facades, 11 August 1967. choreography: Ruth Currier; music: Beethoven and Josef Wittman; cast: Ruth Currier, Alice Condodina, Joan Miller, Edward Effron, Jennifer Scanlon, James May, Ann Vachon

Help, 11 August 1967. choreography: Paul Draper; music: Purcell; a solo for Draper

Agathe's Tale, 12 August 1967. choreography: Paul Taylor; music: Carlos Surinach; costumes: Julian Tomchin; cast: Agathe: Eileen Cropley; Satan: Paul Taylor; Raphael: Cliff Keuter; Orphan Pan: Daniel Williams

Psalm, 19 August 1967. choreography: José Limón; music: Eugene Lester; costumes: Pauline Lawrence; cast: Burden Bearer: Louis Falco; Expiatory Figures: Sally Stackhouse, Jennifer Muller; Psalmists: Lenore Latimer, Jennifer Scanlon, Laura Glenn, Carla Maxwell, Tamara Woshakiwsky, Diane Mohrmann, Alice Condodina, Daniel Lewis, Fritz Ludin, Clyde Morgan, Avner Vered, Jim May, Edward DeSoto

---

1968

7 July–18 August 1968

Advisory board: Charles E. Shain, chairman; Emily Genauer, Martha Hill, José Limón, Pauline Lawrence Limón, Mary Anna L. Meyer, Rosemary Park, Vincent Persichetti, Jeanette Schlottmann Roosevelt, Theodora Wiesner (director)

Festival committee: Charles E. Shain, chairman; Warrine Eastburn, Martha Hill, Rosemary Park, Jeanette Schlottmann Roosevelt, Theodora Wiesner

Teaching staff: Bonnie Bird, Percival Borde, Douglas G. Campbell, Selma Jeanne Cohen, Norma Dalby, Bill Dixon, Judith Dunn, Louis Falco, Susan Fitzgerald, Laurie Freedman, Peggy Hackney, Ned Hitchcock II, Hazel Johnson, Susan Lasovick, Daniel Lewis, José Limón, Muriel Manings, Jennifer Muller, Martha E. Myers, Wendy Perron, Michael Rabbit, Helen Priest Rogers, Carolyn Rosenfield, Bessie Schönberg, Nancy Spanier, Sally Stackhouse, Paul Taylor, Marian Van Tuyl, Lucy Venable, Theodora Wiesner, John Wilson, Josef and Martha Wittman

Repertoire

José Limón and Company: *La Malinche, The Traitor, There Is a Time*

Lotte Goslar and Company: *Clowns and Other Fools*

First Chamber Dance Quartet: *Nagare* (Charles Bennett), *Part II* (Lois Bewley), *The Miller's Dance* (Ramon de los Reyes), *Qualcosa di Carino* (Bewley), *Visions Fugitives* (Bewley), *Panaderos Antiquos* (Manolo Vargas), *Largo* (Bennett), *Suite from Carmina Burana* (William Carter)

Paul Taylor Dance Company: *Lento, Agathe's Tale, Scudorama*

Doris Humphrey Fellows Concert: *In a Dark Grove* (Kazuko Hirabayashi), *The Brood* (Dick Kuch), *Songs Remembered* (Jack Moore), premiere by Kathryn Posin

Premieres

Comedy, 10 August 1968. choreography: José Limón; music: Josef Wittman; cast: Sarah Stackhouse, Louis Falco, Jennifer Muller, Jennifer Scanlon, Lenore Latimore, Laura

Glenn, Carla Maxwell, Diane Mohrmann, Tamara Woshakiwsky, Alice Condodina, Daniel Lewis, Clyde Morgan, Edward DeSoto, Louis Solino, Avner Vered, Charles Hayward

Legend, 17 August 1968. choreography: José Limón; music: tape music selected by Simon Sadoff; cast: Slave: Clyde Morgan; Master: Daniel Lewis; Dark Angel: Louis Falco

40 amp. Mantis, 18 August 1968. choreography: Kathryn Posin; music: Stockhausen; costumes: David Krohn; cast: Irene Feigenheimer, Kathryn Posin, Ulysses Dove, Edward Effron, Whittaker Sheppard

---

1969

7 July–18 August 1968

Administration: Charles L. Reinhart, director; Martha Myers, dean; Fred Grimsey, administrative director

Festival committee and advisory board: Charles E. Shain, chairman; Warrine Eastburn, Emily Genauer, Martha Hill, José Limón, Pauline Lawrence Limón, Mary Anna L. Meyer, Rosemary Park, Vincent Persichetti, Charles L. Reinhart, Jeanette Schlottmann Roosevelt, Theodora Wiesner (this advisory body was dissolved during the course of the year)

Teaching staff: Robert Abramson, Alvin Ailey, Talley Beatty, James Clouser, Selma Jeanne Cohen, James Cunningham, Richard Gain, Linda Grandy, Al Huang, Richard Kuch, June Lewis, John Herbert McDowell, Muriel Manings, Martha Myers, Suzanne Pierce, Michael Rabbit, Yvonne Rainer, Helen Priest Rogers, Paul Taylor, Twyla Tharp, Dorothy Vislocky

Repertoire

Paul Taylor Dance Company: *Party Mix, Orbs, Aureole, Private Domain, Public Domain*
Al Huang Dance Company: *Flower in the Mirror, Cicada Song, Dandelions and Sunflowers, Changes, Dragon Play, The Monkey and the Moon, Phantom Landscape*
Alvin Ailey American Dance Theater: *Toccata* (Talley Beatty), *Icarus* (Lucas Hoving), *Quintet, Blues Suite, Road of the Phoebe Snow* (Beatty), *Dance for Six* (Joyce Trisler), *Poeme* (Pauline Koner), *Metallics* (Paul Sanasardo), *Reflections in D, Revelations*

Premieres

Medley, 19 July 1969. choreography: Twyla Tharp; cast: Sara Rudner, Theresa Dickinson, Margery Tupling, Sheila Raj, Graciella Figueroa, Rose Marie Wright, and festival students

Connecticut Composite, 19 July 1969. choreography: Yvonne Rainer; cast: Becky Arnold, Douglas Dunn, David Gordon, Barbara Lloyd, Yvonne Rainer, and festival students

The Zoo at Night, 1 August 1969. choreography: James Cunningham; costumes: William Florio; cast: James Cunningham, Lauren Persichetti, Linda Tarnay, Lucy Kostelanetz, Leslie Berg, Arawana Campbell, Patricia Catterson, Lee Harper, Thomas Groover, Billy Siegenfeld, Peter Woodin

Work in Progress: Duets, 2 August 1969. choreography: Paul Taylor; music: medieval; cast: Carolyn Adams, Daniel Williams

The Kiss of the Mome Rath: A Febrile Farad, 15 August 1969. choreography and costumes: James Clouser; music: Shostakovich; cast: The Small of It: Joel Rogo; A Blue Lady: Bess Saylor; Three Beautys [sic]: Lise Greer, Ellyn Mason, Ruby Shang; The Tall of It: Jeffrey Kerner; A Busy Lady: Kate Lacy; Three Furies: Mary Alice Kunel, Beth Lessard, Jill Gellerman; Poet in a Blue Cape: Dav Roach; A Couple in Dispute: Lee Harper, James Clouser; Three Uglies: Victoria Conklin, Nancy Mimms, Molly Wentworth; The Fellow in Tails: Ben Dolphin

*Lovely in the Dances, 15 August 1969. choreography: James Clouser; music: Sonja Zarek; cast: Katherine Fisher, Thomas Manning, James Clouser, Kate Lacy, Victoria Conklin, David James Wood, Bess Saylor, Dav Roach, Ben Dolphin

Owari, 15 August 1969. choreography: Al Huang; music: Mantle Hood; setting: Rob Fisher; costumes: Suzanne Pierce; cast: Al Huang, Suzanne Pierce, William Hansen

*Bring My Servant Home, 15 August 1969. choreography: Talley Beatty; music: Palestrina and spirituals; cast: Lee Harper, Vicky Kaufman, Asha Coolawala, Marianne Handy, Jeanne Jones, Per-Olof Fernlung, Deborah Allen, Nancy Lyon, Linda Cleveland, Karen Williams

*Masekela Langage, 16 August 1969. choreography: Alvin Ailey; music: Hugh Masekela; costumes: Christina Giannini; cast: Kelvin Rotardier, Judith Jamison, George Faison, Renee Rose, John Medeiros, Sylvia Waters, Michele Murray

──────────────── **1970** ────────────────

27 June–9 August 1970

Administration: Charles L. Reinhart, director; Martha Myers, dean; Olive Johns, administrator

Teaching staff: Ray Cook, Norma Dalby, Gay Delanghe, Cecily Dell, Richard Englund, Martha Graham Dance Company members, Fred Grimsey, Henley Haslam, Lucas Hoving, June Lewis, Erin Martin, Donald McKayle, Meredith Monk, Seamus Murphy, Martha Myers, Walter Nicks, Dora Sanders, Peter Saul, Clay Taliaferro, Dorothy Vislocky, Gwendolyn Watson, Kayla Kazahn Zalk

Repertoire

Lucas Hoving Dance Company: *Aubade II, Uppercase, Opus '69, Icarus, Satiana*
James Cunningham and Dancers: *Lauren's Dream: October 8, 1969*
Martha Graham Dance Company: *Cave of the Heart, Diversion of Angels, Deaths and Entrances, El Penitente, Every Soul Is a Circus, Oases* (Bertram Ross)
June Lewis: *Pearl*
Martha Myers: *Time-Stop*
Richard Englund: *Crazy Quilt*

Premieres

*The Junior Birdsmen, 17 July 1970. choreography: James Cunningham; costumes: William Florio; cast: Arawana Campbell, James Cunningham, Candice Lerman, Edward Love, Lauren Persichetti, Ted Striggles, and festival students

Needle-Brain Lloyd and the Systems Kid, 18 July 1970. choreography: Meredith Monk; cast: John Chong, Lanny Harrison, Meredith Monk, Susan Larrison, Mark Monstermaker, Blondell Cummings, Daniel Ira Sverdlik, Signe Hammer, Monica Moseley, Barbara Greer Gordier, Beverly Emmons, and festival students

Beach Piece, 24 July 1970. environmental piece for festival students devised by Erin Martin

Genesis 3, 31 July 1970. choreography: Ray Cook; music: Kazimierz Serocki; setting: Fred Grimsey; costumes: Susan Sweet; cast: Laura Segal, Marshall Blake, Ernest Griffin, Bill Holcomb, Ed Love, Christopher Pilafian, Curtis Ryan, James Teeters, David Chase, Tom Holt, Alonzo King, Jon Peasenelli, Stan Roberts, Patric Segalovitch, Woody Wilson

If I Am I, 31 July 1970. choreography: June Lewis; music: Jimmy Giuffre; cast: June Lewis, Raymond Evans, Howard Hormann

Suite of Things, 7 August 1970. choreography: Dorothy Vislocky; music: Morton Subotnik and Alvin Lucier; slides: William Monroe; cast: Sally Crowell, Mary Ann Grafmueller, Carla Murgia, Joanne Petroff, Katherine Fisher, Deborah Lessen, Gilda Peress, Anne Marie Ridgway, Sue Robbins, Norrye Caldwell, Dennis Dubin, Elaine Evans, Hathaway Gamble, William Munroe, Rolinda Rochlin, Virginia Weenink, Paul A. Corman, Nicole Dufresne, Betsy Galt, Bonnie Kissam, Betsy Ogden, Peggy Tansey, Dale Zink

Simple Fractions, 7 August 1970. choreography: Peter Saul; cast: Patricia: Judith Fram; Sara: Ruth Barnes; Nancy: Christine Maira; Joyce: Joan Kohout; Marilyn: Barbara Stephens; Anne: Ann Hutchinson Medina; Margaret: Sharon Ann Ferjanec; Beatrice: Barbara Dickinson; Mary Louise: Dale Zink; Wendy: Dawn Clark; Grace: Karlynn Landen; Dorothy: Catharine Williams; Frank: Billy Siegenfeld; Charles: Peter Woodin; Jane: Andrea Borek; Elizabeth: Susan Creitz; Helen: Susan Fitzgerald; Claire: Judy Gregg; Sally: JoAnne Hewlett; Paula: Sheila Korman; Natalie: Fae Rubenstein; Harriet: Gail Simon; Janet: Fran Spector

Reflections, 7 August 1970. choreography: Lucas Hoving; music: Gwendolyn Watson; costumes: Mylo Guam; cast: Prodigal Son: Charles Phipps; His Brother: Peter Woodin; Anne Marie Ridgway, Randall Faxon, Gay Delanghe, Margaret Beals, Milne Bail, Laurie Cameron

---

1971

10 July–8 August 1971

Administration: Charles L. Reinhart, director; Martha Myers, dean; Kay McGrath, administrator

Teaching staff: Robert Abramson, Art Bauman, Margaret Beals, James Clouser, Moss Cohen, Robert Conley, Frances Cott, Gay Delanghe, Randall Faxon, Sally Fitt, Fred Grimsey, Peggy Hackney, Patric Hickey, Mildred Hill, Lucas Hoving, Lavina Hovinga, June Lewis, Michele Murray, Martha Myers, Walter Nicks, Juli Nunlist, Charles Phipps, Marcia Roud, Colin Russell, Peter Saul, Bessie Schönberg, Clint Shelby, Clay Taliaferro, Sonja Zarek

Repertoire

Rudy Perez Dance Theatre: *New Editions, Monumental Exchange, Center Break, Topload/Offprint, Arcade, Coverage, Transit, Countdown*

Bella Lewitzky Dance Company: *Orrenda, On the Brink of Time, Kinaesonata, Landscapes* (Murray Louis), *Trio for Saki, Bags and Things* (Fred Strickler)
Paul Taylor Dance Company: *Insects and Heroes, Big Bertha, Aureole*
Lucas Hoving Dance Company: *Recueil* (Jean Cébron), *Icarus, Assemblage, Satiana*

Premieres

Annual, 10 July 1971. choreography and sound collage: Rudy Perez; cast: Barbara Roan, Anthony LaGiglia, Stephen Buck, Alice Canglelia, Leonard Hanitchak, John Moore, Wendy Summit, Rudy Perez

Pietas, 17 July 1971. choreography: Bella Lewitzky; music: Cara Bradbury Rhodes; cast: Lynda Davis, Jan Day, Sean Greene, Teresa Nielsen, Iris Pell, Rebecca Bobele, Fred Strickler

The Book of Beasts, 24 July 1971. choreography: Paul Taylor; music: Schubert, Weber, Saint-Saëns, Mozart, Beethoven, Boccherini, Falla, Tchaikovsky; costumes: John Rawlings; cast: Illuminations: Paul Taylor; The Shadows: Bettie de Jong, Daniel Williams, Earnest Morgan, Carolyn Adams, Nicholas Gunn, Senta Driver, Britt Swanson

Zip Code, 31 July 1971. choreography: Lucas Hoving (additional choreography: Pina Bausch); music: tape collage; cast: Pina Bausch, Margaret Beals, Ron Cunningham, Gay Delanghe, Randall Faxon, Louise Frank, Lucas Hoving, Lionel Kilner, Charles Phipps, Marcia Rand, Peter Woodin, Michael Bruce, James Cutting, Jane Lowe, Candy Prior, Ann Marie Ridgway

West/East Stereo (Bo'u'lu-Bo'ici Bo'ee), 7 August 1971. choreography: Ann Halprin; co-art director: Patric Hickey; cast: festival students

---

1972

30 June–6 August 1972

Administration: Charles L. Reinhart, director; Martha Myers, dean; Kay McGrath, administrator

Twenty-fifth Connecticut College ADF committee: Martha Hill, Jeanette Schlottmann Roosevelt, Walter Terry, Theodora Wiesner

Teaching staff: Robert Abramson, Margaret Beals, Miriam Brunner, Moss Cohen, Alfredo Corvino, Frances Cott, Robyn Cutler, Gay Delanghe, Robert Dunn, Fred Grimsey, Peggy Hackney, Lavina Hovinga, Toni Lacativa, June Lewis, Martha Myers, Walter Nicks, Rudy Perez, Janet Plastino, Don Redlich, Shirley Ririe, Clay Taliaferro

Repertoire

José Limón Dance Company: *The Unsung, Dances for Isadora, The Moor's Pavane, There Is a Time, The Winged*
Don Redlich Dance Company: *Jibe, Air Antique, Cahoots, Dance for One Figure, Four Objects and Film Sequence* (Anna Nassif), *Slouching Towards Bethlehem, Passin' Through, Estrange*
Louis Falco Dance Company: *The Sleepers, Nostalgia* (Jennifer Muller), *Huescape, Caviar*

Murray Louis Dance Company: *Chimera, Continuum, Hoopla, Calligraph for Martyrs, Proximities, Personnae*
Alvin Ailey American Dance Theatre: *Dance for Six* (Joyce Trisler), *Journey* (Trisler), *Lark Ascending, Revelations, Streams, Rainbow 'Round My Shoulder* (Donald McKayle), *Mary Lou's Mass, A Song for You*
Dance June Lewis and Company: *Living Field, Idols of the Marketplace, The Weaving*
Margaret Beals: *Wild Swans in Epitaph, 3 Etudes, Horizon Line 1 and 2*

Twenty-fifth Anniversary Repertory Company Performances: 30 June–2 July and 28–30 July

El Penitente: choreography: Martha Graham; music: Louis Horst; designs: Isamu Noguchi; cast: Penitente: Marc Stevens; Christ Figure: Ryland Jordan; Mary: Phyllis Gutelius
Flickers: choreography and costumes: Charles Weidman; music: Lionel Nowak; cast: Marc Stevens, Nina Watt, Peter Woodin, Rael Lamb, Ted Striggles, Linda Tarnay, Randall Faxon, Nancy Scher, Pamela Knisel, Dalienne Majors, Debra Zalkind, Ann DeGange, Raymond Johnson
New Dance: choreography: Doris Humphrey; choreography for Prelude and Third Theme: Charles Weidman; music: Wallingford Riegger; cast: Linda Tarnay, Peter Woodin, Edward DeSoto, Ann DeGange, Dian Dong, Randall Faxon, Phyllis Gutelius, Raymond Johnson, Ryland Jordan, Pamela Knisel, Rael Lamb, Dalienne Majors, Nancy Scher, Marc Stevens, Ted Striggles, Clay Taliaferro, Nina Watt, Debra Zalkind
Emperor Jones: choreography: José Limón; music: Villa-Lobos; setting: Charles Tomlinson; costumes: Pauline Lawrence; cast: The Emperor Jones: Clay Taliaferro; The White Man: Edward DeSoto; The Emperor's Subjects: Raymond Johnson, Ryland Jordan, Rael Lamb, Marc Stevens, Ted Striggles, Peter Woodin
With My Red Fires: choreography: Doris Humphrey; music: Wallingford Riegger; costumes: Pauline Lawrence; cast: The Matriarch: Dalienne Majors; Young Lovers: Nina Watt, Raymond Johnson; Ann DeGange, Edward DeSoto, Dian Dong, Randall Faxon, Ryland Jordan, Pamela Knisel, Rael Lamb, Marc Stevens, Ted Striggles, Linda Tarnay, Peter Woodin, Debra Zalkind, and festival students
*Asparagus Beach (premiere)

Premieres

*Asparagus Beach, 28 July 1972. choreography and score: Rudy Perez; projections: Stephen Price; costumes: Charles Tomlinson; cast: Ann DeGange, Edward DeSoto, Dian Dong, Randall Faxon, Raymond Johnson, Ryland Jordan, Pamela Knisel, Dalienne Majors, Nancy Scher, Marc Stevens, Ted Striggles, Linda Tarnay, Nina Watt, Peter Woodin, Debra Zalkind, Susan Ishino
A Salute to the 25th (comprising *Thank You General Motors, Steeple People*, and *Lot Piece/Lawn 1971*), 29 July 1972. choreography and score: Rudy Perez; cast: Anthony LaGiglia, Ellen Robbins, Peggy Hackney, Nancy Scher, festival students, and the Surfer Drum and Bugle Corps
**She Often Goes for a Walk Just After Sunset*, 2 August 1972. choreography: Don Redlich; sound collage: Miriam Brunner; cast: Lavina Hovinga and festival students

-- **1973** --

28 June–4 August 1973

Administration: Charles L. Reinhart, director; Martha Myers, dean; Kay McGrath, administrator

Teaching staff: Barbara Bennion, Penny Bernstein, Ingrid Brainard, Constance Cook, Frances Cott, Gay Delanghe, Robert Dunn, Katia Geleznova, Claudia Gitelman, Fred Grimsey, Thelma Hill, Wendy Hilton, Steve Karlin, Lenore Latimer, Bruce Lieberman, Nancy Meehan, Martha Myers, Daniel Nagrin, Walter Nicks, Rudy Perez, Doris Rudko, Rhoda Winter Russell, Marta Sanchez, Susan Sandel, Luly Santangelo, Elaine Siegel, Linni Silberman, Clay Taliaferro, Ernest L. Washington

Repertoire

José Limón Dance Company: *Emperor Jones, Orfeo, Choreographic Offering, Dances for Isadora, Carlota, La Malinche, The Moor's Pavane*

Nikolais Dance Theatre: *Somniloquy, Foreplay, Tower, Scenario, Tent*

Erick Hawkins Dance Company: *Angels of the Inmost Heaven, Black Lake, Cantilever, Early Floating, Geography of Noon*

Dance Theatre of Harlem: *Tones* (Arthur Mitchell), *Ancient Voices of Children* (Milko Sparemblek), *Rhythmetron* (Mitchell), *Forces of Rhythm* (Louis Johnson), *Agon* (Balanchine)

Inner City Repertory Dance Company: *Songs of the Disinherited* (Donald McKayle), *Sojourn* (McKayle), *Rainbow 'Round My Shoulder* (McKayle)

Rudy Perez Dance Theatre: *Quadrangle, Countdown*

Marjorie Gamso's Dance Concoctions: *Floatsam and Jetsam, Rough Draft* (Nancy Topf), *Decination, Two Weeks, Chinese Notebook* (Daniel Press), *Circle Solos* (Topf), *Rotogravure/Third Edition, Epilogue*

Pilobolus Dance Theatre: *Pilobolus, Geode, Walklyndon, Syzygy, Aubade, Anaendrom, Ocellus, Cameo, Spyrogyra*

Bruce Becker and Jane Kosminsky's 5 by 2 Dance Company: *There Is a Time*, excerpts (José Limón), *Sola* (Mario Delamo), *Meditations of Orpheus* (Norman Walker), *Negro Spirituals* (Helen Tamiris), *A Cold Sunday Afternoon a Little Later* (Cliff Keuter)

Nora Guthrie and Ted Rotante: *Frank* (Guthrie), *Faith* (Guthrie), *Undercurrents* (Rotante), *Break* (Meredith Monk)

Premieres

Choros of the Daughters of Okeanos, 7 July 1973. choreography: Erick Hawkins; music: Yoritsune Matsudaira; sculptures: Ralph Dorazio; costumes: Raya; cast: Beverly Brown, Carol Conway, Nada Reagan, Natalie Richman

A Suite of Psalms, 13 July 1973. choreography: Carla Maxwell; music: John W. Gertman; cast: Carla Maxwell, Jennifer Scanlon

Haiku (A Dream for Brown Eyes), 20 July 1973. choreography and costumes: Walter Raines; music: Tania Leon; projections and masks: Gary Fails; cast: Gayle McKinney, Melva Murray-White, Virginia Johnson, Sheila Rohan, Yvonne Hall, Derek Williams,

William Scott, Gerald Banks, Paul Russell, Samuel Smalls, Ronald Perry, Homer Bryant, Joseph Wyatt, Edward Moore

Walla-Walla, 26 July 1973. choreography and sound collage: Rudy Perez; cast: John Moore, David Varney, Susan Ishino, Timothy Haynes, Rudy Perez, and festival students

Delicate Negotiations, 27 July 1973. choreography: Marjorie Gamso; cast: Elizabeth Fain, Marjorie Gamso, Jonathan Hollander, Janaki Patrik, Daniel Press, Dana Reitz, Karen Robbins, Nancy Topf

Work-in-Progress: Untitled (Ciona), 27 July 1973. choreography: Pilobolus; music: Jon Appleton; cast: Robby Barnett, Alison Becker Chase, Lee Harris, Robb Pendelton, Martha Clarke, Jonathan Wolken

Americana Plaid, 28 July 1973. choreography and sound collage: Rudy Perez; cast: John Moore, David Varney, Susan Ishino, Timothy Hughes, Rudy Perez, and festival students

Corporate Images, 29 July 1973. choreography: Ted Rotante; music: John McLaughlin Mahavishnu Orchestra; cast: Nora Guthrie, Ted Rotante

Caravanserai, 3 August 1973. choreography: Talley Beatty; music: Santana; costumes: Cleveland Pennington; cast: Gail Benedict, Edwin Brown, Ron Bush, Barry D'Angelo, Clif de Raita, Jacqueline DeRoven, Wanda Evans, Anita Littleman, Ruby Millsap, Stanley Perryman, Marvin Tunney, Anthony White

---

1974

22 June–3 August 1974

Administration: Charles L. Reinhart, director; Martha Myers, dean; Celia Halstead, coordinator; Cordette Grimsey, coordinator (winter)

Teaching staff: Mary Barnett, Mercedes Batista, Chuck Davis, Edward DeSoto, Claudia Gitelman, Kathleen Stanford-Grant, Fred Grimsey, Thelma Hill, Marilyn Hinson, Stuart Hodes, Elizabeth Kagan, Joy Kane, Stephen Karlin, Lenore Latimer, Yurek Lazowski, Bruce Lieberman, Nancy Meehan, Daniel Nagrin, Walter Nicks, Kathryn Posin, Edward Roll, Elaine Siegel, Linni Silberman, Manolo Vargas, James Waring, Lance Westergard

Repertoire

Paul Taylor Dance Company: *3 Epitaphs*, *Post Meridian*, *Party Mix*, *Untitled Quartet*, *So Long Eden*, *Duet*, *Big Bertha*, *Public Domain*

Kathryn Posin Dance Company: *Nuclear Energy I & II*, *Days*, *Ghost Train*, *Bach Pieces*

Trisha Brown and Company: *Skymap*, *Group Primary Accumulation*, *Accumulation*

Nikolais Dance Theatre: *Suite from "Sanctum," Scenario*, *Tent*, *Divertissement*, *Cross-Fade*

Nora Guthrie and Ted Rotante: *Corporate Images II* (Rotante)

Sara and Jerry Pearson: *Vis-à-Vis* (Gladys Bailin), *Auras*, *Amnesia*, *A Mild Mannered Reporter*, *Magnetic Rag*

Meredith Monk/The House: *Education of the Girl Child*, *Paris/Chacon* (Monk and Ping Chong), *Our Lady of Late*

Daniel Nagrin: *Changes: A Retrospective of Solo Dances, 1948–1974*

Ritha Devi: Dances of India

Chuck Davis Dance Company: Dances of Africa

Anna Aragno and George de la Peña: *Bluebird Pas de Deux* (Marius Petipa)

Lynne Charles and Victor Barbee: *Flower Festival Pas de Deux* (August Bournonville)
Louis Falco Dance Company: *Twopenny Portrait, Sleepers, Speeds* (Jennifer Muller), *Biography* (Muller), *Caviar*
Pilobolus Dance Theatre: *Ciona, Triptych, Pseudopodia, Spyrogyra, Dispretzled*
Laura Dean and Dance Company: *Spinning Dance, Response Dance*
Campus events also included performances by theater companies

Premieres

*Pamplona Stones, 30 June 1974. choreography: Trisha Brown; cast: Trisha Brown, Sylvia Whitman
*Buff Her Blind—To Open the Light of the Body, 11 July 1974. choreography and setting: Stephanie Evanitsky; sound: Richard Hayman, David Rossiter; costumes: Nils Eklund; fire elements: Hayman; cast: Barbara Salz, Donald Porteous, Bronya Wajnberg, Kay Gainer, Suellen Epstein, Arthur-George Hurray
*Five, 26 July 1974. choreography: Bella Lewitzky; music: Max Lifchitz; designs: Darlene Neel; cast: Lynda Davis, Sean Greene, Iris Pell, Bruce Taylor, Nora Reynolds
*Yemaya, 26 July 1974. choreography: Manuel Alum; music: Ira Taxin; cast: Felicia Norton, Joan Lombardi, Malou Airando, Dominique Mercy, Tony Constantine, Manuel Alum
*Winter Pieces, 26 July 1974. choreography: Jennifer Muller; music: Curtis O. B. Curtis-Smith; costumes: Melissa Greenberg; cast: Georgiana Holmes, Mary Jane Eisenberg, Angeline Wolf, Matthew Diamond, Lance Westergard, Carol-rae Kraus
*Yellow Point, 26 July 1974. choreography: Nancy Meehan; music: Rocco di Pietro; cast: Nancy Meehan, Micki Goodman, Amy Horowitz, Trudé Link, Sara Shelton, Mary Spalding
*Monkshood's Delight (Monkshood's Farewell), 28 July 1974. choreography: Pilobolus; music: tape collage; cast: Jonathan Wolken, Michael Tracy, Alison Chase, Moses Pendleton, Martha Clarke, Robby Barnett
*Changing, 2 August 1974. choreography: Laura Dean; musician: John Smead; costumes: Kristin Holby; cast: Laura Dean, Grethe Holby, Diane Johnson
*Learn To, 3 August 1974. choreography: Nora Guthrie; music: Charles Hansen and his orchestra, E. J. Miller; slides: Nicholas Wolff Lyndon; cast: Nora Guthrie, Ted Rotante
*Exposure, 3 August 1974. choreography: Sara and Jerry Pearson; music: Dennis Cochrane; slides: Bruce Margolies; cast: Sara and Jerry Pearson

--------------------------------- **1975** ---------------------------------

21 June–2 August 1975

Administration: Charles L. Reinhart, director; Martha Myers, dean; Celia Halstead, coordinator; Cordette Grimsey, coordinator (winter)

Teaching staff: Chuck Davis, Edward DeSoto, Irene Dowd, Consuelo Durr, Elaine Giguere, Fred Grimsey, Nora Guthrie, Elizabeth Kagan, Elizabeth Keen, Pauline Koner, Lenore Latimer, Lynn Levine, Bruce Lieberman, Phyllis Luberg, Nancy Meehan, Nala Najan, Walter Nicks, Kirk Nurock, Libby Nye, Terry Ross, Ted Rotante, Linni Silberman, Manolo Vargas, Lance Westergard, Ethel Winter, Mel Wong

Repertoire

Raymond Johnson: *Fieldgoal* (Rudy Perez), *Scherzo* (James Waring), *Three Faces*

Ze'eva Cohen: *Three Landscapes, 32 Variations in C Minor* (James Waring), *Escape, from "Rooms"* (Anna Sokolow)

Dance Theatre of Harlem: *Every Now and Then* (William Scott), *Allegro Brillante* (Balanchine), *Le Corsaire Pas de Deux* (Karel Shook, after Marius Petipa), *Dougla* (Geoffrey Holder)

Elizabeth Keen Dance Company: *Line Drawing, Poison Variations, Parentheses*

Bhaskar: Dances of India

Alvin Ailey Junior Company: *Night Creature, Icarus* (Lucas Hoving), *Echoes in Blue* (Milton Myers), *Revelations, 40* (Gus Solomons, Jr.), *Dance for Six* (Joyce Trisler)

Twyla Tharp Dances and Dancers: *Sue's Leg, The First Fifty, The Bach Duet, Ocean's Motion*

Iolani Luahine: Traditional dances of Hawaii

Chuck Davis Dance Company: *Experiment with Death, Loving You, Today, Personal Statement, Peace and Love*, dances of Africa

Trisha Brown and Company: *Spiral, Structured Pieces, Floor of the Forest and Other Miracles, Locus, Theme and Variations*

Violette Verdy and Helgi Tomasson: *Raymonda Pas de Deux* (Balanchine), *Tchaikovsky Pas de Deux* (Balanchine)

Nancy Meehan Dance Company: *Split Rock, Bones Cascades Scapes, Grapes and Stones*

Pilobolus Dance Theatre: *Monkshood's Farewell*

Kathryn Posin Dance Company: *Bach Pieces*

Nora Guthrie and Ted Rotante: *Dessert, 159-13 85th St.*

Campus events also included performances by theater companies

Premieres

Solitary Songs, 3 July 1975. choreography: Pauline Koner; music: Berio; costumes: Evelyn Miller; cast: Deborah Pratt, Sam Tampoya, Michael Freed, Tamara Grose, George White, Martha Curtis, Karen Shields

Untitled New Work, 5 July 1975. choreography: Alvin McDuffie; music: Duke Ellington; cast: Marla Bingham, Alistair Butler, Nancy Calahan, Merle E. Holloman, Daniela Malusardi, German Maracara, Lonne Moreton, Delila Moseley, Clayton Palmer, Martial Roumain, Jacqueline Smith-Lee, John Young

Chronology, 19 July 1975. choreography: Trisha Brown; cast: Elizabeth Garrea, Mona Sulzman, Judith Ragir, Trisha Brown, and festival students

Going to the Sun Road, 22 July 1975. choreography: Ted Rotante; music: Joe Clark; an environmental piece for festival students

Howard Beach, 22 July 1975. choreography: Nora Guthrie; music: Paul Bley; cast: Nora Guthrie, Ted Rotante

*Waves, 1 August 1975. choreography: Kathryn Posin; music: Laurie Spiegel; cast: Bill Gornel, Kathryn Posin, Holly Reeve, Ricky Schussel, Susan Thomasson, Lance Westergard, Marsha White

*Untitled, 1 August 1975. choreography: Pilobolus; music: Bob Dennis; cast: Robert Morgan Barnett, Alison Chase, Moses Pendleton, Michael Tracy, Martha Clarke, Jonathan Wolken

────────────────────────── **1976** ──────────────────────────

28 June–7 August 1976 (New London)
22–27 August 1976 (Newport)

Administration: Charles L. Reinhart, director; Martha Myers, dean; Mary Jane Ingram, administrator (New London); Lisa Booth, administrator (New York); Joya Granbery Hoyt, administrator (Newport)

Teaching staff: Marilyn Cristofori, Chuck Davis, Ronnie De Marco, Edward DeSoto, Irene Dowd, Bill Evans, Fred Grimsey, Nora Guthrie, Peggy Hackney, Eleanor Hovda, Lucas Hoving, Denise Jefferson, Gretchen Langstaff, Phyllis Luberg, Nancy Meehan, John Mueller, Kirk Nurock, Libby Nye, Terrence Ross, Ted Rotante, Robert Vickrey, Lance Westergard, Mel Wong

Repertoire

New London
Annabelle Gamson: *Five Waltzes* (Isadora Duncan), *Etude* (Duncan), *Pastorale* (Mary Wigman), *Dance of Summer* (Wigman), *Agave I and II, First Movement, Portrait of Rose*
Pauline Koner Dance Consort: *Concertino In A Major, Cassandra, Solitary Songs*
Chuck Davis Dance Company: Dances of Africa
Metropolitan Opera Ballet Ensemble: *Die Fledermaus Variations* (Norbert Vesak), *Once for the Birth of . . .* (Vesak), *Carnaval* (Michel Fokine), *Belong* (Vesak), *Rich Man's Frug* (Bob Fosse)
Nikolais Dance Theatre: *Temple, Duet from "Somniloquy," Triple Duet from "Grotto," Tensile Involvement, Tribe*
Bella Lewitzky Dance Company: *Ceremony for Three, Spaces Between, Five, On the Brink of Time, Game Plan*
Bill Evans Dance Company: *End of the Trail, The Legacy, Take the "A" Train, Bach Dances, Hard Times*
Guthrie-Rotante Dance Company: *Field* (Rotante), *Brick* (Rotante)
Walter Nicks Dance Theatre Workshop: *Solo Con Salsa, And the Fallen Petals* (Seamus Murphy), *Reflections* (Vendetta Mathea), *Celebration* (Yuriko), *Autumn Dialogue* (Norman Walker), *Roots Revisited*
Nancy Meehan Dance Company: *Live Dragon, Threading the Wave*
Campus events also included theatrical performances by Mabou Mines

Newport
Pilobolus Dance Theatre: *Untitled, Monkshood's Farewell, Ocellus, Alraune, Pagliacco, Lost in Fauna*
American Dance Machine: Tribute to Jack Cole
Judith Jamison: *Cry* (Alvin Ailey)
Paul Taylor Dance Company: *Aureole, 3 Epitaphs, Runes*

Premieres

New London
A Time of Crickets, 2 July 1976. choreography: Pauline Koner; music: Michael Colina;

costumes: Christina Giannini; cast: Martha Curtis, Michael Freed, George White, Harry Grose, Tamara Grose, Don Austen Lowe, Deborah Pratt, Karen Shields, Georgiana Holmes

Greening, 23 July 1976. choreography: Bella Lewitzky; music: Copland; setting: Darlene Neel; cast: Loretta Livingston, Iris Pell, Nora Reynolds, Sean Greene, Kurt Weinheimer, Robert Hughes, Bella Lewitzky

The Dallas Blues, 29 July 1976. choreography: Bill Evans; music: Bessie Smith; cast: Ann Asnes, Jim Coleman, Regina de Corse, Bill Evans, Gregg Lizenbery, Kathleen McClintock

The Five Boons of Life, 1 August 1976. choreography: Nora Guthrie; music: Chick Corea, Jan Hammer, Jerry Goodman; cast: Nora Guthrie, Ted Rotante; Pleasure: Janice Hladki, Susan Mathews; Fame: Jose Sanchez, Jaris Waide, Anne Short, Heather Martin, Jamie Kaplan; Love: Cheryl Spezza, Susan Blankensop, Terry Freedman, Carmen Rozestraten; Riches: Nancy Coenen, Suzanne Stern, Amy Spencer, Rachel Bernstein, Suzanne Costello

* *Glances*, 6 August 1976. choreography: Murray Louis; music: Dave Brubeck; cast: Michael Ballard, Richard Haisma, Helen Kent, Dianne Markham, Anne McLeod, Jerry Pearson, Sara Pearson, Robert Small

Newport

* *Polaris*, 26 August 1976. choreography: Paul Taylor; music: Donald York; designs: Alex Katz; cast: Part I: Carolyn Adams, Elie Chaib, Linda Kent, Victoria Uris, Christopher Gillis; Part II: Nicholas Gunn, Monica Morris, Lila York, Ruth Andrien, Robert Kahn

––––––––––––––––––––––––––– **1977** –––––––––––––––––––––––––––

25 June–6 August 1977 (New London)
19–27 August 1977 (Newport)

Administration: Charles L. Reinhart, director; Martha Myers, dean; Lisa Booth, administrative director; Stephanie Reinhart, administrative director (Newport); Mary Jane Ingram, administrator (Newport)

Faculty: Annette Atwood, Balasaraswati, Isa Bergsohn, Beverly Brown, Irene Dowd, Ralph Farrington, Arthur Hall, Eleanor Hovda, Mieke van Hoek, Denise Jefferson, Gretchen Langstaff, Phyllis Luberg, Daniel Nagrin, Ronnie Ragen, Virginia Reed, Terrence Ross, Peter Saul, Marcus Schulkind, Lee Theodore, Mel Wong

Repertoire

New London
Lakshmi Shanmukham and Balasaraswati: Dances of India
Daniel Nagrin: *Ruminations*
Beverly Brown Dancensemble: *Life in a Drop of Pond Water, The Reason Why: Dragonfly, Cloudspeed, Season of Earth Hush, Body Music*
London Contemporary Dance Theatre: *Diary 2* (Siobhan Davies), *Cell* (Robert Cohan), *Class* (Cohan), *Masque of Separation (Myth)* (Cohan), *Stabat Mater* (Cohan), *Troy Game* (Robert North)
Nikolais Dance Theatre: *Sanctum, Styx, Triad*

Harry (Senta Driver): *Board Fade Except, Second Generation, Memorandum, Matters of Fact, Gallery*

Pilobolus Dance Theatre: *Ciona, Lost in Fauna, Ocellus, Vagabond, Monkshood's Farewell, The Eve of Samhain, Pagliacco, Alraune, Untitled*

Walter Nicks Dance Theatre: *Fanga, Boot Dance, Ancestors, Autumn Dialogues* (Norman Walker), *Aubade* (Lucas Hoving), *Solo Con Salsa, Reflections* (Vendetta Mathea), *Roots Revisited*

Douglas Dunn and Dancers: *Lazy Madge*

Twyla Tharp Dancers and Dances: *Mud, The Fugue, Eight Jelly Rolls, Country Dances, Cacklin' Hen, Simon Medley, Sue's Leg*

Danny Williams Grossman and Dance Company: *Curious Schools of Theatrical Dancing (Part I), Couples, National Spirit, Higher*

American Dance Machine: Excerpts from Broadway musicals

Newport

Dance Theatre of Harlem: *Forces of Rhythm* (Louis Johnson), *Adagietto No. 5* (Royston Maldoom), *Dougla* (Geoffrey Holder)

Don Redlich Dance Company: *Patina, Three Bagatelles, Traces*

Carmen de Lavallade and Group: *Dawn Encounter, Gray Room* (Martha Clarke), *Songs of Bilitis, Pagliacco* (Clarke), *The Prince and the Butterfly* (de Lavallade and Joe Grifasi)

Paul Taylor Dance Company: *Aureole, 3 Epitaphs, Runes, Polaris*

Annabelle Gamson: Dances of Isadora Duncan

Pilobolus Dance Theatre: *Monkshood's Farewell, Untitled, Eve of Samhain*

Premieres

New London

The Fall, 3 July 1977. choreography: Daniel Nagrin; setting: Beverly Owen; costume: Sally Ann Parsons; a solo for Nagrin

*Sudden Death, 17 July 1977. choreography: Senta Driver; cast: Timothy Knowles, Senta Driver

*Bella, 24 July 1977. choreography: Danny Williams Grossman, Judy Jarvis; music: Puccini; designs: Mary Kerr; cast: Judy Jarvis, Danny Williams Grossman

*Ecce Homo, 24 July 1977. choreography: Danny Williams Grossman; music: Bach; costumes: Mary Kerr; cast: Eric Bobrow, Judith Hendin, Greg Parks

*Celeste, 31 July 1977. choreography: Douglas Dunn, in collaboration with Tal Streeter; cast: Ruth Alpert, Michael Bloom, Meg Eginton, Diane Frank, Jennifer Moscall, Daniel Press, Ellen Webb, David Woodberry, and festival students

Newport

*Untitled, 20 August 1977. choreography: Arthur Mitchell; music: Primous Fountain; costumes: Zelda Wynn; cast: Lydia Abarca, Ronald Perry, Yvonne Hall, Susan Lovelle, Allen Samson, Homer Bryant, Stephanie Dabney, Eddie Shellman, Virginia Johnson, Paul Russell, Brenda Garrett, Roman Brooks

*Finisterre, 21 August 1977. choreography: Don Redlich; music: Stephen Burton; cast: Jennifer Donohue, Irene Feigenheimer, Barbara Roan, Billy Siegenfeld

Veranda, 25 August 1977. choreography: Martha Clarke; music: Rimsky-Korsakov; costumes: Kate Carmel; cast: Carmen de Lavallade, Wesley Fata

Shizen, 26 August 1977. choreography: Pilobolus; music: Riley Lee; cast: Alison Chase, Moses Pendleton

Renelagh on the Randon, 26 August 1977. choreography: Jonathan Wolken; music: Telemann; a solo for Wolken

Wakefield (Harvest), 26 August 1977. choreography: Martha Clarke; music: William Sidney Mount; a solo for Clarke

-- **1978** --

17 June–29 July 1978

Administration: Charles L. Reinhart, director; Martha Myers, dean; Isa Bergsohn, assistant to the dean; Lisa Booth, administrative director; June Batten Arey, consultant for programing and development; Steve Gaddis, school administrator; Julia Wray, academic liaison with Duke University; Stephanie Reinhart, performance coordinator

Teaching staff: Annette Atwood, Balasaraswati, Fred Benjamin, Isa Bergsohn, Beverly Brown, Martha Curtis, Jennifer Donohue, Irene Feigenheimer, Jessica Fogel, Julie French, Alfred Gallman, Arthur Hall, Adrienne Hawkins, Mieke van Hoek, Betty Jones, Pauline Koner, Pearl Lang, Didi Levy, Bettze McCoy, Daniel Nagrin, Beverly Rackoff, Ronnie Ragen, Don Redlich, Barbara Roan, Terry Ross, Dora Sanders, Billy Siegenfeld, Marcus Schulkind, Roger Tolle, Missy Vineyard, Elizabeth Walton, Nancy Wanich, Ethel Winter

Repertoire

José Limón Dance Company: *The Moor's Pavane*

José Greco, Nana Lorca, and Friends: An evening of Spanish dance

Jane Goldberg and Charles Cook: Jazz and tap dancing

Eliot Feld Ballet: *The Consort, At Midnight, A Footstep of Air, Harbinger, La Vida, Impromptu*

Daniel Nagrin: *Spanish Dance, Strange Hero, Dance in the Sun, Indeterminate Figure, With My Eye and With My Hand, A Gratitude, Not Me, But Him*

North Carolina Dance Theatre: *Allegro Brillante* (Balanchine), *The Grey Goose of Silence* (Norbert Vesak), *Sun Flowers* (Antony Tudor), *Brandenburg Three* (Charles Czarny)

Pauline Koner Dance Consort: *Mosaic, A Time of Crickets*

Lakshmi Shanmukham: Dances of India

Twyla Tharp Dance Foundation: *Country Dances, The Bach Duet, Simon Medley, Eight Jelly Rolls*

Arthur Hall Afro-American Dance Ensemble: Dance demonstration

American Dance Machine: Excerpts from Broadway musicals

Paul Taylor Dance Company: *Airs, Private Domain, Esplanade*

Don Redlich Dance Company: *Patina, Finisterre, Traces*

Harry (Senta Driver): *Star Games, Second Generation, Exam, Sudden Death*

Pilobolus Dance Theatre: *Moonblind, Pseudopodia, Solo from "The Eve of Samhain," Shizen, Untitled*

Premieres

Cantigas, 1 July 1978. choreography: Pauline Koner; music: George Crumb, medieval music; costumes: A. Christina Giannini; cast: Carl Bailey, Martha Curtis, Valerie Farias, Sharon Filone, Michael Freed, Paco Garcia, Jeffry Judson, Evelyn Shepard, Karen Shields

* *On Doing*, 16 July 1978. choreography: Senta Driver; music: Tom Johnson; costumes: A. Christina Giannini; cast: Senta Driver, Jorge Ledesma, Jeffery Clark, Nicole Riche

Time Writes Notes on Us, 23 July 1978. choreography: Daniel Nagrin; music: Copland; costume: Sally Ann Parsons; a solo for Marcus Schulkind

Getting Well, 23 July 1978. choreography: Daniel Nagrin; music: medieval and Renaissance; costume: Sally Ann Parsons; a solo for Nagrin

One Guiding Life, 27 July 1978. choreography: Don Redlich; music: arranged; costumes: Sally Ann Parsons; cast: Jennifer Donohue, Irene Feigenheimer, Barbara Roan, Billy Siegenfeld, Don Redlich

* *Molly's Not Dead*, 28 July 1978. choreography: Pilobolus; music: traditional; costumes: Kitty Daly; cast: Martha Clarke, Alison Becker Chase, Robby Barnett, Moses Pendleton, Michael Tracy, Jonathan Wolken

---

1979

---

19 June–28 July 1979

Administration: Charles L. Reinhart, director; Martha Myers, dean; Isa Bergsohn, assistant to the dean; Steve Gaddis, school administrator; Julia Wray, academic liaison with Duke University; Lisa Booth, administrative director; Stephanie Reinhart, director of development

Teaching staff: Annette Atwood, Bernard Brechenmacher, Tina Charney, Aileen Crow, Jacqueline Davis, Gemze de Lappe, Cynthia Green, Arthur Hall, Carol Hansen, Mieke van Hoek, Lucas Hoving, Sharon Kinney, Norma Leistiko, Anna Leo, Didi Levy, Don Lowe, Walter Nicks, Pamela Risenhoover, Judith Rosenberg, Terrence Ross, Marcus Schulkind, Gregory Tye, Nancy Wanich, Ethel Winter

Repertoire

Traditional dances of North Carolina

Alvin Ailey American Dance Theatre: *Streams, Cry, Flowers, Revelations, Night Creature, Myth, Butterfly* (Rael Lamb), *District Storyville* (Donald McKayle)

Kathryn Posin Dance Company: *Clear Signals, Waves*

Pilobolus Dance Theatre: *Monkshood's Farewell, Shizen, Ocellus, Untitled, Moon Blind, Solo from "The Eve of Samhain," Lost in Fauna, Geode, Pseudopodia, Molly's Not Dead, Ciona*

Dancers from Bali: Traditional Balinese dances

José Limón Dance Company: *A Choreographic Offering, Figura* (Murray Louis), *The Exiles, The Moor's Pavane, Carlota, Dances for Isadora, Psalm* (excerpts)

Arthur Hall Afro-American Dance Ensemble: Dances of Africa

Crowsnest: *Vagabond, Bone*

Merce Cunningham Dance Company: *Torse, Changing Steps Et Cetera, Summerspace, Sounddance, Signals, Fractions, Rainforest*

Paul Taylor Dance Company: *Diggity, Cloven Kingdom, Esplanade, Book of Beasts, Big Bertha, Airs*

Premieres

*Windowsill, 26 June 1979. choreography: Kathryn Posin; music: Keith Jarrett; setting: Philip Matsu; costumes: David Lewis Phelps; cast: Yael Barash, Yveline Cottez, Joyce Herring, Michael Kane, Mark Morris, Kathryn Posin, Anthony J. Rizzo

The Detail of Phoebe Strickland, 29 June 1979. choreography: Pilobolus; music: Robert Dennis; setting: Neil Peter Jampolis; masks: Carole Sivin; costumes: Kitty Daly; cast: Kammy Brooks, Alison Chase

*Music, 12 July 1979. choreography and music: Laura Dean; costumes: Miguel Cruz; cast: Laura Dean, Angela Caponigro, Perry Couchuk, Peter Healey, John Proto, Monica Solem

*Haiku, 17 July 1979. choreographed and performed by Martha Clarke, Felix Blaska, Robert Barnett; costumes: Lawrence Casey

*Fallen Angel, 17 July 1979. choreography: Martha Clarke; music: Worcester Cathedral; mask: Hunter Nesbitt Spence; costume: Kitty Daly; a solo for Clarke

*La Marquise de Solana, 17 July 1979. choreographed and performed by Martha Clarke and Felix Blaska; music: Jan Radzynski; costumes: Lawrence Casey

*Nachturn, 17 July 1979. choreography: Martha Clarke; music: Mendelssohn; costume: Kitty Daly; a solo for Clarke

*Roadrunners, 19 July 1979. choreography: Merce Cunningham; music: Yasunao Tone; designs: Mark Lancaster; cast: Karole Armitage, Louise Burns, Ellen Cornfield, Merce Cunningham, Meg Eginton, Susan Emery, Lisa Fox, Lise Friedman, Alan Good, Catherine Kerr, Chris Komar, Robert Kovich, Joseph Lennon, Robert Remley, Jim Self

*Profiles, 26 July 1979. choreography: Paul Taylor; music: Jan Radzynski; designs: Gene Moore; cast: Ruth Andrien, Christopher Gillis, Monica Morris, Elie Chaib

--- **1980** ---

14 June–25 July 1980

Administration: Charles L. Reinhart, director; Martha Myers, dean; Lisa Booth, administrative director; Paula Sofras, assistant to the dean; Julia Wray, academic liaison with Duke University; Stephanie Reinhart, director of development

Teaching staff: Annette Atwood, Marianne Bachman, Ruth Currier, Norma Dalby, Creseda Douglas, Lisa Ellyne, Diane Gray, Sharon Kinney, Daniel Nagrin, Jerry and Sara Pearson, Ronnie Ragen, Lawrence Rhodes, Terrence Ross, Diana Schnitt, Pamela Sofras, Kei Takei, Bruce Taylor, Jessica Wolf

Repertoire

Nikolais Dance Theatre: *Divertissement, Guignol, Suite from "Sanctum," Temple, Aviary, Gallery*

Dizzy Gillespie, Scoby Stroman, Honi Coles, Rutgers/Livington Jazz Professors: An evening of jazz and dance

Crowsnest: *Haiku, Nachturn, Pagliacco, Solana, Bone, Fallen Angel*

Erick Hawkins Dance Company: *Agathlon, Plains Daybreak, Parson Weems and the Cherry Tree Etc., Cantilever, Early Floating, Lords of Persia, Greek Dreams,* with Flute

Kei Takei's Moving Earth: *Light Parts 5 and 12*

Twyla Tharp Dance Foundation: *Ocean's Motion, Brahms' Paganini, Sue's Leg, Country Dances, The Fugue*

Paul Taylor Dance Company: *Piece Period, Images, Esplanade, Cloven Kingdom, Le Sacre du Printemps, (The Rehearsal), Airs, Aureole, 3 Epitaphs, Dust*

Chuck Davis Dance Company: *Lamb, African Cookbook, The Bittercup Heals, Sea Ritual*

Bella Lewitzky Dance Company: *Game Plan, Recesses, Pas de Bach, Suite Satie, Five, Kinaesonata*

Pilobolus Dance Theatre: *Ciona, Momix, Bone, Shizen, Untitled, Molly's Not Dead, Alraune, Ocellus, Monkshood's Farewell, A Miniature, The Empty Suitor, Walklyndon*

Premieres

* *The Garden of Villandry,* 24 June 1980. choreographed and performed by Martha Clarke, Felix Blaska, Robert Barnett; music: Schubert; setting: Robert Andrew Parker; costumes: Lawrence Casey

* *Avanti,* 26 June 1980: choreography. Erick Hawkins; music: Lucia Dlugoszewski; designs: Ralph Dorazio; cast: Cathy Ward, Laura Pettibone, Rand Howard, Jesse Duranceau, Cynthia Reynolds, Cori Terry, Douglas Andresen, Craig Nazor

* *The Second Windfield (Light Part 15),* 1 July 1980. choreography: Kei Takei; music: Maldwyn Pate and Japanese folk song; cast: Julie Balliett, Lori Boulanger, Kiken Chin, Richmond Johnstone, Karen Lashinsky, Elsi Miranda, Maldwyn Pate, Kei Takei, Howard Vichinsky

* *Black and Blue,* 24 July 1980. choreographed and performed by Moses Pendleton and Alison Chase; music: Stormin' Norman and Suzy and the Frugstones

——————————————— **1981** ———————————————

18 June–25 July 1981

Administration: Charles L. Reinhart, president; Martha Myers, vice-president; Judith Sagan, chairman, American Dance Festival board of directors; Pamela Sofras, assistant to the dean; David Rich, academic coordinator; Julia Wray, academic liaison with Duke University; Stephanie Reinhart, director of development

Teaching staff: David Chapman, John Colman, Chuck Davis, Irene Dowd, Marcia Esposito, Robert Esposito, Toni Ann Gardella, Adrienne Hawkins, Gerri Houlihan, Shizuko Ijuin, Betty Jones, Kenneth King, Norma Leistiko, Eliza Mallouk, Jacqui Miyahara, Klarna Pinska, Doris Rudko, Donald Saddler, Diana Schnitt, Michael Schwartz, Ruby Shang, Pamela Sofras, François Szony, Jonathan Watts

Repertoire

North Carolina Dance Theatre: *Square Dance* (Balanchine), *Women* (Oscar Araiz), *Piano*

Concerto No. 1 (Salvatore Aiello), *Meadow Dances* (Norbert Vesak), *Dreamscapes* (Charles Czarny), *Clowns and Others* (Aiello)

Johnny Griffin Quartet, Scoby Stroman, Jofar Abdullah: An evening of jazz and dance

Dance Theatre of Harlem: *Four Temperaments* (Balanchine), *Manifestations* (Arthur Mitchell), *Le Corsaire* (Karel Shook, after Petipa), *Troy Game* (Robert North), *Serenade* (Balanchine), *Mirage* (Billy Wilson), *Adagietto No. 5* (Royston Maldoom), *Dougla* (Geoffrey Holder)

May O'Donnell Concert Dance Company: *Homage to Shiva, Dance Concerto, Pursuit of Happiness*

Laura Dean Dancers and Musicians: *Song, Pattern III, Dance*

Marleen Pennison: *Fat Monday, In Absentia, Tante Jeanne*

Molissa Fenley: *Peripheral Vision, Direct Effect, Energizer #2*

Charles Moulton: *Nine Person Precision Ball Passing, Opposite Arch, Motor Fantasy*

Johanna Boyce: *Pass, Only (Pass) Connect*

Bill T. Jones: *Untitled*

Paul Taylor Dance Company: *Aureole, 3 Epitaphs, Le Sacre du Printemps (The Rehearsal), Arden Court*

Vaudeville Alive and Dancing, with Elisa Monte, Joe Roth, Betsy Baytos, Toni Ann Gardella, Jay Marshall, Sandman Sims, François Szony, Michael Tracy

Pilobolus Dance Theatre: *Molly's Not Dead, Bonsai, Momix, Untitled, The Empty Suitor, Geode*

Chuck Davis Dance Company: *Homage*

Premieres

*Resettings, 18 June 1981. choreography: Senta Driver; music: Purcell; costumes: T. Augustine; cast: Rick Guimond, Rebecca McLain, Traci Owens, Pearl Potts, Richard Prewitt, Charles Devlin, Dayna Fox, Todd Goodman, David Herriott, Gwendolyn Leonard, Rick Michalek, Steven Pasco, Laurie Worrill

*Tympani, 2 July 1981. choreography and music: Laura Dean; costumes: Nicholas Romanelli; cast: Angela Caponigro, Peter Healey, Ching Gonzalez, Erin Matthiessen, Sarah Brumgart, Mark Morris

*Waterbodies, 10 July 1981. choreography: Johanna Boyce; music: Jack Eric Williams; film: John Schabel; cast: Claudia Bader, Johanna Boyce, Dean Corren, Bill Ingram, John Kramer, Kate Nichols, Harty Read, Robbyn Scott, Linda Siconolfi

*Social Intercourse, 10 July (Part IV) and 11 July 1981 (Parts I–III). choreography: Bill T. Jones; music: Joe Hannan; slides: Lois Greenfield, Bill T. Jones, Arnie Zane; cast: Caren Calder, Bill T. Jones, Harry Sheppard

*Free Way, 11 July 1981. choreography: Marleen Pennison; sound: Phil Lee; photography: Gerald Murrell; cast: Ronnie: Peter Bass; Hank: Thomas Wilkinson; Cindy: Holly Cavrell; Jean: Marleen Pennison; Ronnie, Jr.: Adam Reinhart

*Gentle Desire, 11 July 1981. choreography: Molissa Fenley; music: Mark Freedman; costumes: Yousun Pak; cast: Lynne Allard, Deni Bank, Molissa Fenley

*Expanded Ball Passing, 11 July 1981. choreography: Charles Moulton; music: A. Leroy; cast: Barbara Allen, Beatrice Bogorad, Charles Moulton

*Rites of Passage, 14 July 1981. choreography: Chuck Davis and Yarabi-Lynette White; music: traditional; costumes: Diana Lansana, Chuck Davis, Carole Lynch; masks:

Komori, Terry White; cast: Initiators: Abbel Salaam, Albert Williams, Tony Williams; High Elder: Chuck Davis; Chief Elder: Tony Davis; Elders: Greg Jenkins, Brett Chambers; Guardians: Thaddeus Bennett, James K. Green III, Tommy Newman, Sherone Price, Lee White, Terry Lainer White; Young Women: Roslyn Davis, Lisa Dockery, Anita Lamberty, Chiqui Santiago

Day 2, 23 July 1981. choreography: Pilobolus; music: Brian Eno, David Byrne, Talking Heads; cast: Robert Faust, Jamey Hampton, Carol Parker, Peter Pucci, Cynthia Quinn, Michael Tracy

*Untitled II, 23 July 1981. choreography: Alison Chase; music: Paul Sullivan; costume: Kitty Daly; a solo for Chase

--------------------------------- **1982** ---------------------------------

12 June–23 July 1982

Administration: Charles L. Reinhart, director; Martha Myers, dean; Stephanie Reinhart, director of planning and development; Sandra Dilley, administrative director; Nancy Trovillion, director of operations; Pamela Anderson Sofras, assistant to the dean; Julia Wray, academic liaison with Duke University

Teaching staff: Fred Benjamin, Nina H. Crumm, Joel Dabin, Chuck Davis, Irene Dowd, Jamal Hardeman, Gerri Houlihan, Betty Jones, Mark Litvin, Eliza Mallouk, Nancy Meehan, Carol-Lynne Moore, Daniel Nagrin, Klarna Pinska, Pamela Anderson Sofras, Gus Solomons, Jr., Kei Takei, Linda Tarnay, John Wilson

Repertoire

Merce Cunningham Dance Company: *Fielding Sixes, Locale, Roadrunners, 10's With Shoes, Trails, Duets, Gallopade*
Johanna Boyce and Performance Group: *Incidents (in Coming of Age)*
Paul Taylor Dance Company: *Esplanade, Profiles, 3 Epitaphs, Mercuric Tidings, Airs, Lost, Found and Lost, Le Sacre du Printemps (The Rehearsal), Cloven Kingdom, House of Cards, Arden Court*
Kei Takei's Moving Earth: *Light Part 12: The Stonefield, Light Part 14: The Pine Cone Field*
Charles Moulton Dance Company: *Stepwise Motion, Display*
Jennifer Muller and the Works: *Beach (Act I), Armless, Speeds, Terrain, Chant*
Waka Dance Company: *A Poem: Forest* (Shigeka Hanayagi)
Bonjin Atsugi Dance Company: *Standing*
Miyako Kato and Dancers: *Arabesque, Point, Distant View and Cantata*
Dai Rakuda Kan: *Sea Dappled Horse* (Akaji Maro)
Chuck Davis Dance Company: *Griot, Djembe and Chant, Isicathwo, Ganza, Lamb*
Nikolais Dance Theatre: *Sanctum (Group Dance), Vaudeville (Trio), Mechanical Organ I, Guignol, Pond, Tensile Involvement, Countdown, Mechanical Organ II*
Pilobolus Dance Theatre, with Crowsnest and Momix: *Haiku, Nachturn, Tarleton's Resurrection, The Empty Suitor, Untitled, Molly's Not Dead, Bonsai, Garden of Villandry, Fromages Dangereuses, It Don't Mean a Thing, Walklyndon, Day Two*

Premieres (American companies)

*Kinscope, 21 June 1982. choreography: Johanna Boyce; music: Richard Munson; cast:
Johanna Boyce, Dean Corren, Bob Gober, Bill Ingram, Laszlo Kertesz, John Kramer,
Kate Nichols, Chuck Riley, Robbyn Scott

*Light Part 17: Dreamcatcher's Diary, 28 June 1982. choreography: Kei Takei; music:
Norma Reynolds Dalby; cast: Lori Boulanger, Lazuro Brezer, David Dorfman, Luis
Gonzalez, Michael Kasper, Brian Laurier, Carol McDowell, Elsi Miranda, Kei Takei,
Cydney Wilkes, John Wilson

*Motor Party, 29 June 1982. choreography: Charles Moulton; music: A. Leroy; cast:
Barbara Allen, Beatrice Bogorad, Kenneth DeLap, Peggy Florin, Charles Moulton

*Perpetrator, 12 July 1982. choreography: Jim Self; music: Frankie Mann; costumes: Naomi
Lane; cast: Jon Mensinger, Jim Self, Ellen van Schuylenburch, Teri Weksler

*Dances of Identity, 12 July 1982. choreography: Charlie Vernon; music: David Felder;
text: Marybeth Schroeder and Vernon; cast: Jan Bartoszek, Sharon Thacker, Charlie
Vernon, Richard Woodbury

* On the Side of Light, 12 July 1982. choreography: Danny Buraczeski; music: Eric Valinsky;
cast: Becky Bowden, Danny Buraczeski, Les Johnson, Abby Levine, Michael McNeill,
Janice Redman, Lee Smilek

Premieres (Japanese companies)

Tearing Sign 8, 7 July 1982. choreography: Bonjin Atsugi; cast: Bonjin Atsugi, Tukiko
Tanegashima, Gen Watanabe

Snow Don't Be Stopping, 7 July 1982. choreography: Shigeka Hanayagi; music: Suihoh
Tosha; costumes: Tetsuhiko Maeda; cast: Omote Hanayagi, Isao Gokita

———————————————— **1983** ————————————————

13 June–23 July 1983

Administration: Charles L. Reinhart, director; Martha Myers, dean; Stephanie Reinhart,
associate director; Nancy Trovillion, administrative director; Pamela Anderson Sofras,
associate dean; Julia Wray, academic liaison with Duke University

Teaching staff: Ze'eva Cohen, Lee Connor, Chuck Davis, Ed Di Lello, Irene Dowd, Jan
Dunn, Simone Forti, Gerri Houlihan, Betty Jones, Richard Levi, Mark Litvin, Eliza
Mallouk, Ronnie Ragen, Ruby Shang, Pamela Anderson Sofras, Kei Takei, Linda Tarnay,
Jaclynn Villamil

Repertoire

Paul Taylor Dance Company: *Diggity, Snow White, Dust, Images, Sunset, Airs, Esplanade,
Book of Beasts, Arden Court*

Pilobolus Dance Theatre: *Molly's Not Dead, What Grows in Huygen's Window, Day Two,
Ciona, Moonblind, Scribble, Walklyndon, Elegy for the Moment, The Empty Suitor,
Bonsai, Untitled*

Maria Benitez Spanish Dance Company: Traditional Spanish dances

Festival Africa: African dances by Calabash Dance Company, Kombo Omolara, Dinizulu
and His African Dancers, Drummers and Singers, Art of Black Dance and Music Inc.,

Chuck Davis Dance Company, Olukose Wiles, Weaver Street Dancers, The Cultural Movement

Charles Moulton Dance Company: *Pascal's Triangle, Instant Six, Fold Out*

Kei Takei's Moving Earth: *Light Part 11: The Stone Field, Light Part 18: The Wheat Field*

Lar Lubovitch Dance Company: *Cavalcade, Gears Align* (Charles Moulton), *Beau Danube, Tabernacle, North Star, Scriabin Dances, Chicago*

Eiko and Koma: *Fur Seal*

José Limón Dance Company: *Air for the G String* (Humphrey), *The Unsung, Orfeo, The Moor's Pavane, Sonata* (Carla Maxwell), *Magritte Magritte* (Anna Sokolow), *There Is a Time*

Ballet Théâtre de l'Arche: *May B* (Maguy Marin)

Compagnie de Danse l'Esquisse: *Terre Battue* (Joëlle Bouvier and Régis Obadia), *Tête Close* (Bouvier and Obadia), *Les Noces d'Argile* (Bouvier and Obadia)

Compagnie Karine Saporta: *Escale I, Hypnotic Circus*

Compagnie Dominique Bagouet: *Insaisies*

Caroline Marcadé et Compagnie: *Pierre Robert*

Premieres

Fonki (Konko Kwesi Adae), 1 July 1983. choreography: Chuck Davis; music: traditional; cast: Chuck Davis Dance Company (individual performers unlisted in program)

Drum Awakening, 2 July 1983. choreography: Chuck Davis, Ayanna Frederick, Yao Odom, Deama Battle, Olukose Wiles; music: traditional; cast: Mother: Cathy Jackson; Father: Al Smith; Elders: Terry White, Chuck Davis, Nana Dinizulu, Ivy Burch, Sherone Price, Kombo Omdara, Olukose Wiles, and members of Art of Black Dance and Music Inc., Calabash Dance Company, Chuck Davis Dance Company, Dinizulu and His African Dancers, Drummers and Singers

*Fireworks, 4 July 1983. choreography: Charles Moulton; cast: Barbara Allen, Mia Babalis, Beatrice Bogorad

*The Daikon Field Solo II from Light Part 16: Vegetable Fields, 5 July 1983. choreography: Kei Takei; music: Buddhist drumming; designs: Tetsu Maeda; cast: Kei Takei, assisted by Lazuro Brezer

*Panel, 18 July 1983. choreography: Claire Porter; music: Laura Clayton; cast: Bill McKinley, LeAnn Schmidt, Mackie Boblette, Claire Porter

*Chorines, 18 July 1983. choreography: Gina Buntz; music: Mary Ellen Childs; costumes: Ann Lindsay; cast: Gina Buntz, Nancy Coenen, Deborah Monlux

*Blanca, 18 July 1983. choreography and slides: Catlin Cobb; music: Dan Handelsman; poetry: Pablo Neruda; cast: Bill Bissel, Catlin Cobb, Lauren Dong, David Dorfman

*Beam, 20 July 1983. choreographed and danced by Eiko and Koma; music: Asian folk

---

1984

---

10 June–21 July 1984

Administration: Charles L. Reinhart, director; Martha Myers, dean; Stephanie Reinhart, associate director; Nancy Trovillion, administrative director; Jan Dunn, assistant dean; Julia Wray, academic liaison with Duke University

Teaching staff: Shelley Berg, Lee Connor, Gail Corbin, Chuck Davis, Nada Diachenko, Ralf Haze, Betty Jones, Sharon Kinney, Mark Litvin, Peggy Lyman, Alvin McDuffie, Mishele Mennett, Dawn Moir, Martha Partridge, Isa Partsch-Bergsohn, Don Redlich, Ernestine Stodelle, Linda Tarnay, Jaclynn Villamil

Repertoire

Uday Shankar India Cultural Centre Dance Company: *Homage* (Amala Shankar), *Snanam, Astra Puja, Apsara* (Mamata Shankar), *Rasa Leela, Harvest, Kartikeya, Harmony*

Ballet Philippines: *Mutya Ng Pasig* (Edna Vida), *Amada* (Alice Reyes), *Awakening* (Brando Miranda), *Vision of Fire* (Vida)

Susan Buirge Project: *Des Sites*

London Contemporary Dance Theatre: *Run Like Thunder* (Tom Jobe), *New Galileo* (Siobhan Davies), *Sighs, Lamentations and Praises* (Robert Cohan), *The Dancing Department* (Davies), *Forest* (Cohan), *Class* (Cohan)

Astad Deboo and Bharat Sharma: *Nataraj* (Guru Krishna Chandra Naik), *Reaching Out* (Deboo), *Mukhote* (Narendra Sharma), *Duel* (Deboo), *Hem Lalit* (B. Sharma), *Awakening (Deboo), Untitled* (B. Sharma), *Asylum* (Deboo)

Dance Indonesia: *Awan Bailau* (Deddy Luthan and Tom Ibnur), *Hhhhhuuuuu* (Noerin Daud and Marzuki Hasan)

Marleen Pennison Company: *The Routine, River Road Sweet*

Eiko and Koma: *Grain*

Merce Cunningham Dance Company: *Inlets 2, Pictures, Quartet, Roadrunners*

Twyla Tharp Dance: *Eight Jelly Rolls, Nine Sinatra Songs, The Fugue, Sue's Leg*

Chuck Davis Dance Company, with the African-American Dance Ensemble: Traditional African dances

Groupe Emile Dubois: *Ulysse* (Jean-Claude Gallotta)

Nikolais Dance Theatre: *Divertissement, The Mechanical Organ, Kaleidoscope, Gallery, Tensile Involvement, Video Game*

Pilobolus Dance Theatre: *Molly's Not Dead, Day Two, Ciona, A Miniature, Stabat Mater, Mirage*

Premieres

Muybridge/Frames, 14 June 1984. choreography: Denisa Reyes; music: Fabian Obispo; costumes; Salvador Bernal; cast: Brando Miranda, Jinn Ibarrola, Ric Culack, Conrad Dy-Liacco, Nonoy Froilan, Ramon Victoria, Jojo Lucila

*Elegy, 19 June 1984. choreographed and danced by Eiko and Koma

*The Hurricane: Dedans l'Année de Cinquante-Sept, 26 June 1984. choreography: Marleen Pennison; music: Ambrose Thibodeaux; cast: Peter Bass, Cynthia Bonnett, Marleen Pennison, Thomas Wilkinson

*Doubles, 28 June 1984. choreography: Merce Cunningham; music: Takehisa Kosugi; designs: Mark Lancaster; cast: Louise Burns, Alan Good, Megan Walker, Lise Friedman, Neil Greenberg, Susan Quinn Young, Rob Remley

*Sorrow Floats, 5 July 1984. choreography: Twyla Tharp; music: Bizet; designs: Kermit Love; cast: John Carrafa, Jennifer Way, Shelley Washington, Katie Glasner

*War of the Guardians, 9 July 1984. choreography: Chuck Davis; music: Bill Paul and traditional African; costumes: Brenda Hayes; cast: P2BHers: Michael Bonsignore, Lil

Fen, Paul Holmbeck, David Kirkpatrick, Tim McGloin, Harry Nagel, Erin Sweeney, Peter Wood; Community Folks: Chuck Davis, David Gedzelman, Darryl Jackson, Linda McGloin, Venita Ashford, Eric Hurlburt, Karen Hurlburt, Seth Hurlburt, Crystal Jones, Emile McGloin, Adrianne Muldrow, Tanya Spain

Wild-Fields, 10 July 1984. choreography: Pooh Kaye; music: Michael Kosch; cast: Claire Bernard, Amy Finkel, Ginger Gillespie, Pooh Kaye, Jennifer Monson, Sanghi Wagner

Climbing the Waltz, 10 July 1984. choreography: Stephanie Skura; music: Frank McCorty; cast: Fred Holland, Lisa Kraus, Yvonne Meier, Stephanie Skura

Forty Arms, Twenty Necks, One Writhing, 10 July 1984. choreography: Mark Morris; music: Herschel Garfein; cast: Erin Matthiessen, Penny Hutchinson, Guillermo Resto, Mark Morris, Betsy Babcock, David Beadle, Monica D'Agostino, Emily Fraenkel, Orna Franti, Sara Johnson, Lara Kohn, Jennifer Kinnier, Kaela Lee, Gabriel Masson, Amy McCall, Mark Nimkoff, Fairfax O'Riley, Marsha Pabalis, Vanessa Player, Debbie Warner

Return to Maria La Baja, 12 July 1984. choreography: Pilobolus; music: Paul Sullivan; costumes: Lawrence Casey; masks: Robert Faust and Carole Sivin; cast: Robby Barnett, Alison Chase, Robert Faust, Lisa Giobbi

The Small Wall Project, 14 July 1984. choreography: Ruby Shang; music: David Friedman; sculptures: Pat Dougherty; flags: Bryant Holsenbeck; an environmental event for Ruby Shang Company, festival students, and staff members

Graph, 19 July 1984. choreography, music, and designs: Alwin Nikolais; cast: Gerald Otte, Jung Auyang, Timothy Harling, Susie Goldman, Joy Hintz, Susan Kline, Christine Lamb, Lynn Lesniak, James Murphy, Raul Trujillo

Tokyo Premiere
Trio, 17 August 1984. choreography and music: Laura Dean; cast: Ching Gonzalez, Elizabeth Maxwell, Mary Anne Schultz

———————————————— **1985** ————————————————

8 June–20 August 1985

Administration: Charles L. Reinhart, director; Martha Myers, dean; Stephanie Reinhart, associate director; Nancy Trovillion, administrative director; Jan Dunn, assistant to the dean; Julia Wray, academic liaison with Duke University

Teaching staff: Jill Beck, Shelley Berg, Helen Closset, Chuck Davis, Nada Diachenko, Cathy Ellich, David Gordon, Kay Gross, David Hochoy, Betty Jones, Sharon Kinney, Mark Litvin, Alvin McDuffie, Nancy Nasworthy, Martha Partridge, Isa Partsch-Bergsohn, Kenneth Rinker, Valda Setterfield, Catherine Sharpe, James Sutton, Clarence Teeters

Repertoire

Nikolais Dance Theatre: *Mechanical Organ, Pond, Graph, Tensile Involvement, Liturgies, Noumenon, Tower*
Martha Clarke: *The Garden of Earthly Delights*
G.R.C.O.P. (Groupe de Recherche Chorégraphique de l'Opéra de Paris): *Aureole* (Paul Taylor), *Density 21.5* (Carolyn Carlson), *On Doute la Nuit* (Jacques Garnier), *Pas de*

Deux (Garnier), *Beethoven and Boothe* (David Gordon), *Le French Revolting* (Michael Clark), *La Couleur du Secret* (Jean Christophe Pare), *Aunis* (Jacques Garnier), *Slow, Heavy and Blue* (Carolyn Carlson)

Paul Taylor Dance Company: *Roses, Last Look, Esplanade, Equinox, Runes, Arden Court*

Pooh Kaye/Eccentric Motions: *The River Sticks, Swept Up, Wild Fields, Inside the House of Floating Paper, Bring Home the Bacon*

Eiko and Koma: *Before the Cock Crows, Fission*

Deborah Carr Theater Dance Ensemble: *Christmas Oratorio* (Charles Weidman), *Flickers* (Weidman), *Traditions* (Weidman), *Lynchtown* (Weidman), *Brahms Waltzes* (Weidman)

David Gordon/Pick Up Company: *Offenbach Suite, My Folks*

Pilobolus Dance Theatre: *Bonsai, Pseudopodia, Can't Get Started, What Grows in Huygen's Window, Ocellus, Mirages, Elegy for the Moment,* solo from *The Empty Suitor*

Desrosiers Dance Theatre: *Brass Fountain* (Robert Desrosiers), *Mille Millions de Tonneres (Bad Weather)* (Desrosiers), *L'Hotel Perdu* (Desrosiers)

Chuck Davis African-American Dance Ensemble: *Welcoming, Africa Is, Drought, Brende Sidibe, Mandiani, Ritual of Peace*

Premieres

*Crucible, 13 June 1985. choreography, music, designs: Alwin Nikolais; cast: Alberto Del Saz, Susie Goldman, Timothy Harling, William Harren, Joy Hintz, Susan Kline, Christine Lamb, Lynn Lesniak, James Murphy, Raul Trujillo

Drought 17 June 1985. choreography and poetry: Chuck Davis; music: Khalid Saleem, Weather Report; costumes: Brenda Hayes; cast: African Griot: Vieux Diop; American Griot: Chuck Davis; The Victims: ensemble; Children: Afi Noni, Adrianne Saddler

Saturday Night/Sunday Morning, 18 June 1985. choreography: Chuck Davis; music: Jimmy McGriff, Linda Hopkins, Nona Hendrix, Wilson Pickett, Inspirational Stars, James Cleveland, Roberta Flack, Les Baxter; costumes: Brenda Hayes; cast: Leah Wise, S. Price, B. Hayes, J. Green, J. Wiliams, I. Burch, A. McFarlane, Dan Jacobs, and unidentified ensemble

Carmina Bananas, 27 June 1985. choreography: Pilobolus; music: Orff's *Carmina Burana*; costumes: Kitty Daly; cast: Austin Hartel, Carol Parker, Josh Perl, Peter Pucci, Jude Sante, Michael Tracy

Nine Lives, 1 July 1985. choreography: David Gordon; music: Western swing; cast: Valda Setterfield, Keith Marshall, Dean Moss, David Gordon, Janice Bourdage, Chuck Finlon, Kenneth Kirkland, Kay McCabe

Weather Over Baguio, 15 July 1985. choreographed and performed by Kinematic (Tamar Kotoske, Maria Lakis, Mary Richter); music: Robert Sprayberry; designs: Robin Klingensmith

Forest, 15 July 1985. choreography and setting: Ralph Lemon; music: Linda Bouchard; costumes: Charles Schoonmaker; cast: Woman with Oranges: Veta Goler; Hunter: Hetty King; Shepherd: Ralph Lemon

*Rebound About, 15 July 1985. choreography: Eccentric Motions and Pooh Kaye; music: Michael Kosch; costumes: Mario Camacho; cast: Claire Bernard, Ginger Gillespie, Amy Finkel, Courtney Conner, Mark Dendy, David Zambrano, Sanghi Wagner

Faculty Premieres

Celtic Suite (Dance in Two Parts), Part I: *Duet for One* (1982); *Part II *Lost Lullabye*, 17 July 1985. choreography: James Sutton; music: Alan Stivel; cast: James Sutton (Part I), Sarah M. DeGunther (Part II)

**If It's Magic*, 17 July 1985. choreography: David Hochoy; music: Stevie Wonder; cast: Kimberly Bartosik, Mario Camacho

**Boxtops*, 17 July 1985. choreography: Martha Partridge, Tigger Benford; cast: Martha Partridge, Tigger Benford

NOTES

I The Founding of the Festival

1 Quotation from Martha Hill made in conversation. The account of Bennington is summarized from Sali Ann Kriegsman, *Modern Dance in America: The Bennington Years*. (Complete publication information for all book titles cited in the notes may be found in the Selected Bibliography.)

2 Sali Ann Kriegsman, *Modern Dance in America: The Bennington Years*, p. 11.

3 Conversation with Martha Hill. All other statements for which no printed source is given were made in conversation with the author.

4 Gertrude E. Noyes, *A History of Connecticut College*, pp. 110–12.

5 Biographical details taken from "Ruth Bloomer Dies," *Dance Observer*, June–July 1959, p. 87; "Ruth Bloomer Dead at 52," *Dance News*, May 1959, p. 13; "In Memoriam Ruth Bloomer," *Dance Magazine*, May 1959, p. 4; and an undated obituary announcement prepared by Theodora Wiesner.

6 "College Correspondence," *Dance Observer*, May 1947, p. 51.

7 This account of Connecticut College is summarized from Noyes, *A History of Connecticut College*.

8 Ibid., pp. 143, 171–72.

9 Statements in festival program for 16 August 1956 and in *A Decade of Dance 1948–1957*, p. 3.

10 Tom Borek, "The Connecticut College American Dance Festival 1948–1972: A Fantastical Documentary," *Dance Perspectives* 50 (Summer 1972): 29.

11 *New York Times*, 15 February 1948.

II Season by Season: 1948 to 1958

1 New York University–Connecticut College School of the Dance, 1948 bulletin and 1948 festival programs. Details concerning festival premieres can be found in the festival chronicle.

2 Modern dancers, until recently, were often capricious about the way they named companies and would change the names of their groups slightly for no apparent reason. Thus, one year, a hypothetical choreographer named John Smith might head the John

Smith Dance Company; the next year he might call his troupe John Smith and Dancers, and the year after that it might be the John Smith Dance Theatre. Many variants exist for the names of the Martha Graham and José Limón companies. Thus, in 1948, the Graham troupe was simply listed on programs as "Martha Graham," followed by the names of her dancers. Therefore companies will usually be referred to in the text as "the Graham company," "the Limón company," etc.; details about companies and their offerings can be found in the festival chronicle.

3   Belitt quotation in *A Decade of Dance 1948–1957*, p. 12. *Diversion of Angels* reviews: Doris Hering, "An American Dance Festival," *Dance Magazine*, October 1948, p. 39; Nik Krevitsky and Cecil Smith in *A Decade of Dance 1948–1957*, p. 36.

4   Program note, 1948 program. *The Strangler* reviews: Walter Terry, *New York Herald Tribune*, 23 August 1948; Robert Sabin, "Review of American Dance Festival," *Dance Observer*, August–September 1948, pp. 86–87; Doris Hering, "An American Dance Festival," *Dance Magazine*, October 1948, p. 41.

5   Nik Krevitsky, "Review of American Dance Festival," *Dance Observer*, August–September 1948, p. 86; Doris Hering, "An American Dance Festival," *Dance Magazine*, October 1948, p. 40; Louis Horst, *New London Evening Day*, 18 August 1949; Walter Terry, *New York Herald Tribune*, 19 August 1948. The Limón quotation appears in the 1967 festival program.

6   Sali Ann Kriegsman, *Modern Dance in America: The Bennington Years*, p. 26.

7   Carl Miller, "A New American Dance Center," *Dance Observer*, August–September 1948, pp. 84–85; Walter Terry, *New York Herald Tribune*, 22 August 1948.

8   Don McDonagh, *Martha Graham*, p. 209.

9   John Martin, *New York Times*, 14 November 1948, and conversation with Martha Hill.

10 John Martin, *New York Times*, 28 August 1949; Doris Hering, *The Daily Compass*, 22 August 1949.

11 Selma Jeanne Cohen, *Doris Humphrey: An Artist First*, pp. 198–99.

12 Walter Terry, *New York Herald Tribune*, 15 August 1949; Doris Hering, "Reflections on the 2nd American Dance Festival," *Dance Magazine*, October 1949, p. 25.

13 Doris Hering, "Reflections on the 2nd American Dance Festival," *Dance Magazine*, October 1949, p. 31; Walter Terry, *New York Herald Tribune*, 14 August 1949; Louis Horst, *New London Evening Day*, 15 August 1949; John Martin, *New York Times*, 14 August 1949.

14 Doris Hering, "Reflections on the 2nd American Dance Festival," *Dance Magazine*, October 1949, p. 31, and conversation with Jane Dudley.

15 John Martin, *New York Times*, 14 August 1949.

16 Nik Krevitsky, "American Dance Festival," *Dance Observer*, August–September 1949, pp. 98–99.

17 Walter Terry, *New York Herald Tribune*, 15 August 1949; John Martin, *New York Times*, 15 August 1949; Nik Krevitsky, "American Dance Festival," *Dance Observer*, August–September 1949, pp. 98–99.

18 Carl Miller, "The N.Y.U.–Connecticut College Second Summer Session," *Dance Observer*, August–September 1949, pp. 96–97.

19 Walter Terry, *New York Herald Tribune*, 27 August 1950.

20 Walter Terry, *New York Herald Tribune*, 14 August 1950; Nik Krevitsky, "American Dance Festival," *Dance Observer*, August–September 1950, p. 103.
21 John Martin, *New York Times*, 21 August 1950; Nik Krevitsky, "American Dance Festival," *Dance Observer*, August–September 1950, p. 104.
22 Nik Krevitsky, "American Dance Festival," *Dance Observer*, August–September 1950, p. 102, and conversation with Sophie Maslow.
23 Walter Terry, *New York Herald Tribune*, 14 August 1950; Nik Krevitsky, "American Dance Festival," *Dance Observer*, August–September 1950, p. 102; Doris Hering, "The 3d Annual American Dance Festival," *Dance Magazine*, October 1950, p. 11, and conversation with Jane Dudley.
24 Walter Terry, *New York Herald Tribune*, 6 August 1950.
25 Nik Krevitsky, "American Dance Festival," *Dance Observer*, August–September 1950, p. 103.
26 Jean Battey Lewis, *Washington Post*, 17 December 1972; Walter Terry, *I Was There*, p. 250; John Martin, *New York Times*, 6 December 1952.
27 Walter Terry, *New York Herald Tribune*, 2 September 1951.
28 The 1951 Connecticut College School of the Dance bulletin; John Martin, *New York Times*, 24 June 1951; conversation with Theodora Wiesner.
29 General Mexican program information: Walter Terry, *New York Herald Tribune*, 2 September 1951. Reviews: Doris Hering, "Outlook from New London," *Dance Magazine*, October 1951, p. 50; Nik Krevitsky, "American Dance Festival," *Dance Observer*, August–September 1951, p. 104.
30 Nik Krevitsky, "American Dance Festival," *Dance Observer*, August–September 1951, p. 104.
31 John Martin, *New York Times*, 2 September 1951; Selma Jeanne Cohen, *Doris Humphrey: An Artist First*, p. 201; conversation with Pauline Koner.
32 Walter Terry, *New York Herald Tribune*, 2 September 1951; John Martin, *New York Times*, 9 September 1951; conversation with Sophie Maslow.
33 John Martin, *New York Times*, 21 August 1951; Nik Krevitsky, "American Dance Festival," *Dance Observer*, August–September 1951, p. 105.
34 *Amorous Adventure* description: Conversation with Pauline Koner; Helen Dzhermolinska, "Blueprint for a Ballet," *Dance Magazine*, April 1951, pp. 14–15, 42–43. Reviews: Nik Krevitsky, "American Dance Festival," *Dance Observer*, August–September 1951, p. 105; John Martin, *New York Times*, 9 September 1951.
35 Nik Krevitsky, "American Dance Festival," *Dance Observer*, August–September 1951, p. 105.
36 John Martin, *New York Times*, 26 August 1951.
37 Walter Terry, *New York Herald Tribune*, 31 August 1952.
38 Doris Hering, "Changing Currents," *Dance Magazine*, October 1952, p. 43; Walter Terry, *New York Herald Tribune*, 23 August 1952.
39 Doris Hering, "Changing Currents," *Dance Magazine*, October 1952, p. 41; Walter Terry, *New York Herald Tribune*, 23 August 1952.
40 *A Decade of Dance 1948–1957*, pp. 38–39, and conversation with Pauline Koner.
41 Louis Horst, "American Dance Festival," *Dance Observer*, August–September 1952, p. 102; Doris Hering, "Changing Currents," *Dance Magazine*, October 1952, p. 17.

42 Walter Terry, *New York Herald Tribune*, 31 August 1952, and conversation with Jane Dudley.

43 On Dietz: John Martin, *New York Times*, 24 May 1953. On Tanner: Walter Terry, *I Was There*, pp. 280–81.

44 Walter Terry, *New York Herald Tribune*, 23 August 1953; Louis Horst, "American Dance Festival," *Dance Observer*, August–September 1953, p. 103.

45 Doris Hering, "American Dance Festival, 1953," *Dance Magazine*, October 1953, p. 29.

46 Louis Horst, "American Dance Festival," *Dance Observer*, August–September 1953, p. 102.

47 Conversation with Pauline Koner. *Cassandra* reviews: Louis Horst, "American Dance Festival," *Dance Observer*, August–September 1953, p. 102; Doris Hering, "American Dance Festival: 1953," *Dance Magazine*, October 1953, p. 29; Walter Terry, *New York Herald Tribune*, 21 August 1953.

48 Conversation with Sophie Maslow. *Manhattan Transfer* reviews: Walter Terry, *New York Herald Tribune*, 22 August 1953; Doris Hering, "American Dance Festival: 1953," *Dance Magazine*, October 1953, p. 27.

49 Louis Horst, "American Dance Festival," *Dance Observer*, August–September 1953, p. 102; José Limón, statement in 1967 festival program.

50 Pauline Koner, "Working with Doris Humphrey," pp. 261–66; John Martin, *New York Times*, 30 August 1953; José Limón, statement in 1967 festival program; Selma Jeanne Cohen, "Doris Humphrey's 'Ruins and Visions,'" *Dance Observer*, December 1950, pp. 148–50; conversation with Pauline Koner.

51 John Martin, *New York Times*, 30 August 1953.

52 *The Traitor*, descriptive remarks: Selma Jeanne Cohen, *The Modern Dance: Seven Statements of Belief*, p. 26; José Limón, statement in 1967 festival program. Reviews: Walter Terry (first Terry quotation), *I Was There*, pp. 293–94; Walter Terry (second Terry quotation), *New York Herald Tribune*, 20 August 1954; Doris Hering, "New London Festival," *Dance Magazine*, October 1954, p. 23; Louis Horst, "American Dance Festival," *Dance Observer*, August–September 1954, p. 101.

53 John Martin, *New York Times*, 29 August 1954; Doris Hering, "New London Festival," *Dance Magazine*, October 1954, p. 26.

54 Doris Hering, "New London Festival," *Dance Magazine*, October 1954, p. 44.

55 Ibid., p. 26.

56 Walter Terry, *New York Herald Tribune*, 22 August 1954; Doris Hering, "New London Festival," *Dance Magazine*, October 1954, p. 44.

57 Campus activities summarized from "College Correspondence," *Dance Observer*, December 1955, p. 151; John Martin, *New York Times*, 17 April 1955; Louis Horst, "American Dance Festival," *Dance Observer*, August–September 1955, p. 97.

58 Doris Hering, "Eighth American Dance Festival," *Dance Magazine*, October 1955, pp. 12–13; Walter Terry, *New York Herald Tribune*, 22 August 1955.

59 Walter Terry, *New York Herald Tribune*, 28 August 1955.

60 Louis Horst, "American Dance Festival," *Dance Observer*, August–September 1955, p. 97; Walter Terry, *New York Herald Tribune*, 28 August 1955.

61 Quoted in *A Decade of Dance 1948–1957*, p. 41.

62 Doris Hering, "Eighth American Dance Festival," *Dance Magazine*, October 1955, p. 13; John Martin, *New York Times*, 28 August 1955.

63 Quoted in *A Decade of Dance 1948–1957*, p. 41.

64 John Martin, *New York Times*, 18 August 1956; Walter Terry, *New York Herald Tribune*, 26 August 1956; Louis Horst, "American Dance Festival," *Dance Observer*, August–September 1956, p. 101; George Beiswanger, "New London: Residues and Reflections (Part III)," *Dance Observer*, January 1957, p. 6.

65 John Martin, *New York Times*, 20 August 1956; Doris Hering, "Reviews," *Dance Magazine*, October 1956, p. 74; George Beiswanger, "New London: Residues and Reflections (Part I)," *Dance Observer*, November 1956, p. 133.

66 Walter Terry, *New York Herald Tribune*, 26 August 1956; George Beiswanger, "New London: Residues and Reflections (Part I)," *Dance Observer*, November 1956, p. 134.

67 Margaret Lloyd, *Christian Science Monitor*, 1 September 1956; Walter Terry, *New York Herald Tribune*, 26 August 1956; Louis Horst, "American Dance Festival," *Dance Observer*, August–September 1956, p. 101; George Beiswanger, "New London: Residues and Reflections (Part II)," *Dance Observer*, December 1956, pp. 149–50; conversation with Pauline Koner.

68 Doris Hering, "Reviews," *Dance Magazine*, October 1956, p. 10.

69 Walter Terry, *New York Herald Tribune*, 14 July 1957; Tom Borek, "The Connecticut College American Dance Festival: A Fantastical Documentary," *Dance Perspectives* 50 (Summer 1972): 25; "The Lecture Series," *Dance Observer*, August–September 1957, pp. 106–7.

70 Louis Horst, "10th American Dance Festival," *Dance Observer*, August–September 1957, pp. 102–3; Louis Horst, "The Little Concert Series," *Dance Observer*, August–September 1957, p. 104; Doris Hering, "New London: Tenth Summer," *Dance Magazine*, October 1957, p. 29; P. W. Manchester, *New York Herald Tribune*, 25 August 1957.

71 Doris Hering, "New London: Tenth Summer," *Dance Magazine*, October 1957, p. 29; Louis Horst, "10th American Dance Festival," *Dance Observer*, August–September 1957, p. 102.

72 P. W. Manchester, *New York Herald Tribune*, 25 August 1957; Louis Horst, "10th American Dance Festival," *Dance Observer*, August–September 1957, p. 102.

73 P. W. Manchester, *New York Herald Tribune*, 25 August 1957; Louis Horst, "10th American Dance Festival," *Dance Observer*, August–September 1957, p. 102; Louis Horst, *New London Evening Day*, 19 August 1957.

74 Louis Horst, "10th American Dance Festival," *Dance Observer*, August–September 1957, p. 103.

75 P. W. Manchester, *New York Herald Tribune*, 25 August 1957; John Martin, *New York Times*, 25 August 1957.

76 "Notes on Dance Events," *New York Herald Tribune*, 23 March 1958.

77 Margaret Lloyd, *Christian Science Monitor*, 23 August 1958; Walter Terry, *New York Herald Tribune*, 24 August 1958; Louis Horst, "11th American Dance Festival," *Dance Observer*, August–September 1958, pp. 101–2; Merce Cunningham, "Summerspace Story," *Dance Magazine*, June 1966, pp. 52–54.

78 Louis Horst, "11th American Dance Festival," *Dance Observer*, August–September 1958, p. 101; Walter Terry, *New York Herald Tribune*, 24 August 1958.

79 Louis Horst, "11th American Dance Festival," *Dance Observer*, August–September 1958, p. 101; Walter Terry, *New York Herald Tribune*, 24 August 1958; Doris Hering, "American Dance Festival #11," *Dance Magazine*, October 1958, p. 33.

80 Walter Terry, *New York Herald Tribune*, 24 August 1958; Doris Hering, "American Dance Festival #11," *Dance Magazine*, October 1958, p. 64.

81 Dorothy Madden, "Ruth Bloomer Dies," *Dance Observer*, June–July 1959, p. 87; conversations with Martha Hill, Jeanette Schlottmann, Theodora Wiesner.

III Overview 1948 to 1958: A Festival in Connecticut

1 Conversation with Jane Dudley. Henceforth, all statements for which no printed source is given were made in conversation with the author. Particularly valuable for this chapter have been conversations with Selma Jeanne Cohen, Jane Dudley, Martha Hill, Pauline Koner, Sophie Maslow, Helen Priest Rogers, Doris Rudko, Jeanette Schlottmann, Paul Taylor, Lucy Venable, and Theodora Wiesner.

2 Ruth Bloomer, "A View of Dance Education in Colleges Today," *Dance Magazine*, January 1958, p. 82.

3 Letter from Dorothy Berea Silver to the author, 13 June 1983.

4 Doris Hering, "Reflections on the 2nd Annual American Dance Festival," *Dance Magazine*, October 1949, p. 24.

5 Tom Borek, "The Connecticut College American Dance Festival 1948–1972: A Fantastical Documentary," *Dance Perspectives* 50 (Summer 1972): 56; conversation with Jeanette Schlottmann.

6 Helen Priest Rogers, "Films for Notation," *Dance Magazine*, September 1965, p. 57; Patricia Mandell, *New London Day*, 28 April 1976; conversation with Helen Priest Rogers.

7 Gertrude E. Noyes, *A History of Connecticut College*, pp. 73, 156, 205; conversations with Martha Hill, Jeanette Schlottmann, Helen Priest Rogers.

8 The board and faculty meetings: conversations with Martha Hill, Pauline Koner, Helen Priest Rogers, Jeanette Schlottmann, Theodora Wiesner.

9 Jean Battey Lewis, *Washington Post*, 17 December 1972; Deborah Jowitt, *Dance Beat*, p. 51.

10 José Limón, "Young Dancers State Their Views," *Dance Observer*, January 1946, p. 7; Selma Jeanne Cohen, *The Modern Dance: Seven Statements of Belief*, pp. 23–24.

11 George Beiswanger, "New London: Residues and Reflections (Part V)," *Dance Observer*, March 1957, pp. 38–39.

12 Tom Borek, "The Connecticut College American Dance Festival 1948–1972: A Fantastical Documentary," *Dance Perspectives* 50 (Summer 1972): 26.

13 Selma Jeanne Cohen, *The Modern Dance: Seven Statements of Belief*, p. 24.

14 Doris Humphrey, in "Declaration."

15 Walter Terry, *New York Herald Tribune*, 15 August 1949; Ernestine Stodelle, "With Her Red Fires," *Dance Observer*, January 1961, pp. 5–6; Deborah Jowitt, *Dance Beat*, p. 80.

16 Selma Jeanne Cohen, *Doris Humphrey: An Artist First*, p. 209; summarized from Pauline Koner, "With Doris Humphrey"; José Limón, statement in 1967 festival program; conversations with Selma Jeanne Cohen, Pauline Koner, Paul Taylor, Lucy Venable.

17   Summarized from Doris Humphrey, *The Art of Making Dances*.
18   Norma Stahl, "Concerning José Limón," *Saturday Review*, 16 April 1958, p. 33.
19   Selma Jeanne Cohen, *Doris Humphrey: An Artist First*, pp. 218–19, and conversations with Selma Jeanne Cohen, Pauline Koner, Jeanette Schlottmann, Lucy Venable.
20   John Martin, *New York Times*, 11 September 1955; Pauline Koner, "Working with Doris Humphrey," pp. 235–48, and conversation with Pauline Koner.
21   Lawrence: Sali Ann Kriegsman, *Modern Dance In America: The Bennington Years*, p. 321; Sadoff: Eugene Palatsky, "Meet Simon Sadoff," *Dance Magazine*, December 1963, pp. 19–20.
22   Biographical sketch of Louis Horst in 1964 festival program; Doris Hering, "The $130,000 Anniversary Waltz," *Dance Magazine*, October 1972, p. 67; Sali Ann Kriegsman, *Modern Dance in America: The Bennington Years*, p. 319; Robert Sabin, "Louis Horst and Modern Dance in America (Part I)," *Dance Magazine*, January 1953, p. 21; conversations with Doris Rudko, Jeanette Schlottmann, Paul Taylor.
23   *A Decade of Dance 1948–1957*, p. 8; Louis Horst, *Pre-Classic Dance Forms*, pp. 51, 68; summarized from Louis Horst and Carroll Russell, *Modern Dance Forms in Relation to the Other Modern Arts*; Robert Sabin, "Louis Horst and Modern Dance in America (Part IV)," *Dance Magazine*, April 1953, pp. 39–40; conversations with Doris Rudko, Jeanette Schlottmann, Paul Taylor, Theodora Wiesner.
24   John Martin, *New York Times*, 26 August 1956.

IV   Season by Season: 1959 to 1968

1   Conversation with Jeanette Schlottmann.
2   Louis Horst, "12th American Dance Festival," *Dance Observer*, August–September 1959, p. 102; Doris Hering, "The 'Good Guys' Versus the 'Bad Guys,'" *Dance Magazine*, October 1959, pp. 32–33.
3   Louis Horst, "12th American Dance Festival," *Dance Observer*, August–September 1959, p. 101; P. W. Manchester, "The Season in Review," *Dance News*, September 1959, p. 11.
4   Doris Hering, "The 'Good Guys' Versus the 'Bad Guys,'" *Dance Magazine*, October 1959, p. 85; Louis Horst, "12th American Dance Festival," *Dance Observer*, August–September 1959, p. 101; P. W. Manchester, "The Season in Review," *Dance News*, September 1969, p. 11.
5   Margaret Lloyd, *Christian Science Monitor*, 5 September 1959; Doris Hering, "The 'Good Guys' Versus the 'Bad Guys,'" *Dance Magazine*, October 1959, p. 35.
6   Doris Hering, "Reviews," *Dance Magazine*, September 1957, p. 13, and "The 'Good Guys' Versus the 'Bad Guys,'" *Dance Magazine*, October 1959, pp. 33–34.
7   Louis Horst, "12th American Dance Festival," *Dance Observer*, August–September 1959, p. 102; Doris Hering, "The 'Good Guys' Versus the 'Bad Guys,'" *Dance Magazine*, October 1959, p. 34.
8   Louis Horst, "12th American Dance Festival," *Dance Observer*, August–September 1959, p. 101.
9   "Report on the Thirteenth Season of the Connecticut College School of Dance" (annual festival report).
10   Doris Hering, "Silences and Sounds," *Dance Magazine*, October 1960, p. 25; P. W.

Manchester, "New London, Connecticut Festival," *The Dancing Times*, October 1958, p. 25.

11 *Crises* description: Don McDonagh, *The Complete Guide to Modern Dance*, pp. 285–86. Reviews: Louis Horst, "13th American Dance Festival," *Dance Observer*, August–September 1960, p. 103; Doris Hering, "Silences and Sounds," *Dance Magazine*, October 1960, p. 24.

12 Don McDonagh, *The Complete Guide to Modern Dance*, pp. 197–98; Walter Terry, *New York Herald Tribune*, 22 August 1960; Doris Hering, "Silences and Sounds," *Dance Magazine*, October 1960, p. 22.

13 Louis Horst, "13th American Dance Festival," *Dance Observer*, August–September 1960, p. 103; Doris Hering, "Silences and Sounds," *Dance Magazine*, October 1960, p. 23; Walter Terry, *New York Herald Tribune*, 20 August 1960.

14 Doris Hering, "Fourteenth American Dance Festival," *Dance Magazine*, October 1961, p. 21; P. W. Manchester, *Christian Science Monitor*, 2 September 1961.

15 Louis Horst, "14th American Dance Festival," *Dance Observer*, August–September 1961, p. 102.

16 Ibid., p. 101; Doris Hering, "Fourteenth American Dance Festival," *Dance Magazine*, October 1961, p. 26; Walter Terry, *New York Herald Tribune*, 21 August 1961.

17 Louis Horst, "14th American Dance Festival," *Dance Observer*, August–September 1961, p. 101; Doris Hering, "Fourteenth American Dance Festival," *Dance Magazine*, October 1961, p. 22.

18 Doris Hering, "Fourteenth American Dance Festival," *Dance Magazine*, October 1961, p. 61 (on Wood), p. 22 (on Moore).

19 Ibid., p. 22; Louis Horst, "14th American Dance Festival," *Dance Observer*, August–September 1961, p. 101; Walter Terry, *New York Herald Tribune*, 21 August 1961; Allen Hughes, *New York Times*, 21 August 1961.

20 Walter Terry, *New York Herald Tribune*, 10 September 1961; Louis Horst, "14th American Dance Festival," *Dance Observer*, August–September 1961, p. 101; Doris Hering, "Fourteenth American Dance Festival," *Dance Magazine*, October 1961, pp. 60–61.

21 *Aeon* description: Don McDonagh, *The Complete Guide to Modern Dance*, pp. 286–87, and conversation with Jeanette Schlottmann. Reviews: Walter Terry, *New York Herald Tribune*, 10 September 1961; Doris Hering, "Fourteenth American Dance Festival," *Dance Magazine*, October 1961, p. 27; Louis Horst, "14th American Dance Festival," *Dance Observer*, August–September 1961, p. 101.

22 "Schlottmann Weds Roosevelt," *Dance Magazine*, June 1961, p. 5.

23 Walter Terry, *New York Herald Tribune*, 25 August 1962.

24 "From Connecticut College," *Dance Observer*, February 1963, pp. 26–27.

25 Gertrude E. Noyes, *A History of Connecticut College*, p. 177, and conversation with Jeanette Schlottmann. All quotations for which no source is given were made in conversation with the author.

26 Doris Hering, "Reviews," *Dance Magazine*, October 1962, pp. 44–45; Allen Hughes, *New York Times*, 18 August 1962; Walter Terry, *New York Herald Tribune*, 25 August 1962; Jill Johnston, *Village Voice*, 6 September 1962.

27 Allen Hughes, *New York Times*, 6 August 1962; George Beiswanger, in *Dance 62*,

p. 14; Louis Horst, "The American Dance Festival," *Dance Observer*, August–September 1962, p. 104; conversations with Jeanette Schlottmann and Paul Taylor.

28 Walter Terry, *New York Herald Tribune*, 25 August 1962; Louis Horst, "The American Dance Festival," *Dance Observer*, August–September 1962, p. 105. A description of *I, Odysseus* is also provided by Allen Hughes, *New York Times*, 20 August 1962.

29 Lillian Moore, *New York Herald Tribune*, 13 August 1962.

30 Lillian Moore, *New York Herald Tribune*, 6 August 1962.

31 "Dance Notes," *New York Herald Tribune*, 7 April 1963; Connecticut College School of Dance press release dated 9 March 1963; conversation with Theodora Wiesner.

32 Allen Hughes, *New York Times*, 29 July 1963; Walter Sorell, "The American Dance Festival," *Dance Observer*, August–September 1963, p. 101.

33 *Scudorama* description: Allen Hughes, *New York Times*, 19 August 1963; Don McDonagh, *The Complete Guide to Modern Dance*, pp. 320–21; Marcia B. Siegel, *At the Vanishing Point*, p. 203; conversations with Paul Taylor and Charles L. Reinhart. Reviews: Walter Sorell, "The American Dance Festival," *Dance Observer*, August–September 1963, p. 103; Doris Hering, "Where Do They Come From?", *Dance Magazine*, October 1963, p. 24.

34 Doris Hering, "Where Do They Come From?", *Dance Magazine*, October 1963, p. 66; Allen Hughes, *New York Times*, 19 August 1963.

35 Walter Sorell, "The American Dance Festival," *Dance Observer*, August–September 1963, p. 103; Doris Hering, "Where Do They Come From?", *Dance Magazine*, October 1963, p. 25.

36 Walter Sorell, "The American Dance Festival," *Dance Observer*, August–September 1963, p. 103; Walter Terry, *New York Herald Tribune*, 19 August 1963.

37 Walter Terry, *New York Herald Tribune*, 16 August 1963.

38 Philharmonic Hall programs for 6, 13, and 20 August 1963; conversation with Theodora Wiesner.

39 Don McDonagh, *Martha Graham*, p. 275; Lillian Moore, "Honoring Louis Horst," *The Dancing Times*, October 1964, p. 27; P. W. Manchester, *Christian Science Monitor*, 22 August 1964; Doris Hering, "Campus in Ferment," *Dance Magazine*, October 1964, pp. 36–37; Jill Johnston, *Village Voice*, 27 August 1964.

40 Doris Hering, "Campus in Ferment," *Dance Magazine*, October 1964, pp. 36–37; Jill Johnston, *Village Voice*, 10 September 1964.

41 Doris Hering, "Campus in Ferment," *Dance Magazine*, October 1964, pp. 36–37; Allen Hughes, *New York Times*, 17 August 1964.

42 *Primitive Mysteries* revival: Don McDonagh, *Martha Graham*, pp. 274–76; conversation with Sophie Maslow. Reviews: Allen Hughes, *New York Times*, 17 August 1964; Doris Hering, "Campus in Ferment," *Dance Magazine*, October 1964, pp. 36–37; Jill Johnston, *Village Voice*, 27 August 1964; Eugene Palatsky, *Newark Evening News*, 23 August 1964; Walter Terry, *New York Herald Tribune*, 17 August 1964.

43 P. W. Manchester, *Christian Science Monitor*, 22 August 1964; Doris Hering, "Campus in Ferment," *Dance Magazine*, October 1964, pp. 37–38.

44 Walter Terry, *New York Herald Tribune*, 14 August 1964; Doris Hering, "Campus in Ferment," *Dance Magazine*, October 1964, p. 39.

45 Eugene Palatsky, *Newark Evening News*, 23 August 1964.

46 P. W. Manchester, *Christian Science Monitor*, 22 August 1964; Doris Hering, "Campus in Ferment," *Dance Magazine*, October 1964, p. 38.

47 Walter Terry, *New York Herald Tribune*, 30 August 1964.

48 Allen Hughes, *New York Times*, 23 August 1964.

49 Walter Terry, *New York Herald Tribune*, 29 August 1965.

50 Doris Hering, "Eighteenth American Dance Festival," *Dance Magazine*, October 1965, p. 68.

51 Allen Hughes, *New York Times*, 2 August 1965.

52 Doris Hering, "Eighteenth American Dance Festival," *Dance Magazine*, October 1965, p. 70.

53 Ibid.

54 Allen Hughes, *New York Times*, 9 August 1965.

55 Allen Hughes, *New York Times*, 16 August 1965; Doris Hering, "Eighteenth American Dance Festival," *Dance Magazine*, October 1965, pp. 68–69.

56 Doris Hering, "For Dreaming, For Searching," *Dance Magazine*, October 1966, p. 44.

57 P. W. Manchester, *Christian Science Monitor*, 26 August 1966; Doris Hering, "For Dreaming, For Searching," *Dance Magazine*, October 1966, p. 44; Don McDonagh, *New York Times*, 21 August 1967.

58 Doris Hering, "For Dreaming, For Searching," *Dance Magazine*, October 1966, p. 42; P. W. Manchester, *Christian Science Monitor*, 26 August 1966.

59 "College News," *Dance Magazine*, October 1967, p. 97.

60 Don McDonagh, "American Dance Festival," *Dance and Dancers*, December 1967, p. 40; Doris Hering, "José and Others," *Dance Magazine*, October 1967, p. 35; conversation with Paul Taylor.

61 Doris Hering, "José and Others," *Dance Magazine*, October 1967, p. 33; P. W. Manchester, "American Dance Festival," *Dance News*, October 1967, p. 9.

62 Jack Anderson, "American Dance Festival," *Ballet Today*, November–December 1967, p. 26.

63 Doris Hering, "José and Others," *Dance Magazine*, October 1967, p. 73; Don McDonagh, "American Dance Festival," *Dance and Dancers*, December 1967, p. 42.

64 Doris Hering, "José and Others," *Dance Magazine*, October 1967, p. 73.

65 Ibid., p. 74, and conversation with Doris Hering.

66 "Statistics: Connecticut College School of Dance 1968" (bulletin prepared by the school).

67 Conversation with Bonnie Bird.

68 Anna Kisselgoff, *New York Times*, 12 August 1968; Doris Hering, "Reviews," *Dance Magazine*, October 1968, pp. 32, 82.

69 Don McDonagh, *New York Times*, 19 August 1968; Marcia Marks, "Reviews," *Dance Magazine*, October 1968, pp. 92–93.

70 Doris Hering, "Reviews," *Dance Magazine*, October 1968, pp. 31, 83–84.

71 Marcia Marks, "Reviews," *Dance Magazine*, October 1968, p. 85.

V Overview 1959 to 1968: A Steady, Secure Place

1 Conversation with Selma Jeanne Cohen. All other statements for which no printed source is given were made in conversation with the author. Particularly useful for this

chapter have been conversations with Bonnie Bird, Trisha Brown, Nathan Clark, Selma Jeanne Cohen, Martha Hill, Sophie Maslow, Charles Reinhart, Jeanette Schlottmann Roosevelt, Lucy Venable, and Theodora Wiesner.

2   Tom Borek, "The Connecticut College American Dance Festival 1948–1972: A Fantastical Documentary," *Dance Perspectives* 50 (Summer 1972): 56.

3   Allen Hughes, *New York Times*, 23 August 1964.

4   Doris Hering, "Reviews," *Dance Magazine*, October 1968, p. 31; John Martin, *New York Times*, 20 July 1952, and conversations with Sophie Maslow and Jeanette Schlottmann Roosevelt.

5   Doris Hering, "Campus in Ferment," *Dance Magazine*, October 1964, pp. 34–35, and conversations with Bonnie Bird, Selma Jeanne Cohen, and Doris Hering.

6   Louis Horst and Carroll Russell, *Modern Dance Forms in Relation to the Other Modern Arts*, p. 22; Don McDonagh, "American Dance Festival," *Dance and Dancers*, December 1967, p. 38.

7   Selma Jeanne Cohen, *Doris Humphrey: An Artist First*, pp. 218–19.

8   Festival program for 7 August 1962; information on the *Trillium* incident from conversations with Trisha Brown and Jeanette Schlottmann Roosevelt.

9   Walter Sorell, "Louis Horst," *Dance Magazine*, March 1964, p. 39.

10 Sally Banes, *Terpsichore in Sneakers: Post-Modern Dance*, pp. 98–99; conversation with Jeanette Schlottmann Roosevelt.

11 Margaret Lloyd, *Christian Science Monitor*, 27 August 1955.

12 Sali Ann Kriegsman, *Modern Dance in America: The Bennington Years*, p. 27.

13 Doris Hering, "Eighth American Dance Festival," *Dance Magazine*, October 1955, p. 12.

14 Allen Hughes, *New York Times*, 30 August 1964.

15 Allen Hughes, *New York Times*, 23 August 1964.

16 Walter Terry, *New York Herald Tribune*, 10 September 1961.

17 Doris Hering, "Eighteenth American Dance Festival," *Dance Magazine*, October 1965, pp. 70–71.

18 Sali Ann Kriegsman, *Modern Dance in America: The Bennington Years*, p. 12.

19 Quoted in Tom Borek, "The Connecticut College American Dance Festival 1948–1972: A Fantastical Documentary," *Dance Perspectives* 50 (Summer 1972): 56.

20 Doris Hering, "Fourteenth American Dance Festival," *Dance Magazine*, October 1961, p. 61.

21 Janice Berman, "Flagwaver," *Ballet News*. July 1984, p. 20; Walter Terry, "One of the New Breed—Manager Charles Reinhart," *Dance Magazine Annual 1969*, pp. 114–17; Nancy Vreeland, "ADF's Charles Reinhardt [*sic*]," *Dance Magazine*, May 1985, summer calendar insert, p. SC-30; conversations with Charles and Stephanie Reinhart.

22 ADF official biography dated 28 April 1984; conversation with Martha Myers.

23 Conversation with Charles Reinhart.

VI Season by Season: 1969 to 1977

1   All statements for which no printed source is given were made in conversation with the author. Particularly helpful in the preparation of this chapter have been conversations with Selma Jeanne Cohen, Doris Hering, Martha Myers, Charles and Stephanie Reinhart, and Paul Taylor.

2 Jack Anderson, *New York Times*, 18 June 1978.

3 Doris Hering, "Next Year, Keep the Baby," *Dance Magazine*, October 1969, pp. 40–41.

4 Kathleen Cannell, *Christian Science Monitor*, 22 August 1969; Stephen Smoliar, "The Festival," *Dance Magazine*, October 1969, p. 77.

5 Doris Hering, "Next Year, Keep the Baby," *Dance Magazine*, October 1969, pp. 40–41; Stephen Smoliar, "The Festival," *Dance Magazine*, October 1969, p. 41.

6 *Medley* description: Don McDonagh, *The Complete Guide to Modern Dance*, pp. 482–83. Reviews: Kathleen Cannell, *Christian Science Monitor*, 22 August 1969; Don McDonagh, *New York Times*, 21 July 1969; Stephen Smoliar, "The Festival," *Dance Magazine*, October 1969, p. 42.

7 Stephen Smoliar, "The Festival," *Dance Magazine*, October 1969, p. 42; Marcia B. Siegel, *At the Vanishing Point*, pp. 268–69; Don McDonagh, *New York Times*, 21 July 1969.

8 Stephen Smoliar, "The Festival," *Dance Magazine*, October 1969, pp. 42, 76–77; conversation with Paul Taylor.

9 Don McDonagh, "Revolution in Connecticut," *Ballet Review*, vol. 4, no. 1, 1971, pp. 60–61.

10 Don McDonagh, *New York Times*, 25 July 1970.

11 Tom Borek, "The Connecticut College American Dance Festival 1948–1972: A Fantastical Documentary," *Dance Perspectives* 50 (Summer 1972): 56; Ellen W. Jacobs, "Learning to Look," *Dance Magazine*, October 1970, pp. 24, 76; conversation with Selma Jeanne Cohen.

12 Anna Kisselgoff, *New York Times*, 14 July 1970.

13 Don McDonagh, *New York Times*, 19 July 1970; John Mueller quoted in Ellen W. Jacobs, "Learning to Look," *Dance Magazine*, October 1970, p. 77.

14 Don McDonagh, *New York Times*, 9 August 1970; Kathleen Cannell, *Christian Science Monitor*, 12 August 1970.

15 Don McDonagh, *New York Times*, 9 August 1970; Kathleen Cannell, *Christian Science Monitor*, 12 August 1970.

16 Ibid.

17 Laura Shapiro, *Boston Phoenix*, 15 August 1970.

18 Ibid.

19 Laura Shapiro, *Boston Phoenix*, 1 August 1970.

20 Doris Hering, "A Myth Any Thursday," *Dance Magazine*, November 1971, p. 38.

21 Sali Ann Kriegsman, *Modern Dance in America: The Bennington Years*, p. 267; Frances Alenikoff, "American Dance Festival: Lucas Hoving and Ann Halprin," *Dance News*, October 1971, p. 7; Doris Hering, "San Francisco Dancers' Workshop," *Dance Magazine*, November 1971, pp. 40–41; Marcia B. Siegel, *At the Vanishing Point*, pp. 300–302; James Monahan, "Reflections on an American Dance Festival," *The Dancing Times*, October 1971, p. 17; James Kennedy, quoted in Tom Borek, "The Connecticut College American Dance Festival 1948–72: A Fantastical Documentary," *Dance Perspectives* 50 (Summer 1972): 47.

22 Frances Alenikoff, "American Dance Festival: Perez, Lewitzky and Taylor," *Dance News*, September 1971, p. 3; Deborah Jowitt, *Village Voice*, 29 July 1971; Nancy Mason, "Bella Lewitzky Dance Company," *Dance Magazine*, November 1971, p. 41.

23 Frances Alenikoff, "American Dance Festival: Lucas Hoving and Ann Halprin," *Dance*

News, October 1971, p. 7; Doris Hering, "Lucas Hoving Dance Company," *Dance Magazine*, November 1971, p. 87.

24 Frances Alenikoff, "American Dance Festival: Perez, Lewitzky and Taylor," *Dance News*, September 1971, p. 3; Kathleen Marner, "Rudy Perez Dance Theatre," *Dance Magazine*, November 1971, p. 41.

25 Frances Alenikoff, "American Dance Festival: Perez, Lewitzky and Taylor," *Dance News*, September 1971, p. 3; Deborah Jowitt, *Village Voice*, 29 July 1971; James Monahan, "Reflections on an American Dance Festival," *The Dancing Times*, October 1971, p. 17.

26 Ellen W. Jacobs, "Introducing a New Company," ADF 1972 program; Anna Kisselgoff, *New York Times*, 16 April 1972; Doris Hering, "The $130,000 Anniversary Waltz," *Dance Magazine*, October 1972, p. 68.

27 Deborah Jowitt, *Village Voice*, 13 July 1972; Clive Barnes, *New York Times*, 30 July 1972.

28 Don McDonagh, *New York Times*, 2 August 1972.

29 Deborah Jowitt, *Village Voice*, 3 August 1972; Doris Hering, "The $130,000 Anniversary Waltz," *Dance Magazine*, October 1972, pp. 69–70; Clive Barnes, *New York Times*, 30 July 1972; Frances Alenikoff, "Doris Humphrey, José Limón, Rudy Perez," *Dance News*, October 1972, p. 4.

30 Doris Hering, "The $130,000 Anniversary Waltz," *Dance Magazine*, October 1972, p. 70.

31 Ibid.; Clive Barnes, *New York Times*, 30 July 1972.

32 Doris Hering, "The $130,000 Anniversary Waltz," *Dance Magazine*, October 1972, p. 70.

33 Ibid.; Anna Kisselgoff, *New York Times*, 2 July 1972.

34 Frances Alenikoff, "Doris Humphrey, José Limón, Rudy Perez," *Dance News*, October 1972, p. 4; Deborah Jowitt, *Village Voice*, 3 August 1972.

35 The 1973 festival program.

36 Don McDonagh, *New York Times*, 15 July 1973.

37 "Applications Being Accepted for Dance/Television Workshop," *Dance Magazine*, April 1974, p. 4.

38 Deborah Jowitt, *Village Voice*, 9 August 1973; Anna Kisselgoff, *New York Times*, 31 July 1973.

39 Deborah Jowitt, *Village Voice*, 9 August 1973.

40 Ibid.; Anna Kisselgoff, *New York Times*, 31 July 1973.

41 Anna Kisselgoff, *New York Times*, 31 July 1973.

42 Anna Kisselgoff, *New York Times*, 24 July 1973.

43 Don McDonagh, *New York Times*, 6 August 1973; Ernestine Stodelle, "26th American Dance Festival," *Dance Magazine*, October 1973, p. 26.

44 Dorothy Stowe, *Hartford Times*, 21 July 1973; Ernestine Stodelle, "26th American Dance Festival," *Dance Magazine*, October 1973, p. 25.

45 Leslie Pfeil, *Groton News*, 9 July 1973.

46 Summarized from Rose Anne Thom, "Innovation or Inundation?" *Dance Magazine*, October 1974, p. 20; "American Dance Festival," *Dance Magazine*, July 1974, pp. 10–11; "Applications Being Accepted for Dance/Television Workshop," *Dance Magazine*, April 1974, p. 4; "Applications Being Accepted for Dance Educators' Workshop,"

Dance Magazine, May 1974, p. 4; 1974 festival programs.

47   Anna Kisselgoff, *New York Times*, 3 August 1974.

48   Gertrude E. Noyes, *A History of Connecticut College*, p. 209; *Who's Who in America 1982–1983* (vol. 1), p. 62; conversation with Charles Reinhart.

49   Rose Anne Thom, "Innovation or Inundation?" *Dance Magazine*, October 1974, pp. 21–22.

50   Deborah Jowitt, *Village Voice*, 15 August 1974; information on dancers' "disappearance" supplied by Dean company's office.

51   Ibid.

52   Ibid.; Rose Anne Thom, "Innovation or Inundation?" *Dance Magazine*, October 1974, p. 22.

53   Deborah Jowitt, *Village Voice*, 15 August 1974.

54   Ibid.; Rose Anne Thom, "Innovation or Inundation?" *Dance Magazine*, October 1974, p. 22.

55   "American Dance Festival to Run June 21–August 2 in Connecticut," *Dance Magazine*, May 1975, pp. 4–5; 1975 festival program.

56   Deborah Jowitt, *Village Voice*, 4 August 1975.

57   Robb Baker, "New London, Connecticut," *Dance Magazine*, October 1975, pp. 79–80.

58   Laura Shapiro, *Boston Globe*, 5 August 1975.

59   Patricia Mandell, *New London Day*, 5 July 1975.

60   Patricia Mandell, *New London Day*, 2 August 1975.

61   Deborah Jowitt, *Village Voice*, 4 August 1975.

62   Dinovelli, *Hartford Courant*, 24 July 1975; conversation with Charles Reinhart.

63   Anna Kisselgoff, *New York Times*, 31 August 1975.

64   Anna Kisselgoff, *New York Times*, 22 August 1976; conversation with Charles Reinhart.

65   Anna Kisselgoff, *New York Times*, 22 August 1976.

66   Amanda Smith, "Newport," *Dance Magazine*, February 1977, pp. 77–78; Christopher Pavlakis, *The American Music Handbook*, pp. 408–10; conversation with Paul Taylor.

67   Amanda Smith, "Newport," *Dance Magazine*, February 1977, p. 78; conversation with Paul Taylor.

68   Amanda Smith, "Newport," *Dance Magazine*, February 1977, p. 78.

69   Jackie Coleman, "New London," *Dance Magazine*, February 1977, p. 76.

70   Doris Hering, "New London," *Dance Magazine*, October 1976, p. 74.

71   Jackie Coleman, "New London," *Dance Magazine*, February 1977, p. 77.

72   Anna Kisselgoff, *New York Times*, 9 August 1976.

73   Jackie Coleman, "New London," *Dance Magazine*, February 1977, p. 77.

74   Donna Dinovelli, *Hartford Courant*, 2 August 1976.

75   Jackie Coleman, "New London," *Dance Magazine*, February 1977, p. 76.

76   American Dance Festival press release dated 9 November 1976 (contains Reinhart quotation); Connecticut College press release dated 10 November 1976 (contains Ames quotation).

77   "American Dance Festival Schedules Full Lineup of Performances in New London and Newport," *Dance Magazine*, July 1977, p. 4; Anne P. Kearns, "American Dance Festival —The Modern Tradition," 1977 program.

78   Don McDonagh, *New York Times*, 12 July 1977.

79 Anna Kisselgoff, *New York Times*, 2 and 3 July 1977.

80 Clive Barnes, *New York Times*, 26 July 1977.

81 Clive Barnes, *New York Times*, 19 July 1977.

82 Joyce Mariani, *Norwich Bulletin*, 1 August 1977.

83 Clive Barnes, *New York Times*, 29 August 1977; Jack Anderson, "New York Newsletter," *The Dancing Times*, September 1977, p. 687.

84 Don McDonagh, *New York Times*, 2 August 1977.

85 Don McDonagh, *New York Times*, 22 August 1977.

86 Ernestine Stodelle, *New Haven Register*, 24 July 1977.

87 "American Dance Festival to Move to Duke U. in Durham, N.C.," *Dance Magazine*, December 1977, p. 4.

VII   Overview 1969 to 1977: A New Beginning

1   Tom Borek, "The Connecticut College American Dance Festival 1948–1972: A Fantastical Documentary," *Dance Perspectives* 50 (Summer 1972): 56; Anne P. Kearns, "New London—Summer Dance Capital," 1976 program; Jack Anderson, *New York Times*, 18 June 1978; "American Dance Festival," *Dance Magazine*, July 1974, pp. 10–11; James Kennedy, *Manchester Guardian Weekly*, 4 September 1971.

2   Doris Hering, "Next Year, Keep the Baby," *Dance Magazine*, October 1969, p. 40.

3   Anna Kisselgoff, *New York Times*, 31 August 1975.

4   Hawkins quoted in Sali Ann Kriegsman, *Modern Dance in America: The Bennington Years*, p. 260; conversation with Martha Hill.

5   James Kennedy, *Manchester Guardian Weekly*, 4 September 1971; James Monahan, "Reflections on an American Dance Festival," *The Dancing Times*, October 1971, p. 17.

6   Anna Kisselgoff, *New York Times*, 31 August 1975; Reinhart quoted in Tom Borek, "The Connecticut College American Dance Festival 1948–1972: A Fantastical Documentary," *Dance Perspectives* 50 (Summer 1972): 47.

7   Anna Kisselgoff, *New York Times*, 3 August 1974.

8   David Newton, *Greensboro Daily News*, 17 June 1979.

9   Patricia Mandell, *New London Day*, 3 August 1976.

10 "Director Says He Missed Dance Pleas," *New London Day*, 3 August 1976.

11 Jack Anderson, *New York Times*, 18 June 1978; Anna Kisselgoff, *New York Times*, 15 November 1976. I have also drawn upon conversations with Edgar Mayhew, Martha Myers, Charles Reinhart, and Theodora Wiesner for this account of the differences between the festival and the college.

12 Letter from Oakes Ames to Charles Reinhart, 3 August 1977 (in ADF files).

13 Jack Anderson, *New York Times*, 18 June 1978.

14 Patricia Mandell, *New London Day*, 4 August 1976.

15 Questions to Duke University, University of Massachusetts–Amherst, and University of Wisconsin–Milwaukee, 1977 (ADF files).

16 Duke history summarized from Jon Phelps, *I Have Selected Duke University*; Duke facilities: *Report Prepared for the American Dance Festival*, 30 August 1977, pp. 8–9; conversation with Terry Sanford.

17 Conversations with Terry Sanford and Vicky Patton.

18   *Report Prepared for the American Dance Festival*, 30 August 1977, p. 4.

19   Jack Anderson, *New York Times*, 18 June 1978; conversation with Charles Reinhart.

VIII   Season by Season: 1978 to 1985

1   Accounts of Durham in 1978 can be found in Jack Anderson, "New York Newsletter," *The Dancing Times*, September 1978, p. 707; Jack Anderson, *New York Times*, 18 June 1978; Deborah Jowitt, *Village Voice*, 21 August 1978; Anna Kisselgoff, *New York Times*, 12 November 1978; *New York Times*, 24 June 1978.

2   Quoted by Anna Kisselgoff, *New York Times*, 9 November 1980.

3   Linda Small, "Durham," *Dance Magazine*, December 1978, p. 47; Deborah Jowitt, *Village Voice*, 21 August 1978.

4   Anna Kisselgoff, *New York Times*, 19 June 1978.

5   *New York Times*, 9 July 1978; Giora Manor, "Music and Dance Workshop at American Dance Festival," *Dance News*, October 1978, p. 4.

6   Giora Manor, "American Dance Festival's First Season in Durham," *Dance News*, September 1978, p. 3.

7   Deborah Jowitt, *Village Voice*, 21 August 1978; Linda Small, "Durham," *Dance Magazine*, December 1978, p. 48.

8   Deborah Jowitt, *Village Voice*, 21 August 1978.

9   Ibid.

10   Jack Anderson, *New York Times*, 3 July 1978.

11   Linda Small, "Durham," *Dance Magazine*, December 1978, pp. 47–48; Giora Manor, "American Dance Festival's First Season in Durham," *Dance News*, September 1978, p. 3.

12   "American Dance Festival to Stay at Duke, Despite Deficit," *Dance Magazine*, December 1978, p. 9; Anna Kisselgoff, *New York Times*, 12 November 1978. Durham and New London: Jack Anderson, *New York Times*, 18 June 1978; conversations with Charles Reinhart and Edgar Mayhew.

13   *Variety*, 5 May 1979; conversation with Charles Reinhart.

14   Anna Kisselgoff, *New York Times*, 21 June 1979.

15   David Newton, *Greensboro Daily News*, 17 June 1979; Gordon Fancher and Gerald Myers, eds., *Philosophical Essays on Dance*.

16   Susan Reiter, "Durham," *Ballet News*, November 1979, p. 43.

17   Robert Greskovic, "TV," *Ballet News*, November 1979, p. 53; conversation with Paul Taylor.

18   Susan Reiter, "Durham," *Ballet News*, November 1979, p. 42.

19   Jack Anderson, *New York Times*, 23 July 1979.

20   Charles Horton, *Chapel Hill Newspaper*, 28 June 1979.

21   *Chapel Hill Newspaper*, 24 June 1979; Roy Dicks, *Spectator*, 4 July 1979.

22   Clive Barnes, *New York Post*, 19 June 1980; season's flyers.

23   Jack Anderson, *New York Times*, 29 June 1980; Charles Horton, "Durham," *Ballet News*, October 1980, p. 40.

24   Charles Horton, "Durham," *Ballet News*, October 1980, p. 40.

25   Jack Anderson, *New York Times*, 26 June 1980.

26   Charles Horton, "Durham," *Ballet News*, October 1980, p. 40.

27 Anna Kisselgoff, *New York Times*, 9 November 1980.

28 The 1981 ADF program; "ADF Announces Cash Awards," *Dance Magazine*, June 1981, p. 4.

29 The 1981 ADF program.

30 "Emerging Generation" accounts: Susan Reiter, *New York Times*, 5 July 1981; Jack Anderson, *New York Times*, 13 July 1981. Reviews: Jack Anderson, *New York Times*, 13 July 1981; J. D. Reed, "Synthesizer Chic in North Carolina," *Time*, 27 July 1981, p. 73.

31 North Carolina Dance Theatre: Susan Broili, *Durham Sun*, 18 June 1981; Debra Fowler, *Durham Sun*, 19 June 1981; Trip Purcell, *Durham Morning Herald*, 19 June 1981. *Resettings*: Dee Dee Hooker, *Raleigh News and Observer*, 20 June 1981.

32 Charles Horton, "Durham," *Ballet News*, November 1981, p. 37.

33 *Untitled II*: Charles Horton, "Durham," *Ballet News*, November 1981, p. 37. *Day Two*: Susan Broili, *Durham Sun*, 30 July 1981; Elizabeth Lee, *Durham Morning Herald*, 24 July 1981.

34 Charles Horton, "Durham," *Ballet News*, November 1981, p. 37; Elizabeth Lee, *Durham Morning Herald*, 17 July 1981.

35 The 1982 festival programs; "ADF Offers Third Annual Dance Medicine Seminar," ADF press release 1984; "Liggett Gives $30,000 to Durham Festival," *New York Times*, 31 January 1982; "Dance Projects Get Exxon's $60,000," *New York Times*, 13 May 1982; Jim Wise, *Durham Morning Herald*, 27 July 1982.

36 Jack Anderson, *New York Times*, 16 July 1982.

37 Elizabeth Lee, *Durham Morning Herald*, 2 July 1982 (*Motor Party* review) and 30 July 1982 (other comments).

38 Elizabeth Lee, *Durham Morning Herald*, 2 July 1982.

39 "Summer Festival Sneak Previews," *Dance Magazine*, February 1982, p. 5; Ichikawa quoted in Ruby Shang, *New York Times*, 4 July 1982; Anna Kisselgoff, *New York Times*, 10 July 1982; Elizabeth Lee, *Durham Morning Herald*, 7 July 1982; Annalyn Swan, "A Dazzling Feast from Japan," *Newsweek*, 19 July 1982, p. 61.

40 *Variety*, 22 June 1983.

41 Information on French companies: David Stevens, *New York Times*, 10 July 1983; Beverly Walter, *North Carolina Leader*, 14 July 1983; Jim Wise, *Durham Morning Herald*, 9 July 1983. Reviews: Susan Broili, *Durham Sun*, 21 July 1983; Anna Kisselgoff, *New York Times*, 13, 14, and 15 July 1983; Elizabeth Lee, "Durham," *Ballet News*, November 1983, pp. 37–38.

42 David Newton, *Greensboro Record*, 30 June 1983; Susan Broili, *Durham Sun*, 7 July 1983; Elizabeth Lee, "Durham," *Ballet News*, November 1983, p. 37.

43 Jack Anderson, *New York Times*, 21 July 1983; Elizabeth Lee, *Durham Morning Herald*, 19 July 1983.

44 Allison Adams, *Durham Sun*, 7 July 1983; Elizabeth Lee, *Durham Morning Herald*, 8 July 1983.

45 Elizabeth Lee, *Durham Morning Herald*, 8 July 1983.

46 Jack Anderson, *New York Times*, 24 July 1983.

47 Janice Berman, "Flagwaver," *Ballet News*, July 1984, pp. 21–22; "ADF Offers Third Annual Dance Medicine Seminar," "American Dance Festival Gathers Renowned

Professionals for Golden Anniversary Season Educational Programs," "A Golden Anniversary to Mark a Golden Age" (ADF press releases, 1984).

48 Jennifer Dunning, *New York Times*, 14 July 1984.

49 Elizabeth Lee, "Durham," *Ballet News*, November 1984, p. 40; Anne Levin, *Oak Ridger*, 13 July 1984.

50 La Fleur Paysour, *Charlotte Observer*, 2 July 1984; Linda Belans, *Spectator*, 26 July 1984.

51 Elizabeth Lee, "Durham," *Ballet News*, November 1984, p. 40; Linda Belans, *Spectator*, 26 July 1984.

52 Jennifer Dunning, *New York Times*, 13 July 1984; Elizabeth Lee, *Durham Morning Herald*, 11 July 1984; Elizabeth Lee, "Durham," *Ballet News*, November 1984, p. 40.

53 Elizabeth Lee, "Durham," *Ballet News*, November 1984, p. 40.

54 Elizabeth Lee, *Durham Morning Herald*, 29 June 1984.

55 Elizabeth Lee, *Durham Morning Herald*, 3 July 1984.

56 Linda Belans, *Spectator*, 28 June 1984.

57 Anna Kisselgoff, *New York Times*, 26 June 1984; Linda Belans, *Spectator*, 28 June 1984; Elizabeth Lee, *Durham Morning Herald*, 17 July 1984.

58 Japan: Terry Trucco, *New York Times*, 28 August 1984. Statistics: Jim Wise, *Durham Morning Herald*, 24 July 1984. Quotation: Dee Dee Hooker, "Pirouettes in the Melting Pot," *Carolina Lifestyle*, June 1983, p. 58.

59 Linda Belans, *Spectator*, 27 June 1985.

60 Ibid.

61 Anna Kisselgoff, *New York Times*, 21 July 1985.

IX Since 1978: A New Home

1 *New York Times*, 14 June 1980; Dee Dee Hooker, "Pirouettes in the Melting Pot," *Carolina Lifestyle*, June 1983, p. 57; Lynn Johnson, *Raleigh Times*, 21 June 1983. Valuable material for this chapter has been gained from conversations with Selma Jeanne Cohen, Martha Myers, Vicky Patton, Charles Reinhart, Terry Sanford, and Paul Taylor. All statements for which no printed source is given were made in conversation with the author.

2 Jim Wise, *Durham Morning Herald*, 9 July 1984; *New York Times*, 14 June 1980.

3 *New York Times*, 3 October 1981.

4 Jack Anderson, *New York Times*, 18 June 1978.

5 Deborah Jowitt, *Village Voice*, 21 August 1978.

6 Taylor discusses his own work in Selma Jeanne Cohen, *The Modern Dance: Seven Statements of Belief*, pp. 91–102. Critical assessments of Taylor include Jack Anderson, "Choreographic Fox: Paul Taylor," *Dance Magazine*, April 1980, pp. 68–73; Jack Anderson, "Paul Taylor: Surface and Substance," *Ballet Review*, vol. 6, no. 1, 1977–78, pp. 39–44; Allen Hughes, in *Dance 62*, p. 31; Deborah Jowitt, *Village Voice*, 29 July 1971.

7 Deborah Jowitt, *Dance Beat*, p. 146; Deborah Jowitt, *Village Voice*, 21 August 1978.

8 Dee Dee Hooker, "Pirouettes in the Melting Pot," *Carolina Lifestyle*, June 1983, p. 57; Anna Kisselgoff, *New York Times*, 9 November 1980.

X   A Summing Up

1   Quoted in *Dance 62*, p. 13.
2   For a detailed historical account of modern dance in colleges, see Richard Kraus and Sarah Alberti Chapman, *History of the Dance in Art and Education*, 2d ed., chapters 7, 13, 14, and 16.
3   This point is discussed in Sali Ann Kriegsman, *Modern Dance in America: The Bennington Years*, p. 12.
4   Conversation with Paul Taylor. All quotations for which no printed source is given were made in conversation with the author. Particularly helpful for this chapter have been comments by Harriet Berg, Selma Jeanne Cohen, Pauline Koner, Martha Myers, Charles Reinhart, Marcia B. Siegel, and Paul Taylor.
5   Selma Jeanne Cohen, *The Modern Dance: Seven Statements of Belief*, p. 21.
6   Lincoln Kirstein, *Ballet: Bias and Belief*, p. x.
7   Selma Jeanne Cohen, *The Modern Dance: Seven Statements of Belief*, p. 101.
8   John Martin, *New York Times*, 30 August 1953; Jack Anderson, *New York Times*, 18 June 1978.

SELECTED BIBLIOGRAPHY

This bibliography is restricted to books and lengthy magazine articles. The sources of news items and brief newspaper and magazine reviews quoted in the text are cited in the notes to each chapter.

Anderson, Jack. "Choreographic Fox: Paul Taylor." *Dance Magazine*, April 1980, pp. 68–73.

———. "Paul Taylor: Surface and Substance." *Ballet Review*, vol. 6, no. 1, 1977–78, pp. 39–44.

Banes, Sally. *Terpsichore in Sneakers: Post-Modern Dance*. Boston: Houghton Mifflin, 1980.

Beiswanger, George. "New London: Residues and Reflections" (six parts). *Dance Observer*, November 1956, pp. 133–35; December 1956, pp. 149–51; January 1957, pp. 5–6; February 1957, pp. 21–23; March 1957, pp. 37–39; May 1957, pp. 69–71.

Berman, Janice. "Flagwaver." *Ballet News*, July 1984, pp. 20–22.

Bloomer, Ruth. "A View of Dance Education in Colleges Today." *Dance Magazine*, February 1958, pp. 45, 82–83.

Borek, Tom. "The Connecticut College American Dance Festival 1948–1972: A Fantastical Documentary." *Dance Perspectives* 50, Summer 1972.

Cohen, Selma Jeanne. *Doris Humphrey: An Artist First*. Middletown, Conn.: Wesleyan University Press, 1972.

———. "Doris Humphrey's 'Ruins and Visions.'" *Dance Observer*, December 1953, pp. 148–50.

———, ed. *The Modern Dance: Seven Statements of Belief*. Middletown, Conn.: Wesleyan University Press, 1966.

Cunningham, Merce. "Summerspace Story." *Dance Magazine*, June 1966, pp. 52–54.

Dance 62, January 1963. Brooklyn: Dance Perspectives Inc., 1963.

"A Decade of Dance 1948–1957." (Souvenir program of the 10th American Dance Festival, 1957.)

Dzhermolinska, Helen. "Blueprint for a Ballet." *Dance Magazine*, April 1951, pp. 14–15, 22–23.

Fancher, Gordon and Gerald Myers, eds., *Philosophical Essays on Dance*. Brooklyn: Dance Horizons, 1981.

Hooker, Dee Dee. "Pirouettes in the Melting Pot." *Carolina Lifestyle*, June 1983, pp. 57–58.

Horst, Louis. *Pre-Classic Dance Forms*. Brooklyn: Dance Horizons, 1968.

———, and Carroll Russell. *Modern Dance Forms in Relation to the Other Modern Arts*. San Francisco: Impulse Publications, 1961.

Humphrey, Doris. *The Art of Making Dances*. New York: Rinehart, 1959.

———. "Declaration." In Doris Humphrey–Charles Weidman and Dance Group souvenir program, n.d. (In Dance Collection of the New York Public Library at Lincoln Center.)

Jacobs, Ellen W. "Learning to Look," *Dance Magazine*, October 1970, pp. 24, 76–78.

Jowitt, Deborah. *Dance Beat: Selected Views and Reviews 1967–1976*. New York: Marcel Dekker, 1977.

Kearns, Anne P. "New London—Summer Dance Capital," (In 1976 ADF programs.)

Kirstein, Lincoln. *Ballet: Bias and Belief*. New York: Dance Horizons, 1983.

Koner, Pauline. "Working With Doris Humphrey." *Dance Chronicle*, vol. 7, no. 3, 1984–85, pp. 235–78.

Kraus, Richard, and Sarah Alberti Chapman. *History of the Dance in Art and Education*. 2d ed. Englewood Cliffs, N.J.: Prentice-Hall, 1981.

Kriegsman, Sali Ann. *Modern Dance in America: The Bennington Years*. Boston: G. K. Hall, 1981.

McDonagh, Don. *The Complete Guide to Modern Dance*. Garden City, N.Y.: Doubleday, 1976.

———. *Martha Graham*. New York: Praeger, 1973.

———. "Revolution in Connecticut," *Ballet Review*, vol. 4, no. 1, 1971, pp. 58–63.

Maynard, Olga. "Pauline Koner: A Cyclic Force." *Dance Magazine*, April 1973, pp. 55–70.

Noyes, Gertrude E. *A History of Connecticut College*. New London: Connecticut College, 1982.

Palatsky, Eugene. "Meet Simon Sadoff." *Dance Magazine*, December 1963, pp. 19–20.

Pavlakis, Christopher. *The American Music Handbook*. New York: Free Press, 1974.

Phelps, Jon. *"I Have Selected Duke University . . .": A Short History*. Durham: Duke University, 1973.

"A Proposal for the American Dance Festival." Amherst: Office of the Chancellor, University of Massachusetts, September 1977.

"Report Prepared for the American Dance Festival." Durham: Duke University, Loblolly-Summer Performing Arts Program, 30 August 1977.

Rogers, Helen Priest. "Films for Notation." *Dance Magazine*, September 1965, pp. 55–57.

Sabin, Robert. "Louis Horst and Modern Dance in America" (four parts). *Dance Magazine*, January 1953, pp. 21–22; February 1953, pp. 23–24; March 1953, pp. 30–31; April 1953, pp. 38–40.

Siegel, Marcia B. *At the Vanishing Point: A Critic Looks at Dance*. New York: Saturday Review Press, 1972.

Sorell, Walter. "Louis Horst." *Dance Magazine*, March 1964, p. 39.

Stahl, Norma. "Concerning José Limón." *Saturday Review*, 16 April 1955, pp. 33–34.

Stodelle, Ernestine. "Louis Horst, Father-Image." *Dance Magazine*, January 1953, pp. 54–56.

———. "With Her Red Fires." *Dance Observer*, January 1961, pp. 5–6.

Terry, Walter. *I Was There*. New York: Marcel Dekker, 1978.

————. "One of the New Breed—Manager Charles Reinhart." *Dance Magazine Annual* 1969, pp. 114–17.

"Time to Walk in Space." *Dance Perspectives* 34, Summer 1968.

Vreeland, Nancy. "ADF's Charles Reinhardt [*sic*]." *Dance Magazine*, May 1985 (summer calendar insert), p. SC30.

INDEX